# MARINE REFRIGERATION
## AND AIR-CONDITIONING

# MARINE REFRIGERATION
## AND AIR-CONDITIONING

James A. Harbach

## CORNELL MARITIME PRESS

A Division of Schiffer Publishing, Ltd.

ISBN: 978-0-87033-565-5
Printed in China

Library of Congress Cataloging-in-Publication Data:

Harbach, James A.
    Marine refrigeration and air-conditioning / James A. Harbach.—1st ed.
        p. cm.
    Includes bibliographical references and index.
    ISBN-13: 978-0-87033-565-5
    1. Marine refrigeration. 2. Ships–Air conditioning. I. Title.
VM485.H37 2005
623.8'53—dc22
                            2005009901

Published by Schiffer Publishing, Ltd.
4880 Lower Valley Road
Atglen, PA 19310
Phone: (610) 593-1777; Fax: (610) 593-2002
E-mail: Info@schifferbooks.com

*Marine Refrigeration and Air-Conditioning* originally published by Cornell Maritime Press in 2005

For our complete selection of fine books on this and related subjects, please visit our website at www.schifferbooks.com. You may also write for a free catalog.

This book may be purchased from the publisher. Please try your bookstore first.

We are always looking for people to write books on new and related subjects. If you have an idea for a book, please contact us at proposals@schifferbooks.com.

Schiffer Publishing's titles are available at special discounts for bulk purchases for sales promotions or premiums. Special editions, including personalized covers, corporate imprints, and excerpts can be created in large quantities for special needs. For more information, contact the publisher.

To the graduates of the United States Merchant
Marine Academy, who have never failed to step forward to serve the
nation in times of war or national crisis.

The author would like to acknowledge the U.S. Merchant Marine
Academy for granting sabbatical leave that provided the release time
needed to prepare the draft of this book.

# Contents

CONTENTS

## CHAPTER 3

# Refrigerants

## CHAPTER 4

# Compressors

## CHAPTER 5

# Evaporators and Condensers

## CHAPTER 6
# Controls and Accessories

## CHAPTER 7
# Psychrometry and HVAC Processes

## CHAPTER 8
# Cooling and Heating Load Calculations

CHAPTER 9

# HVAC Systems and Components

CHAPTER 10

# Absorption Systems, Multi-Pressure Systems, and Low-Temperature Systems

CHAPTER 11

# Operation and Maintenance

# Appendix

# Preface

This book was written to serve three distinct audiences: (1) students and faculty at maritime schools and colleges for use in their undergraduate course, (2) practicing marine engineers at sea and ashore looking for a comprehensive reference on the subject, and (3) engineers and technicians preparing for the EPA refrigerant certification exam. This results in a book with a unique coverage of both the theoretical and practical aspects of refrigeration and air-conditioning. There are a number of undergraduate texts on air-conditioning, but they do not cover refrigeration cycles in any depth. There are books that cover the applied aspects of refrigeration, but they are focused on technicians and don't contain coverage of theory and design topics. There are books available for preparing for the EPA exam, but they are typically limited to exam preparation for practicing professionals and do not cover basic refrigeration and air-conditioning topics.

Engineers and technicians preparing for the EPA exam will find most of the material covering the topics tested in chapter 3 and chapter 11. Chapter 3 covers both old and new refrigerants, including the impact environmental concerns has had on their use in refrigeration and air-conditioning systems. Chapter 11 covers the techniques for properly handling refrigerants, and for operating and maintaining refrigeration systems to minimize the loss of refrigerants to the atmosphere. The appendix following chapter 11 contains information on the EPA exam including several hundred sample test questions.

The coverage of the theoretical and design topics assumes a knowledge of undergraduate thermodynamics, fluid mechanics, and heat transfer. It was decided to not expand the size of the book with a superficial overview of these topics. Any good undergraduate text covering these subjects will

1

serve as a suitable reference. The theory and design topics can be skipped over by those only interested in the applied aspects of the subject.

It is hoped this book finds an important place on many marine engineers' bookshelves.

James A. Harbach
Professor of Engineering
U.S. Merchant Marine Academy

CHAPTER 1

# Introduction

Refrigeration is defined as the branch of science and engineering that deals with the process of reducing and maintaining the temperature of a space or material below that of the surroundings. Since heat flows naturally from a region of higher temperature to one of lower temperature, there is always a flow of heat from the surroundings into the refrigerated area. The amount of this flow of heat can be minimized by proper insulation, but to maintain a constant temperature in the refrigerated space, the refrigeration system must remove heat from the space at the same rate as the heat is entering from the surroundings.

## MARINE APPLICATIONS OF MECHANICAL REFRIGERATION

Mechanical refrigeration is used aboard ship for many purposes, including (1) refrigerated ship's stores, (2) air-conditioning, and (3) refrigerated cargo storage. Most marine refrigeration systems use reciprocating compressors; however, systems using rotary and centrifugal compressors are becoming more common. The reciprocating and rotary types are positive displacement while the centrifugal type uses the centrifugal force created by a high-speed impeller to provide the compression. Reciprocating compressors are especially flexible. They are used in high temperature (air-conditioning) as well as low temperature (cryogenic) applications, and in sizes from less than 1 ton to 250 tons or more. This flexibility when considered along with the reciprocating compressor's reliability and efficiency accounts for its widespread popularity. Screw compressors are replacing reciprocating compressors in certain applications, while centrifugal compressors are used primarily in large tonnage air-conditioning or refrigerated cargo applications. Scroll compressors have become popular in small capacity applications where reciprocating compressors were commonly selected.

Environmental concerns have had a significant impact on refrigeration and air-conditioning systems during the 1990s. The Montreal Protocols and the resulting amendments to the Clean Air Act dramatically changed the refrigerants used and the procedures for handling them. Refrigerants in common use for many years (such as R-12) are now no longer in production and have become very expensive. Owners of systems using these refrigerants had to consider retrofitting the existing system with one of the new refrigerants or complete replacement of the condensing units. Personnel servicing the systems had to become trained in the use of the new recovery equipment and pass an EPA test to become certified in the handling of refrigerants to minimize their release into the atmosphere.

## REFRIGERATED SHIP'S STORES

Ship's stores refrigeration equipment is installed to preserve the food required for consumption by the crew and passengers. The food is typically stored in insulated walk-in type storage compartments. The installation for a commercial ship such as a tanker or containership commonly consists of a freeze room, dairy room, fruit and vegetable room, with two condensing units. The system is designed to maintain the freeze room at 0°F (−18°C) and chill rooms at 33°F (0.5°C). Unit coolers or natural convection bare tube evaporators are commonly used. Most ship's stores systems are designed with two separate condensing units. Each condensing unit consists of a compressor, condenser, receiver, heat exchanger, controls, valves, and associated piping. Figure 1-1 shows a condensing unit for a ship's stores refrigeration system. Each condensing unit can handle the entire plant load during normal steady-state operation, while both units can be used for pull-down operation after loading new stores. The maximum system capacity is based on lowering the product temperature to design in two days after loading product. Provisions must be made for the defrosting of freeze box evaporator coils to permit removal of accumulated ice to maintain efficiency. Defrosting can be accomplished by electric heaters or by the use of hot refrigerant gas from the compressor.

## AIR-CONDITIONING

Air-conditioning is the control of the temperature and humidity of enclosed spaces to make the environment more comfortable for the people living and

Fig. 1-1. Ship's stores refrigeration system.

working there. While technically it includes winter heating, air-condition-ing is normally taken to mean cooling and dehumidifying during warm weather. A typical air-conditioning system is similar to that used for re-frigerated ship's stores except that higher temperatures are involved and the system tonnage is larger. The evaporators operate above 32°F (0°C) and, therefore, no defrosting provisions are required. Evaporators of smaller systems are usually of the direct expansion type while larger sys-tems typically are of the chilled water type. Integrated packages called chiller units deliver water at 45°F to 50°F (7°C to 10°C). The chilled water is then circulated to the remotely located cooling coils.

Air-conditioning applications are different from refrigerated storage applications in that standby condensing capacity is normally not fur-nished. The system capacity is selected based on the estimated peak load with all condensing units in service. The plant is typically arranged to per-mit cross connection of condensing units thus allowing securing unneeded units. Figure 1-2 shows a 60-ton condensing unit for a merchant ship air-conditioning system. A 200-ton condensing unit for a naval ship air-conditioning system is shown in figure 1-3.

Fig. 1-2. 60-ton condensing unit for merchant ship AC system.

Fig. 1-3. 200-ton condensing unit for naval air-conditioning system.
Courtesy York International-Marine Systems.

# REFRIGERATED CARGO

Refrigerated cargo spaces are installed to permit the shipment of perishable cargo. These systems vary in size from the small self-contained unit on a refrigerated container to a complex brine system on a refrigerated cargo vessel. The systems on refrigerated cargo vessels are usually designed for maximum flexibility to permit the carriage of different cargoes at different temperatures. Defrosting provisions are required for all evaporators designed for below 32°F (0°C) operation. Where the installation is extensive and uses forced air cooling coils, hot seawater defrosting is common. Hot seawater is heated and sprayed over the coils to melt the frost and carry it away down the drains. The fans are shut down during defrosting to minimize the carryover of heat into the storage area.

Some cargoes such as fruit and vegetables give off carbon dioxide ($CO_2$) during storage. To prevent dangerous concentrations, ventilation systems are commonly provided to force fresh air into the refrigerated space and exhaust stale compartment air to the outside. Since the introduction of warm outside air imposes a significant load on the refrigeration system, the ventilation fans are commonly sized for about one air change per hour and operated for 20 minutes per hour during normal operation (not pulldown) only.

In large systems, it is frequently economical to employ brine as a secondary refrigerant in an indirect system. The primary refrigerant evaporator is employed to chill the secondary refrigerant, the brine, which is then circulated to the refrigerated spaces. Calcium chloride and sodium chloride are the most common types of brine used. Calcium chloride brine can achieve temperatures as low as –67°F (–55°C) while sodium chloride brine can achieve temperatures as low as –6°F (–21°C).

Refrigerated containers are fitted with self-contained electric heating and cooling units. The typical unit is mounted flush with the front face of a standard-size container. Cooling is provided by a vapor-compression refrigeration system with a semi-hermetic reciprocating compressor and an air-cooled condenser. Figure 1-4 is a diagram of the refrigeration system for a refrigerated container. One axial flow fan circulates cooling air from the atmosphere across the condenser while a second fan circulates the air across the evaporator and to the product in the container. Figure 1-5 shows the air flow through the unit. Heating and defrosting are accomplished with electric resistance heating elements located in the evaporator section. The heating and cooling cycles are controlled automatically by a thermostat, while the defrost cycle is initiated by a timer or a differential pressure switch monitoring the air pressure across the evaporator. The evaporator fan is secured automatically during the defrost cycle. Electric power to run the units can be supplied from the ship's electrical system, from deck-mounted packaged diesel generators, or from individual diesel generators mounted in the container front. Some units are built with a diesel as the primary drive and an electric motor backup. The units with diesel engines or diesel generators can be carried over land by trucks without generating capacity.

An increasingly important refrigerated cargo is liquefied natural gas (LNG). Natural gas, which is primarily methane, is liquefied in shoreside facilities to increase its density and thus the quantity that can be carried in the tanker. The LNG tanker carries the cargo in insulated tanks at atmospheric pressure at a temperature of $-160°C$. Almost all LNG tankers built to date have been powered by geared steam turbine propulsion plants. The tanks are not mechanically refrigerated, with the gas vaporized by heat transfer (called "boiloff") being used as fuel in ship's boilers. New tanker

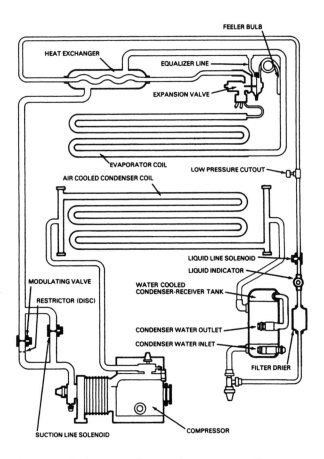

Fig. 1-4. Refrigerated container system diagram.
Courtesy Thermo King Corp.

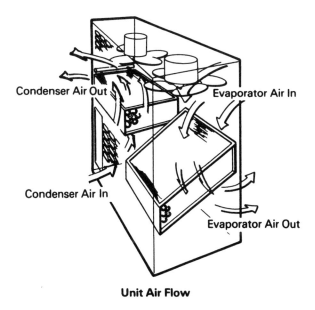

**Unit Air Flow**

Fig. 1-5. Refrigerated container air flow. Courtesy Thermo King Corp.

designs are being considered powered by diesel engines with onboard systems for reliquefaction of the boiloff. Recent advances in the efficiency of the tank insulation systems have reduced the amount of boiloff and thus the required size of the reliquefaction system.

## CHAPTER 2

# The Vapor Compression Cycle

The task of a refrigeration or air-conditioning system is to maintain the temperature of an enclosed space below its surroundings. Since heat naturally flows from higher temperature areas to lower temperature areas, a device must be constructed to move the thermal energy in the opposite direction. The rate at which heat must be removed from the cooled space is the refrigeration (or cooling) load. This load is the sum of a variety of loads including (1) heat transferred through the walls of the cooled space, (2) heat from outside air entering the space, and (3) heat from sources within the space such as people and equipment. Chapter 8 covers some methods and techniques for estimating cooling and heating loads.

The first means of refrigeration used by humans was the melting of ice blocks. When mechanical refrigeration systems were developed, it was natural to express the cooling capacity of the new systems in terms similar to that of melting ice. A common unit of refrigeration is the cooling effect of 1 ton (2,000 lbm) of ice melting at a constant rate in one day. The latent heat of fusion of ice is 144 Btu/lbm (334.9 kJ/kg), and so the refrigeration produced by 2,000 lbm (907.18 kg) or 1 ton of ice is 288,000 Btu ($3.0384 \times 105$ kJ). One ton of refrigeration is thus 288,000 Btu divided by 24 hours. Hence:

$$1 \text{ ton of refrigeration} = \frac{288{,}000 \text{ Btu}}{24 \text{ hrs}} = 12{,}000 \text{ Btu/hr}$$

$$= 3.516 \text{ kW} = 200 \text{ Btu/min}$$

It should be noted that the field of air-conditioning covers more than cooling the air, but also includes heating in cold weather and matters of air quality, distribution, and human comfort. In this chapter we are primarily concerned with the cooling function of air-conditioning. Chapters 7 and 9 will cover these and other considerations in some detail.

## THE REVERSED CARNOT CYCLE

The Carnot cycle operating as a heat engine is commonly used in thermodynamics to compare the performance of other engine cycles. The efficiency of a Carnot cycle cannot be exceeded by any other cycle operating between the same temperatures, and thus it provides a measure of maximum possible performance. Figure 2-1 shows a Carnot cycle operating as a heat engine and the cycle plotted on a temperature-entropy diagram. The Carnot cycle consists of the following four processes:

|||
|---|---|
| 1–2 | Isentropic Compression |
| 2–3 | Constant Temperature Heat Addition |
| 3–4 | Isentropic Expansion |
| 4–1 | Constant Temperature Heat Rejection |

When operating as an engine, the Carnot cycle converts the maximum amount of heat supplied from the high temperature source into power, thus having the highest possible thermal efficiency for the given conditions.

By operating the cycle in reverse, it is possible to devise a refrigeration system with the highest possible performance. The four processes remain the same, but work must be supplied to the cycle, and heat is removed from the low temperature source and rejected to the high temperature source. Figure 2-2 shows a reversed Carnot cycle, in other words, a Carnot cycle operating as refrigeration system and the associated temperature-entropy diagram.

The performance of a refrigeration system is expressed as a coefficient of performance (COP), and is defined as the heat supplied to the cycle at the low temperature (the desired cooling effect) divided by the net work supplied (what it "costs" to operate the cycle). Thus:

$$COP_R = \frac{Q_L}{W_{NET}} = \frac{Q_L}{Q_H - Q_L} \tag{2.1}$$

It should be noted that the above expression is valid for all refrigeration systems, both ideal and actual.

From the temperature-entropy diagram in figure 2-2, the COP for the reversed Carnot cycle can be determined. Remember from thermodynamics that the heat transferred in a reversible process is $q_{rev} = \int T \, ds$. Since the temperatures of the heat addition and rejection processes are constant and s4 = s1 and s3 = s2, the integrations reduce to calculating the areas of the rectangles on the T-s diagram.

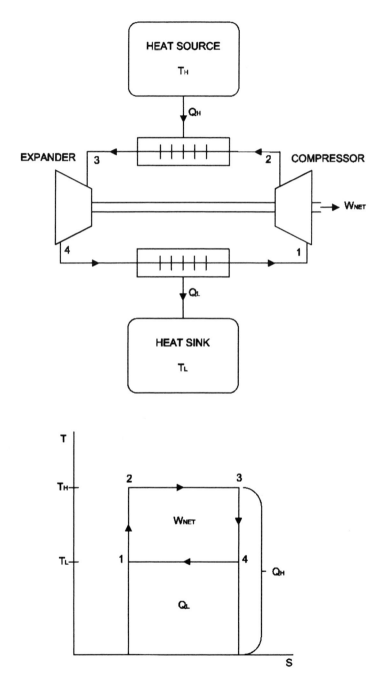

Fig. 2-1. Carnot cycle operating as a heat engine.

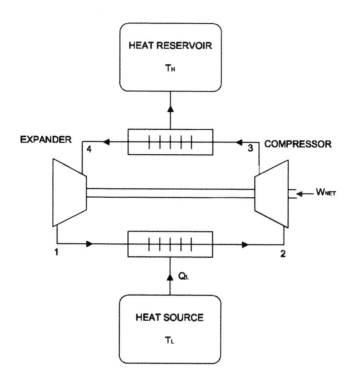

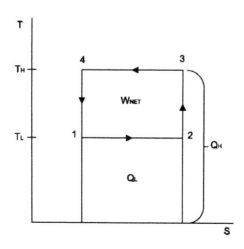

Fig. 2-2. Reversed Carnot cycle operating as a refrigeration system.

$$COP_R = \frac{T_L(s2 - s1)}{T_H(s3 - s4) - T_L(s2 - s1)} = \frac{T_L(s2 - s1)}{T_H(s2 - s1) - T_L(s2 - s1)}$$

$$COP_R = \frac{T_L}{T_H - T_L} \tag{2.2}$$

Since the performance of the reversed Carnot cycle is the highest that can possibly be achieved, the reversed Carnot COP is often used as a basis of comparison with actual system COP values. It is only necessary to know the high and low temperatures to calculated its value.

A heat pump is a refrigeration system used for heating rather than cooling. The system transfers heat from the colder surroundings into the warmer building. The heat rejected from the system becomes the desired effect of the system and the COP for a heat pump can thus be defined as follows.

$$COP_{HP} = \frac{Q_H}{W_{NET}} = \frac{Q_H}{Q_H - Q_L} \tag{2.3}$$

If a reversed Carnot cycle is being used as a heat pump, a relationship for its COP can be determined as was done for the Carnot refrigeration system above.

$$COP_{HP} = \frac{T_H(s2 - s1)}{T_H(s2 - s1) - T_L(s2 - s1)} = \frac{T_H}{T_H - T_L} \tag{2.4}$$

Heat pumps are used in many mild climates for winter heating. The systems are essentially a conventional air-conditioning system with added hardware and controls to permit the shift from cooling to heating by rearranging the flow of the refrigerant in the system.

An examination of equations 2.2 and 2.4 will reveal that the closer the temperatures $T_H$ and $T_L$ are to one another, the higher the COP will be. However, these temperatures are not arbitrary but are determined by the temperature of the surroundings and the temperature of the space being cooled or heated. For a refrigeration system to function, the temperature of the cycle during heat addition must be below the cooled space temperature, and the temperature of the cycle during heat rejection must be below the surroundings temperature. The cycle high and low temperatures can be brought closer together by reducing the temperature differences during heat addition and rejection. However for the temperature differences to approach zero, the heat exchangers must be be made extremely large. In a real system, this becomes an economic tradeoff between cycle efficiency and the size and cost of the system heat exchangers.

EXAMPLE PROBLEM 2.1. A reversed Carnot air-conditioning system is used to maintain a ship control room at 23°C when the surroundings are 35°C. If 10 kW of heat must be removed from the control room to maintain the temperature, determine the power required to operate the system.

SOLUTION.

SKETCH AND GIVEN DATA:

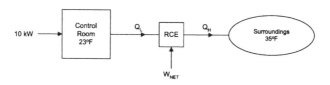

ASSUMPTIONS:

1. The surroundings temperature is $T_H$ and the control room temperature is $T_L$.
2. The cycle heat exchanger temperature differences are zero.

ANALYSIS:

Convert the temperatures to Kelvin: $T_H = 35 + 273 = 308°K$
$$T_L = 23 + 273 = 296°K$$

The COP of a reversed Carnot refrigerator is:

$$COP_R = \frac{T_L}{T_H - T_L} = \frac{296}{308 - 296} = 24.7$$

From the definition of $COP_R$:

$$COP_R = \frac{Q_L}{W_{NET}}$$

$$24.7 = \frac{10 \text{ kW}}{W_{NET}}$$

$$W_{NET} = 0.405 \text{ kW}$$

COMMENTS:

1. Absolute temperatures must be used in the calculations.
2. The power required for an actual air-conditioner will be higher.

## THE VAPOR-COMPRESSION CYCLE

The reversed Carnot cycle has a number of disadvantages that prevent it from being employed in a real system. First, in order to maintain constant high-side temperature, the compressor would have to compress a mixture to saturation at the discharge. See figure 2-3. Controlling the refrigerant flow to ensure this is very difficult. Second, the work performed by the expander is very small in comparison to the compressor work, and the cost for such an expander would not be economically justified.

While other cycles such as the absorption cycle are sometimes used for refrigeration systems, almost all marine refrigeration and air-conditioning systems operate on the vapor-compression cycle. Any cycle consists of a repetitive series of thermodynamic processes. The operating fluid starts at a particular state or condition, passes through the series of processes, and returns to the initial condition. The vapor-compression cycle consists of the following processes: (1) expansion, (2) vaporization, (3) compression, and (4) condensation.

A simple vapor-compression cycle is shown in Figure 2-4. Starting at the receiver at point 4, high-temperature, high-pressure liquid refrigerant flows from the receiver to the expansion valve. The pressure of the refrigerant is reduced by the expansion valve so that the evaporator temperature will be below the temperature of the refrigerated space. Some of the liquid refrigerant flashes to a vapor as the pressure is reduced. In the evaporator, the liquid vaporizes at a constant temperature and pressure as heat is picked up through the walls of the cooling coils. The compressor draws the vapor from the evaporator through the suction line into the compressor inlet. In the compressor, the refrigerant vapor pressure and temperature are increased and the high-temperature, high-pressure vapor is discharged

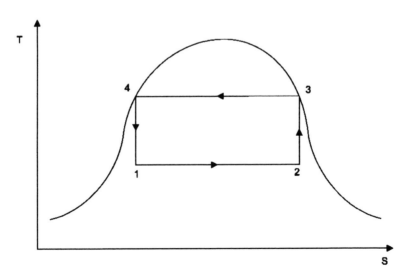

Fig. 2-3. Temperature-entropy diagram for two-phase substance operating on the reversed Carnot cycle.

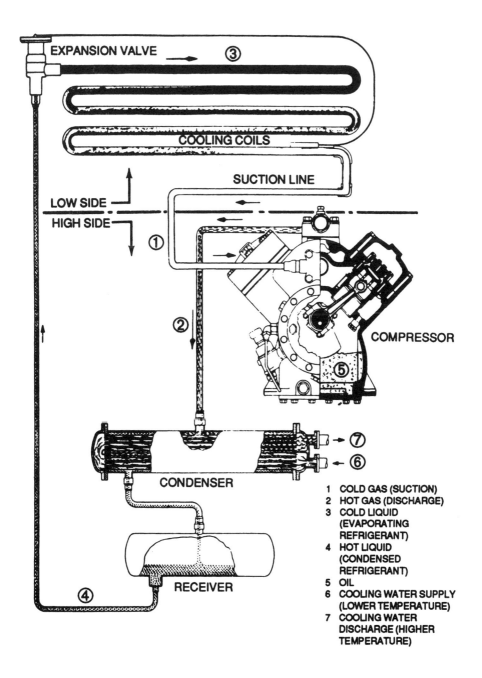

Fig. 2-4. Basic vapor-compresssion refrigeration cycle.
Courtesy Carrier Corporation.

into the hot gas line. The vapor then flows to the condenser where it comes in contact with the relatively cool condenser tubes. The refrigerant vapor gives up heat to the condenser cooling medium, condenses to a liquid, and drains from the condenser into the receiver, ready to be recirculated.

One question to consider is what type of working substance, or refrigerant, can be used in a refrigeration system? Some of the factors that must be considered are thermodynamic properties, cost, safety, efficiency, and environmental concerns. It is also desirable, but not essential, to have the compressor inlet pressure equal to or greater than atmospheric pressure, so that air is not likely to leak into the refrigeration system. There are many choices available, as table 3-1 illustrates in chapter 3. In the appendix, property charts and tables are given for several common refrigerants. Chapter 3 contains much additional information about refrigerants.

### High Side/Low Side
A refrigerating system can be divided into two parts according to the pressure exerted by the refrigerant. The low-pressure portion of the system (the "low side") consists of the expansion valve, the evaporator, and the suction line. This is the pressure at which the refrigerant is vaporized in the evaporator. The high-pressure portion of the system (the "high side") consists of the compressor, the hot gas line, the condenser, the receiver, and the liquid line. This is the pressure at which the refrigerant is condensed in the condenser. The dividing points between the high side and the low side are the expansion valve and the compressor.

### Evaporator Temperature
In order for refrigeration to take place, the evaporator coil temperature must be below that of the refrigerated space. The evaporator temperature is controlled by varying the pressure in the evaporator since the vaporization of the refrigerant occurs at the saturation temperature corresponding to the evaporator pressure. Raising the evaporator pressure raises the evaporator temperature, and lowering the pressure lowers the temperature.

### Condensing Temperature
In order for the refrigerant gas to condense to a liquid in the condenser, its saturation temperature must be above that of the condenser cooling medium. Raising the condenser pressure raises the condensing temperature, and lowering the pressure lowers the temperature. To provide continuous refrigeration, the refrigerant vapor must be condensed at the same rate as the refrigerant liquid is vaporized in the evaporator. Obviously, any increase in the rate of vaporization will increase the required rate of heat transfer in the condenser. Heat transfer in the condenser is a function of (1) the condenser surface area, (2) the condenser heat transfer coefficient, and (3) the temperature difference between the condensing

refrigerant vapor and condensing medium. Since the first two items are normally fixed, it follows that the condenser heat transfer varies with the temperature difference. The condensing temperature thus varies directly with the cooling medium temperature and the rate of refrigerant vaporization in the evaporator.

## THE IDEAL SATURATED VAPOR-COMPRESSION CYCLE

It is useful to have a simple theoretical cycle to use for comparison to actual vapor compression cycles. In the ideal saturated vapor-compression cycle shown in figure 2-5, it is assumed the vapor leaving the evaporator and the liquid leaving the condenser are saturated (no superheating and subcooling), and that there are no frictional pressure losses in the system. The cycle consists of the following four processes.

1–2     Constant pressure heat addition in the evaporator to a saturated vapor.

2–3     Isentropic compression to the condenser pressure.

3–4     Constant pressure heat rejection in the condenser to a saturated liquid.

4–1     Expansion at constant enthalpy to the evaporator pressure.

The superheat horn as shown in the T-s diagram in figure 2-5 illustrates the additional work required of dry compression as compared to wet compression as in the Carnot cycle. The area a-b-c-1 represents the loss of refrigerating effect due to the irreversible throttling process compared with the constant-entropy expansion process of the Carnot cycle. In refrigeration practice, a pressure-enthalpy (p-h) diagram is often used to analyze cycles rather than the temperature-enthalpy (T-s) diagram common in thermodynamic work. Figure 2-6 shows a p-h diagram for an ideal saturated vapor-compression system. A p-h diagram for R-134a and property tables for R-12, R-22, and R-134a can be found in the appendix.

---

EXAMPLE PROBLEM 2.2. An ideal saturated vapor-compression refrigeration system produces 20 kW of refrigeration using R-12 as a refrigerant while operating between a condenser pressure of 1,000 kPa and an evaporator temperature of 0°C. Determine (a) the refrigerating effect in kilojoules per kilogram, (b) the circulating rate of R-12 in kilograms per second, (c) the power required, (d) the $COP$, (e) the heat rejected in kilowatts, (f) the volume flowrate of refrigerant at the compressor inlet, and (g) the $COP$ of a reversed Carnot cycle operating under the same conditions.

SOLUTION.
   SKETCH AND GIVEN DATA:

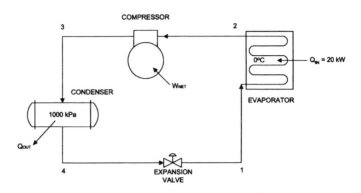

ASSUMPTIONS:
1. The changes in kinetic and potential energies may be neglected.
2. The condenser and evaporator processes are constant-pressure.
3. The expansion process is a constant enthalpy process.
4. Saturated vapor enters the compressor, and saturated liquid leaves the
   condenser.

ANALYSIS:
Before the energy terms associated with each component and for the
entire system can be determined, first find the enthalpy values for each
point around the cycle using the R-12 property tables in the appendix.
   From assumption 4 you know that $h4$ is the enthalpy of saturated liquid at 1,000 kPa (Tsat = 41.7°C) and $h2$ is the enthalpy of saturated vapor at 0°C. Using the saturated R-12 tables, $h4$ = 77.15 kJ/kg and
$h2$ = 188.95 kJ/kg.
   Process 4–1 is a throttling process; hence, $h1 = h4$ = 77.15 kJ/kg.
   Process 2–3 is isentropic. The pressure at state 3 must be equal to the
saturated pressure at state 4, as process 3–4 is constant-pressure. Thus,
$p3 = p4 = psat$ = 1,000 kPa. The value of entropy at state 2 can be looked
up in the saturated tables, and because the entropy is constant from state 2
to state 3, $s3 = s2 = sg$ at 0°C = 0.7017 kJ/kg-°K. Entering the superheated
R-12 tables with the pressure and entropy, find the enthalpy at point 3 by
interpolating to be $h3$ = 209.95 kJ/kg.
   The refrigerating effect is the heat added per unit mass in the evaporator, hence,

$$qin = h2 - h1 = 188.95 - 77.15 = 111.8 \ \text{kJ/kg} \tag{a}$$

   The system capacity provides information regarding the mass flow rate
required.

$$20 \text{ kW} = m(h2 - h1) = m(111.8 \text{ kJ/kg})$$
$$m = 0.179 \text{ kg/s} \tag{b}$$

The power is found from a first-law analysis of the compressor, subject to the assumptions.

$$Wnet = m(h3 - h2) = (0.179 \text{ kg/s})(209.95 - 188.95 \text{ kJ/kg})$$
$$Wnet = 3.76 \text{ kW} \tag{c}$$

Using the definition of the *COP* of a refrigerator:

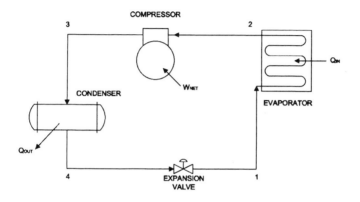

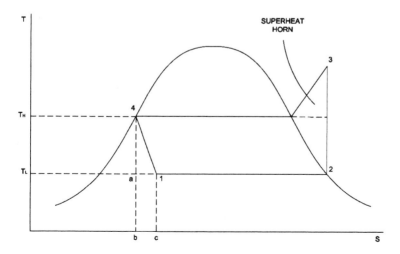

Fig. 2-5. Schematic diagram and T-s diagram for the ideal saturated vapor-compresson cycle.

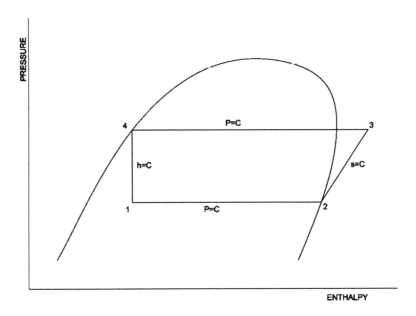

Fig. 2-6. Pressure-enthalpy (p-h) diagram for the ideal saturated vapor-compression cycle.

$$COP_R = \frac{Qin}{Wnet} = \frac{20 \text{ kW}}{3.76 \text{ kW}} = 5.32 \qquad \text{(d)}$$

The heat rejected occurs in the condenser, from a first-law analysis

$$Qout = m\,(h4 - h3)$$
$$Qout = (0.179 \text{ kg/s})(209.95 - 77.15 \text{ kJ/kg}) = 23.77 \text{ kW} \qquad \text{(e)}$$

The specific volume at compressor inlet conditions is equal to the saturated-vapor specific volume at 0°C or 0.05595 m³/kg. The volume flow rate is thus

$$V = m\,v2 = (0.179 \text{ kg/s})\left(0.05595 \text{ m}^3/\text{kg}\right)$$
$$V = 0.010 \text{ m}^3/\text{s} \qquad \text{(f)}$$

The saturation temperature at the condenser pressure of 1,000 kPa is 41.7°C from the tables. Converting the two temperatures to Kelvin and using the equation for a reversed Carnot refrigerator:

$$COP_R = \frac{T_L}{T_H - T_L} = \frac{273}{314.7 - 273} = 6.55 \qquad \text{(g)}$$

COMMENTS:
1. Knowing the temperature allows the determination of the pressure, and vice versa, when the refrigerant is in the saturated region. This assists us when analyzing the condenser and evaporator.
2. The required physical dimensions of a compressor depend on the refrigerant volume flow rate it must handle at the inlet conditions.
3. The ideal saturated cycle $COP$ is about 20 percent lower than the reversed Carnot $COP$.

### Deviations from the Ideal Saturated Cycle

Actual refrigeration cycles deviate somewhat from the ideal saturated cycle discussed above. For example, pressure drops occur in the piping, across the condenser and evaporator, and across other components due to the flow of refrigerant through them. Subcooling of liquid refrigerant can occur in the receiver and liquid line. Superheating of the refrigerant gas can occur in the evaporator and suction line. Figure 2-7 compares an actual

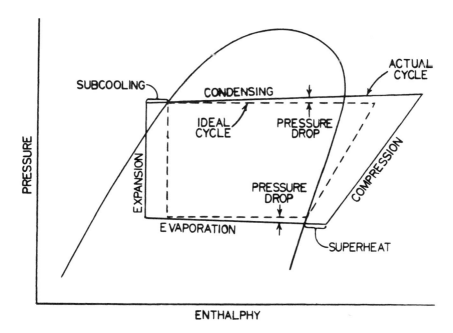

Fig. 2-7. Comparison of ideal saturated cycle and actual cycle.

cycle with the simple cycle on a pressure-enthalpy diagram. In general, pressure drops are kept to a minimum consistent with economic pipe sizes. The effect of superheating the refrigerant gas on cycle performance depends on where the superheating occurs. In general, superheating is kept to a minimum consistent with complete vaporization and avoiding liquid refrigerant flooding back to the compressor. Some superheating is necessary to ensure proper operation of the thermostatic expansion valve commonly used in vapor-compression systems. Subcooling of the liquid refrigerant generally has a desirable effect on cycle performance. It reduces flashing across the expansion valve and increases the refrigerating effect in the evaporator.

It is common on many modern systems to install a liquid-suction heat exchanger (heat interchanger). Figure 2-8 shows a system with a liquid-suction heat exchanger installed. The relatively cool refrigerant gas coming from the evaporator is used to subcool the liquid refrigerant flowing to the expansion valve. The subcooling of the liquid results in an increase in the refrigerating effect, but this is offset by the increased compressor work caused by the superheating. It is difficult to predict the net effect of these two changes on the system efficiency. In some instances, the COP will increase, in others it will decrease, and in others there will be no measurable change.

Due to friction and other losses, the actual compression process will deviate from the ideal isentropic process. The actual compressor will require more power to compress the same amount of refrigerant gas between the same suction and discharge pressures. The overall compressor efficiency ($\eta_{oc}$) that compares the ideal compressor work to the actual compressor is defined as follows:

$$\eta_{oc} = \frac{\text{ideal compressor work}}{\text{actual compressor work}} \times 100$$

Further information on the efficiency and performance of compressors is contained in chapter 4.

---

EXAMPLE PROBLEM 2.3. A vapor-compression system operating on R-134a operates with an evaporating temperature of 0°F and a condensing temperature of 105°F. The cooling load is 10 tons. The superheat at the compression suction and the subcooling at the condenser outlet are 10°F. Determine (a) the COP, (b) the refrigerant mass flow rate, and (c) the compressor power. Compare the COP to those for an ideal saturated cycle with the same evaporator and condenser temperatures.

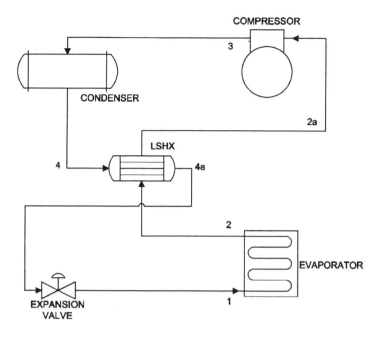

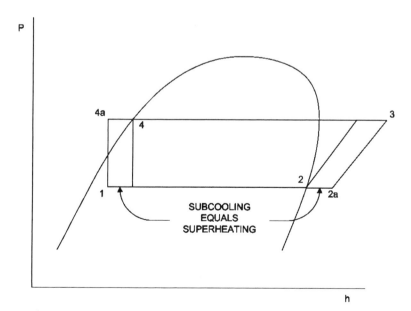

Fig. 2-8. Vapor-compression cycle with liquid-suction heat exchanger.

SOLUTION.

SKETCH AND GIVEN DATA:

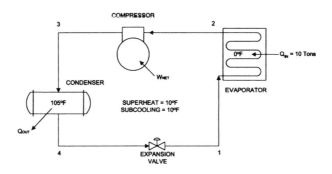

ASSUMPTIONS:

1. The system is closed, but each component may be treated as an open system.
2. The changes in kinetic and potential energies may be neglected.
3. The expansion process is constant-enthalpy.
4. The compression process is isentropic.

ANALYSIS:

First determine the enthalpy values using the R-134a tables. The subcooled liquid at point 4 has the same enthalply as a saturated liquid at the same temperature of 95°F.

$$h4 = hf \text{ at } 95° F = 43.39 \text{ Btu/lbm}$$

Since the process from point 4 to point 1 is constant enthalpy.

$$h1 = h4 = 43.39 \text{ Btu/lbm}$$

Using the superheat tables, determine the enthalpy and entropy at the evaporator outlet (point 2) for 21.2 psia and 10°F.

$$h2 = 105.12 \text{ Btu/lbm} \qquad s2 = 0.2298 \text{ Btu/lbm-°F}$$

Using the superheat tables, determine the enthalpy of the compressor outlet (point 3) for 149.7 psia and $s$ = 0.2298 Btu/lbm-°F.

$$h3 = 123.18 \text{ Btu/lbm}$$

Determine the refrigerant mass flow from an energy balance of the evaporator.

$$QL = m(h2 - h1)$$
$$(10 \text{ tons})(12{,}000 \text{ Btu/hr-ton}) = m(105.12 - 43.34 \text{ Btu/lbm})$$
$$m = 1{,}943.95 \text{ lbm/hr} = 32.4 \text{ lbm/min} \qquad \text{(b)}$$

The compressor power can now be calculated.

$$Wnet = m(h3 - h2) = (1{,}943.95 \text{ lbm/hr})(123.18 - 105.12 \text{ Btu/lbm})$$
$$Wnet = 35{,}108 \text{ Btu/hr} = 13.8 \text{ hp} \qquad \text{(c)}$$

The COP is thus.

$$COP_R = \frac{Q_L}{Wnet} = \frac{120{,}000 \text{ Btu/hr}}{35{,}108 \text{ Btu/hr}} = 3.42 \qquad \text{(a)}$$

Analyzing the ideal saturated cycle for 0°F and 105°F as in example problem 2.2

$$COP_R = 3.2$$

COMMENTS:
1. The refrigerating effect greater than in the standard cycle due to the subcooling and superheating.
2. The *COP* is slightly higher than for the standard cycle indicating the increased refrigerating effect more than compensated for the increased compressor work.
3. We assumed that all superheating results in useful cooling. This may not be true in many real installations.

---

EXAMPLE PROBLEM 2.4. An ideal saturated vapor-compression system operating under the same conditons as example problem 2.3 is modified by the addition of a liquid-suction heat exchanger. The vapor leaving the evaporator is superheated to 50°F. Determine (a) the *COP*, (b) the refrigerant mass flow rate, and (c) the compressor power. Compare the *COP* with that for the ideal saturated cycle without the heat exchanger.

SOLUTION.

SKETCH AND GIVEN DATA:

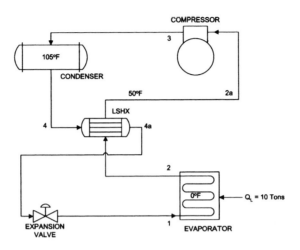

ASSUMPTIONS:

1. The system is closed, but each component may be treated as an open system.
2. The changes in kinetic and potential energies may be neglected.
3. The expansion process is constant-enthalpy.
4. The compression process is isentropic.
5. The subcooling equals the superheating ($h4 - h4a = h2a - h2$).

ANALYSIS:

First it is necessary to determine the enthalpy values using the R-134a tables in the appendix.

$h2 = hg$ at $0°F = 103.16$ Btu/lbm

$h4 = hf$ at $105°F = 46.93$ Btu/lbm

$h2a$ and $s2a$ are found from the superheat tables by interpolating for 21.2 psia and 50°F.

$h2a = 113.06$ Btu/lbm          $s2a = 0.2460$ Btu/lbm-°F

The subcooling is assumed to equal the superheating.

$$h4 - h4a = h2a - h2$$
$$46.93 - h4a = 113.06 - 103.16$$
$$h4a = 37.03 \text{ Btu/lbm}$$

Since the expansion process is constant enthalpy.

$$h1 = h4a = 37.03\,\text{Btu/lbm}$$

Find $h3$ from the superheat tables by interpolating for 149.7 psia and $s = 0.2460$ Btu/lbm-°F.

$$h3 = 133.04\,\text{Btu/lbm}$$

Determine the refrigerant mass flow from an energy balance of the evaporator.

$$Q_L = m(h2 - h1)$$
$$120{,}000\,\text{Btu/hr} = m(103.16 - 37.03\,\text{Btu/lbm})$$
$$m = 1{,}814.6\,\text{lbm/hr} = 30.24\,\text{lbm/min} \tag{b}$$

The compressor power can now be calculated.

$$Wnet = m(h3 - h2a)$$
$$Wnet = (1{,}841.6\,\text{lbm/hr})(133.04 - 113.06\,\text{Btu/lbm})$$
$$Wnet = 36.256\,\text{Btu/hr} = 14.25\,\text{hp} \tag{c}$$

The $COP_R$ is thus.

$$COP_R = \frac{Q_L}{Wnet} = \frac{120{,}000\,\text{Btu/hr}}{36{,}256\,\text{Btu/hr}} = 3.31 \tag{a}$$

This compares with a $COP_R$ of 3.2 for the ideal saturated cycle (see example problem 2.3).

COMMENTS:

1. The refrigerating effect is about 8% greater than for the standard cycle.
2. The $COP$ is slightly higher than for the ideal saturated cycle. Some refrigerants may experience a slight decline.
3. It is assumed that all superheating results in useful cooling. This may not be true in many real installations.

---

# MULTIPLE EVAPORATORS WITH ONE COMPRESSOR

In refrigeration systems it is not economical to have a separate refrigeration compressor for installations that have more than one evaporator. One compressor may be used to receive the refrigerant from several evaporators operating at different pressures, and thus different temperatures. Figure 2-9 illustrates a compressor receiving refrigerant from two evaporators.

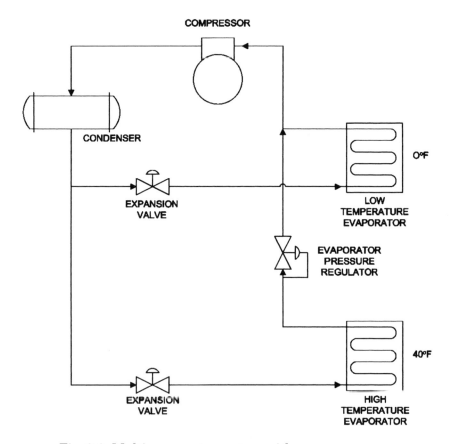

Fig. 2-9. Multi-evaporator system with one compressor.

The compressor intake pressure must be at the pressure of the lowest-temperature evaporator, in this case the evaporator set at 0°F. Such a situation would occur when an evaporator is used for maintaining frozen foods. In this case the pressure corresponding to 0°F is 23.8 psia. The other evaporator could maintain a space 40°F. This would correspond to refrigerated dairy and vegetable produce, where the temperature of the refrigerant in the evaporator coils should be above 32°F to prevent dehydration of the produce. If the refrigerant in the coils is below 32°F, ice will form on the coils due to the condensing of water in the air. This lowers the relative humidity, accelerating the dehydration of the produce.

To prevent dehydration in the high-temperature box, a back-pressure valve is located on the higher-temperature box evaporator's exit piping. The back-pressure regulator maintains a higher pressure in the evaporator coils exists at the compressor suction. The pressure at the

compressor inlet must be high enough to maintain the correct temperature in the lowest-temperature space pressure in the high-pressure
evaporator rises above the set point, the valve will open, allowing some
refrigerant to leave the evaporator and flow to the compressor inlet. The
saturated refrigerant temperature in any evaporator coil may be adjusted by regulating the back pressure; the higher the pressure, the
higher the saturated temperature.

---

EXAMPLe PROBLEM 2.5. A refrigeration system using R-12 has two evaporators operating at different temperatures and one compressor. One evaporator provides 5 tons of cooling at 40°F, and the second provides 7 tons of
cooling at 0°F. The condenser pressure is 150 psia. Determine (a) refrigerant flow through each evaporator and (b) the *COP* for the system.

SOLUTION.

SKETCH AND GIVEN DATA:

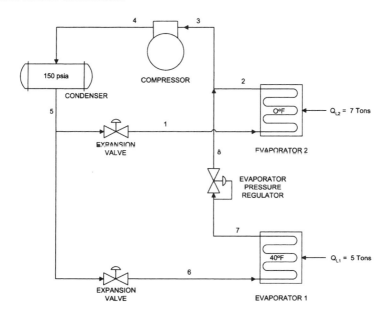

ASSUMPTIONS:
1. The changes in kinetic and potential energies may be neglected.
2. Refrigerant leaves the condenser as a saturated liquid; it leaves the evaporators as a saturated vapor.
3. The compression process is isentropic; the condensation and evaporation
   processes are at constant pressure.
4. The condenser and evaporator processes are constant-pressure.
5. The expansion process is a constant enthalpy process.

ANALYSIS:

Determine the enthalpy states around the cycle:

$h5 = hf$ at 150 psia = 33.81 Btu/lbm
$h5 = h6 = h1$ = 33.81 Btu/lbm for throttling processes
$h2 = hg$ at 0°F = 77.80 Btu/lbm
$h7 = hg$ at 40°F = 82.13 Btu/lbm
$h8 = h7$ = 82.13 Btu/lbm since this is a throttling process

Before $h3$ and $h4$ can be determined, the flow rates through the evaporators must be calculated. Performing a first-law analysis for each.
For the 40°F evaporator.

$$Q_{L1} = m1(h7 - h6)$$
$$(5 \text{ tons})(200 \text{ Btu/min-ton}) = m1(82.13 - 33.81 \text{ Btu/lbm})$$
$$m1 = 20.7 \text{ lbm/min} \tag{a}$$

For the 0°F evaporator.

$$Q_{L2} = m2(h2 - h1)$$
$$(7 \text{ tons})(200 \text{ Btu/min-ton}) = m2(77.8 - 33.81 \text{ Btu/lbm})$$
$$m2 = 31.83 \text{ lbm/min} \tag{a}$$

Performing a mass and energy balance for the mixing of the evaporator outlets to determine $h3$.

$$m2 \, h2 + m1 \, h8 = (m1 + m2)h3$$
$$(31.83 \text{ lbm/min})(77.8 \text{ Btu/lbm}) + (20.7 \text{ lbm/min})(82.13 \text{ Btu/lbm})$$
$$= (20.7 + 31.83 \text{ lbm/min})(h3 \text{ Btu/lbm})$$
$$h3 = 79.5 \text{ Btu/lbm} \tag{a}$$

Since the saturation temperature at point 3 is 0°F and $hg$ at that temperature is 77.8 Btu/lbm, the refrigerant at point 3 is superheated. Using the superheat tables knowing the pressure and enthalpy, interpolate to find the entropy at point 3.

$$s3 = 0.1737 \text{ Btu/lbm-°F}$$

Now with the entropy known and with the discharge pressure of 150 psia, interpolate using the superheat tables in the appendix to find the enthalpy.

$$h4 = 94.11 \text{ Btu/lbm}$$

The compressor power can now be calculated.

$$Wnet = (m1 + m2)(h4 - h3)$$
$$Wnet = (20.7 + 31.83 \, \text{lbm/min})(94.11 - 79.5 \, \text{Btu/lbm})$$
$$Wnet = 767.5 \, \text{Btu/min} = 18.1 \, \text{hp}$$

The $COP_R$ is thus.

$$COP = \frac{(12 \, \text{tons})(200 \, \text{Btu/min-tons})}{(767.5 \, \text{Btu/min})} = 3.13 \qquad \text{(b)}$$

COMMENTS:
The $COP$ is calculated by using the basic definition.

# PROBLEMS (ENGLISH UNITS)

2.1E  A reversed Carnot cycle maintains a refrigerated space at 40°F while in a room at 80°F. A wattmeter measuring the power being delivered to the unit reads 3kW. How much cooling is being provided?

2.2E  A reversed Carnot cycle operating as a heat pump delivers 90,000 Btu/hr to a house being maintained at 70°F when the outside temperature is 32°F. The heat pump maintains the hose temperature by cycling on and off. When running, the heat pump requires 15 hp. If electricity to run the heat pump costs $0.11 per kWhr, determine (a) the number of hours the heat pump runs each day, (b) the cost of electricity each day, and (c) the cost of electricity if the house was heated by electric resistance baseboard heating.

2.3E  An ideal saturated vapor-compression refrigeration system uses R-12 as the refrigerant. The R-12 leaves the evaporator at −15°F, and the condenser pressure is 150 psia. The flow rate is 45 lbm/min. Determine (a) the tons of refrigeration, (b) the power required, and (c) the $COP_R$.

2.4E  A refrigeration compressor receives 40 ft³/min of R-134a at −10°F from the evaporator of a standard vapor-compression refrigeration system. The condenser pressure is 150 psia. Determine (a) the mass flow rate, (b) the power required, (c) the tons of refrigeration, and (d) the $COP_R$.

2.5E  Redo the problem above using R-22 as the refrigerant. All conditions are the same except the condenser pressure is 250 psia.

2.6E  An ideal saturated vapor-compression refrigerating system is modified by the addition of a liquid-suction heat exchanger, providing 10°F of superheating of the vapor leaving the evaporator. The evaporator operates at −20°F, and the condenser operates at 240 psia. The cooling load is 50 tons. If the refrigerant is R-12, determine (a) the refrigerant mass flow rate, (b) the $COP_R$, (c) the refrigerating effect, (d) the degrees of subcooling, and (e) the power required.

2.7E In a vapor-compression refrigeration system, the R-12 leaves the evaporator at 20 psia and 20°F, enters the compressor, and is compressed isentropically to 200 psia. The discharge from the condenser is subcooled by 10°F. The refrigerant flow rate is 100 lbm/min. Determine (a) the tons of refrigeration, (b) the $COP_R$, and (c) the increase in the refrigerating effect compared to the standard cycle.

2.8E A 10-ton vapor-compression refrigeration system uses R-134a. The vapor enters the compressor with 20°F of superheating and exits the condenser with 10°F of subcooling. The evaporator pressure is 15 psia, and the condenser pressure is 175 psia. The compressor isentropic efficiency is 80%. Determine (a) the power, (b) the $COP_R$, and (c) the refrigerant mass flow rate.

2.9E A compressor serves two evaporators, one providing 5 tons of cooling at −20°F and the other, 10 tons of cooling at 10F. The system is a vapor-compression refrigeration system using R-12 with the condenser pressure at 200 psia. Assume saturated conditons leaving the condenser and evaporators and isentropic compression. Determine (a) the refrigerant flow through each evaporator, (b) the R-12 state entering the compressor, and (c) the compressor power.

2.10E A home uses a vapor-compression heat pump operating on R-12 as the means for providing heating. The house requires 48,000 Btu/hr of heat when the inside temperature is 70°F and the outside temperature is 30°F. The minimum temperature difference between the heat exchangers and air is 20°F. Determine (a) the evaporator and condenser pressures, (b) the cycle $COP_{HP}$, (c) the mass flow rate of R-12, and (d) the compressor power required.

2.11E A vapor-compression air-conditioning system provides cooling to the crew quarters of a containership. The cooling load is 200,000 Btu/hr and the $COP_R$ is 3.0. The electricity to drive the system comes from diesel generators with a thermal efficiency of 40%. The diesel generators use fuel with a heating value of 19,000 Btu/lbm and costs $200 per metric ton. Determine (a) the system electic load and (b) the cost of fuel each day to operate the system.

# PROBLEMS (SI UNITS)

2.1S A reversed Carnot cycle operates between temperature limits of −5°C and 30°C. The power supplied to the cycle is 4 kW and the refrigerating effect is 30 kJ/kg. Determine (a) the $COP_R$ and (b) the refrigerant flow rate.

2.2S A reversed Cannot cycle is used for heating and cooling. The work supplied is 10 kW. If the $COP_R$ = 3.5 for cooling and $T_L$ is 0°C, determine (a) $T_H$, (b) the refrigeration (tons), and (c) the $COP_{HP}$ for heating.

2.3S  An ideal saturated vapor-compression refrigeration system uses R-134a as the refrigerant. The refrigerant leaves the evaporator at –20°C, and the condenser pressure is 800 kPa. The flow rate is 20 kg/min. Determine (a) the tons of refrigeration, (b) the power required, and (c) the $COP_R$.

2.4S  An ideal saturated vapor-compression refrigeration system uses R-12 as the refrigerant. The R-12 leaves the evaporator at –20°C, and the condenser pressure is 800 kPa. The flow rate is 20 kg/min. Determine (a) the tons of refrigeration, (b) the power required, and (c) the $COP_R$.

2.5S  A refrigeration compressor receives 1.2 m3/min of R-12 at –10°C from the evaporator of an ideal saturated vapor-compression refrigeration system. The condenser pressure is 1.2 MPa. Determine (a) the refrigerant mass flow rate, (b) the compressor power, (c) the tons of refrigeration, and (d) the $COP_R$.

2.6S  Redo the above problem using R-22 as the refrigerant. All conditions are the same except the condenser pressure is 1.6 MPa.

2.7S  A vapor-compression refrigeration system uses R-12 and has an evaporator pressure of 100 kPa and a condenser pressure of 900 kPa. The temperature of the refrigerant entering the compressor is –10°C and entering the condenser is 90°C. The refrigerant leaving the condenser is subcooled 5°C, and the compressor power is 5 kW. Determine (a) the tons of refrigeration, (b) the $COP$, and (c) the change of availability across the compressor.

2.8S  A vapor-compression refrigeration system uses a liquid-suction heat exchanger located after the evaporator to subcool the liquid refrigerant entering the expansion valve. The refrigerant vapor leaving the evaporator is superheated in the process. Assume the refrigerant leaves the evaporator as a saturated vapor and the condenser as a saturated liquid and that no pressure drops occur in the heat exchangers. The evaporator temperature is –10°C, the condenser pressure is 1,000 kPa, and the flow rate of R-12 is 20 kg/min. Determine (a) the compressor power, (b) the tons of refrigeration, and (c) the $COP_R$.

2.9S  An ideal saturated vapor-compression refrigeration system is modified by the addition of a liquid-suction heat exchanger is operating with 10°C of superheat. The evaporator operates at –10°C and the condenser at 1.2 MPa. The cooling load is 50 tons. If the fluid is R-134a, determine (a) the refrigerant mass flow rate, (b) the $COP_R$, (c) the refrigerating effect, (d) the degrees of subcooling, (e) the compressor power required, and (f) the required compressor volumetric capacity .

2.10S  A 10-ton vapor-compression refrigeration system uses R-12. The vapor enters the compressor with 10°C of superheat and exits the condenser with 5°C of subcooling. The evaporator pressure is 150 kPa, and the condenser pressure is 1,000 kPa. The compressor isentropic efficiency is 80%. Determine (a) the compressor power, (b) the $COP_R$, and (c) the refrigerant flow rate.

2.11S  A vapor-compression refrigerator has a 1.5 kW motor driving the compressor. The compressor efficiency is 70% and has inlet pressure and temperature of 50 kPa and −20°C and a discharge pressure of 900 kPa. The condenser exit pressure is 800 kPa, and the expansion valve exit pressure is 60 kPa. Determine (a) the flow rate, (b) the $COP$, and (c) the tons of refrigeration for R-12.

2.12S  A compressor serves two evaporators, one providing 5 tons of cooling at −20°C and the other 10 tons of cooling at 0°C. The system is a vapor-compression refrigeration system with the condenser pressure at 1.2 MPa. Determine (a) the refrigerant flow through each evaporator, (b) the R-12 state entering the compressor, and (c) the compressor power.

2.13S  A vapor-compression heat pump system uses R-12. The compressor receives 0.75 kg/min at 250 kPa and 0°C and discharges it at 900 kPa and 60°C. The refrigerant leaves the condenser as a saturated liquid. Determine (a) the heat output in kW, (b) the power required, and (c) the $COP_{HP}$.

2.14S  A home uses a vapor-compression heat pump operating on R-22 as the means for providing heat. The house requires 15 kW of heat when the inside air temperature is 20°C and the outside air temperature is 0°C. The minimum temperature difference between the heat exchangers and inside and outside air is 10°C. Determine (a) the evaporator and condenser pressures, (b) the cycle $COP_{HP}$, (c) the mass flow rate of R-12, and (d) the compressor power required.

CHAPTER 3

# Refrigerants

A refrigerant is the working fluid that picks up the heat from the enclosed refrigerated space and transfers it to the surroundings. It should be understood that there is no such thing as an ideal refrigerant. Factors that enter into the selection of a refrigerant for a particular application include thermodynamic properties, cost, safety aspects, and environmental considerations. In the early part of the twentieth century, substances such as carbon dioxide ($CO_2$) and ammonia ($NH_3$) were commonly used. For most of the last half of the twentieth century, the fluorocarbon refrigerants R-12 (dichlordifluoromethane-$CCl_2F_2$), R-11 (trichloromonofluoromethane $CCl_3F$), and R-22 (monochlorodifluoromethane-$CHClF_2$) have been the most popular for industrial and marine applications. Fluorocarbons are based on the substances methane ($CH_4$) or ethane ($C_2H_6$) in which one or more of the hydrogen atoms has been replaced by fluorine or chlorine atoms. An examination of figure 3-1 shows the relationship of some common refrigerants to methane and ethane. If all the hydrogen atoms in the molecule have been replaced by fluorines and chlorines, the refrigerant is referred to as a chlorofluorocarbon (CFC). If some hydrogen atoms remain along with chlorines and flourines, the refrigerant is referred to as a hydrochlorofluorocarbon (HCFC). R-12 and R-11 are examples of CFCs, and R-22 is an example of a HCFC. A substance with no chlorine atoms at all is referred to as a hydrofluorocarbon (HFC). R-134a is an example of an HFC. Table 3-1 summarizes the characteristics of a number of different refrigerants, both older ones that are being phased out and new replacements. Table 3-2 compares the saturation pressure-temperature properties for several once popular refrigerants with their newer replacements.

37

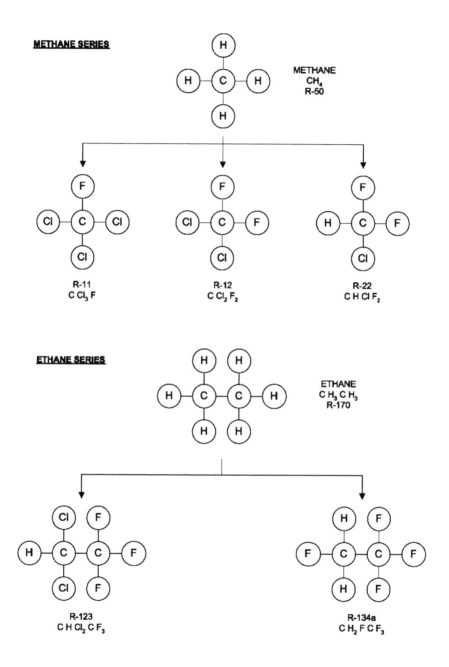

Fig. 3-1. Fluorocarbon refrigerants based on methane and ethane.

**TABLE 3-1**
**Refrigerant Characteristics**

| Refrigerant Number | Chemical Formula or Composition | Type | MW | Boiling Point at 1 Atm. (°F) | Safety Class |
|---|---|---|---|---|---|
| R-11 | CCl₃F | CFC | 137.4 | 74.8 | A1 |
| R-12 | CCl₂F₂ | CFC | 120.9 | −21.6 | A1 |
| R-22 | CHClF₂ | HCFC | 86.5 | −41.4 | A1 |
| R-123 | CHCl₂CF₃ | HCFC | 153 | 83.7 | B1 |
| R-134a | CF₃CH₂F | HFC | 102 | −15.1 | A1 |
| R-404A | R-125/R-143a/R-134a | HFC blend | 97.6 | −51.6 | A1 |
| R-507 | R-125/R-143a | HFC blend | 98.9 | −52.1 | A1 |
| R-717 | NH₃ | Inorganic | 17 | −28.0 | B2 |
| R-744 | CO₂ | Inorganic | 44 | −109 | A1 |

## PROPERTIES

The important thermodynamic properties that enter into the selection of a refrigerant are the latent heat of vaporization, the saturation temperatures and pressures, the specific volume of the vapor, and the specific heat of the vapor and liquid. High latent heat is desirable in all but small systems because it reduces the amount of refrigerant that must be circulated for a given system capacity. This affects the size and thus the cost of the compressor. The specific volume of the vapor is also an important factor in the compressor size. A low specific volume will result in a smaller compressor in a given system. The specific heats of the liquid and vapor affect the performance of the liquid-suction heat exchanger. A refrigerant with a low liquid specific heat and a high vapor specific heat will see increased subcooling (and thus refrigeration effect) with a minimum increase in compressor work. The appendix contains tables of the saturation and superheat thermodynamic properties for R-12, R-22 and R-134a. Included are tables for both English and SI units. The properties tabulated are pressure, temperature, density/specific volume, enthalpy, and entropy. Saturation tables versus both temperature and pressure are included. The values tabulated for the saturated pressure tables were selected to correspond with the pressure values in the superheat tables to reduce the need for interpolation when solving problems.

## SAFETY

Safety is obviously a concern when selecting a refrigerant for an application. Refrigerants are rated for two important safety characteristics—toxicity and flammability—in accordance with ASHRAE Standard 34. While

## TABLE 3-2
## Refrigerant Saturated Pressure-Temperature Data

| Temperature (°F) | R-12 Pressure (psig) | R-134 Pressure (psig) | R-11 Pressure (psig) | R-123 Pressure (psig) | R-22 Pressure (psig) | R-404A Bubble Pressure (psig) | R-507 (AZ-50) Bubble Pressure (psig) |
|---|---|---|---|---|---|---|---|
| -40.00 | 11.0 ("Hg Vac) | 14.8 ("Hg Vac) | 28.4 ("Hg Vac) | 28.9 ("Hg Vac) | 0.6 | 5.2 | 5.7 |
| -30.00 | 5.5 ("Hg Vac) | 9.8 ("Hg Vac) | 27.8 ("Hg Vac) | 28.4 ("Hg Vac) | 4.9 | 10.7 | 11.3 |
| -20.00 | 0.5 | 3.7 ("Hg Vac) | 27.0 ("Hg Vac) | 27.8 ("Hg Vac) | 10.2 | 17.2 | 18.0 |
| -10.00 | 4.5 | 1.9 | 26.0 ("Hg Vac) | 27.0 ("Hg Vac) | 16.5 | 25.0 | 26.0 |
| 0.00 | 9.1 | 6.5 | 24.7 ("Hg Vac) | 25.9 ("Hg Vac) | 24.0 | 34.1 | 35.4 |
| 10.00 | 14.6 | 11.9 | 23.1 ("Hg Vac) | 24.6 ("Hg Vac) | 32.8 | 44.8 | 46.3 |
| 20.00 | 21.0 | 18.4 | 21.1 ("Hg Vac) | 22.9 ("Hg Vac) | 43.1 | 57.2 | 58.9 |
| 30.00 | 28.4 | 26.1 | 18.6 ("Hg Vac) | 20.8 ("Hg Vac) | 55.0 | 71.4 | 73.4 |
| 40.00 | 36.9 | 35.0 | 15.6 ("Hg Vac) | 18.2 ("Hg Vac) | 68.6 | 87.6 | 90.0 |
| 50.00 | 46.6 | 45.4 | 12.0 ("Hg Vac) | 15.0 ("Hg Vac) | 84.1 | 106.0 | 108.8 |
| 60.00 | 57.6 | 57.4 | 7.7 ("Hg Vac) | 11.2 ("Hg Vac) | 101.6 | 126.7 | 130.0 |
| 70.00 | 70.1 | 71.1 | 2.7 ("Hg Vac) | 6.6 ("Hg Vac) | 121.4 | 150.0 | 153.8 |
| 80.00 | 84.0 | 86.7 | 1.6 | 1.2 ("Hg Vac) | 143.6 | 176.1 | 180.4 |
| 90.00 | 99.6 | 104.3 | 5.0 | 2.5 | 168.4 | 205.2 | 210.1 |
| 100.00 | 116.9 | 124.2 | 8.9 | 6.1 | 195.9 | 237.4 | 243.0 |
| 110.00 | 136.1 | 146.4 | 13.4 | 10.3 | 226.4 | 273.1 | 279.5 |
| 120.00 | 157.3 | 171.2 | 18.5 | 15.1 | 260.0 | 312.5 | 319.7 |
| 130.00 | 180.5 | 198.7 | 24.2 | 20.6 | 296.9 | 355.9 | 354.1 |
| 140.00 | 206.0 | 229.2 | 30.7 | 26.8 | 337.4 | 403.8 | 413.2 |

all substances are toxic if the concentration is high enough to reduce the oxygen to an unacceptable level, some substances cause problems at much lower levels or for short time exposures. A refrigerant with a Class A rating has not exhibited toxicity at concentrations up to 400 ppm. A refrigerant with a Class B rating has exhibited some toxicity problems at concentrations below 400 ppm. Flammability is ranked by three classes. A refrigerant rated Class 1 has exhibited no flame propagation when tested in air at 14.7 psia and 70°F. Class 2 refrigerants have a lower flammability limit (LFL) of more than 0.00625 lbm/ft$^2$ at 14.7 psia and 70°F and a heat of combustion of less than 8,174 Btu/lbm. Class 3 refrigerants are highly flammable and have an LFL of less than or equal to 0.00625 lbm/ft$^2$ at 14.7 psia and 70°F or a heat of combustion equal to or more than 8,174 Btu/lbm. Figure 3-2 shows the six safety group classifications for refrigerants: A1, A2, A3, B1, B2, and B3. The refrigerants selected for marine applications all have a safety group classification of A1, meaning low toxicity and no flame propagation at normal temperature and pressure. The Material Safety Data Sheet (MSDS) for the refrigerant should be consulted for more detailed information.

|                      | *Lower Toxicity* | *Higher Toxicity* |
|----------------------|:----------------:|:-----------------:|
| No flame propagation | A1               | B1                |
| Lower flammability   | A2               | B2                |
| Higher flammability  | A3               | B3                |

Fig. 3-2. ASHRAE refrigerant safety classification.

## LUBRICANTS

The compatibility of the oil used for lubrication of the compressor and the system refrigerants is important as the two come into contact in the compressor crankcase. The refrigerant and the oil should not react with one another, and oil and refrigerant should have the ability to dissolve in the oil and vice versa. This ability to dissolve is called miscibility and is important to aid in the return of oil carried along with the refrigerant back to the compressor crankcase. Traditionally mineral-based oils have been used in refrigeration compressors. While suitable for use with CFCs and many HCFCs, mineral oils are not compatible with CFC refrigerants.

A variety of synthetic lubricating oils are available that are compatible with the new refrigerants. The most common types of synthetic oils are alkylbenzene, glycols, and ester-based oils. Alkylbenzene has been used for many years with HCFCs and HCFC blends because of their higher miscibility with these refrigerants compared to mineral oils. One advantage of alkylbenzene is that it can be mixed with up to 20% mineral oil and still retain its miscibility, thus simplifying a retrofit of an HCFC blend to an existing system without excessive oil flushing. One of the more popular glycol-based lubricants is polyalkylene glycol (PAG). PAG was one of the lubricants first evaluated for use with CFCs like R-134a, and many automotive air conditioning systems use PAG oils. However, it was found that the polyolester (POE) lubricants had better compatibility with fewer problems and are recommended for HFC and HFC blends such as R-134a and R-404A. When converting a system from a mineral oil to POE, the system must be carefully flushed to reduce the mineral oil content to below 5 percent. Ester-based oils are highly hygroscopic and careful handling is necessary to avoid water absorption. Use only new sealed oil containers when adding oil to the compressor. Do not leave the oil container open any longer than absolutely necessary. Further information on compressor lubrication and oil return is contained in chapter 4, and information on converting system refrigerants is contained in chapter 11.

## REFRIGERANT NUMBERING SYSTEM

In the 1950s DuPont developed a standard numbering system for refrigerants based on their chemical composition. This system has become an industry standard. The system for numbering single component halocarbon refrigerants is explained as follows:

A refrigerant is given the number R-XYZ where

X = the number of carbon atoms minus one (omitted if zero)
Y = the number of hydrogen atoms plus one
Z = the number of fluorine atoms

Take for example dichlorodifluoromethane, $CCl_2F_2$:

There is one carbon thus X = 1 − 1 = 0 (omit)
There are no hydrogen atoms thus Y = 0 + 1 = 1
There are two fluorine atoms thus Z = 2

Therefore the refrigerant is R-12.

In some cases the designation CFC, HCFC, or HFC rather than just "R" is used along with the refrigerant number. Thus R-12 becomes CFC-12, R-22 becomes HCFC-22, and R-134a becomes HFC-134a. Note that a refrigerant with a two-digit number will be based on methane with one carbon at the center of the molecule, while a one-hundred series refrigerant will be based on ethane with two carbons at the center. While no refrigerants based on propane are in current use, such a substance would be a two-hundred series refrigerant.

The letter at the end of the number of some refrigerants indicates that it is an isomer. Isomers have the same chemical composition but differ in the arrangement of the atoms that make up the molecule. An example of two isomers are the refrigerants R-134 and R-134a. Both have the same atoms that make up the molecules: two carbons, two hydrogens, and four flourines. Figure 3-3 shows the arrangement of the atoms in the two isomers. The symmetry of the molecule determines the numbering of the isomers. This is done by comparing the distribution of the atomic masses bonded to each carbon atom. Note that R-134 is symmetrical with two fluorine atoms and one hydrogen atom around each carbon. R-134a is not symmetrical with three flourines around one carbon and two hydrogens and one fluorine around the other. If there was a third possible arrangement of the atoms in the molecule that was even less symmetrical, it would be designated R-134b. An examination of Figure 3-3 shows that there is no other possible arrangement of the atoms in the molecule. Keep in mind that the atoms and molecules are in constant movement and the figures are merely depictions of the atoms relative positions within the molecule. Moving the two hydrogens to the other carbon in R-134a doesn't create another molecule, just a different point of reference for the same one. The same applies to the sequence of the fluorine and hydrogen atoms around each carbon.

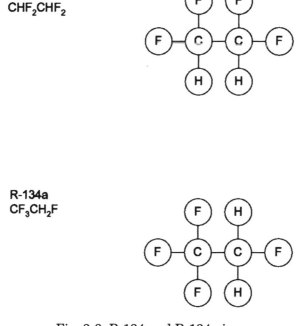

R-134
$CHF_2CHF_2$

R-134a
$CF_3CH_2F$

Fig. 3-3. R-134 and R-134a isomers.

As will be shown in the next section, refrigerant blends are given numbers in the 400s and 500s. Refrigerant numbers are also given to a wide variety of substances other than halocarbons. Inorganic compounds are given numbers in the 700s. For example ammonia ($NH_3$) is R-717, water ($H_2O$) is R-718, air is R-729, and carbon dioxide ($CO_2$) is R-744. The second and third digits in the number are the molecular weight of the substance. Saturated organic substances are given numbers in the 600s and unsaturated organic compounds are given numbers in the 1100s. For example ethylamine is R-631 and ethylene is R-1150.

## REFRIGERANT BLENDS

Mixing two or more different substances together can develop new refrigerants. This is usually done because existing single component refrigerants don't have the required properties for a particular application, or to develop a refrigerant superior to existing refrigerants. Such refrigerants are called blends. Blends can be classified as azeotropes or zeotropes. An azeotrope is a mixture of two or more liquids of precise proportions such that the blend has a constant boiling temperature point at a constant pressure during a phase change and maintains a nearly constant chemical composition throughout the refrigeration cycle. It behaves almost as if it was a single substance. It should be noted that if the percentage of the substances in the blend were changed, it would no longer behave as a zeotrope. Two zeotropes blends that have been used in refrigeration systems are R-500 and R-502. R-500 is a blend of 73.8% R-12 and 26.2% R-152a. R-502 is a blend of 48.8% R-22 and 51.2% R-115. Because one of the components in each of these blends is a CFC, they are no longer being produced and are being phased out of use in existing systems.

A zeotrope is a blend of two or more substances that will experience a change in mixture ratio during phase changes and exhibit a variation in temperature during phase changes at constant pressure. This change in temperature during boiling or condensing at constant pressure is referred to as temperature glide. The saturation temperature of the vapor at a particular pressure is called the "dew" point (temperature). The saturation temperature of the liquid at the same pressure is called the "bubble" point. The difference between the two temperatures is called the "temperature glide." A blend that exhibits only a small temperature glide and approaches the characteristics of an azeotrope is referred to as "near-azeotropic." Table 3-3 contains saturation pressure and temperature data for two different blends, R-404A and R-407C. Note in each case the bubble temperature is lower than the dew temperature. This means the temperature of the refrigerant will drop as it condenses at constant pressure and rise as it boils at constant pressure. This is characteristic of all zeotropes.

An examination of table 3-3 shows that R-404A has a temperature glide of only about 1°F, while that for R-407C is 9 to 12°F.

### TABLE 3-3
### Pressure-Temperature Data for Refrigerant Blends R-404A and R407C

| Pressure (psig) | R-404A Bubble Temperature (°F) | R-404A Dew Temperature (°F) | R-407C Bubble Temperature (°F) | R-407C Dew Temperature (°F) |
|---|---|---|---|---|
| 0.0 | −51.81 | −50.40 | −46.86 | −34.10 |
| 10.0 | −31.13 | −29.84 | −26.22 | −13.89 |
| 20.0 | −16.22 | −15.02 | −11.39 | 0.63 |
| 30.0 | −4.33 | −3.19 | 0.43 | 12.18 |
| 40.0 | 5.67 | 6.77 | 10.36 | 21.88 |
| 50.0 | 14.37 | 15.42 | 18.98 | 30.30 |
| 60.0 | 22.10 | 23.12 | 26.64 | 37.78 |
| 70.0 | 29.09 | 30.07 | 33.56 | 44.53 |
| 80.0 | 35.48 | 36.44 | 39.89 | 50.69 |
| 90.0 | 41.39 | 42.32 | 45.73 | 56.38 |
| 100.0 | 46.89 | 47.79 | 51.17 | 61.67 |
| 110.0 | 52.04 | 52.91 | 56.26 | 66.61 |
| 120.0 | 56.89 | 57.74 | 61.06 | 71.27 |
| 130.0 | 61.47 | 62.31 | 65.59 | 75.67 |
| 140.0 | 65.83 | 66.64 | 69.90 | 79.85 |
| 150.0 | 69.98 | 70.78 | 74.01 | 83.82 |
| 160.0 | 73.95 | 74.72 | 77.93 | 87.62 |
| 170.0 | 77.75 | 78.51 | 81.69 | 91.25 |
| 180.0 | 81.40 | 82.14 | 85.30 | 94.74 |
| 190.0 | 84.91 | 85.64 | 88.78 | 98.10 |
| 200.0 | 88.30 | 89.01 | 92.13 | 101.33 |

As the manufacturers develop blends, they are initially given proprietary designations such as MP-39, HP-62, Klea 60, and AZ-50. As blends receive wide use, they are given "R" numbers. Zeotropes are given numbers in the 400s and azeotropes are given numbers in the 500s. The numbers are merely given out in sequence. If a blend with different percentages of the same constituents is developed and approved, a letter (A, B, C) is used to differentiate between the two. For example, R-402A is a blend of 38% R-22, 60% R-125, and 2% R-290. R-402B is a blend of 60% R-22, 38% R-125, and 2% R-290.

A leak in a system charged with a refrigerant blend causes a unique problem. The substances that make up the blend have different boiling points and exert different partial pressures. Any refrigerant leak can result in more of one component being lost than others, changing the ratio of the components in the mixture, and potentially affecting the performance of the system. This change in composition is called "fractionation." Fractionation is more of a problem with blends that have a large temperature glide and thus change composition significantly during phase changes. Leaks occurring in the evaporator or condenser where phase changes occur are of greater concern than areas where the refrigerant is entirely liquid or vapor. Topping off a system charge using a near azeotropic blend normally will not have a significant effect on system performance. If performance is affected after repeated partial recharging, the charge must be recovered and the system recharged with new refrigerant. Blends should only be charged as a liquid to avoid fractionation during the process. More details on charging and recovering refrigerants, leak detection, and other service and maintenance procedures are contained in chapter 11.

## OZONE DEPLETION AND THE MONTREAL PROTOCOLS

In the 1970s, two scientists at the University of California, Dr. Sherwood Rowland and Dr. Mario Molina, raised concerns that some chlorinated compounds were destroying ozone in the upper atmosphere. Ozone ($O_3$) is formed when high-energy ultraviolet light breaks apart an oxygen ($O_2$) molecule, liberating two single oxygen ions, which may then bind with an ($O_2$) molecule to form ozone. Ozone in the stratosphere scatters and absorbs UV radiation, reducing the levels that reach the earth's surface. Reduction of ozone levels in the upper atmosphere leads to increased ultraviolet radiation reaching the earth's surface that can result in increased rates of skin cancer and cataracts, and also possible suppression of the body's immune system. Increased levels of ultraviolet light can also affect the growth of photo plankton, disrupting the marine food chain. The Rowland-Molina theory states that certain chlorinated compounds will remain intact in the atmosphere for years, eventually reaching the stratosphere where the high-energy UV radiation levels will break down the molecule, releasing the chorine atoms. While the process of ozone depletion is complex, it can be explained by the following simplified process as shown in Figure 3-4. The free chlorine atoms react with ozone ($O_3$), forming chlorine monoxide (CIO) and oxygen ($O_2$). A free oxygen atom will then react with the chlorine monoxide, forming oxygen and releasing the chlorine atom to repeat the process. The chlorine acts as a catalyst in the process, and a single chlorine atom can destroy thousands of ozone molecules.

These concerns led to the banning of CFCs for propellants in aerosol sprays in 1978. In 1987, the United States and many other countries signed the "Montreal Protocol on Substances That Deplete the Ozone" that regulates the production and use of CFCs. Subsequent agreements included HCFCs in the substances under control, and in 1990 President Bush signed amendments to the Clean Air Act that put in place schedules for the phase out of the production of CFCs and HCFCs, regulations on their use and disposal, specifies service practices to minimize the release of refrigerants into the atmosphere, certification of equipment used in the recovery of refrigerants from systems, and requirements for the licensing of

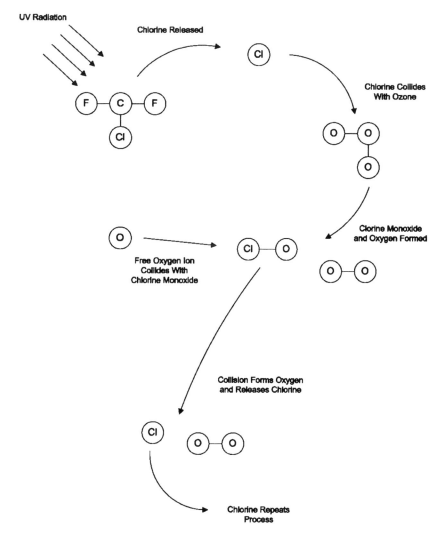

Fig. 3-4. Ozone depletion by cholorinated compound.

technicians involved in the repair and maintenance of refrigeration and air-conditioning systems. The most important section of the amendments to the Clean Air Act for the marine industry is Section 608, which pertains to refrigeration equipment common on ships and other marine vehicles. Violations of the Clean Air Act can carry penalties up to $27,500 per day, so it is essential that all owners and operators of the equipment using refrigerants understand the various requirements. Chapter 11 of this text contains information on venting prohibitions, recovery/recycling equipment and procedures, and other aspects of Section 608 that pertain to equipment operation and maintenance. The appendix contains information on technician certification including information on the certification test.

In general, CFCs like R-11 and R-12 are more damaging to the ozone layer than HCFCs. This is because CFCs are very stable substances and a high percentage survives intact into the upper atmosphere where the ozone destruction process described above can proceed. HCFCs are less stable and a much smaller percentage makes it to the stratosphere. HFCs have no effect on ozone depletion because the molecule does not contain any chlorine. A factor called the Ozone Depletion Potential (ODP) has been developed to quantify the danger of substances to the ozone. The factor is defined as 1.0 for R-11, and the factor for other substances are related to that for R-11. Table 3-4 contains the ODP for a number of refrigerants. Note that HCFCs have only a fraction of the ODP of CFCs. For example R-22 has an ODP of 0.05 whereas R-12 has an ODP of 1.0.

**TABLE 3-4**
**Ozone Depletion Potential and**
**Global Warming Potential for Common Refrigerants**

|        | ODP<br>(R-11 = 1.0) | GWP Direct<br>(R-11 = 1.0) | GWP Indirect<br>($CO_2$ = 1.0) |
|--------|------|------|-------|
| R-11   | 1.0  | 1.0  | 1,300 |
| R-12   | 1.0  | 3.0  | 3,700 |
| R-22   | 0.05 | 0.34 | 570   |
| R-123  | 0.02 | 0.02 | 28    |
| R-134a | 0.0  | 0.28 | 400   |
| R-404A | 0.0  | 0.94 | —     |

Because of their greater danger to the ozone layer, CFCs, halons, and other substances classified by the EPA as Class 1 were targeted for early phaseout. As of December 31, 1995, CFC production has ceased. In recognition that safe alternatives are not available yet for all refrigerant applications, HCFCs are being allowed to remain in use for an extended period while chlorine-free replacements are developed. Table 3-5 shows the phaseout schedule for HCFC consumption. Consumption is defined as production plus imports minus exports. The baseline (cap) is based on 100% of the HCFC consumption plus 3.1% of the CFC consumption in 1989. Note that reduction in HCFC consumption begins in 2004 and is not ended until 2030. It is important to note that HCFCs may continue to be used after 2030 and will continue to be sold, though the cost will certainly rise as happened with CFCs after their phase out.

A second environmental concern related to the release of refrigerants into atmosphere is global warming, commonly referred to as the greenhouse effect. Global warming is the reradiation of heat from the earth by certain gases in the atmosphere back to the earth, resulting in gradual increases in the earth's average temperature. Scientists are concerned about the effects global warming will have on the weather and on water levels as the ice caps melt. The most significant substance affecting global warming is carbon dioxide released from the combustion of hydrocarbon fuels. However, halocarbon refrigerants are hundreds of times more effective in trapping heat compared to carbon dioxide, and, therefore, this effect also must be considered in selecting and controlling refrigerants. There are direct and indirect effects that must be considered. The release of refrigerants into the atmosphere is a direct effect. Indirect effects are related to the energy efficiency of the equipment using the substance and the carbon dioxide released by the energy production. A factor called the Global Warming Potential (GWP) quantifies the effect different substances have on reradiating thermal energy back to the earth.

For the direct effects, the GWP is defined as 1.0 for R-11 and the factor for other substances are referenced to R-11. Note that R-12 has a GWP of 3.0 while that for R-134a is only 0.28. For the indirect effects, the base of 1.0 is defined for carbon dioxide. Table 3-4 contains the direct and indirect GWP for several common refrigerants.

## ALTERNATIVE REFRIGERANTS

In response to the phase out of CFCs, refrigerant manufacturers have introduced a number of new compounds for use in new systems and also as replacements in existing systems after the necessary conversion process. Some of these new refrigerants are chlorine free (HFCs) and are expected to be used far into the future. Others contain HCFCs and are considered interim refrigerants, designed for use as retrofits to existing equipment or in new systems where a chlorine-free substance is not yet available. Some of these new refrigerants are single component types containing only one type of molecule, while others are blends of two or three different substances.

R-134a is an HFC and is the most widely used of the new single component refrigerants. It has a similar pressure-temperature relationship to R-12 and has been used in many new applications where R-12 was used in the past. It is not recommended for applications with evaporator temperatures below −10°F because the low side pressure can drop below atmospheric and air can be drawn in. Like most HFCs, it is not compatible with traditional mineral lubricating oil, requiring the use of synthetic oils such as polyolester (POE). This refrigerant may be used in retrofit applications but requires complete flushing of the old mineral oil and replacement of certain system components. An alternative for retrofit applications is to use an HCFC blend discussed below.

R-123 is an HCFC and has been proposed as an interim replacement for R-11 in centrifugal chillers because of its similar temperature-pressure characteristics. Caution must be taken when using this refrigerant as it has been shown to have toxic properties and has a safety rating of B1. Refrigerant leakage alarms must be installed and technicians must be trained in the use of breathing apparatus and go through annual fit testing. Retrofit in an existing R-11 system is an engineered conversion requiring significant parts replacement.

As many R-12 compressors are also designed for use with R-22, it should be considered a possible retrofit for such systems. R-22 is an HCFC and is not scheduled for complete production phaseout until 2030. One possible difficulty is that operating pressures are higher than with R-12 and compressor speed may have to be reduced to avoid motor overloads. More information on refrigerant retrofits is contained in chapter 11.

A wide variety of refrigerant blends are being marketed for retrofit and new applications. Two blends that have become popular as replacements for R-22 and R-502 in new low and medium temperature applications are R-404A and R-507. R-404A is a near azeotropic blend of 44% R-125, 52% R-143a, and 4% R-134a also sold as Forane FX 70 and Suva HP-62. R-507 is an azeotropic blend of 50% R-125 and 50% R-143a. Both are blends of HFCs and thus are potential long-term replacements. Neither R-404A nor R-507 is considered a "drop-in" replacement for R-22 or R-502 as they require the removal of the mineral oil and replacement with a polyolester (POE) lubricant. Other blends are termed "service" blends and are intended primarily for retrofit applications. They typically contain HCFCs and thus are suitable only as interim replacements. Examples are R-401A, R-401B, and R-409A, which are replacements for R-12 and R-500, and R-402A and R-402B, which are replacements for R-502. These blends are compatible with alkylbenzene and in some cases mineral oil, and thus do not require the complete flushing required with conversion to POE lubricants.

## SECONDARY REFRIGERANTS

In larger systems with loads located far from the condensing unit, the use of secondary refrigerants is common. Many air-conditioning chillers use chilled water as a heat transfer medium. Chilled water cannot be used for systems operating below 32°F (0°C), so brine or anti-freeze mixtures are used to prevent freezing. Brine solutions are mixtures of salts such as calcium chloride or sodium chloride and water. Anti-freeze mixtures such as ethylene glycol and propylene glycol are commonly used. Further information on secondary refrigerants and their use in chiller systems is contained in chapter 5.

# PROBLEMS (ENGLISH UNITS)

3.1E  Determine standard refrigerant number for the following substances (a) methane $CH_4$, (b) trichloromonofluoromethane $CCl_3F$, and (c) trichlorotrifluoroethane $CCl_2FCClF_2$.

3.2E  Using the standard refrigerant numbering system, determine the chemical formula for (a) R-12, (b) R-22, and (c) R-123. For each, determine if the refrigerant is a CFC, HCFC, or HFC.

3.3E  Draw the arrangement of the molecules for the two isomers of trichlorotrifluoroethane. Identify the isomer that is least symmetric and thus should be identified with an "a" suffix.

3.4E  Draw the arrangement of the molecules for the three isomers of R-142. Identify the isomer that should be identified with an "a" suffix and the one that should be identified with a "b" suffix.

3.5E  Calculate the temperature glide for R-404A and R-407C at temperatures of 0°F and 75°F.

# PROBLEMS (SI UNITS)

3.1S  Determine standard refrigerant number for the following substances (a) methane $CH_4$, (b) trichloromonofluoromethane $CCl_3F$, and (c) trichlorotrifluoroethane $CCl_2FCClF_2$.

3.2S  Using the standard refrigerant numbering system, determine the chemical formula for (a) R-12, (b) R-22, and (c) R-123. For each, determine if the refrigerant is a CFC, HCFC, or HFC.

3.3S  Draw the arrangement of the molecules for the two isomers of trichlorotrifluoroethane. Identify the isomer that is least symmetric and thus should be identified with an "a" suffix.

3.4S  Draw the arrangement of the molecules for the three isomers of R-142. Identify the isomer that should be identified with an "a" suffix and the one that should be identified with a "b" suffix.

CHAPTER 4

# Compressors

Three types of compressors are used in refrigeration systems: (1) reciprocating, (2) rotary, and (3) centrifugal. The reciprocating and rotary types are positive displacement machines. In the reciprocating compressor, the gas is compressed by a piston, while in a rotary compressor a screw, roller, vane, or scroll traps the gas and reduces its volume and increases its pressure. A centrifugal compressor uses a high-speed impeller to generate the compression force by dynamic action. Each compressor type has certain advantages and disadvantages. The type selected depends on such factors as the size and type of the installation and on the refrigerant used.

## RECIPROCATING COMPRESSORS

The reciprocating compressor is the most common type found in marine refrigeration systems. It is found in systems rated from less than one ton to several hundred tons and in high, medium, and low temperature applications. It is durable and efficient and can be manufactured economically.

The basic components of a reciprocating compressor include the piston, cylinder, crankshaft, connecting rod, intake valves, and discharge valves. Figure 4-1 shows a reciprocating compressor at several points in the cycle. It is important to remember that the compressor valves that control the flow of gas into and out of the cylinder are operated by the difference in pressure across them, similar to the way a check valve in a pipe only allows fluid flow in one direction. As the piston moves downward from top dead center, the pressure in the cylinder drops to the suction pressure and the suction valves open, and refrigerant gas is drawn into the cylinder. As the piston begins to move up from bottom dead center, the gas pressure increases slightly, closing the suction valve, and the pressure of the trapped

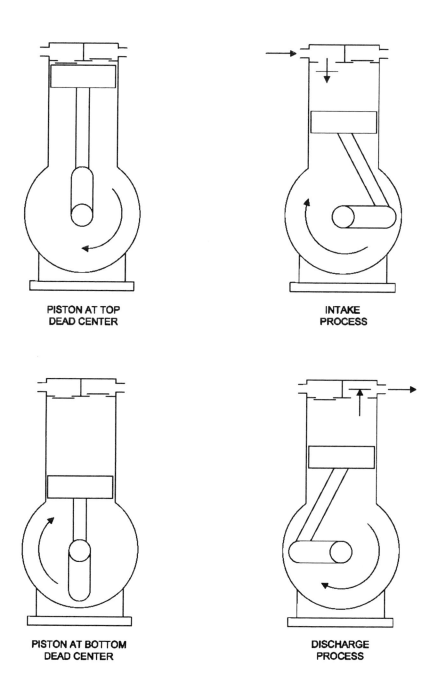

PISTON AT TOP
DEAD CENTER

INTAKE
PROCESS

PISTON AT BOTTOM
DEAD CENTER

DISCHARGE
PROCESS

Fig. 4-1. Reciprocating compressor cycle.

gas begins to increase. When the pressure reaches the discharge pressure, the discharge valve opens, allowing the high-pressure gas to escape into the discharge manifold. Discharge continues until the piston reaches top dead center and the cycle begins again.

A small amount of clearance is necessary between the top of the piston and the bottom of the cylinder head that contains the valves to prevent the piston from striking the cylinder head as it approaches top dead center. The volume of this space is called the clearance volume. At top dead center, a small volume of high-pressure gas will remain in the cylinder as the piston begins moving down. It is necessary to re-expand this gas to the suction pressure before the suction valve will open on the intake stroke. Figure 4-2 is a pressure-volume diagram for a complete cycle of an ideal reciprocating compressor. The cycle consists of four processes: re-expansion, intake, compression, and discharge. The clearance volume and the resulting re-expansion process have a significant effect on the

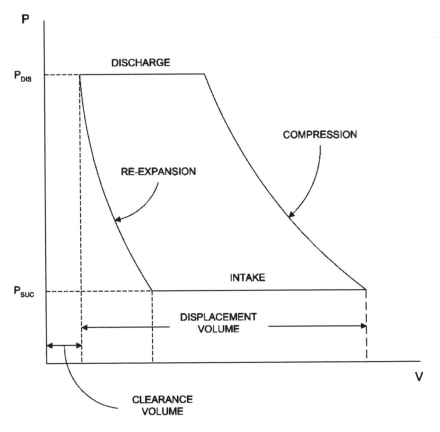

Fig. 4-2. Pressure-volume diagram of ideal reciprocating compressor.

performance of a reciprocating compressor. The larger the clearance volume, the longer the re-expansion process and the shorter the intake process will be. A large clearance volume in combination with a large difference between the suction and discharge pressure can result in the re-expansion process occupying most of the stroke from top dead center to bottom dead center, significantly reducing the compressor capacity. The compressor volumetric efficiency that quantifies this performance characteristic will be defined later.

Marine reciprocating compressors are typically of the single-acting enclosed type. In single-acting compressors, vapor compression occurs on only one side of the piston, while in double-acting compressors, vapor compression occurs on both sides of the piston. Double-acting compressors are only found on older large industrial installations. Enclosed-type compressors drive the piston by a connecting rod driven by the crankshaft. The crankcase is airtight and exposed to the system refrigerant. Reciprocating compressors can be further classified as open, hermetic, or semi-hermetic. An open type unit as shown in figure 4-3 has a separate motor and compressor. A hermetic unit as shown in figure 4-4a is a sealed motor-compressor assembly and is common in smaller units. A semi-hermetic or "accessible hermetic" is a unit in which the shell of the assembly is bolted rather than welded. This allows for field servicing. See figure 4-4b.

The number of cylinders varies from one to as many as twelve or more. In multi-cylinder units, the cylinders may be arranged in-line, radially, or in a V or W pattern. A V-type compressor has the cylinders arranged in two banks while a W-type has the cylinders arranged in three banks. Figure

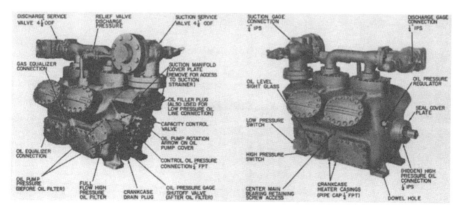

Fig. 4-3. Open-type W pattern compressor. Courtesy Carrier Corporation.

Fig. 4-4a. Hermetic compressor.

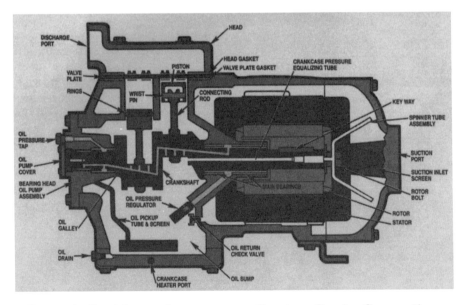

Fig. 4-4b. Semi-hermetic compressor. Courtesy Carrier Corporation.

4-3 shows a modern open-type W pattern compressor while figure 4-5 shows a typical V-type compressor. The construction details of a typical reciprocating compressor are shown in figures 4-5 and 4-6. Pistons can be of the automotive or the double-trunk type. The piston assembly shown in figure 4-6 is of the automotive type while figures 4-7a and 4-7b show an in-line reciprocating compressor with double-trunk pistons. When automotive type pistons are used, the gas enters and exits through valves located at the top of the cylinder. In double-trunk piston units, the gas enters through ports in the cylinder wall and enters the center of the piston. The gas passes into the cylinder through suction valves located in the top of the piston and discharges through valves located at the top of the cylinder.

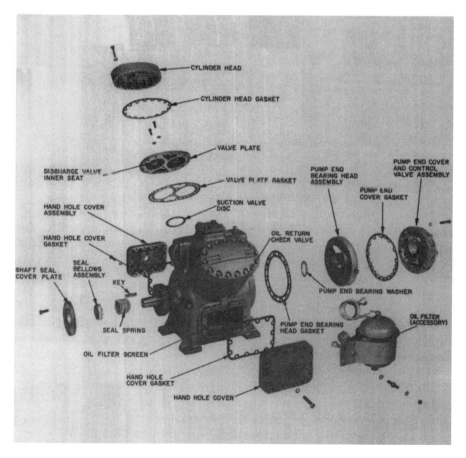

Fig. 4-5. V-type compressor assembly. Courtesy Carrier Corporation.

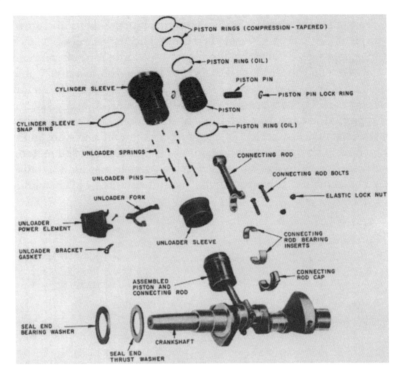

Fig. 4-6. Reciprocating compressor internal parts. Courtesy
Carrier Corporation.

### Intake and Discharge Valves

The valve types used in refrigeration compressors are the reed, the ring,
and the poppet. All three types open and close automatically based on the
pressure differential across the valve. Reed valves are flexible metal strips
that fit over slots in the valve seat. Ring valves consist of one or more circular rings, valve springs, and a retainer. The poppet valve is similar in construction to an automobile valve that is spring loaded. Poppet valves are
used only in low-speed compressors while reed and ring valves can be used
in both low-speed and high-speed machines. Figure 4-8 shows the gas flow
through a typical compressor. Figure 4-9 shows a typical suction and discharge valve assembly using ring valves. The arrangement of common
reed valve and ring valve installations are shown in figure 4-10.

Many larger compressors are fitted with a spring-loaded safety head.
Under normal operating conditions, the head is held in place by heavy
springs rather than bolts. The small clearance volume in the compressor
increases the possibility of damage due to the intake of liquid refrigerant.
In the event that a slug of liquid refrigerant should enter the cylinder, the
safety head will rise and prevent damage to the compressor.

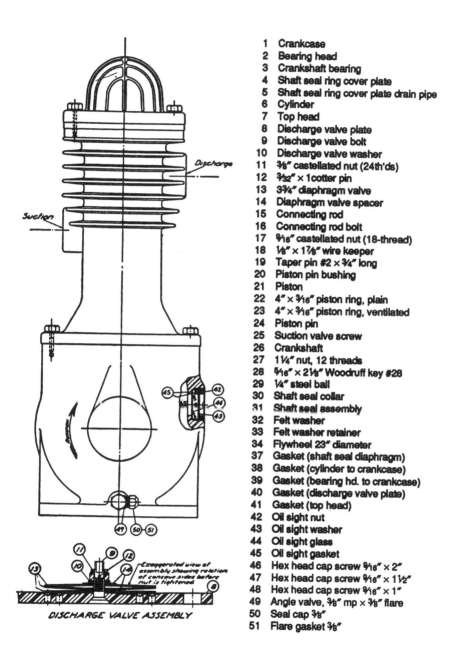

1 Crankcase
2 Bearing head
3 Crankshaft bearing
4 Shaft seal ring cover plate
5 Shaft seal ring cover plate drain pipe
6 Cylinder
7 Top head
8 Discharge valve plate
9 Discharge valve bolt
10 Discharge valve washer
11 3/8" castellated nut (24th'ds)
12 3/32" × 1 cotter pin
13 3¾" diaphragm valve
14 Diaphragm valve spacer
15 Connecting rod
16 Connecting rod bolt
17 9/16" castellated nut (18-thread)
18 1/8" × 1⅛" wire keeper
19 Taper pin #2 × ¾" long
20 Piston pin bushing
21 Piston
22 4" × 3/16" piston ring, plain
23 4" × 3/16" piston ring, ventilated
24 Piston pin
25 Suction valve screw
26 Crankshaft
27 1¼" nut, 12 threads
28 5/16" × 2⅛" Woodruff key #28
29 ¼" steel ball
30 Shaft seal collar
31 Shaft seal assembly
32 Felt washer
33 Felt washer retainer
34 Flywheel 23" diameter
37 Gasket (shaft seal diaphragm)
38 Gasket (cylinder to crankcase)
39 Gasket (bearing hd. to crankcase)
40 Gasket (discharge valve plate)
41 Gasket (top head)
42 Oil sight nut
43 Oil sight washer
44 Oil sight glass
45 Oil sight gasket
46 Hex head cap screw 9/16" × 2"
47 Hex head cap screw 9/16" × 1½"
48 Hex head cap screw 9/16" × 1"
49 Angle valve, 3/8" mp × 3/8" flare
50 Seal cap 3/8"
51 Flare gasket 3/8"

DISCHARGE VALVE ASSEMBLY

Fig. 4-7a. Two-cylinder in-line compressor. Courtesy York
Ice Machinery Corp.

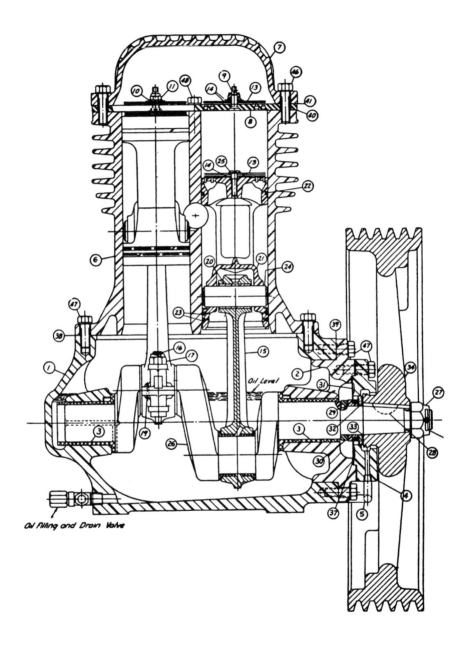

Fig. 4-7b.  Two-cylinder in-line compressor. Courtesy York
Ice Machinery Corp.

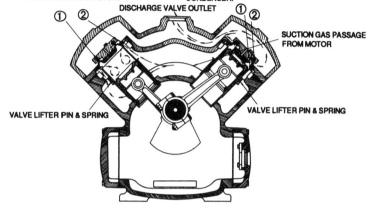

LEFT CYLINDER

1 ON DOWNWARD STROKE OF THE PISTON, THE DISCHARGE VALVE CLOSES, AND THE PRESSURE ABOVE THE PISTON AND THE SUCTION VALVE DISCS DROPS BELOW THE SUCTION (CRANKCASE) PRESSURE.

2 THE REDUCTION IN PRESSURE CAUSES THE SUCTION VALVES TO LIFT OPEN AND ALLOWS VAPOR TO PASS INTO THE CYLINDER ABOVE THE PISTON.

RIGHT CYLINDER

1 ON THE UPSTROKE, THE PISTON COM-PRESSES THE VAPOR WHICH IN TURN CLOSES THE SUCTION VALVES. THE PRESSURE INCREASES AS THE PISTON RISES UNTIL IT EXCEEDS THE CONDENSING PRESSURE.

2 THIS INCREASE IN PRESSURE OPENS THE DISCHARGE VALVES ALLOWING THE COM-PRESSED VAPOR TO PASS INTO THE CONDENSER.

DISCHARGE VALVE OUTLET

SUCTION GAS PASSAGE FROM MOTOR

VALVE LIFTER PIN & SPRING

VALVE LIFTER PIN & SPRING

Fig. 4-8. Compressor gas flow. Courtesy Carrier Corporation.

## Shaft Seals

Open-type compressors require a crankshaft seal where the shaft exits the casing to prevent refrigerant from escaping or air entering. While a variety of crankshaft seals have been used in refrigeration compressors, the most popular type is the spring-loaded mechanical seal, figures 4-11 and 4-12. The seal consists of a spring-loaded carbon or bronze rotating seal that runs against a stationary seal plate with a highly polished face. A rubber gasket seals the crankshaft and the rotating seal, and another gasket seals the seal plate and the compressor casing. The spring maintains the rotating seal in firm contact with the stationary seal plate. An oil film lubricates the two smooth mating seal surfaces and forms a vapor-tight seal.

## Lubrication

There are two basic types of lubrication systems found on refrigeration compressors: splash and forced feed. Splash lubrication is common on smaller compressors (10 hp and less) while larger compressors typically have some form of forced lubrication. A combination of splash and forced lubrication can sometimes be found on a single compressor. In splash lubrication, the crankcase is filled with oil to approximately the level of the crankshaft. As the crankshaft turns, oil is splashed onto the bearings, the cylinder walls, and other surfaces. Oil scoops are sometimes used to force

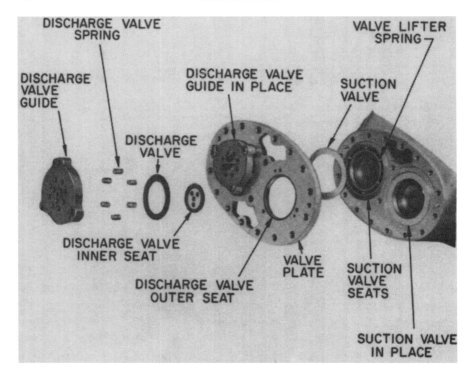

DISCHARGE VALVE
SPRING

VALVE LIFTER
SPRING

DISCHARGE
VALVE
GUIDE

DISCHARGE VALVE
GUIDE IN PLACE

SUCTION
VALVE

DISCHARGE
VALVE

DISCHARGE VALVE
INNER SEAT

DISCHARGE VALVE
OUTER SEAT

VALVE
PLATE

SUCTION
VALVE
SEATS

SUCTION VALVE
IN PLACE

Fig. 4-9. Suction and discharge valve assemblies. Courtesy
Carrier Corporation.

oil through drilled passages to lubricate the connecting rod bearings. Oil
cavities usually are located above the main bearings to collect oil, which
then feeds the bearings by gravity.

In forced-feed lubrication, a pump is used to deliver the oil to the various parts requiring lubrication. The pump is typically a small positive displacement unit driven by gears from the crankshaft. The oil is delivered
under pressure through oil tubes and/or drilled passages in the crankshaft
and connecting rods. Oil strainers are located at the pump suction, and oil
filters are usually installed at the pump discharge. An oil pressure failure
switch is installed to warn of loss of proper lubrication. Figure 4-13 shows a
typical refrigeration compressor forced lubrication system. The oil selected
for lubrication of refrigeration compressors must be chemically stable,
have low pour and cloud points, have the proper viscosity for the operating
temperature range, and be compatible with the system refrigerant. In addition the oil used in hermetic units must have a high dielectric strength to
avoid grounding or shorting of the motor windings. Traditionally, mineral
oils have been used in refrigeration compressors, but the new chlorine-free
refrigerants such as R-134a are not compatible with them. They require

synthetic oils such as polyalkylene glycol (PAG) or polyolester (POE). Further information on the compatibility of oils with various refrigerants is discussed in chapter 3. Consult the manufacturer's technical manual for the recommended oils for each compressor.

A certain amount of refrigerant will always be dissolved in the lubricating oil. However, large amounts of refrigerant in the oil are undesirable. Excessive dilution can result in inadequate lubrication. In addition, during compressor start-up, the lowering of the crankcase pressure will cause oil foaming due to the vaporization of the refrigerant. In severe cases, this

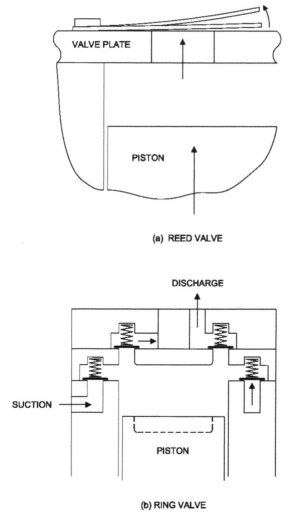

Fig. 4-10. Arrangement of compressor reed and ring valves.

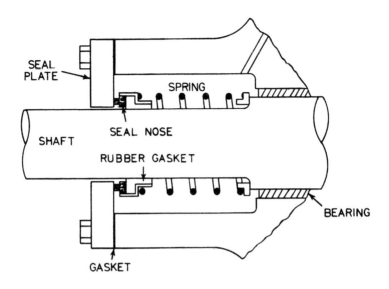

Fig. 4-11. Mechanical shaft seal.

can disrupt lubrication and can cause carryover of the liquid refrigerant and oil into the cylinder. Since marine systems typically operate on the pumpdown cycle, the low crankcase pressure at shutdown limits refrigerant absorption by the oil. Crankcase heaters that come on automatically during the compressor off cycle can be used to keep the oil warm and further reduce refrigerant absorption. A common cause of excessive oil dilution by liquid refrigerant is an improperly adjusted thermostatic expansion that which allows overfeeding of the evaporator. The liquid refrigerant then carries over into the compressor suction and enters the crankcase.

## Capacity Control

Any refrigeration or air-conditioning system must be designed to handle the maximum refrigeration load anticipated. In a refrigeration system, this typically occurs when warm cargo or stores are loaded and the temperature of the stores must be lowered to the desired storage temperature. The total refrigeration load is the sum of energy to be removed from the stores plus the heat leakage into the refrigerated space from the surroundings. As the stores temperature decreases and reaches the desired storage temperature, the system load is reduce to just the heat infiltration from the surroundings. This is considerably less load than the initial load. If the compressor continues to operate at full capacity, it would short-cycle, starting and stopping with short running times. This is inefficient and the space conditions will not be maintained consistently. A similar situation will exist in an air-conditioning system when the outside conditions are warm but well below the design values. The system is oversized for the existing conditions and will short cycle if the system capacity is not reduced.

There are a number of methods of controlling the capacity of reciprocating compressors. Some of the methods that can be used include: (1) variable speed operation, (2) cylinder unloading by holding suction

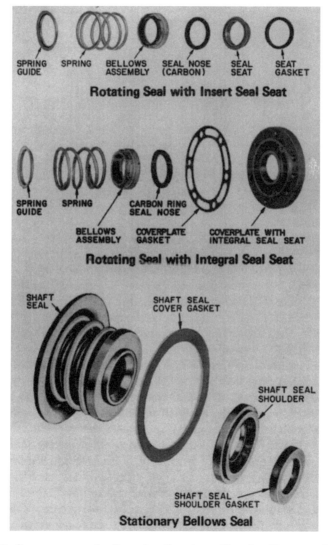

Fig. 4-12. Compressor shaft seals. Courtesy Carrier Corporation.

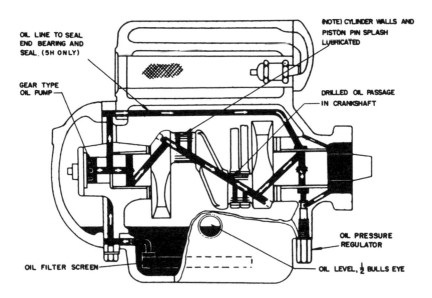

Fig. 4-13. Compressor lubrication system. Courtesy Carrier Corporation.

valves open, (3) cylinder bypass, (4) hot gas bypass, and (5) multiple compressors. Operating a reciprocating compressor at different speeds is an effective technique for varying the compressor capacity. Like other positive displacement compressors, the capacity of a reciprocating compressor varies directly with its speed. For example, reducing the compressor speed to half will reduce the refrigerant flow and thus the system capacity to one-half. Multi-speed motors provide speed reduction in steps, typically two or three. A two-speed motor would typically provide operation at 100 percent and 50 percent, while a three-speed motor would typically provide operation at one third, two thirds, and full capacity. A continuously variable speed drive such as a wound rotor induction motor, a steam turbine, or an induction motor with variable frequency controller provides stepless variation in capacity.

A common method of varying the capacity of multicylinder compressors is to vary the number of active cylinders by holding the suction valves open. The capacity control system unloads cylinders (that is, cuts cylinders out of operation) in response to changes in refrigeration load based on monitoring the suction pressure. Figure 4-14 shows a typical compressor capacity control system. Compressor lubricating oil is used to operate the valve lifting mechanism. Under high loads (high-suction pressures), oil is admitted to the actuating cylinders and the suction valves are allowed to operate normally. As the load decreases (and the suction pressure drops), the oil pressure is cut off to the actuating cylinder and the suction valves are held open, stopping the compression of the controlled cylinders. Typically, compressor cylinders are unloaded in pairs, or in banks, by having different set points on the hydraulic mechanism, thus maintaining an even load on the crankshaft. If the suction pressure continues to fall off after all controlled cylinders are cut out, the compressor will stop on the low pressure switch. Since oil pressure is required to load the cylinder, the compressor will start with all controlled cylinders unloaded, thus reducing the starting load on the compressor motor.

Another method of unloading some cylinders in a multicylinder compressor is to install a bypass valve in a line connecting the discharge of one cylinder bank to its suction as shown in figure 4-15. When the cylinder bypass valve is opened, gas discharged from the cylinder is returned to the suction where it mixes with the inlet vapor. The check valve in the discharge line between the cylinders prevents the gas from the other cylinder from being bypassed as well. The bypass valve is operated by the suction pressure in a manner similar to the suction valve bypass system described above. As the suction pressure drops, the bypass valve is opened and the compressor capacity is reduced.

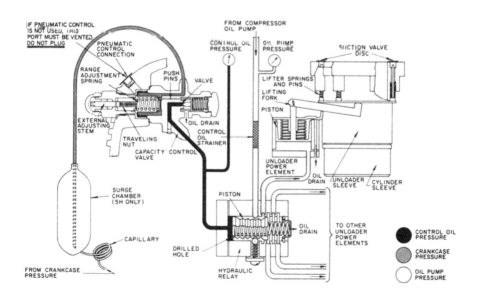

Fig. 4-14. Compressor capacity control system. Courtesy
Carrier Corporation.

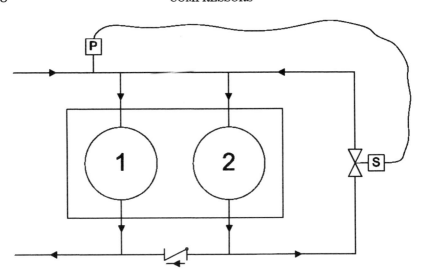

Fig. 4-15. Cylinder bypass capacity control.

Hot gas bypass is a technique sometimes used on small systems for capacity control. It has the disadvantage of not reducing the compressor power under reduced capacity operation as happens with the previous techniques. The compressor discharge is returned to the compressor suction or the evaporator inlet using a constant pressure (automatic) expansion valve. Returning the gas to the evaporator inlet is preferred as it eliminates compressor overheating, which can occur if the gas is bypassed to the compressor suction.

If the system is fitted with multiple compressors, they can be operated either singly or simultaneously depending on the system load. For example, in a refrigerated stores application, both compressors could be used during pulldown after stores have just been loaded and the boxes need to be reduced to design temperatures. Once the box and product temperatures have been reduced to the proper level, one compressor can be secured. Oil return can be a problem with compressors operating in parallel, so it is important that the compressors are designed for such operation. Either oil separators or a system for equalizing the sump oil levels should be fitted to avoid one sump from being drained while the other is overfilled.

### Reciprocating Compressor Performance Factors
The performance of the compressor in a refrigeration system has a significant impact on the overall system performance. A variety of factors can be defined to express the performance of real compressors and account for losses that increase the compressor power requirements and reduce the

compressor capacity. This section will analyze the performance of reciprocating compressors, but much of the analysis is applicable to other positive displacement types such as screw, vane, and scroll compressors. The two most important compressor performance factors are the volumetric efficiency and the overall compressor efficiency.

In the earlier section of this chapter describing the operation and construction of reciprocating compressors, the four processes that make up the compressor cycle and the effect of the clearance volume on the compressor capacity was described. It was noted that due to re-expansion of the high-pressure gas as the piston moves down from top dead center, the volume of gas compressed per cycle is reduced. In addition, such things as pressure drops across the compressor valves and manifolds, heating of the cold intake gas by the warm cylinder, and leakage past the valves and piston rings will also reduce the volume of gas compressed. The volumetric efficiency ($\eta_{vol}$) is defined as follows:

$$\eta_{vol} = \frac{V_{act}}{V_{dis}} \times 100 \tag{4.1}$$

where

$\eta_{vol}$ = volumetric efficiency, in percent
$V_{act}$ = actual volume of suction vapor compressed, in $ft^3/min$ or $m^3/sec$
$V_{dis}$ = the compressor displacement rate, in $ft^3/min$ or $m^3/sec$

The compressor displacement rate is the maximum possible volume of gas displaced per unit time based on the cylinder bore and stroke, the number of cylinders, and compressor operating speed. The compressor displacement rate for a single-acting compressor can be calculated as follows:

$$V_{dis} = (\pi/4)(d^2)(L)(N)(n) \tag{4.2}$$

where

$V_{dis}$ = compressor displacement rate in $ft^3/$min or $m^3/min$
$d$ = bore of the cylinder, in ft or m
$L$ = stroke of the cylinder, in ft or m
$N$ = operating speed, in revolutions per minute or second
$n$ = number of cylinders

EXAMPLE PROBLEM 4.1. A 4-cylinder compressor with a 30 mm bore and a 35 mm stroke is operating at 1150 rpm. Calculate: (a) the compressor displacement rate and (b) the volumetric efficiency if 0.075 $m^3/min$ are being compressed.

SOLUTION.

SKETCH AND GIVEN DATA:

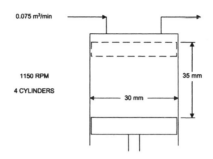

0.075 m³/min

1150 RPM

4 CYLINDERS

35 mm

30 mm

ASSUMPTIONS:

The compressor operates at steady-state conditions.

ANALYSIS:

Using equation 4.2, calculate the compressor displacement rate.

$$V_{dis} = (\pi/4)(d^2)(L)(N)(n) = (0.7854)(0.030\ m)^2(0.035\ m)(1{,}150\ rpm)(4\ cyls.)$$

$$V_{dis} = 0.1138\ m^3/min \tag{a}$$

Using equation 4.1, calculate the volumetric efficiency.

$$\eta_{vol} = \frac{V_{act}}{V_{dis}} \times 100 = \frac{\left(0.075\ m^3/min\right)}{\left(0.1138\ m^3/min\right)}(100) = 65.9\% \tag{b}$$

COMMENTS:

The displacement rate must be greater than the actual volume of refrigerant gas that is to be compressed to overcome losses.

It was noted above that the clearance volume and the re-expansion of the trapped refrigerant vapor have a significant impact on the compressor volumetric efficiency. By assuming the vapor behaves like an ideal gas and assuming isentropic expansion, the volumetric efficiency that would result from the effect of the clearance volume can be derived. The clearance volumetric efficiency ($\eta_{cv}$) can be estimated using the following equation:

$$\eta_{cv} = \left(1 - \left(V_{cl}/V_{dpl}\right)\left(P_{dis}/P_{suc} - 1\right)\right) \times 100 \tag{4.3}$$

where

$\eta_{cv}$ = clearance volumetric efficiency, in percent
$V_{cl}$ = clearance volume in ft$^3$ or m$^3$

$V_{dpl}$ = displacement volume, in ft$^3$ or m$^3$
$P_{dis}$ = absolute discharge pressure, in psia or kPa
$P_{suc}$ = absolute suction pressure, in psia or kPa

Any compressor's actual volumetric efficiency will be lower than the clearance volumetric efficiency due to the factors listed above. Figure 4-16 compares the estimated clearance volumetric efficiency with the typical actual volumetric efficiency for medium-sized reciprocating compressors handling halocarbon refrigerants. The efficiency for small compressors will be somewhat lower, and that for large compressors will be somewhat higher.

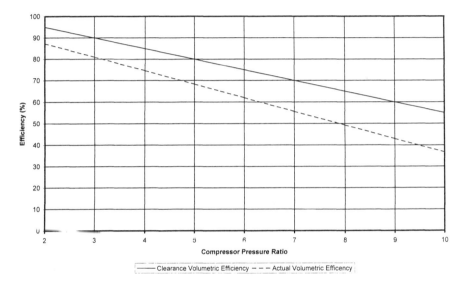

Fig. 4-16. Compressor volumetric efficiency.

EXAMPLE PROBLEM 4.2. Calculate the clearance volumetric efficiency of a reciprocating compressor operating on R-22 with a condensing temperature of 110°F and a clearance volume of 5 percent of the displacement, for evaporating temperatures of: (a) 0°F and (b) 40°F.

SOLUTION.

SKETCH AND GIVEN DATA:

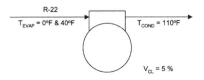

ASSUMPTIONS:

The refrigerant vapor behaves like an ideal gas.

ANALYSIS:

From the R-22 saturated property tables at the three temperatures:

$$0°F = 38.7 \text{ psia} \qquad 40°F = 83.3 \text{ psia} \qquad 110°F = 241.1 \text{ psia}$$

Using equation 4.3 for the two suction pressures:

$$\eta_{cv} = \left(1 - \left(V_{cl}/V_{dpl}\right)\left(P_{dis}/P_{suc} - 1\right)\right) \times 100$$
$$\eta_{cv} = \left(1 - (0.05)(241.1/38.7 - 1)\right)(100) = 73.8\%$$
$$\eta_{cv} = \left(1 - (0.05)(241.1/83.3 - 1)\right)(100) = 90.5\%$$

COMMENTS:

The actual volumetric efficiency will be lower due to various losses.

In an actual compressor, irreversibilities and losses of various kinds occur, and the power that must be supplied to the compressor is greater than the power that an ideal compressor would require. The overall compressor efficiency ($\eta_{oc}$) is a measure of how closely the actual compressor work (or power) approaches the ideal compressor work (or power):

$$\eta_{oc} = \frac{\text{ideal compressor work}}{\text{actual compressor work}} \times 100 \qquad (4.4)$$

Chapter 2 introduced the ideal saturated vapor-compression cycle and based the ideal compressor work on an isentropic process. Thus the overall compressor efficiency compares the power that an isentropic compressor would require to the actual power being delivered to the compressor. Refer to chapter 2 for the procedures for calculating the isentropic work and the ideal compressor power.

EXAMPLE PROBLEM 4.3. An R-134a reciprocating compressor operates between an evaporating temperature of 0°F and a condensing temperature of 100°F. The overall compressor efficiency is 65 percent. If the suction vapor is saturated and the suction flow rate is 20 ft/min, calculate the compressor power.

SOLUTION.

SKETCH AND GIVEN DATA:

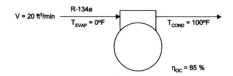

ASSUMPTIONS:

1. The compressor operates at steady-state conditions.
2. The changes in kinetic and potential energy can be neglected.

ANALYSIS:

From the R-134a saturated property tables at 0°F:

$$v_g = 2.158 \text{ ft}^3/\text{lbm} \qquad h_g = 103.2 \text{ Btu/lbm} \qquad s_g = 0.2256 \text{ Btu/lbm} ° \text{F}$$

For an isentropic process, from the superheated property tables at the pressure corresponding to 100°F (139 psia) and the suction entropy (0.2256 Btu/lbm-°F), interpolating as necessary:

$$h = 120.4 \text{ Btu/lbm}$$

The ideal compressor work is thus:

$$\Delta h_{\text{ideal}} = 120.4 = 103.2 - 17.2 \text{ Btu/lbm}$$

Using equation 4.4, the actual compressor work is calculated:

$$\Delta h_{\text{actual}} = \frac{17.2 \text{ Btu/lbm}}{0.65} = 26.46 \text{ Btu/lbm}$$

Calculating the refrigerant mass flow using the suction specific volume:

$$m = \frac{\left(20 \text{ ft}^3/\text{min}\right)}{\left(2.158 \text{ ft}^3/\text{lbm}\right)} = 9.268 \text{ lbm/min}$$

The compressor power is thus:

$$W_c = m \, \Delta h_{\text{actual}} = (9.268 \text{ lbm/min})(26.46 \text{ Btu/lbm})$$
$$= 245.2 \text{ Btu/min} = 5.78 \text{ hp}$$

COMMENTS:

A p-h diagram or computer software can also be used to determine the compressor outlet enthalpy for the isentropic compression process. This will eliminate the need for interpolation.

---

The overall compressor efficiency can be broken down into two components: the compression efficiency ($\eta_c$) and the mechanical efficiency ($\eta_m$). Thus

$$\eta_{oc} = \eta_c \, \eta_m$$

The compression efficiency accounts for deviation from the ideal compression process including such things as pressure drops across the compressor valves, heat exchange between the refrigerant gas and cylinder walls, and turbulence and friction of the gas within the cylinder. The mechanical efficiency accounts for friction within the compressor including the compressor bearings, seals, and pistons. Note that the factors that affect the compression efficiency are very similar to those that affect the volumetric efficiency, thus the compression efficiency and volumetric efficiency are usually fairly similar. The mechanical friction losses of a typical compressor are in the range of 5 to 15 percent of the total compressor power, with larger compressors towards the lower end of the range and smaller ones towards the higher end. If no information is available regarding the overall compressor efficiency in a particular application, it can be estimated by using figure 4-16 for the compression efficiency, and assuming a mechanical efficiency of 85 to 95 percent based on the compressor size.

---

EXAMPLE PROBLEM 4.4. A reciprocating compressor for a 20-ton air-conditioning system using R-134a is selected. Assuming an evaporating temperature of 40°F and a condensing temperature of 110°F, estimate: (a) the compressor displacement rate and (b) the compressor power.

SOLUTION.

SKETCH AND GIVEN DATA:

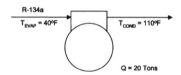

ASSUMPTIONS:
1. The mechanical efficiency is 90 percent.
2. The compression efficiency is equal to the volumetric efficiency.
3. The compressor suction is a saturated vapor and the condenser outlet is saturated liquid.

ANALYSIS:

From the R-134a saturated tables at the evaporating and condensing temperatures:

40°F:      $p = 49.7$ psia     $v_g = 0.9528 \, \text{ft}^3/\text{lbm}$     $h_g = 108.9 \, \text{Btu}/\text{lbm}$

$s_g = 0.2221 \, \text{Btu}/\text{lbm-}^\circ\text{F}$

0°      $p = 161.1$ psia     $h_f = 48.7 \, \text{Btu}/\text{lbm}$

Using figure 4-16 to estimate the volumetric efficiency:

$$\frac{P_{dis}}{P_{suct}} = \frac{161.1 \text{ psia}}{49.7 \text{ psia}} = 3.24 \qquad \eta = 79.5\%$$

The overall compressor efficiency is estimated using equation 4.5, assuming the compression efficiency is equal to the volumetric efficiency and mechanical efficiency is 90 percent:

$$\eta_{oc} = \eta_c\, \eta_m = (0.795)(0.9) = 0.716 = 71.6\%$$

Using the R-134a superheat tables to determine the discharge enthalpy for an isentropic compression process knowing the pressure (161.1 psia) and entropy (0.2221 Btu/lbm-°F):

$$h_3 = 119.4 \text{ Btu/lbm}$$

Calculating the ideal compressor work:

$$\Delta h_{ideal} = h_3 - h_2 = 119.4 - 108.9 = 10.5 \text{ Btu/lbm}$$

Calculating the refrigerant flow rate using the required cooling capacity of 20 tons:

$$Q = m\,(h_2 - h_1)$$
$$(20 \text{ tons})(12{,}000 \text{ Btu/hr-ton}) = (m)(108.9 - 48.7 \text{ Btu/lbm})$$
$$m = 3{,}986.7 \text{ lbm/hr} = 66.45 \text{ lbm/min}$$

The suction volume flow rate is thus:

$$V_{act} = (66.45 \text{ lbm/min})(0.9528 \text{ ft}^3/\text{lbm}) = 63.31 \text{ ft}^3/\text{min}$$

The compressor displacement rate based on the 79.5% volumetric efficiency calculated above is:

$$V_{dis} = \frac{63.31 \text{ ft}^3/\text{lbm}}{0.795} = 79.6 \text{ ft}^3/\text{lbm} \qquad \text{(a)}$$

The compressor power based on the overall compressor efficiency calculated above is:

$$W_c = \frac{m\,\Delta h_{ideal}}{\eta_{oc}} = \frac{(66.45 \text{ lbm/min})(10.5 \text{ Btu/lbm})}{0.716}$$
$$W_c = 974.5 \text{ Btu/min} = 23.0 \text{ hp} \qquad \text{(b)}$$

COMMENTS:
1. The actual cycle will include superheat at the compressor suction and possibly subcooling on the condenser outlet. This will affect the required compressor displacement.
2. If available, manufacturer's data should be used to estimate the compressor efficiencies.

## Refrigeration System Performance
## Under Varying Evaporator Pressure

In order to properly design a refrigeration or air-conditioning system, it is important to understand how the performance of a compressor varies under changing operating conditions. Varying the evaporator pressure in particular can have a significant impact on the system capacity and compressor power requirements. Using the relationships developed above for compressor efficiencies, the performance of a reciprocating compressor can be developed and used to establish various system characteristics.

Figures 4-17 and 4-18 present the results of an analysis of an ideal compressor in ideal saturated vapor compression cycle using R-134a. The compressor was assumed to have a displacement rate of 100 ft³/min with a clearance volume of 5 percent of the displacement volume. The condensing temperature was held constant at 110°F and the evaporating temperature was varied from –40°F to 50°F. It was assumed that re-expansion was the only factor affecting the compressor's volumetric efficiency and equation 4.3 was used to calculate the clearance volumetric efficiency.

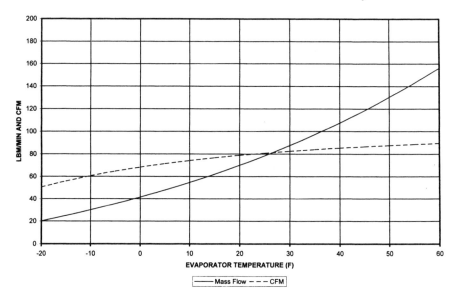

Fig. 4-17. Refrigerant flow versus evaporator temperature.

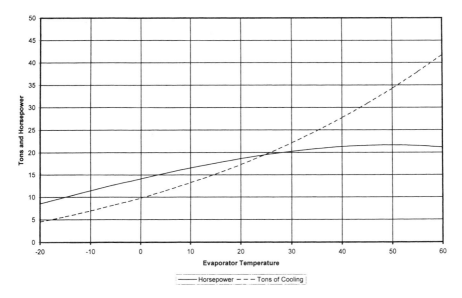

Fig. 4-18. Compressor power and tons of cooling versus
evaporator temperature.

Some significant trends can be noted from a study of Figures 4-17 and
4-18. As expected, the compressor volumetric efficiency increases with increasing evaporating temperature due to the reduced pressure ratio. However as the evaporating temperature increases, the mass flow of refrigerant
increases at a rate much greater than might be expected due to the increasing refrigerant density in combination with the increasing volumetric efficiency. The large increase in mass flow results in similar increases in
refrigerating capacity and compressor power since each is calculated by
multiplying the mass flow rate times a change in enthalpy. While the compressor work decreases and the refrigerating effect increases as the evaporating temperature increases, the changes are small in comparison to the
large increase in refrigerant mass flow.

These trends have important implications. The compressor motor on a
refrigeration system can easily be overloaded if the evaporating temperature rises above the design value. On small systems, the compressor motor
can be oversized to handle this condition. On large systems, this probably
does not make sense. Instead larger systems can include a suction pressure regulating valve to limit the increase in the suction pressure during
start-up of pulldown conditions. This will limit the compressor power requirements and prevent overloading of the motor.

The decrease in system capacity as the evaporating temperature decreases is exactly opposite to what usually happens to the system load. As

the temperature difference between the inside and outside temperatures increases, the amount of heat transferred increases. As Figure 4-18 shows, as the difference between the evaporator and condenser increases, the system capacity decreases. Thus the two trends are opposite: as the temperature difference increases, the system load increases while the system capacity decreases. Just when you need to remove more heat from the space, the system has less ability to do so. These opposite trends have implications for system sizing. The system must have adequate capacity at the worst conditions it will experience. If the system design conditions are not established correctly, the system will not be able to maintain the desired space temperature.

## ROTARY COMPRESSORS

Rotary compressors are positive displacement machines like the reciprocating compressor. While they have had limited usage in marine systems, they are more common in industrial installations and are starting to be used in marine applications. The three most common types are screw, vane, and scroll compressors. Each type will be discussed in the following sections.

Screw compressors first became popular for refrigeration service in Europe during the 1950s and 1960s. They are now popular in the United States for use in systems of 50 to 500 tons capacity. The most common construction is the twin-screw type as shown in figure 4-19a. A condensing unit using a screw compressor is shown in figure 4-19b. While some early compressors used timing gears to avoid lubrication of the rotors, common practice today is to drive one rotor and have the second driven by the first. The refrigerant vapor enters through a port at one end of the compressor and discharges through a port at the other end. As the screws rotate, a void is formed and gas enters, filling the entire length of the screw. Continued rotation closes off the void and the gas volume is reduced axially towards the outlet end by the meshing of the screws. At some point in the rotation of the screws, the outlet port is uncovered and the trapped gas begins discharging. Oil is injected between the rotors for lubrication, cooling, and sealing of the rotors. Because of the quantity of oil injected, an oil separator must be located in the system after the compressor discharge to recover the oil. The lubrication system will also typically include a pump, oil sump, cooler, filter, and associated controls and safety devices.

An important characteristic of a screw compressor is the volume ratio, defined as the trapped volume as the intake port just closes divided by the trapped volume as the outlet port just opens. The ideal volume ratio for a particular application is based on the ratio of the condenser pressure to the evaporator pressure. The higher system the pressure ratio, the higher the compressor volume ratio should be for maximum efficiency. Many screw

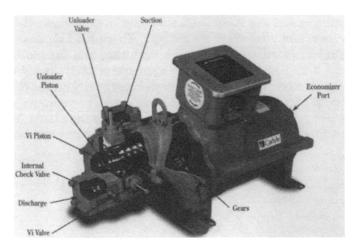

Fig. 4-19a. Twin-screw compressor. Courtesy Carrier Corporation.

Fig. 4-19b. 125-ton screw compressor condensing unit. Courtesy York International-Marine Systems.

compressors are fitted with a sliding valve in the casing. As the valve is opened, it delays the position at which compression begins along the rotor, thus effectively reducing the volume ratio. This is done for capacity control, not to maximize efficiency. Screw compressor are very efficient machines, and there is little loss in efficiency for moderate deviations from the optimum pressure ratio. The sliding valve permits smooth stepless capacity reduction down to about 10 percent of rated capacity. The slide valve can also be used to permit unloaded starting of the compressor.

Vane compressors are most commonly used in small domestic refrigerators, freezers, and room air conditioners. There are two basic types of vane compressors available: the single-vane type and the multiple-vane type. Figure 4-20 illustrates the arrangement of each type. In the single-vane type, a circular rotor is mounted eccentrically on the compressor shaft. As the shaft rotates, the circular rotor moves in a manner similar to a cam with the rotor tip having close clearance with the casing. The single vane is mounted in the stationary casing and separates the suction and

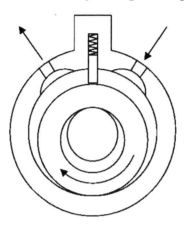

**(a) SINGLE-VANE TYPE**

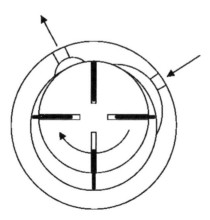

**(b) MULTIPLE-VANE TYPE**

Fig. 4-20. Vane compressors.

discharge sections. The vane is held against the rotor by a spring. A check valve is installed in the discharge port to prevent high-pressure gas from backing up into the compressor. In the multiple-vane type, the vanes are mounted in slots in the circular rotor. The rotor is mounted off-center in the circular cylinder so that rotor almost touches the cylinder at one point. The vanes are held against the cylinder wall by centrifugal force and move in and out as they follow the shape of the cylinder wall. As in the single-vane type, a check valve is installed in the discharge port to prevent high-pressure gas from backing up.

A recent design that is becoming popular in sizes from below one horsepower to about 25 horsepower is the scroll compressor. The scroll compressor is a positive displacement compressor employing two involute scrolls—one stationary and one rotating. The refrigerant gas is trapped in a series of pockets that are formed between the two scrolls. The suction gas enters the scrolls at the outer periphery. As the scroll rotates, gas is trapped and its volume is reduced as the pocket is moved towards the center of the scrolls. A discharge port is located at the center, and the high-pressure gas is discharged when the port is exposed. Figure 4-21 illustrates the interaction of the scrolls and the compression process. There are multiple pockets of gas being trapped simultaneously, and the gas flow is very smooth and nearly continuous. The smooth gas discharge in combination with a lack of suction and discharge valves and smooth rotary motion results in a very quiet, low vibration machine. Figure 4-22 shows the construction of a typical scroll compressor. Scroll compressors have higher volumetric and overall compressor efficiencies as compared to similar-sized reciprocating compressors.

The scroll compressor is a constant volume ratio machine similar to the screw compressor. Thus like the screw compressor, a scroll compressor will be most efficient at one system pressure ratio. However, the scroll compressor is an efficient machine and the reduction for off-design operation is small. The volume ratio can be varied during the design phase by increasing the number of wraps of the spirals. In order to maintain high efficiency, internal leakage of gases from the high pressure areas to the lower pressure areas must be minimized. The major locations of potential

1 Gas enters an outer opening as one scroll orbits the other.

2 The open passage is sealed as gas is drawn into the compression chamber.

3 As one scroll continues orbiting, the gas is compressed into an increasingly smaller "pocket."

4 Gas is continually compressed to the center of the scrolls, where it is discharged through precisely machined ports into the condenser.

Fig. 4-21. Scroll compression process.

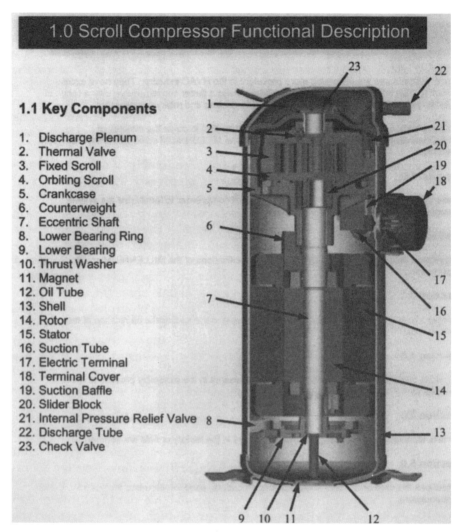

## 1.0 Scroll Compressor Functional Description

### 1.1 Key Components

1. Discharge Plenum
2. Thermal Valve
3. Fixed Scroll
4. Orbiting Scroll
5. Crankcase
6. Counterweight
7. Eccentric Shaft
8. Lower Bearing Ring
9. Lower Bearing
10. Thrust Washer
11. Magnet
12. Oil Tube
13. Shell
14. Rotor
15. Stator
16. Suction Tube
17. Electric Terminal
18. Terminal Cover
19. Suction Baffle
20. Slider Block
21. Internal Pressure Relief Valve
22. Discharge Tube
23. Check Valve

Fig. 4-22. Scroll compressor. Courtesy Carrier Corporation.

leakage are the clearance between the mating scrolls, and between the tips of the scrolls and the mating face plate. Leakage between the mating scrolls is controlled by careful machining of the scrolls. Leakage between the scroll tips and the face plates can be controlled by applying an axial force to maintain contact between the two. This technique automatically compensates for wear and allows the scrolls to move apart should liquid enter the suction.

# CENTRIFUGAL COMPRESSORS

Centrifugal compressors are similar in construction to centrifugal pumps. Figure 4-23 shows the construction of a typical centrifugal compressor. One or more impellers mounted on a shaft rotating at high speed impart kinetic energy to the refrigerant gas. In the casing, the high-velocity gas is slowed down, converting the kinetic energy to pressure. Centrifugal compressors are generally high capacity machines and thus are commonly used on systems of 300 tons and larger, though units of under 100 tons are available. They are especially suitable for large chilled water air-conditioning systems. While not common on commercial vessels, centrifugal compressor systems are used on many larger naval vessels.

For an impeller with radial blades, an analysis of the energy transfer in the rotor shows that the theoretical enthalpy increase of the gas is primarily related to the square of the peripheral velocity of the rotor.

$$\Delta h = V^2/C \qquad (4.6)$$

where

$\Delta h$ = enthalpy change in Btu/lbm or kJ/kg
$V$ = rotor peripheral velocity in ft/sec or m/sec
$C$ = conversion constant, $32.2 \times 778.2 = 25{,}058$ for English units, and 1,000 for SI units

The actual enthalpy increase in the impeller will be lower due to various losses. Most impellers are built with blades that curve backwards. This will result in a further decrease in the enthalpy developed at other than very low flow rates.

The pressure developed by a centrifugal rotor is dependent on the peripheral velocity and the density of the fluid being handled. Due to the low density of the typical refrigerant gas compared to a liquid, the pressure developed per stage in a centrifugal compressor is fairly low compared to a centrifugal pump. The rotor peripheral speed is proportional to the diameter of the impeller and the rotational speed of the rotor. The maximum peripheral speed is limited by the centrifugal stress and material strength, and by the sonic velocity of the refrigerant. This means that compressors with two to four stages are common, even when relatively modest discharge pressures are required. Refrigerants that have a relatively large displacement per ton such as R-11 and R-123 are especially suitable for these systems, particularly in smaller system sizes. R-11 is a CFC and is no longer being used in new installations. R-123 is being considered as a replacement for R-11, but there are safety concerns with R-123, so it is not likely to be used in marine applications. Centrifugal machines using R-134a are available. Because of the lower capacity per ton required with

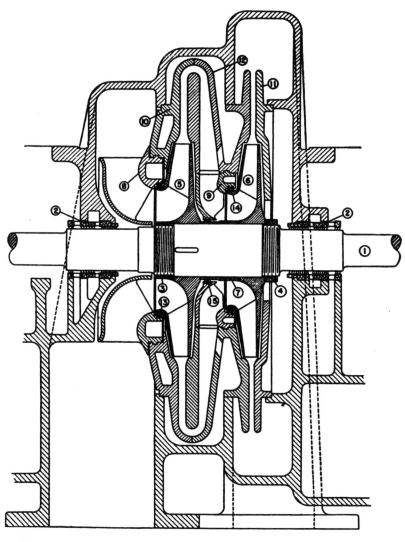

| 1 | Shaft | 6 | Impeller, second stage | 11 | Discharge wall |
|---|---|---|---|---|---|
| 2 | Shaft labyrinth, either end | 7 | Impeller spacer | 12 | Diaphragm, first stage |
| 3 | Impeller lock nut, suction end | 8 | Inlet guide vane, first stage | 13 | Inlet labyrinth, first stage |
| 4 | Impeller lock nut, discharge end | 9 | Inlet guide vane, second stage | 14 | Inlet labyrinth, second stage |
| 5 | Impeller, first stage | 10 | Intake wall | 15 | Spacer labyrinth |

Fig. 4-23. Centrifugal compressor.

high-pressure refrigerants like R-134a, such refrigerants are normally used in only in units with larger capacities.

---

EXAMPLE PROBLEM 4.5. A centrifugal compressor is to be in a system with an evaporator temperature of 40°F and a condensing temperature of 110°F. The refrigerant is R-134a and the compressor rpm is 3,500. Estimate the rotor peripheral speed and rotor diameter, for a one-stage compressor and a two-stage compressor.

SOLUTION.

SKETCH AND GIVEN DATA:

ASSUMPTIONS:
1. The suction vapor is saturated.
2. The compression is isentropic.
3. The impeller vanes are radial.

ANALYSIS:

Using the R-134a tables in the appendix, the enthalpy and entropy for saturated vapor at 40°F are:

$$hg = 108.8 \, \text{Btu/lbm} \qquad sg = 0.222 \, \text{Btu/lbm-}°\text{R}$$

Using the R134a superheat tables for the pressure corresponding to 110°F and an entropy of 0.222 Btu/lbm-°R, the enthalpy at the discharge for isentropic compression is:

$$h = 118.5 \, \text{Btu/lbm}$$

The ideal compressor work is thus:

$$\Delta h = 118.5 - 108.9 \, \text{Btu/lbm} = 9.7 \, \text{Btu/lbm}$$

Using equation 4.6 to calculate the peripheral speed and rotor diameter for a single stage compressor:

$$\Delta h = V^2/C$$

$$9.7\,\text{Btu/lbm} = V^2/25{,}058$$

$$V = 493\,\text{ft/sec}$$

$$V = \text{rotor circumference} \times \text{revolutions per second}$$

$$493\,\text{ft/sec} = (\Pi)(D)(3{,}500\ \text{rpm})(60\ \text{sec/min})$$

$$D = 2.69\,\text{ft}$$

For two stages, the total enthalpy change will be split equally between the two stages:

$$\Delta h = V^2/C$$

$$9.7/2 = 4.85\,\text{Btu/lbm} = V^2/25{,}058$$

$$V = 348.6\,\text{ft/sec}$$

$$348.6\,\text{ft/sec} = (\Pi)(D)(3{,}500\ \text{rpm})(60\ \text{sec/min})$$

$$D = 1.90\,\text{ft}$$

COMMENTS:
The actual rotor peripheral speed and thus diameter will need to be larger to account for losses and for backward curved vanes on the impeller.

Figure 4-24 is a diagram of a multistage centrifugal compressor system. The unit includes the compressor, evaporator, condenser, and associated controls. Like most centrifugal units, it is close-coupled to minimize pressure drops between the various system components and employs a secondary refrigerant (chilled water, glycol antifreeze, or brine) for distribution to the various cooling loads. It shows the use of flash gas removal during the expansion process that improves the cycle efficiency. The refrigerant is reduced from the high side to low side pressure in two steps by float valves. The gas that flashes in the pressure reduction across the first float valve is introduced into the compressor between the two stages. This reduces the work of compression due to the intercooling effect and the fact that the gas only needs to be compressed by one stage rather than two. Figure 4-25 shows a typical centrifugal compressor chiller unit.

Centrifugal compressors are pressure lubricated either by a shaft-driven or external motor-driven oil pump. The system is arranged to avoid contact of the oil by the system refrigerant, thus simplifying lubrication. The system also includes an oil cooler to maintain oil temperature during operation and an oil filter to remove contaminants. An oil heater is commonly installed in the oil sump to reduce refrigerant dilution of the lubricating oil during shutdown periods. If the system operates with low side pressures below atmospheric, a purge recovery unit is commonly installed to continuously remove noncondensable gases and to recover and return refrigerant mixed with the purged gases. The purge system consists of a small reciprocating compressor, a condenser, and a separating tank. The suction of the compressor is connected to the main system condenser. The gases flow to the purge condenser where the refrigerant condenses. In the separating tank, a float valve controls the return of the liquid refrigerant to the main system, and a relief valve vents the noncondensable gases to the atmosphere.

Centrifugal compressor systems are controlled by sensing (or monitoring) the secondary refrigerant temperature. The system capacity is varied as required to maintain the chiller outlet temperature constant. The methods that can be employed to vary compressor capacity are: (1) prerotation inlet vanes, (2) variable speed operation, (3) varying condenser pressure, and (4) bypassing discharge gas. The first two methods are the most popular, but the latter two are sometimes used in combination with one of the other methods. Prerotation vanes are installed in the compressor inlet and cause the entering vapor to swirl, giving it a tangential velocity in the direction of the impeller rotation. Closing the vanes increases the swirl and

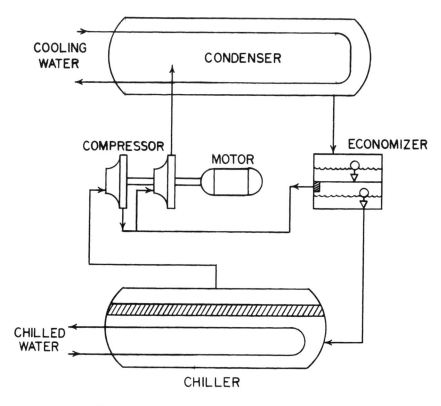

Fig. 4-24. Centrifugal compressor system.

Fig. 4-25. 440-ton chilled water plant. Courtesy York
International-Marine Systems.

reduces the head produced at a given flow rate. Centrifugal compressors
are very sensitive to speed changes, so the use of a steam turbine, wound
rotor induction motor, variable frequency controller, and squirrel cage motor, or other variable speed drive to power the compressor is a very effective
technique to control the capacity.

## PROBLEMS (ENGLISH UNITS)

4.1E. Compute the displacement rate of a 6-cylinder reciprocating compressor
having a 3 inch bore and a 3 inch stroke and rotating at 1,750 rpm.

4.2E  The compressor in the above problem is operating in a system using R-134a
with an evaporating temperature of 0°F and a condensing temperature of 110°F.
The actual compressor flow rate is 70 ft$^3$/min. Calculate the actual compressor volumetric efficiency, and the clearance volumetric efficiency, assuming a clearance
volume of 5 percent of the compressor displacement.

4.3E  It takes 20 hp to drive the compressor in the above problem. Assuming the suction gas is saturated, calculate the overall compressor efficiency.

4.4E  A reciprocating compressor has a displacement rate of 50 ft$^3$/min. The overall compressor efficiency is 65 percent and the volumetric efficiency is 70 percent. The compressor suction is saturated vapor at 40°F. Calculate the refrigerant mass flow and the power required if the refrigerant is R-22. Repeat for R-134a.

4.5E  An R-22 reciprocating compressor for an air-conditioning system is being sized. The system capacity is 10 tons, the evaporator temperature is 40°F, and the condensing temperature is 110°F. Estimate the compressor displacement rate and the compressor power.

4.6E  A 4-cylinder reciprocating compressor with a 2.5 inch bore and 3 inch stroke operates at 3,500 rpm. The refrigerant is R-134a, the evaporating temperature is 0°F, and the condensing temperature is 100°F. Estimate the system cooling capacity in tons.

4.7E  An R-22 reciprocating compressor with a displacement rate of 75 ft$^3$/min operates with a condensing temperature of 110°F. For evaporating temperatures of -20°F, 10°F, and 40°F, estimate the refrigerant mass flow and the compressor power. Plot the results as function of the evaporating temperature.

4.8E  A centrifugal compressor operating at 5,000 rpm uses R-22. The evaporator temperature is 5°F and the condenser temperature is 105°F. How many stages are required if the the the impeller diameter is 18 inches?

# PROBLEMS (SI UNITS)

4.1S  Compute the displacement rate of a 6-cylinder reciprocating compressor having a 75 mm bore and a 75 mm stroke and rotating at 1,750 rpm.

4.2S  The compressor in the above problem is operating in a system using R-134a with an evaporating temperature of -20°C and a condensing temperature of 45°C. The actual compressor flow rate is 2 m$^3$/sec. Calculate the actual compressor volumetric efficiency, and the clearance volumetric efficiency, assuming a clearance volume of 5 percent of the compressor displacement.

4.3S  It takes 15 kW to drive the compressor in the above problem. Assuming the suction gas is saturated, calculate the overall compressor efficiency.

4.4S  A reciprocating compressor has a displacement rate of 1.5 m$^3$/sec. The overall compressor efficiency is 65 percent and the volumetric efficiency is 70 percent. The compressor suction is saturated vapor at 5°C. Calculate the refrigerant mass flow and the power required if the refrigerant is R-22. Repeat for R-134a.

4.5S  An R-22 reciprocating compressor for an air-conditioning system is being sized. The system capacity is 40 kW, the evaporator temperature is 5°C, and the condensing temperature is 45°C. Estimate the compressor displacement rate and the compressor power.

4.6S  A 4-cylinder reciprocating compressor with a 20 mm bore and 25 mm stroke operates at 3,500 rpm. The refrigerant is R-134a, the evaporating temperature is −20°C, and the condensing temperature is 40°C. Estimate the system cooling capacity in tons.

4.7S  An R-22 reciprocating compressor with a displacement rate of 2 m$^3$/min operates with a condensing temperature of 40°C. For evaporating temperatures of −30°C, −10°C, and 10°C, estimate the refrigerant mass flow and the compressor power. Plot the results as function of the evaporating temperature.

4.8S  A centrifugal compressor operating at 5,000 rpm uses R-22. The evaporator temperature is 5°C and the condenser temperature is 35°C. How many stages are required if the the impeller diameter is 0.5m?

CHAPTER 5

# Evaporators and Condensers

Heat exchangers are important components in any refrigeration or air-conditioning system. The most important of these are the evaporator and the condenser. The evaporator is the heat exchanger in which the system cooling is done. Refrigerant boils on one side of the tubes or plates of the evaporator, and heat is removed from fluid (air, water, or brine) on the other side. The condenser is the heat exchanger that receives the refrigerant gas from the compressor turns it back to a liquid for reuse by the system. Air or water on one side of the condenser tubes or plates is heated as the refrigerant condenses on the other side. Other heat exchangers found in refrigeration systems include heat interchangers (liquid-suction heat exchangers) and lubricating oil coolers.

## EVAPORATORS

Evaporators can be described based on the construction of the heat exchanger surface (bare tube, finned tube, or plate) and if the evaporator is direct expansion or flooded. In a direct expansion evaporator, a controlled amount of liquid refrigerant is admitted into the inside of the evaporator tube, and the air or water being cooled flows over the outside. Flooded evaporators are commonly found on chillers used in large air-conditioning systems. The water being chilled flows inside the tubes, and the refrigerant is in the shell, covering the outside of the tubes. Figure 5-1 illustrates the difference between a dry expansion and a flooded evaporator.

Marine evaporators are usually of either the natural convection type or the forced convection type. Natural convection evaporators are bare, finned coils, or plates mounted on the walls or overhead of a refrigerated storage room. They are suitable for applications where low air velocities

91

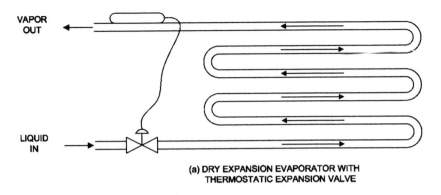

(a) DRY EXPANSION EVAPORATOR WITH
THERMOSTATIC EXPANSION VALVE

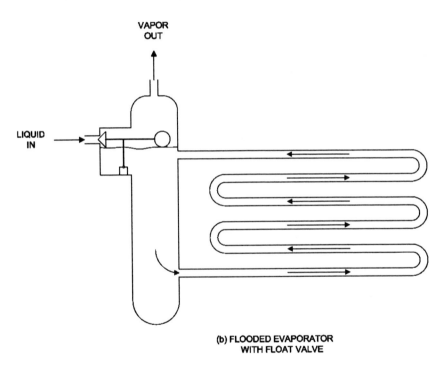

(b) FLOODED EVAPORATOR
WITH FLOAT VALVE

Fig. 5-1. Evaporator types.

and minimum dehydration of the product are desired and thus are especially suited for refrigerated food storage. Natural convection evaporators rely on the difference in density between cool and warm air to circulate air across the coils. The low air velocities in a natural circulation evaporator result in low heat transfer. This increases the amount of surface required for a particular installation in comparison to a forced convection unit. Baffles can be used with roof-mounted evaporators to increase the air circulation and heat transfer as shown in figure 5-2. Natural convection evaporators are less susceptible to frost buildup due to the larger evaporator area and are commonly defrosted manually using a hot gas defrost procedure. See chapter 11 for more information on hot gas defrosting.

Forced convection evaporators are in common use in ship's stores refrigeration, cargo refrigeration, and air-conditioning systems. Names such as "unit coolers," "fan coil units," or "cold diffusers" are used to describe a unit consisting of a metal housing containing a cooling coil with bare or finned tubes, one or more motor-driven fans, and drain pan. The configuration of the unit will depend on whether it is designed for floor or wall or ceiling mounting. Figure 5-3 shows a typical unit cooler used in marine refrigeration applications. Units designed for air-conditioning applications may also contain a heating coil so that the same unit may be used for winter heating as well as air-conditioning. Units designed for domestic refrigeration freeze room applications are susceptible to rapid frosting. These units are usually fitted with an electric resistance defrost system to melt ice and frost from the coil drain pan and drain line. Automatic controls are commonly installed to automate the defrost process. The defrost cycle is typically initiated by a timer that closes the refrigerant solenoid valve, stops the fans, and turns on the heaters. The defrost cycle is terminated by a thermostat sensing a rise in the coil temperature after the ice and frost melt.

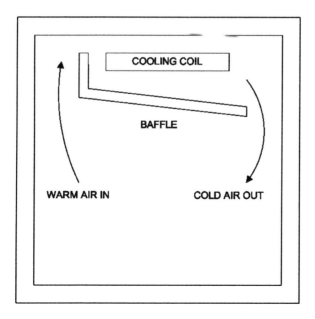

Fig. 5-2. Baffle for ceiling-mounted evaporator.

Fig. 5-3. Unit coolers.

## CONDENSERS

In shoreside refrigeration and air-conditioning applications, condensers are either air-cooled, water-cooled, or evaporative. Because vast quantities of seawater for cooling purposes are readily available, almost all marine refrigeration condensers are of the water-cooled type. The only common exception to this is drinking water coolers that are usually air-cooled. Evaporative condensers using cooling towers to reject heat to the atmosphere are common on larger shoreside systems but are unnecessary on marine systems.

Marine water-cooled condensers are commonly of the multipass, shell-and-tube type as shown in figure 5-4. Seawater is circulated inside the condenser tubes. Baffles in the condenser heads allow for multiple passes of the water back and forth through the tubes in the shell. Two-pass or four-pass configurations are common. More passes result in higher water velocities through the tubes that increase heat transfer at the expense of higher pressure drops that increase the power to circulate the water. Hot refrigerant gas from the compressor discharge is admitted to the top of the shell, condenses on the outer surfaces of the tubes, and is removed as liquid from the bottom of the shell. Tubes can be either bare or finned. A marine condenser is typically constructed of a steel shell, copper-nickel tubes and tube sheets, and bronze waterheads. Gas inlet, liquid outlet, purge, and water regulating valve control connections are provided. The small air-cooled condensers found in drinking water coolers are usually fitted with finned tubes and a cooling fan to circulate air over the outside of the fins.

Smaller water-cooled condensers like those found on systems such as ice machines are commonly of the double-tube (tube-in-tube) type as shown in figure 5-5. Water flow inside the inner tube and the refrigerant is piped to

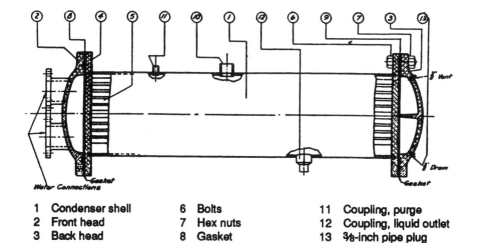

| 1 | Condenser shell | 6 | Bolts | 11 | Coupling, purge |
| 2 | Front head | 7 | Hex nuts | 12 | Coupling, liquid outlet |
| 3 | Back head | 8 | Gasket | 13 | 3/8-inch pipe plug |
| 4 | Tube head | 9 | Gasket | | |
| 5 | Tubes | 10 | Coupling, gas inlet | | |

Fig. 5-4. Condenser.

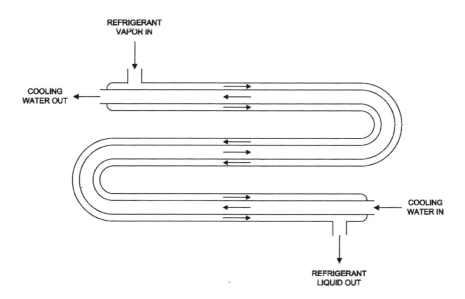

Fig. 5-5. Double-pipe condenser.

the annulus between the inner and outer tubes. The refrigerant and water are connected to flow in opposite directions, increasing the heat transfer.

## LIQUID CHILLERS AND
## SECONDARY REFRIGERANTS

In larger systems it may be uneconomical to install direct expansion evaporators and run refrigerant lines to all locations requiring cooling. In such applications, a central chiller can produce chilled water or brine and the liquid can be pumped to the various locations. This is called an indirect system and the water or brine is called a secondary refrigerant. The chiller is basically a complete refrigeration system with condenser, compressor, evaporator, and controls in a compact package. A large chiller package used for air-conditioning on an aircraft carrier is shown in figure 5-6.

Water is used as a secondary refrigerant in larger air-conditioning systems. Water is inexpensive, noncorrosive, and has excellent heat transfer properties. In air-conditioning applications, the evaporator can operate above the freezing temperatures, permitting water to be used.

Fig. 5-6. Navy 800-ton AC plant for use on CUN.

Chilled water systems for air condition applications are discussed in chapter 9. For systems that operate at lower temperatures, a secondary refrigerant such as a brine or antifreeze solution are necessary. Brine systems have been common on marine refrigerated cargo systems for many years. Two types of brine are in common use: sodium chloride (NaCl) and calcium chloride ($CaCl_2$). The properties of calcium chloride and sodium chloride brine at different concentrations are given in tables 5-1 and 5-2. Note that for each, there is a concentration that results in minimum crystallization temperature. This is called the eutectic point. For calcium chloride brine, the eutectic temperature is –67°F at a concentration of 29.87 percent by weight. For sodium chloride brine, this occurs

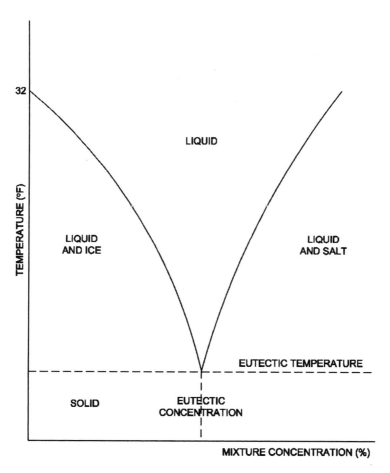

Fig. 5-7. Brine phase diagram.

at −6°F at a concentration of 23 percent by weight. At concentrations below eutectic, the water in the solution freezes first. At concentrations
above eutectic, the salt crystallizes first. Figure 5-7 shows a typical phase
diagram for a brine solution.

### TABLE 5-1
### Properties of Calcium Chloride Brine

| Percent CaCl (by weight) | Specific Gravity (59°F/39°F) | lb CaCl₂/gal | Crystallization Temperature (°F) |
|---|---|---|---|
| 0 | 1.000 | 0.000 | 3.20 |
| 5 | 1.044 | 0.436 | 27.7 |
| 10 | 1.087 | 0.908 | 22.3 |
| 15 | 1.133 | 1.418 | 13.5 |
| 20 | 1.182 | 1.970 | −0.4 |
| 25 | 1.233 | 2.574 | −21.0 |
| 29.87 | 1.290 | 3.16 | −67.0 |
| 30 | 1.295 | 3.22 | −50.8 |
| 32 | 1.317 | 3.49 | −19.5 |
| 34 | 1.340 | 3.77 | 4.3 |

### TABLE 5-2
### Properties of Sodium Chloride Brine

| Percent CaCl (by weight) | Specific Gravity (59°F/39°F) | lb NaCl/gal | Crystallization Temperature (°F) |
|---|---|---|---|
| 0 | 1.000 | 0.000 | 32.0 |
| 5 | 1.035 | 0.432 | 27.0 |
| 10 | 1.072 | 0.895 | 20.4 |
| 15 | 1.111 | 1.392 | 12.0 |
| 20 | 1.150 | 1.920 | 1.8 |
| 23 | 1.175 | 2.256 | −6.0 |
| 25 | 1.191 | 2.488 | 16.1 |

Two common antifreeze solutions that can be used as secondary refrigerants are ethylene glycol and propylene glycol. Unlike brines, both glycols
are noncorrosive, and they are also very stable. Propylene glycol is less
toxic than ethylene glycol and is more commonly used in refrigeration service. The freezing points for different concentrations of both are given in
table 5-3.

## TABLE 5-3
## Ethylene Glycol

| Percent by Volume | °F |
|---|---|
| 15 | 22.4 |
| 20 | 16.2 |
| 25 | 10 |
| 30 | 3.5 |
| 35 | −4 |
| 40 | −12.5 |
| 45 | −22 |
| 50 | −32.5 |

## Propylene Glycol

| Percent by Volume | °F |
|---|---|
| 5 | 29 |
| 10 | 26 |
| 15 | 22.5 |
| 20 | 19 |
| 25 | 14.5 |
| 30 | 9 |
| 35 | 2.5 |
| 40 | −5.5 |
| 45 | −15 |
| 50 | −25.5 |
| 55 | −29.5 |
| 59 | −57 |

# SIZING OF EVAPORATORS AND CONDENSERS

It is necessary to understand the basics of heat transfer to be able to determine the size and configuration of an evaporator or condenser suitable in a particular application. The first step is to determine the rate at which thermal energy must be transferred, in units such as Btu/hr or kW. For a refrigeration system evaporator or condenser, this will come from the cycle analysis. The evaporator load will be the system capacity. A 10 ton refrigeration system will mean the evaporator must transfer 120,000 Btu/hr (10 tons × 12,000 Btu/hr/ton). The condenser for the same system will have a load somewhat greater than the system capacity since it must reject the heat absorbed by the evaporator plus the energy added by the compressor. The condenser load will typically be 15 to 50 percent higher than that for the evaporator. The ratio of the condenser load to the evaporator load is called the heat rejection ratio. The higher the condenser pressure and the lower the evaporator pressure, the higher the heat rejection ratio will be. The efficiency of the compressor also has an effect on the heat rejection ratio. An efficient compressor will have a lower heat rejection ratio than an inefficient one because of the lower compressor power. Table 5-4 shows some typical heat rejection ratios for a range of evaporator and condenser temperatures.

## TABLE 5-4
## Heat Rejection Ratios

| Evaporator Temp. (°F) | Condensing Temperature (°F) | | | |
| --- | --- | --- | --- | --- |
| | 90 | 100 | 110 | 120 |
| −20 | 1.33 | 1.37 | 1.42 | 1.47 |
| −10 | 1.28 | 1.32 | 1.37 | 1.42 |
| 0 | 1.24 | 1.28 | 1.32 | 1.37 |
| 10 | 1.21 | 1.24 | 1.28 | 1.32 |
| 20 | 1.17 | 1.20 | 1.24 | 1.28 |
| 30 | 1.14 | 1.17 | 1.20 | 1.24 |
| 40 | 1.12 | 1.15 | 1.17 | 1.20 |
| 50 | 1.09 | 1.12 | 1.14 | 1.17 |

The first law of thermodynamics states that energy must be conserved. For a heat exchanger with negligible heat transferred to the surroundings, the energy that is given up by one fluid must be equal to the heat picked up by the second fluid. For a heat exchanger with fluids A and B exchanging heat between one another:

$$Q_A = Q_B$$
$$m_A \, \Delta h_A = m_B \, \Delta h_B$$

where

$Q$ = heat transferred, in Btu/hr or kW
$m$ = mass flow, in lbm/hr or kg/sec
$\Delta h$ = change in enthalpy in Btu/lbm or kJ/kg

If a fluid is changing phase, the enthalpy values must be looked up in the appropriate property tables. If a fluid is not changing phase, the change in enthalpy can be calculated from the temperature change and the specific heat for the fluid.

$$Q = m \, \Delta h = m \, Cp \, \Delta T$$

where

$Cp$ = specific heat, in Btu/lbm-°R or kJ/kg-°K
$\Delta T$ = temperature change of the fluid, in °F or °C

Heat transfer in heat exchangers like refrigeration condensers and evaporators is a combination of conduction and convection. Heat is transferred by conduction through the tube (or plate) wall and by convection between the tube or plate and the fluids on the inside and outside of the tube. The heat transferred can be calculated using the following equation:

$$Q = U \ A \ \Delta T_m \qquad (5.1)$$

where

$Q$ = heat transferred, in Btu/hr or kW
$U$ = overall heat transfer coefficient, in Btu/hr-ft$^2$-°F or W/m$^2$-°C
$A$ = heat transfer area, in ft$^2$ or m$^2$
$\Delta T_m$ = mean temperature difference between the fluids inside and outside the tube, in °F or °C

The heat transfer area *(A)* and overall heat transfer coefficient *(U)* can be based either on the inside or outside area, but commonly is based on the outside area ($A_o$ and $U_o$). The value of the overall heat transfer coefficient will vary tremendously based on a variety of factors including the fluid properties, if there is a phase change or not, and if the convection flow is forced or natural. The values of the overall heat transfer coefficient in refrigeration service will range from values of 1 to 3 Btu/hr-ft$^2$-°F for natural convection evaporators to values of 150 to 300 for water-cooled condensers.

The mean temperature difference requires some further discussion. Figure 5-8 shows the temperature variation for several heat exchanger configurations. In parallel flow or counter-flow configurations, one fluid is heated and rises in temperature while the other fluid is cooled and drops in temperature. The only difference is that the two fluids flow in the same direction in parallel-flow heat exchangers and in opposite directions in counter-flow heat exchangers. In condensers or evaporators, one of the fluids changes phase and thus its temperature remains constant. An examination of figure 5-8 will show that the temperature difference between the fluids is constantly changing along the heat transfer surface. That is why the mean temperature difference must be used in the above equation.

Consider a condenser with refrigerant condensing at 105°F and with cooling water entering at 75°F and leaving at 95°F. At the inlet end, the temperature difference is 30°F and at the exit end it's 10°F. The average difference would be (30°+10°)/2 or 20°F. Unfortunately, this is not the mean temperature difference. The cooling water temperature changes faster at the inlet end because of the larger temperature difference between the refrigerant and the water compared to outlet end, and slower at the outlet end due to the smaller temperature difference.

For parallel-flow and counter-flow heat exchangers and for evaporators and condensers, the mean temperature difference is equal to the log mean

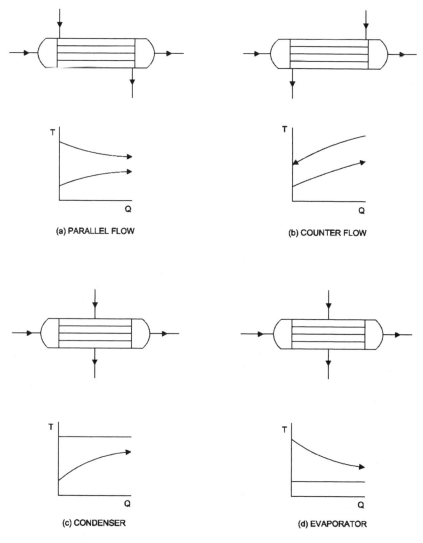

Fig. 5-8. Temperature variation in various heat exchangers.

temperature difference *(LMTD)* and can be calculated using the following equation:

$$LMTD = \frac{\Delta T_1 - \Delta T_2}{ln(\Delta T_1 / \Delta T_2)} \qquad (5.2)$$

where

     $\Delta T_1$ = temperature difference at the inlet end of the heat exchanger

$\Delta T_2$ = temperature difference at the outlet end of the heat exchange
$ln$ = natural logarithm

Thus for our condenser example, the *LMTD* would be 18.2°F versus the average temperature difference of 20°F. Using the average temperature difference rather than the *LMTD* would have overestimated the heat transferred.

If both fluids are changing temperature and the heat exchanger has multiple tube and shell passes, or for cross flow heat exchangers, the mean temperature difference is not equal to the log mean temperature difference and a correction factor *(F)* must be applied as follows:

$$\Delta T_m = F \; LMTD \qquad (5.3)$$

Graphs are available in most books on heat transfer or heat exchangers to permit the determination of the correction factor for a variety of heat exchanger configurations. Since refrigeration condensers and evaporators each involve a fluid changing phase at constant temperature, there is no need to apply a correction factor. Even if there is some subcooling or super-heating of the fluid changing phase, the effect on the mean temperature difference is small and the correction factor can be assumed to be 1.0. The temperature differences should be based on the difference between the sat-uration temperature of the refrigerant and the water or air on the other side of the heat transfer surface.

---

EXAMPLE PROBLEM 5.1. A water-cooled condenser is condensing 20 kg/min of R-134a. The refrigerant enters as a superheated vapor with a pressure of 900 kPa and a temperature of 50°C and exits as a saturated liquid at the same pressure. Cooling water is supplied at 25°C and exits at 30°C. Deter-mine: (a) the cooling load, in kW and (b) the cooling water flow, in kg per second.

SOLUTION.

SKETCH AND GIVEN DATA:

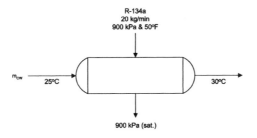

R-134a
20 kg/min
900 kPa & 50°F

$m_{cw}$     25°C

30°C

900 kPa (sat.)

ASSUMPTIONS:
1. The cooling water is freshwater with a specific heat of 4.19 kJ/kg-°K.
2. Conditions are steady-state.

ANALYSIS:
Looking up the enthalpy of R-134a at the two conditions in the appendix tables:

$$h_{in} = 274.17 \text{ kJ/kg} \qquad h_{out} = 101.64 \text{ kJ/kg}$$

From an energy balance for the condenser

$$Q = m_r \Delta h_r = \frac{(20 \text{ kg/min})}{(60 \text{ sec/min})}(274.17 - 101.64 \text{ kj/kg}) = 57.51 \text{ kW} \qquad (a)$$

$$Q = m_{cw} \Delta h_{cw} = m_{cw} C_p \Delta T_{cw}$$

$$m_{cw} = \frac{Q}{Cp \ \Delta T_{cw}} = \frac{57.51 \text{ kW}}{(4.19 \text{ kJ/kg-K})} = 2.745 \text{ kg/sec} \qquad (b)$$

COMMENTS:
None.

---

EXAMPLE PROBLEM 5.2. A water-cooled condenser is being sized for a 10-ton refrigeration system. The condensing temperature is 103°F, and the cooling water enters at 80°F and exits at 93°F. The heat rejection is 1.3 and the overall heat transfer coefficient is 125 Btu/hr-ft²-°F. Determine: (a) the outside surface area, (b) the gpm of cooling water, and (c) the tube length if there are 60 bare 5/8 inch OD tubes.

SOLUTION.
SKETCH AND GIVEN DATA:

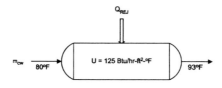

ASSUMPTIONS:
1. The cooling water is fresh with a specific heat of 1.0 Btu/lbm-°F and a density of 62.4 lbm/ft³.
2. No *LMTD* correction is needed (F = 1).
3. All energy from the condensing refrigerant is transferred to the water.

ANALYSIS:
Calculating the heat load.

$$Q = (10 \text{ tons})(12{,}000 \text{ Btu/hr-ton})(1.3) = 156{,}000 \text{ Btu/hr}$$

Calculate the *LMTD* (equation 5.2).

$$\Delta T_1 = 103° - 80° = 23°\text{F} \qquad \Delta T_2 = 103° - 93° = 10°\text{F}$$

$$LMTD = \frac{(23° - 10°)}{ln(23°/10°)} = 15.61°\text{F}$$

Solving for the outside heat transfer area using equation 5.1.

$$A_o = \frac{Q}{U_o \, LMTD} = \frac{156{,}000 \text{ Btu/hr}}{\left(125 \text{ Btu/hr-ft}^2\right)(15.61°\text{F})} = 79.95 \text{ ft}^2 \qquad \text{(a)}$$

From the energy balance for the heat exchanger, solve for the cooling water flow:

$$Q = m \, Cp \, \Delta T$$

$$m = \frac{156{,}000 \text{ Btu/hr}}{(1.0 \text{ Btu/lbm °F})(93° \quad 80°\text{F})} = 12{,}000 \text{ lbm/hr}$$

$$gpm = \frac{(12{,}000 \text{ lbm/hr})\left(7.481 \text{ gal/ft}^3\right)}{\left(62.4 \text{ lbm/ft}^3\right)(60 \text{ min/hr})} = 23.98 \text{ gal/min} \qquad \text{(b)}$$

Solving for the tube length, considering that the total outside heat transfer area is the outside area of each tube (circumference times length) times the number of tubes.

$$A_o = (Pi \, D \, L)(\# \text{ tubes})$$

$$L = \frac{A_o}{Pi \, D \, \# \text{tubes}} = \frac{79.95 \text{ ft}^2}{(Pi)(0.625/12 \text{ ft})(60)} = 8.15 \text{ ft} \qquad \text{(c)}$$

COMMENTS:
Check the units carefully! Note the conversions between hours and minutes and inches and feet required to get the units to work out correctly.

# ESTIMATING OVERALL
# HEAT TRANSFER COEFFICIENTS

The overall heat transfer coefficient can be estimated by combining the effects of conduction through the tube wall and convection on the inside and outside of the tube. Consider a section of a refrigeration condenser tube where inside water is flowing and the refrigerant is condensing on the outside as shown on figure 5-9. First heat is transferred by convection to the outside of the tube, and the refrigerant condenses. Next heat is transferred by conduction through the tube wall. Finally heat is transferred by convection from the inside of the tube to the cooling water by convection causing the water to increase in temperature.

The heat transfer due to conduction through the tube wall can be calculated from the following:

$$Q = x/k \; A \; \Delta T_{tube} \tag{5.4}$$

where

$Q$ = heat transferred, in Btu/hr or kW
$x$ = wall thickness in inches, feet, or meters

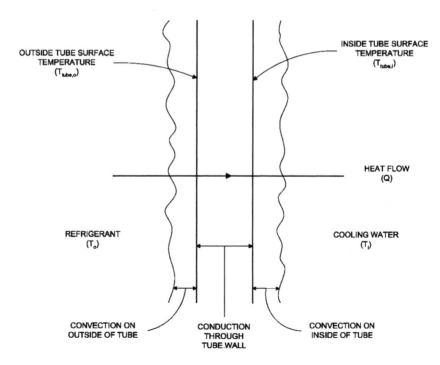

Fig. 5-9. Heat transfer through condenser tube.

$k$ = thermal conductivity of the tube material in Btu/hr-ft$^2$-°F/in,
Btu/hr-ft-°F, or W/m-°C

$A$ = heat transfer area, in ft$^2$ or m$^2$

$\Delta T_{tube}$ = outside tube temperature minus the inside tube temperature,
in °F or °C

Values for the thermal conductivity for some common heat exchanger tube materials are included in table 5-5. It is important to be careful that the units of wall thickness are consistent with those for the thermal conductivity.

**TABLE 5-5**
**Thermal Conductivity of Tube Materials**

| Material | Btu / hr-ft-°F | W/m-°C |
|---|---|---|
| 70-30 Cu-Ni | 18 | 31 |
| Monel | 14.5 | 25 |
| Copper | 225 | 390 |
| Admiralty | 70 | 121 |
| Brass | 60 | 104 |
| Aluminum bronze | 45 | 78 |
| Carbon steel | 28 | 48.5 |
| Stainless steel | 10 | 17.3 |
| Aluminum (pure) | 134 | 232 |
| Aluminum (alloy) | 90 | 156 |

The heat transfer due to convection on the inside and outside of the tube can be calculated for the following:

$$Q = h \; A \; \Delta T_{film} \qquad (5.5)$$

where

$Q$ = heat transferred, in Btu/hr or kW

$h$ = convection film coefficient, in Btu/hr-ft$^2$-°F or W/m$^2$-°C

$A$ = heat transfer area, in ft$^2$ or m$^2$

$\Delta T_{film}$ = temperature difference between the fluid and the inside and outside of the tube wall, in °F or °C

The value of the convection film coefficient depends on a variety of factors such as the fluid properties, the fluid velocity, whether the convection is forced (from a pump or fan) or natural, and if the fluid as it's heated or cooled just changes temperature or changes phase (that is, boils or condenses). Some techniques for estimating film coefficients will be discussed later.

As figure 5-9 indicated, the heat transfer through the outside convection film, the heat transfer by conduction through the tube wall, the heat transfer through the inside convection are all in series and must be the same. They must also be equal to the overall heat transfer predicted by the overall heat transfer coefficient. Thus

$$Q = U \ A \ LMTD = h_o \ A_o \ \Delta T_{film,o} = k/x \ A_{mt} \ \Delta T_{tube} = h_i \ A_i \ T_{film,i}$$

If the areas in each term are the same, from the above it can be shown that the overall heat transfer coefficient is

$$U_o = 1/(1/h_o + x/k + 1/h_i) \tag{5.6}$$

If the areas for each term are not the same, the equation becomes slightly more complicated. For example, for a cylindrical tube, the equation for the overall heat transfer coefficient becomes

$$U_o = 1/\left(1/h_o + (r_o/k) \ ln(r_o/r_i) + (r_o/r_i)/h_i\right) \tag{5.7}$$

where

$r_o$ = outside radius of the tube
$r_i$ = inside radius of the tube

Because the difference in area between the inside and outside areas of a typical heat exchanger tube is small, the simpler equation for equal areas (equation 5.6) can be used with little error.

For finned tube heat exchangers, the difference in area between the inside and outside areas is significant so an adjustment is necessary. For heat exchangers with fins on the outside of the tubes, the equation for the overall heat transfer coefficient becomes

$$U_o = 1/\left(1/(E_o h_o) + (r_o/A_o)/(A_i \ k) \ ln(r_o/r_i) + (A_o/A_i)/h_i\right) \tag{5.8}$$

where

$A_o$ = outside area of the finned tube
$A_i$ = inside tube area
$E_o$ = effectiveness of the outside finned area

Procedures for calculating the effectiveness of finned tubes can be found in most books on heat transfer or heat exchangers.

The equations above will estimate the overall coefficient for a new or carefully cleaned heat exchanger. After the heat exchanger has been in service for some time, fouling will occur on the heat exchange surfaces that will reduce the overall heat transfer coefficient. This can be accounted for using either fouling resistances or a fouling factor. Table 5-6 contains some recommended fouling resistances that can be included in equations 5.6,

5.7, or 5.8 to account for fouling. For example, equation 5.6 with fouling resistances included would become

$$U_o = 1/(1/h_o + r_o + x/k + r_i + 1/h_i)$$

Note that $r_o$ and $r_i$ are the outside and inside fouling resistances. The other equations would be modified in a similar fashion.

**TABLE 5-6**
**Fouling Resistances**

| Fluid | $hr\text{-}ft^2\text{-}°F/Btu$ | $m^2\text{-}°C/W$ |
|---|---|---|
| Seawater | 0.0005 | 0.00009 |
| Freshwater | 0.001 | 0.00018 |
| Refrigerant vapor (oil bearing) | 0.002 | 0.00035 |
| Refrigerant liquid | 0.001 | 0.00018 |

The fouling factor (FF) is essentially an adjustment to the clean overall heat transfer coefficient. The coefficient is calculated using equations 5.6, 5.7, or 5.8 and then multiplied by the fouling factor to obtain the coefficient to use for service operation. A fouling factor of about 0.7 to 0.9 is reasonable for many common heat exchangers.

---

EXAMPLE PROBLEM 5.3. The overall heat transfer coefficient for a refrigeration condenser is being estimated. The outside film coefficient is 300 Btu/hr-ft²-°F and the inside film coefficient is 1,200 Btu/hr-ft²-°F. The tubes are ¾ inch OD, 18 BWG and made of 70-30 Cu-Ni. Calculate the overall heat transfer coefficient based on (a) equal inside and outside areas, (b) a cylindrical tube, (c) considering inside and outside fouling resistances, (d) considering a fouling factor of 0.75.

SOLUTION.

SKETCH AND GIVEN DATA:

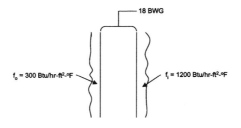

ASSUMPTIONS:

1. Conditions are steady state.
2. The properties are uniform.

ANALYSIS:

The wall thickness for an 18 BWG tube is 0.049 inches and k = 18.0 Btu/hr-ft-°F for 70-30 Cu-Ni.

Using equation 5.6

$$U_o = \frac{1}{(1/300) + (0.049/12)/(18.0) + (1/1,200)} = 227.6 \, \text{Btu}/\text{hr-ft}^2\text{-}°\text{F} \qquad \text{(a)}$$

Using equation 5.7

$$U_o = \frac{1}{(1/300) + ((0.375/12)/18.0)/ln(0.375/0.326) + (0.375/0.326)(1/1,200)}$$

$$U_o = 220.5 \, \text{Btu}/\text{hr-ft}^2\text{-}°\text{F} \qquad \text{(b)}$$

Using equation 5.6 and including the fouling resistances from table 5-6

$$U_o = \frac{1}{(1/300) + 0.002 + (0.049/12)/(18.0) + 0.005 + (1/1,200)}$$

$$U_o = 145.1 \, \text{Btu}/\text{hr-ft}^2\text{-}°\text{F} \qquad \text{(c)}$$

Using equation 5.6 and the results from part (a) and applying the fouling factor

$$U_o = (227.6)(0.75) = 170.7 \, \text{Btu}/\text{hr-ft}^2\text{-}°\text{F} \qquad \text{(d)}$$

COMMENTS:

1. The difference between the overall heat transfer coefficient estimated assuming equal inside and outside areas versus that for a cylinder is only 3 percent in this situation. The difference will be less for larger diameter tubes and a bit more for smaller diameter tubes.
2. Calculating the service overall heat transfer coefficient using fouling resistances is generally more accurate than using a fouling factor.

## ESTIMATING CONVECTION FILM COEFFICIENTS

Estimating the convection film coefficient in a particular situation is a fairly complex subject. The coefficient is dependent on a variety of factors including the fluid properties (which vary with temperature), the physical situation (inside tube, across plate, etc.), and if there is a phase change (boiling or condensing) or just a temperature change taking place. Selecting the best equation for a particular situation from the dozens found in heat transfer books can be daunting. While a detailed coverage of this subject is beyond the scope of this book, a few procedures for estimating heat transfer coefficients are presented below.

Water or air being pumped inside or across tubes and being heated or cooled is a common situation in refrigeration and HVAC systems. A popular equation for estimating the heat transfer coefficient in these situations is

$$Nu = C\, Re^n\, Pr^m \qquad (5.9)$$

where

$Nu$ = Nusselt Number = $fD/k$
$Re$ = Reynolds Number = $VD\rho/\mu$
$Pr$ = Prandtl Number = $Cp\,\mu/k$
$f$ = film coefficient, in Btu/hr–ft$^2$-°F or W/m$^2$-°C
$D$ = tube diameter, in ft or m
$k$ = fluid thermal conductivity, in Btu/hr-ft-°F or W/m-°C
$V$ = velocity, in ft/s or m/s
$\rho$ = fluid density, in lbm/ft$^3$ or kg/m$^3$
$\mu$ = fluid absolute viscosity, in lbm/ft-s or kg/m-s
$Cp$ = fluid specific heat, in Btu/lbm-°F or J/kg-°C

Note that the Nusselt, Reynolds and Prandtl numbers are dimensionless ratios. This can be used to check the units of the various values being used. For flow inside tubes, the values of the constant and exponents are $C$ = 0.023, $n = 0.8$, and $m - 0.4$. For flow across tubes, the values of the constant and exponents are $C = 0.26$, $n = 0.6$, and $m = 0.37$. The properties of water and air needed for calculating convection film coefficients are contained in tables 5-7 and 5-8.

### TABLE 5-7
### Properties of Water (SI Units)

| Temperature (°C) | Density (kg/m$^3$) | Specific Heat (J/kg-°C) | Viscosity (kg/m-s) | Conductivity (W/m-°C) |
|---|---|---|---|---|
| 0 | 999.8 | 4,218 | 0.001791 | 0.5619 |
| 5 | 1,000 | 4,203 | 0.001520 | 0.5723 |
| 10 | 999.8 | 4,193 | 0.001308 | 0.5820 |
| 15 | 999.2 | 4,187 | 0.001139 | 0.5911 |
| 20 | 998.3 | 4,182 | 0.001003 | 0.5996 |
| 25 | 997.1 | 4,180 | 0.000891 | 0.6076 |
| 30 | 995.7 | 4,180 | 0.000798 | 0.6150 |
| 35 | 994.1 | 4,179 | 0.000720 | 0.6221 |
| 40 | 992.3 | 4,179 | 0.000653 | 0.6286 |
| 45 | 990.2 | 4,182 | 0.000596 | 0.6347 |
| 50 | 988.0 | 4,182 | 0.000547 | 0.6405 |

**TABLE 5-7** *(continued)*
**Properties of Water (English Units)**

| Temperature (°F) | Density (lbm/ft³) | Specific Heat (Btu/lbm-°F) | Viscosity (lbm/ft-hr) | Conductivity (Btu/hr-ft-°F) |
|---|---|---|---|---|
| 32 | 62.41 | 1.008 | 4.333 | 0.3247 |
| 40 | 62.42 | 1.004 | 3.742 | 0.3300 |
| 50 | 62.41 | 1.001 | 3.163 | 0.3363 |
| 60 | 62.37 | 1.000 | 2.715 | 0.3421 |
| 70 | 62.31 | 0.999 | 2.361 | 0.3475 |
| 80 | 62.22 | 0.998 | 2.075 | 0.3525 |
| 90 | 62.12 | 0.998 | 1.842 | 0.3572 |
| 100 | 62.00 | 0.998 | 1.648 | 0.3616 |
| 110 | 61.86 | 0.998 | 1.486 | 0.3656 |
| 120 | 61.71 | 0.998 | 1.348 | 0.3693 |

**TABLE 5-8**
**Properties of Air (SI Units)**

| Temperature (°C) | Density (kg/m³) | Specific Heat (J/kg-°C) | Viscosity (kg/m-s) | Conductivity (W/m-°C) |
|---|---|---|---|---|
| −30 | 1.452 | 1,006 | 0.0000157 | 0.0217 |
| −20 | 1.394 | 1,006 | 0.0000162 | 0.0225 |
| −10 | 1.341 | 1,006 | 0.0000167 | 0.0233 |
| 0 | 1.292 | 1,006 | 0.0000172 | 0.0241 |
| 10 | 1.247 | 1,006 | 0.0000177 | 0.0249 |
| 20 | 1.204 | 1,006 | 0.0000182 | 0.0256 |
| 30 | 1.164 | 1,006 | 0.0000186 | 0.0264 |
| 40 | 1.127 | 1,007 | 0.0000191 | 0.0271 |
| 50 | 1.092 | 1,007 | 0.0000196 | 0.0278 |
| 60 | 1.059 | 1,008 | 0.0000200 | 0.0285 |

**Properties of Air (English Units)**

| Temperature (°F) | Density (lbm/ft³) | Specific Heat (Btu/lbm-°F) | Viscosity (lbm/ft-hr) | Conductivity (Btu/hr-ft-°F) |
|---|---|---|---|---|
| −20 | 9.022 | 0.2402 | 0.0381 | 0.01258 |
| 0 | 8.630 | 0.2402 | 0.0395 | 0.01310 |
| 20 | 8.270 | 0.2402 | 0.0408 | 0.01361 |
| 40 | 7.939 | 0.2402 | 0.0422 | 0.01412 |
| 60 | 7.633 | 0.2403 | 0.0435 | 0.01462 |
| 80 | 7.350 | 0.2403 | 0.0447 | 0.01511 |
| 100 | 7.088 | 0.2405 | 0.0460 | 0.01557 |
| 120 | 6.843 | 0.2406 | 0.0472 | 0.01602 |
| 140 | 6.615 | 0.2408 | 0.0485 | 0.01648 |

EXAMPLE PROBLEM 5.4. Water is being heated as it flows at 2 m/s inside a 16.5 mm ID tube. Estimate the convection film coefficient for water temperatures of (a) 0°C and (b) 40°C.

SOLUTION.

SKETCH AND GIVEN DATA:

ASSUMPTIONS:
1. The water flow is steady.
2. The water properties may be determined at the given temperature.

ANALYSIS:
From table 5.7, the properties of water at 0°C are:

$$mu = 0.001791 \text{ kg/m-s} \quad Cp = 4{,}218 \text{ J/kg-°C}$$
$$rho = 999.8 \text{ J/kg-°C} \quad k = 0.5619 \text{ W/m-°C}$$

Using equation 5.9 with the constants and exponents for flow inside a tube:

$$Nu = 0.023 \; Re^{0.8} Pr^{0.4}$$
$$Re = V\,D\,rho/mu = (2 \text{ m/s})(0.0165 \text{ m})(999.8 \text{ J/kg-°C})/(0.001791 \text{ kg/m-s}) = 18{,}422$$
$$Pr = Cp\,mu/k = (4{,}218 \text{ J/kg-°C})(0.001791 \text{ kg/m-s})/(0.5619 \text{ W/m-°C}) = 13.45$$
$$Nu = 0.023\,(18{,}422)^{0.8}(13.45)^{0.4} = 168.1$$
$$f = Nu\,k/D = (168.1)(0.5619 \text{ W/m-°C})/(0.0165 \text{ m}) = 5{,}725 \text{ W/m}^2\text{-°C} \qquad \text{(a)}$$

From table 5.7, the properties of water at 40°C are:

$$mu = 0.0006531 \text{ kg/m-s} \quad Cp = 4{,}179 \text{ J/kg-°C}$$
$$rho = 992.3 \text{ J/kg-°C} \quad k = 0.6286 \text{ W/m-}^0\text{C}$$

Using equation 5.9 with the constants and exponents for flow inside a tube:

$$Nu = 0.023 \; Re^{0.8} Pr^{0.4}$$
$$Re = V\,D\,rho/mu = (2 \text{ m/s})(0.0165 \text{ m})(992.3 \text{ J/kg-°C})/(0.006531 \text{ kg/m-s}) = 50{,}139$$
$$Pr = Cp\,mu/k = (4{,}179 \text{ J/kg-°C})(0.006531 \text{ kg/m-s})/(0.6286 \text{ W/m-°C}) = 4.34$$
$$Nu = 0.023\,(50{,}139)^{0.8}(4.34)^{0.4} = 238.2$$
$$f = Nu\,k/D = (238.2)(0.6286 \text{ W/m-°C})/(0.0165 \text{ m}) = 9{,}073 \text{ W/m}^2\text{-°C} \qquad \text{(a)}$$

COMMENTS:
1. When the fluid is changing temperature, evaluate the properties at the average temperature.
2. At higher temperatures, the reduced viscosity results in higher film coefficient.

---

As a convenience figures 5-10 and 5-11 can be used for estimating film coefficients for two common situations—water flowing inside tubes and air flowing across tubes. Figure 5-10 can be used to estimate the film coefficient for freshwater flowing inside tubes. While the values are based on ¾ inch OD tubes, they will be reasonably accurate for tubes from ½ inch OD to 1 inch OD. Figure 5-11 can be used to estimate the film coefficient for air at atmospheric pressure flowing across tubes. The values are based on air at 70°F, but they will be reasonably accurate for temperatures from about 0°F to 100°F.

When a phase change takes place, the mechanisms governing the heat transfer process are very different from single phase heat transfer. Other fluid properties such as the latent heat of vaporization $(h_{fg})$ become more important in affecting the value of the convective film coefficient. For example, when one pound of steam condenses in a vacuum, about 1,000 Btu of heat are exchanged. It would take 100 pounds of liquid water changing 10°F to exchange the same amount of heat. This results in very high overall heat transfer coefficients for steam condensers. The film coefficients for condensing refrigerants are much lower than those for steam, primarily

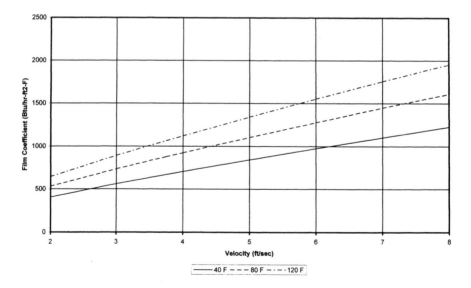

Fig. 5-10. Water inside ¾ inch tube.

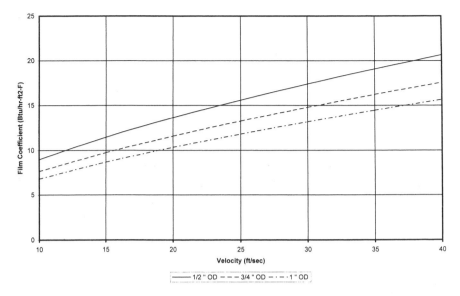

Fig. 5-11. Air across tubes.

because the latent heats for refrigerants are much lower. For example $h_{fg}$ for R-12 at 100 psia is 59.37 Btu/lbm while the value of $h_{fg}$ for steam at that pressure is 889.5 Btu/lbm. Typical values for the heat transfer coefficients for R-12 condensing on horizontal tubes at a temperature of 110°F for changing film temperature differences are given in figure 5-12. The values will be reasonably accurate for temperatures between 90°F and 130°F and for similar refrigerants such as R-22 and R-134a.

Like estimating condensing heat transfer coefficients, estimating the heat transfer coefficient for boiling is a complicated matter. One situation that everyone is familiar with is the boiling of water in a pot on a stove. As the bottom of the pot is heated by the burner, the heat is transferred to the liquid by free convection and bubble agitation. The steam forms at the pot bottom, rises, and is replaced by liquid water. This is referred to as pool boiling. In most refrigeration system evaporators, however, the boiling occurs as the refrigerant flows along the inside a tube. This is referred to as forced convection boiling. The heat transfer process is strongly affected by the velocity and composition of the refrigerant as it flows through the tubes. As the refrigerant boils, the percentage of liquid decreases, the density decreases, and the velocity increases. The heat transfer varies significantly along the length of the tube, starting low then increasing as the liquid changes phase and the velocity increases, then dropping as all the liquid boils to vapor and the vapor becomes superheated. This is shown in figure 5-13.

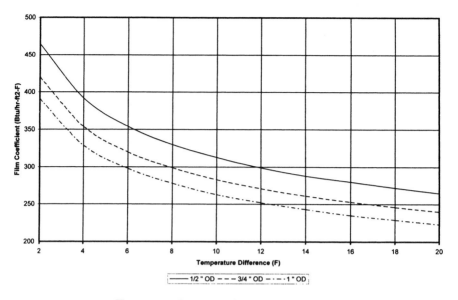

Fig. 5-12. R-12 condensing at 110°F.

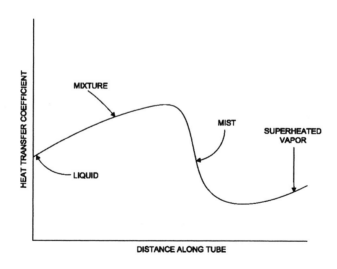

Fig. 5-13. Boiling inside an evaporator tube.

Typical values of the average boiling film coefficient vary from approximately 60 to 300 Btu/hr-ft$^2$-°F (about 350 to 1,700 W/m$^2$-°C) for refrigerants such as R-12, R-22, and R-134a. For evaporators exchanging heat to air, the low film coefficient for the air will control the heat transfer. If the actual boiling coefficient is significantly different from the estimated value, it will have little effect on the overall heat transfer coefficient for the heat exchanger. If the air is being circulated by forced convection, equation 5.9 or figure 5-12 can be used to estimate the air film coefficient. If the air is being circulated by natural convection, the overall heat transfer coefficient will typically be between 1 and 3 Btu/hr-ft$^2$-°F. The manufacturer of the evaporator should be contacted if more accurate estimates are required.

## PROBLEMS (ENGLISH UNITS)

5.1E  The heat being rejected to a water-cooled condenser is 100,000 Btu/hr. If the cooling water flow is 20 gpm and the entering water temperature is 75°F, what will the water temperature exiting the condenser be?

5.2E  A water-cooled condenser is condensing 10 lbm per minute of R-22 at 240 psig and 150°F to a saturated liquid at the same pressure. The cooling water enters the tubes at 70°F and leaves at 85°F. Determine the cooling water flow in gallons per minute.

5.3E  A fan-coil unit used as the evaporator in a cold storage room has a capacity of 2 tons. Air enters the unit at 40°F and exits at 35°F. Determine the air flow in cubic feet per minute.

5.4E A  20-ton air-conditioning system has a heat rejection factor of 1.3. The condensing temperature is 105°F and the cooling water enters at 75°F and exits at 90°F. The overall heat transfer coefficient $(U_o)$ is 140 Btu/hr-ft$^2$-°F. What is the required outside tube surface area? What length will the tubes be if the condenser is constructed of 100 ¾ inch OD tubes?

5.5E  A water-cooled condenser is constructed of ¾ inch OD 18 BWG 70-30 Cu-Ni tubes. The water velocity is 5 ft/sec. Use figures 5-10 and 5-12 to estimate the film coefficients and table 5-6 for the fouling resistances. Estimate the overall heat transfer coefficient.

5.6E  Calculate the convection film coefficient for 80°F water flowing at a velocity of 5 ft/sec inside a 1 inch OD with a 0.049 inch wall thickness. Compare your answer to the results for 3/4 inch tubes presented in figure 5-10.

# PROBLEMS (SI UNITS)

5.1S  The heat being rejected to a water-cooled condenser is 50 kW. If the cooling water flow is 1.5 kg/s and the entering water temperature is 20 °C, what will the water temperature exiting the condenser be?

5.2S  A water-cooled condenser is condensing 5 kg per minute of R-22 at 1,600 kPa and 60°C to a saturated liquid at the same pressure. The cooling water enters the tubes at 20°C and leaves at 30°C. Determine the cooling water flow in kg per minute.

5.3.S  A fan-coil unit is used as the evaporator in a cold storage room has a capacity of 4 kW. Air enters the unit at 5°C and exits at 2°C. Determine the air flow in cubic meters per minute.

5.4S  A 50 kW air-conditioning system has a heat rejection factor of 1.3. The condensing temperature is 40°C and the cooling water enters at 25°C and exits at 33°C. The overall heat transfer coefficient $(U_o)$ is 800 W/m$^2$-°C. What is the required outside tube surface area? What length will the tubes be if the condenser is constructed of 100 2 cm OD tubes?

5.5S  Calculate the film coefficient for air at 0°C flowing across a 2.5 cm tube at a velocity of 10 m/sec.

## CHAPTER 6

# Controls and Accessories

Most marine refrigeration and air-conditioning systems with reciprocating compressors operate on a method of overall system control known as the "pump-down cycle." The refrigerated space temperature is monitored by a thermostat that acts to open and close the solenoid valve in the liquid refrigerant supply line based on space temperature. If the space temperature rises above the temperature set point, the thermostat opens the refrigerant solenoid valve, and if the space temperature drops below the set point, the thermostat closes the solenoid valve. The routine starting and stopping of the compressor is controlled by the low-pressure cutout switch installed in the compressor suction line. If the suction pressure rises above the low-pressure cutout set point, the compressor is started. If the suction pressure drops below the set point, the compressor is stopped.

Let's follow the system through one complete cycle. Figure 6-1 shows a simple refrigeration system with the controls necessary for operation on the pump-down cycle. Begin with the space temperature high. The thermostat contacts close, energizing the solenoid valve and admitting refrigerant to the evaporator. The refrigerant vaporizes, increasing the evaporator pressure. The low-pressure switch closes, starting the compressor. The refrigeration system is now operating with continuous cooling taking place. As cooling continues, the space temperature will gradually drop. When the space temperature is reduced to the set point of the thermostat, the thermostat contacts will open, deenergizing the solenoid valve and stopping the flow of refrigerant to the evaporator. Continued compressor operation reduces the suction pressure to the set point of the low-pressure switch, opening the switch contacts and stopping the compressor. Due to the stopping of refrigeration, cooling has ceased and the space temperature will

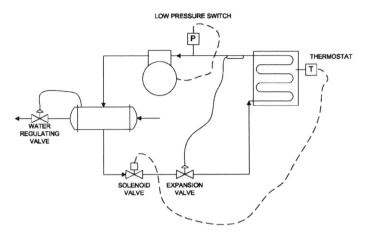

Fig. 6-1. Pump-down cycle.

slowly rise. When the space temperature reaches the thermostat set point, the cycle will begin again.

The pump-down cycle decreases the possibility of liquid refrigerant flooding back to the compressor during start-up and substantially reduces the dilution of crankcase oil by the refrigerant. An understanding of the pump-down cycle control sequence is essential in troubleshooting refrigeration systems.

## EXPANSION DEVICES

The purpose of the expansion device in a refrigeration system is to reduce the refrigerant pressure from the high side pressure to the low side pressure and regulate the flow of the liquid refrigerant admitted to the evaporator. Expansion devices used in various systems include the constant pressure expansion valve, the thermostatic expansion valve, the capillary tube, and the float valve. Of these, the thermostatic expansion valve and the capillary tube are most commonly found in marine systems.

### Constant Pressure Expansion Valve

The constant pressure (or automatic) expansion valve is essentially a reducing valve that maintains a constant evaporator pressure. Figure 6-2 is a schematic of a simplified constant pressure expansion valve. If the evaporator pressure drops, the valve will open wide and feed more refrigerant into the evaporator. An increase in evaporator pressure will cause the valve to close and decrease the flow of refrigerant into the evaporator. Constant pressure expansion valves do not adjust well to changing system

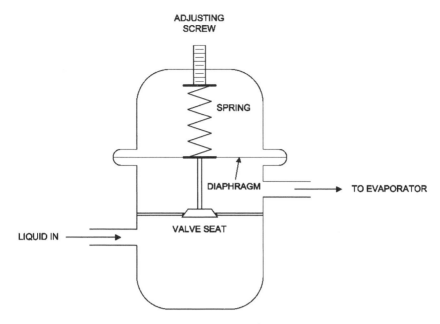

Fig. 6-2. Constant pressure expansion valve.

loads. If the system load decreases, the evaporator pressure will drop and the constant pressure evaporator will open further in an attempt to keep the evaporator pressure constant. This can result in overfeeding and flooding of liquid refrigerant back to the compressor. A load increase will result in the valve closing in an attempt to reduce the evaporator pressure, thus underfeeding the evaporator and reducing the system efficiency. This limits the use of the constant pressure expansion valve to smaller systems that operate at nearly constant load and where a small carefully controlled refrigerant charge reduces the possibility of floodback.

### Thermostatic Expansion Valve

The thermostatic expansion valve responds to both the evaporator pressure and outlet temperature, and thus is able to maintain a constant superheat at the outlet of the evaporator. This allows the valve to respond to varying system loads and avoids underfeeding at high loads and overfeeding at low loads experienced by the constant pressure expansion valve. As refrigerant is fed to the evaporator, the liquid first boils into a vapor. As further heat is absorbed by the evaporator, the refrigerant gas becomes superheated. Feeding more refrigerant to the evaporator will lower the superheat temperature, while feeding less refrigerant will raise the superheat temperature. If the load should increase, the superheat will increase, and the valve will respond by opening to feed more refrigerant into the evaporator. A load decrease would result in a decrease in the superheat, and the valve would respond by closing and reducing the refrigerant feed into the evaporator.

Figure 6-3 shows a typical thermostatic expansion valve. A feeler bulb partially filled with a volatile liquid, typically the system refrigerant, is clamped to the outlet of the evaporator so that the bulb and the power fluid inside closely assume the outlet refrigerant gas temperature. The pressure produced by the feeler bulb will be the saturation pressure based on the outlet temperature. The pressure from the feeler bulb is applied to the top of the valve diaphragm, and the evaporator pressure pushes on the bottom. A spring applies a third force and balances the valve assembly as shown in figure 6-4. When the valve is balanced, the sum of the evaporator pressure times the diaphragm area plus the spring force will equal the feeler bulb pressure times the diaphragm area. For the valve to open and feed refrigerant to the evaporator, the bulb pressure must be higher than the evaporator pressure due to the spring force. Since the bulb pressure responds to the evaporator outlet temperature, this can only occur when the suction gas is superheated. The spring is normally adjusted by the factory to obtain about 10°F (6°C) of superheat in service. Valves set for less than this will not operate properly and may flood back liquid refrigerant to the compressor. Valves set for more than 10°F (6°C) will reduce the effectiveness of the evaporator and will reduce the system capacity.

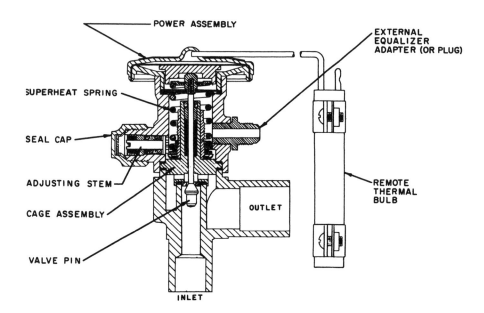

Fig. 6-3. Thermostatic expansion valve. Courtesy Alco Controls.

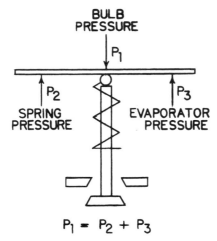

Fig. 6-4. Thermostatic expansion valve equilibrium.

The superheat setting of most thermostatic expansion valves is adjustable. Remove the seal cap on the side of the valve and turn the adjusting stem with a screwdriver. Turning the stem to the right increases the spring pressure, reducing refrigerant flow, and increasing superheat. Turning the stem to the left decreases the spring tension, increasing refrigerant flow, and reducing superheat. Two turns of the stem will typically change the superheat about 1°F (0.5°C). One technique of measuring superheat is to use a contact thermometer to accurately measure the temperatures at the inlet and outlet of the evaporator. This method will yield good results only when the evaporator pressure drop is low. A second technique is to compare the evaporator outlet temperature with the saturation temperature corresponding to the compressor suction pressure. This will yield good results only when the pressure drop between the evaporator and the compressor is low. The best technique will involve taking pressure and temperature readings at the evaporator outlet. For example, referring to figure 6-5, the following data are taken for an R-12 system:

1. Evaporator outlet pressure (from gauge) = 37 psig (255 kPa)
2. Evaporator outlet temperature (from contact thermometer) = 50°F (10°C)
3. Sensing bulb pressure = 61.3 psia (from R-12 table for 50°F)
4. 37 psig = 51.7 psia = 40.1°F (from R-12 table)
5. Thus superheat = 50°F − 40.1°F = 9.9°F

If a check of superheat indicates a problem, valve adjustment is indicated. It should be noted, however, that improper installation of the

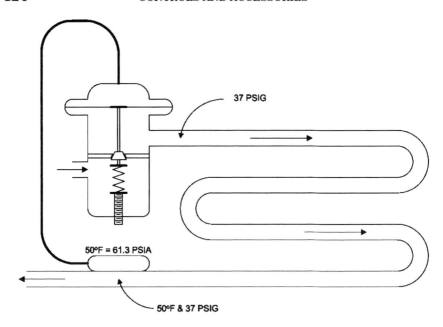

Fig. 6-5. Superheat with internally-equalized thermostatic
expansion valve.

sensing bulb is a common cause of expansion valve problems. Figure 6-6
shows some recommended bulb installations. It is most important that
the bulb make good thermal contact with the suction line. Clean the line
thoroughly and clamp the bulb securely. If the bulb is installed in a location outside the cooled space, it will probably be necessary to insulate the
bulb as shown in figure 6-7.

Thermostatic expansion valves can be purchased as internally equalized or externally equalized. An internally equalized valve has a small port
that admits the valve outlet pressure (that is, the evaporator inlet pressure) to the bottom of the valve diaphragm. Some refrigeration systems
have an appreciable pressure drop across the evaporator. Use of an internally equalized valve in such applications can result in unacceptably high
superheat at the evaporator outlet. The solution is to use an externally
equalized valve that has a fitting for connecting the evaporator outlet pressure rather than the inlet pressure to the bottom of the valve diaphragm.
Assume the valve from the superheat example above is installed in a system with a 3 psi pressure drop across the evaporator. The valve remains
adjusted for 9.9°F of superheat and the evaporator inlet pressure remains at 37 psig. Since the pressure acting on the bottom of the diaphragm is the inlet pressure of 37 psig, the valve will modulate to maintain

EXTERNAL BULB ON SMALL SUCTION LINE

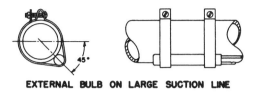

EXTERNAL BULB ON LARGE SUCTION LINE

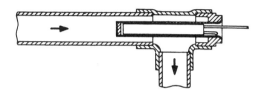

Fig. 6-6. Remote bulb installation.

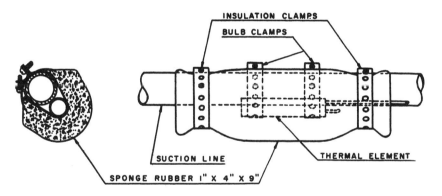

Fig. 6-7. Expansion valve bulb insulation.

an outlet temperature of 50°F that is 9.9°F above the saturation temperature for 37 psig. Refer to figure 6-8 and calculate the superheat:

1. Evaporator outlet pressure = 37 psig – 3 psi = 34 psig = 48.7 psia
2. Evaporator outlet temperature = 50°F (10°C)
3. 34 psig = 48.7 psia = 36.7°F (from R-12 table)
4. Thus superheat = 50°F – 36.7°F = 13.3°F

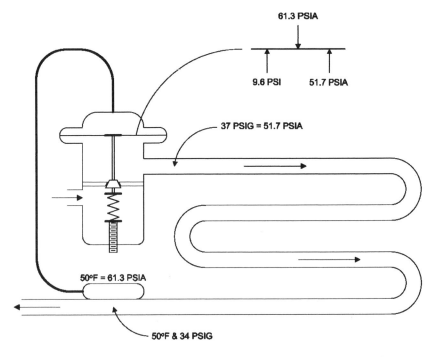

Fig. 6-8. Increased superheat due to evaporator pressure drop.

The superheat has increased from 9.9°F to 13.3°F due to the pressure drop across the evaporator. If the valve were externally actuated, the pressure applied to the bottom of the valve diaphragm will be 34 psig, rather than 37 psig. Note from the first example, the sensing bulb pressure was 61.3 psia when the evaporator pressure acting on the bottom of the diaphragm was 37 psig (51.7 psia). That means the pressure difference across the diaphragm would be 9.6 psi (61.3 – 51.7). Refer to figure 6-9 and calculate the superheat:

    1. Evaporator outlet pressure = 37 psig – 3 psi = 34 psig = 48.7 psia
    2. 48.7 psia = 36.7°F (from R-12 table)
    3. Sensing bulb pressure = 48.7 psia + 9.6 psi = 58.3 psia
    4. 58.3 psia = 47°F (from R-12 table)
    5. Superheat = 47°F – 36.7°F = 10.3°F

The use of an externally equalized expansion valve reduced the superheat from 13.3°F to 10.3°F. In general, an external equalized valve should be used when the evaporator pressure drop is sufficient to change the saturation temperature 3°F (1.5°C) in air-conditioning applications, 2°F (1°C) in refrigeration systems, or 1°F (0.5°C) in low temperature (cryogenic)

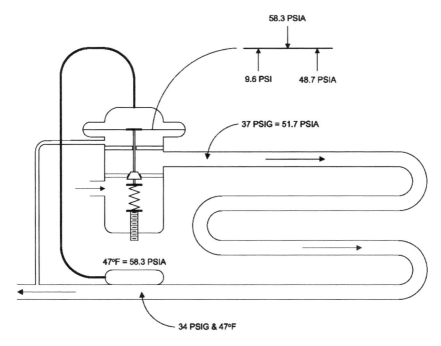

Fig. 6-9. Use of externally-equalized expansion valve to
reduce superheat.

systems. An externally equalized valve is also recommended when a refrigerant distributor is used between the valve and the evaporator.

Thermostatic expansion valves are available with a variety of thermostatic charges. The thermostatic charge is the substance in the expansion
valves sensing bulb that responds to the evaporator outlet temperature.
The bulb pressure will vary based on the evaporator outlet temperature,
and the charge must be selected to allow the valve to maintain a satisfactory level of superheat over the operating range of the system. Thermostatic expansion valves are available with the following types of charges:

- liquid charge
- gas charge
- liquid cross charge
- gas cross charge
- adsorption charge

With a liquid charge, there is sufficient charge such that some liquid
remains in the sensing bulb under all temperature conditions. This prevents charge migration that can occur if the bulb becomes warmer than

the diaphragm chamber. Charge migration will result in loss of valve control. A conventional liquid charge is the use of same substance for the charge as is used for the system refrigerant. It the valve is charged with a substance other than the system refrigerant or a mixture, this is referred to as a cross charge. With a conventional liquid cross charge, the sensing bulb will have the same pressure-temperature characteristics as the saturation characteristic of the system refrigerant. With a liquid cross charge, the pressure-temperature characteristic of the sensing bulb will be different and will cross the system refrigerant saturation curve at some point.

Cross-charged expansion valves are commonly used in low-temperature applications. A check of the saturation properties of any common refrigerant will reveal why. The amount of superheat required to change the bulb pressure a given amount is much greater at low temperatures than at high temperatures. For example, for R-134a, the saturation pressure changes from 45.1 psia to 49.7 psia as the saturation temperature changes from 35°F to 40°F (0.92 psi per °F). Between −40°F and −35°F, the saturation pressure changes from 7.4 to 8.6 psia (0.24 psi per °F). The use of another substance that changes pressure more at desired operating temperature permits the valve to operate satisfactorily with a normal amount of superheat. Cross-charged valves are normally designed to be used in a relatively narrow temperature range. If a cross-charged valve is used at temperatures above the design range, the superheat will increase, reducing system efficiency.

A gas-charged expansion valve is similar to the liquid-charged valve except the bulb charge is limited so that at some particular bulb temperature, all the liquid will have vaporized. Once this happens, changes in the sensed temperature have little effect on bulb pressure and thus the valve movement. This has the effect of limiting the maximum evaporator pressure and thus the compressor load. Gas-charged expansion valves can be installed in systems to limit the compressor load during pull-down conditions. Like liquid-charged valves, gas-charged valves are available charged with the system refrigerant or cross-charged with another substance. Care must be taken in the installation of gas-charged expansion valves to avoid charge migration.

An adsorption charge consists of noncondensable gas and an adsorbent material located in the sensing bulb. If the temperature of the bulb increases, gas is released from the absorbent material, increasing the bulb temperature. If the bulb temperature decreases, gas is adsorbed and the bulb pressure drops. Adsorption charged expansion valves do not limit evaporator pressure.

Because of the wide variety of valves available, it is important to replace a thermostatic expansion valve with one of the same type and size. Check the system manual or consult the expansion valve manufacturer.

## Capillary Tube Systems

Many small refrigeration systems such as those found in drinking fountains, small refrigerators, and small freezers use a capillary tube as the expansion device. These systems commonly use a small hermetic reciprocating compressor and an air-cooled condenser. The systems are designed to be compact and to require little routine maintenance. The use of a hermetic compressor eliminates refrigerant leaks at the shaft seal and also simplifies compressor lubrication. The simplicity and reduced cost of the system is an advantage. An obvious disadvantage of these systems is that repairs are difficult because of the inaccessibility of the moving parts.

The capillary tube has a small diameter, typically 0.030 to 0.050 inches, and it may be from 3 to 20 feet long. Liquid refrigerant enters the tube, and the pressure drops because of friction and the acceleration of the refrigerant as some of it flashes to vapor due to the decreasing pressure. The desired pressure drop determines the length and diameter of tubing—the longer the tubing and/or the smaller the tube diameter, the greater the pressure drop. There are many combinations of length and diameter that will result in the same pressure drop, but once selected, the tube cannot adjust to varying cycle conditions. At the system balance point, the mass flow passed by the capillary tube must equal the mass flow being moved by the compressor. In general, the tube will pass less mass as the pressure difference between the condenser and evaporator decreases, while the compressor will move more mass under those conditions. If the flows do not balance, the system pressures must adjust until they do. Figure 6-10 illustrates the balancing of a refrigeration system fitted with a capillary tube under several conditions.

Like the constant pressure expansion valve, the capillary tube tends to starve the evaporator under high loads and overfeed under low loads. At high loads, the evaporator pressure tends to easily evaporate the refrigerant supplied to it, and the evaporator pressure rises, tending to reduce the tube flow and causing underfeeding of the evaporator. A low loads, the evaporator drops, resulting in increasing the tube flow and decreasing the compressor capacity. This overfeeding can result in liquid floodback to the compressor. This is normally prevented by limiting the size of the refrigerant charge so the evaporator cannot fill completely with liquid refrigerant. This careful control is possible because the system is charged and sealed at the factory by the manufacturer. Another technique used to reduce the possibility of floodback is to install an accumulator in the line between the evaporator and condenser to collect any liquid from the evaporator.

The capillary tubing is commonly bonded to the cold compressor suction line to ensure subcooling of the refrigerant entering the evaporator. The refrigerant in the capillary tube remains a liquid for a longer distance and the capacity of the tube is increased. Due to the superheating of the suction gas, this increases the work of the compressor slightly. Even

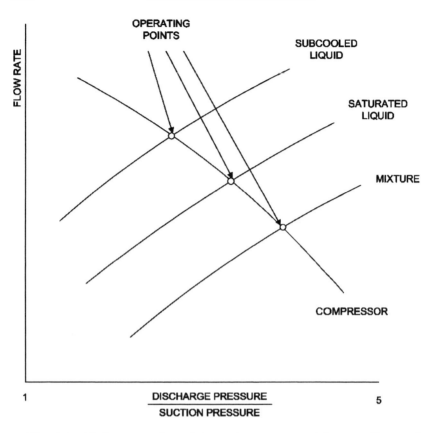

Fig. 6-10. Balancing of a refrigeration system with a capillary tube.

though the refrigerating effect is improved by subcooling, there is a slight decrease in unit performance.

### Float Valve

Float valves are used on flooded evaporators to maintain a constant liquid level in the evaporator or supply receiver. As the level in the evaporator or receiver drops, the float valve will open bringing the refrigerant level back to the desired level. The float valve can be located on either the high pressure side or the low pressure side of the system. A valve located on the high pressure side is called a high-pressure float valve while one located on the low pressure side is called a low-pressure float valve. An alternative to a continuously modulating valve is a level switch that opens a solenoid valve completely when the level is low and closes it completely when the level is high. Most evaporators in marine systems are of the dry-expansion type, and float valves are not commonly used on these applications. Flooded evaporators are most commonly used in large capacity chiller systems like those used for air-conditioning large buildings. A diagram of a system fitted with a high-pressure float valve is shown in figure 6-11. Figure 5-1 shows a flooded evaporator fitted with a low-pressure float valve.

## High- and Low-Pressure Switches

These devices are very similar in construction and operation, but perform very different functions in the refrigeration system. The high-pressure switch is a safety device. It is actuated by the compressor discharge pressure and stops the compressor in the event of high pressure. The low-pressure switch is actuated by the compressor suction pressure. It is the primary control for stopping and starting the compressor during normal system operation when operating on the pump-down cycle. When the suction pressure has been pumped down to the desired level (the cut-out setting), the low-pressure switch opens and stops the compressor. When the pressure rises to the desired level (the cut-in setting), the switch closes and the compressor starts. The low-pressure switch is designed to close on high system pressure and open on low system pressures, while the high pressure switch is designed to open on high system pressure and close on low

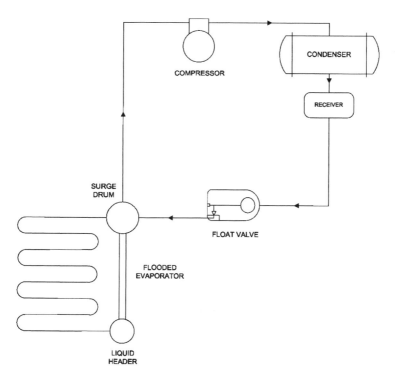

Fig. 6-11. High-float valve installation.

system pressures. Figure 6-12 shows a typical control wiring diagram for a compressor operating on the pump down cycle. Note that all the switches are arranged in series. When all switches are closed, the motor contactor coil is energized and the compressor starts. Under normal operation, the compressor is stopped and started by the low-pressure switch. The high-pressure switch, water-failure switch, and the motor overloads are safety devices and only open if a problem occurs, stopping the compressor. The compressor crankcase heater is turned on automatically as the compressor stops and secured when the compressor starts.

The high- and low-pressure switches can be supplied as separate units or as a single unit with both pressure switches in the same housing. Each switch consists of a sensing element (either a diaphragm or a bellows) balanced by a spring and a snap-action switch. The snap-action is designed to ensure the switch closes smartly without bouncing and preventing excessive arcing at the contacts when the pressure set point is reached. Figure 6-13 is simplified schematic of a pressure switch fitted with a magnet to provide the snap-action feature. The set point (commonly called the range)

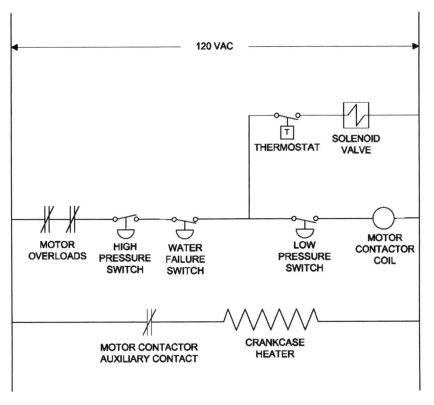

Fig. 6-12. Typical compressor control wiring diagram.

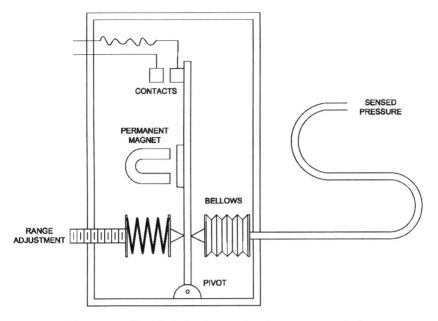

Fig. 6-13. Simplified schematic of pressure switch.

is adjusted by turning the screw that changes the compression on the spring, which acts against the pressure bellows.

Some switches permit independent control of both the cut-in and cut-out pressures. A common way this feature is included is to have a range adjustment and a differential pressure adjustment. The range adjustment permits control of the cut-in (or cut-out) pressure, while the differential adjustment controls the difference between the cut-in and cut-out pressures. Some switches have separate adjustments for the cut-in and cut-out pressures. When adjusting a switch it is important to know if the range adjustment affects the cut-in or cut-out pressure and how the range and differential adjustments interact. In many switches, changing the range affects both the cut-in and cut-out pressures simultaneously, while some change only one pressure. In the second type, a change in the differential adjustment is also required to maintain the same difference between the cut-in and cut-out pressures.

Figure 6-14 shows a typical low pressure switch with range and differential adjustments. The two pressure bellows control a single set of contact that opens when the low-pressure input goes low and when the high-pressure input goes high. The low-pressure switch has range and differential adjustments, while the high-pressure switch has only a range adjustment (the differential is fixed).

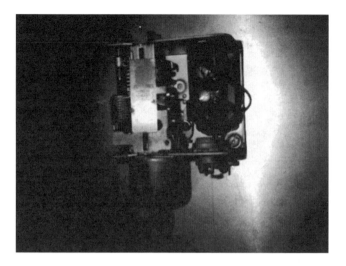

Fig. 6-14. Low pressure control switch.

Before making adjustments to the switch settings, consult the system manual to determine proper cut-in and cut-out pressures. The high-pressure switch set point is determined based on the normal condenser pressure. This pressure will vary based on the system refrigerant and the design of the condenser. If the high-pressure switch set point is set too low, the compressor will stop when system conditions are normal and cooling will cease. If the switch is set too high, the switch will not protect the compressor from excessive pressures. The low-pressure switch set point is determined by the normal evaporator pressure. If more than one evaporator is served by the same compressor, the lowest pressure evaporator determines the proper setting. If the low-pressure switch is set too high, the compressor will stop prematurely and the system will be unable to maintain desired temperatures. If the switch is set too low, the compressor will continue to run when cooling is no longer required, resulting in unnecessary wear and energy cost. A low switch setting can also result in lower than design evaporator temperatures that can cause problems in some applications. The differential adjustment on the low-pressure switch must be set to permit proper system operation. If the differential adjustment is set too low, the compressor may short cycle (start and stop repeatedly). If the differential adjustment is set too high, the compressor may not start (or stop) when desired, and the system may not be able to properly maintain the design system temperatures.

Most pressure switches have a calibrated scale and pointer to display the settings. To check the operation and adjustment of a typical low-pressure switch, proceed as follows:

1. Note the settings on the range and differential adjustments.
2. Start compressor and control the suction pressure by throttling the compressor suction stop valve.
3. Lower the suction pressure until the compressor stops. Note the cut-out pressure. Gradually open the suction valve until the compressor restarts, noting the cut-in pressure.
4. If adjustment to the differential is necessary make this change first, then make changes to the range setting. Repeat step 3 and make further adjustments as required.
5. An alternative way to adjust the cut-out pressure is as follows: Lower the range adjustment to 10 psi below the desired setting. With the compressor running, gradually lower the suction pressure by throttling the suction valve to the desired cut-out pressure and hold it. Turn range screw until the contacts open, stopping the compressor. The cut-out point is now set.

To check the operation and adjustment of a high-pressure switch, proceed as follows:

1. Note the settings on the range adjustment and differential adjustment (if fitted).
2. Turn the differential screw to minimum and range screw to maximum.
3. Start the compressor and carefully control the discharge pressure by manually throttling the condenser water flow. *Caution! Do not exceed the design high side pressure!*
4. Slowly bring discharge pressure to the desired cut-out point. If the compressor does not stop, turn range adjustment down until the contacts open, stopping the compressor.
5. Open the cooling water to lower the condenser pressure, noting the pressure at which the compressor starts. If the switch has a differential adjustment and the difference between the cut-out and cut-in pressures is unsatisfactory, adjust the differential adjustment and repeat the above test.

## Thermostatic Switch

A thermostatic switch (also called a thermostat) is a temperature control device used to open or close an electric contact based on sensing a temperature. These devices are commonly used to maintain the desired space temperature by opening and closing a solenoid valve that starts and stops the flow of refrigerant to the evaporator. The thermostats used in air-conditioning and heating systems have typically used a bimetallic element as the sensing device, though digital thermostats are becoming common today. The unit must be installed in the space being cooled or heated. The construction of the thermostatic switches commonly used in refrigeration systems is very similar to the pressure switches discussed above with the addition of a remote sensing bulb that delivers a pressure to the bellows of the switch. See figure 6-15. The sensing bulb is filled with a volatile liquid charge. This design permits the switch to be located outside of the cooled space. Changes in the sensed temperature cause changes in the pressure exerted by the remote bulb on the bellows that then operates the switch. With a temperature rise, the pressure increases and the bellows closes the switch contact to complete the electric circuit. The circuit is interrupted on a reduction in temperature. Most thermostats will have a set point (range) adjustment and a differential adjustment. Changing the set point adjustment will affect the cut-in and cut-out points an equal amount. The differential adjustment will only affect the cut-out point.

To adjust a thermostatic switch, proceed as follows:

1. Turn the differential adjustment to maximum.
2. Turn the range adjustment to minimum.
3. Bring the compartment down to the desired cut-in temperature. Increase the range adjustment until the contacts open, then decrease it until the contacts just close. This fixes the cut-in point.
4. Lower the compartment to the desired cut-out temperature, then reduce the differential adjustment until the contacts open. This fixes the cut-out point.

The compressor control wiring diagram shown in figure 6-12 includes a thermostat controlling a solenoid valve. The wiring is arranged to secure

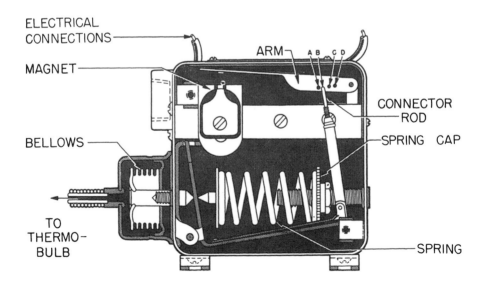

Fig. 6-15. Thermostatic control switch.

the flow of refrigerant to the evaporator if one of the safety switches stops the compressor.

### Solenoid Valve

A solenoid is used where there is a requirement to automatically start and stop the flow of refrigerant. Solenoid valves can be operated by a thermostatic switch, a float switch, a high-pressure switch, a low-pressure switch, or some similar device. The most common use of solenoid valves in reciprocating compressor systems is to control the flow of refrigerant to the evaporator using a thermostat. Figure 6-16 shows a cross section of a typical direct-acting solenoid valve. When the coil is energized, the magnetic field draws a steel plunger towards the center of the coil, lifting the valve off its seat. When the coil is de-energized, the weight of the plunger, and in some designs a spring, causes it to fall and close the valve. The gravity-closing type must be installed with the plunger upright.

In larger capacities, a pilot-operated type is used to avoid large uneconomical coils. In this type of valve, the solenoid coil operates a small pilot valve that uses refrigerant pressure acting on a piston to open the main valve. A small pressure drop across the valve is required for operation.

### Oil Pressure Failure Switch

This device is a differential pressure switch designed to prevent operation of the compressor in the event of low oil pressure. There are two pressure

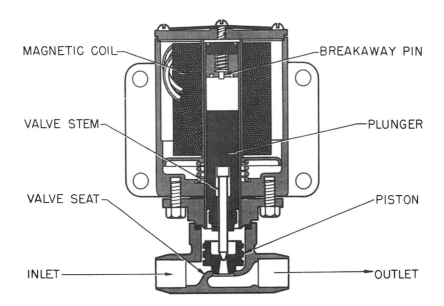

Fig. 6-16. Solenoid valve.

inputs to the switch, the oil pump discharge and the crankcase (suction pressure), and the switch senses the pressure difference between the two pressures. This is necessary because the suction pressure can vary significantly from a high value during pulldown conditions to a low value just before the compressor is stopped by the low-pressure switch. The oil pressure switch stops the compressor motor in the event of low oil pressure. A time delay is incorporated into the motor control circuit to permit compressor start-up. A time delay is sometimes also incorporated in the cut-out mode to avoid premature shutdowns during load changes. A manual reset is commonly installed. The switch is typically factory adjusted and if it does not operate properly, it must be replaced. Never operate the compressor if the oil pressure switch is inoperative. Correct the malfunction because improper lubrication will cause serious damage to the compressor.

### Water Failure Switch

This switch is similar in construction to the low-pressure switch. It senses the condenser water supply pressure and stops the compressor in the event of a loss of condenser cooling water supply. If the switch fails to function, the refrigerant pressure in the condenser increases to the point where the high-pressure switch goes into operation and stops the compressor. Many smaller systems will not have a water failure switch installed and will rely on the high-pressure switch to protect the compressor.

### Evaporator Pressure Regulator

Evaporator pressure regulators are commonly installed at the outlet of the higher temperature evaporators in a multi-box system. Figure 6-17 shows a typical evaporator pressure regulator. Its function is to prevent the evaporator pressure and, therefore, its temperature from falling below a predetermined minimum regardless of the compressor suction pressure. Note that the evaporator pressure regulator limits the minimum pressure, but does not maintain the evaporator pressure constant under high load (pulldown) conditions. Under those conditions the evaporator pressure will rise above the regulator set point. The limiting of evaporator pressure and temperature allows the control of box humidity and prevents the dehydration of the stored product while permitting the compressor to satisfy the requirements of the coldest evaporator. In domestic ships, stores refrigeration systems, evaporator pressure regulators are usually installed on all boxes operating above freezing. This allows the coils to be maintained above freezing and avoid the need for defrosting.

### Suction Pressure Regulator

The suction pressure regulator or "holdback valve" is sometimes installed to limit the suction pressure at the compressor inlet to a predetermined maximum. This prevents overload of the compressor driver during

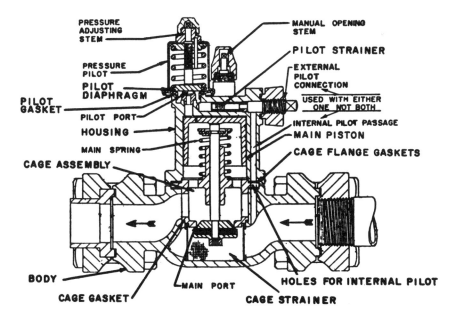

Fig. 6-17. Evaporator pressure regulator. Courtesy Alco Controls.

pull-down or other periods of high evaporator pressure. The valve is similar in construction to the evaporator pressure regulator but senses the downstream rather than the upstream pressure.

### Water-Regulating Valves

Most marine refrigeration systems use seawater-cooled condensers. Water-regulating valves are commonly installed to control the quantity of cooling water circulating through the condenser. Figure 6-18 is a typical water-regulating valve. The valve is actuated by the refrigerant pressure in the condenser. If the condenser pressure should increase, the valve will open, admitting more cooling water, and returning the pressure back to the set point. A decrease in condenser pressure will cause the valve to close and reduce the water flow. Valves on marine systems are typically adjusted to maintain a condensing temperature of about 100°F to 110°F. Consult the system manufacturer's manual for the proper set points. When the compressor stops, the condenser pressure gradually decreases to the saturated vapor pressure corresponding to the ambient temperature. This decrease in pressure is sufficient to close the regulating valve and stop the flow of cooling water.

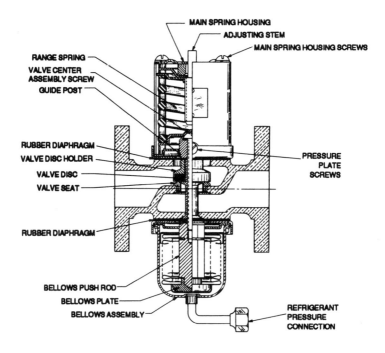

Fig. 6-18. Water-regulating valve. Courtesy Penn Valve.

## Relief Valves and Fusible Plugs

Relief valves are installed in refrigeration systems to relieve unsafe system pressures. Marine systems will have at least one relief valve installed on the condenser with discharge overboard through a rupture disc. If there is an isolation valve between the condenser and the receiver, there will also be a relief valve installed on the receiver with the valve outlet connected to the condenser. This protects the receiver from possible rupture in the event it is isolated and exposed to high temperatures.

Small systems sometimes have a fusible plug installed in place of a relief valve. A fusible plug is simply a pipe plug that has been drilled and filled with a metal alloy designed to melt at a predetermined temperature. See figure 6-19. The design melting point of the alloy is selected based on the saturation temperature of the system refrigerant at the pressure of interest. Since the refrigerant charge is lost if the fusible plug melts, the use of a relief valve to protect the system is recommended in all but very small applications.

## Manual Valves

Manual valves are installed at various locations in the refrigeration system to facilitate system operation, to permit cutting units in and out, to isolate

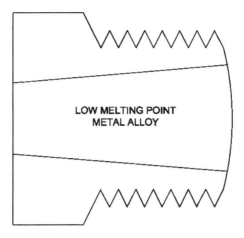

Fig. 6-19. Fusible plug.

components for maintenance, and for other purposes. Two basic types of valves are used, packed and packless. Many of the valves used in refrigeration systems today are of the packless type as shown in figure 6-20. Packless valves employ a diaphragm to isolate the handwheel assembly from the refrigerant to minimize the possibility of leakage that can occur from valve packing. Packed valves are usually of the backseating type. When in the open position, the valve is backseated to minimize the possibility of leakage. The compressor service valves are usually of the packed type and commonly include a connection for attaching a service gauge as shown in figure 6-21.

1  BODY
2  CAP
3  WASHER (BACKSEAT)
4  UPPER STEM
5  WASHER (STEM BRG)
6  STEM BEARING
7  DIAPHRAGM SET
8  BUSHING
9  BUSHING GASKET
10  LOWER STEM
11  WASHER (STEM CAP)
12  STEM CAP
13  BALL CHECK
14  SPRING (BALL CHECK)
15  SPRING
16  HANDWHEEL
17  WASHER (HANDWHEEL)
18  NAMEPLATE
19  SCREW

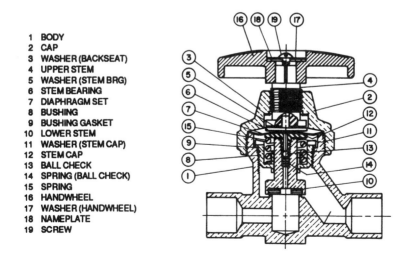

Fig. 6-20. Packing valve. Courtesy Henry Valve Co.

Backseating the valve permits attaching a gauge or repacking the valve without loss of refrigerant. To measure the system pressure with a gauge attached, the valve must be in an intermediate position between the front and back seats. A cap covers the valve stem and minimizes the possibility of loss of refrigerant should there be a leak at the packing.

### Liquid Indicators (Sight Glasses)

Liquid indicators or sight glasses are commonly installed in the liquid line to indicate a proper refrigerant charge. Bubbles appearing in the liquid stream are an indication of a shortage of refrigerant. Some indicators also

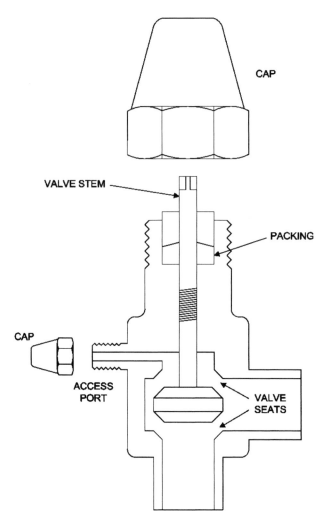

Fig. 6-21. Backseating-type packed valve.

include a moisture indicator. A portion of the indicator will change color based on the relative moisture content of the refrigerant. Figure 6-22 shows a typical refrigerant sight glass.

## Dehydrator

A dehydrator (also called a drier) is installed in the refrigerant liquid line to remove moisture from the systems. In other than very small systems, the dehydrator is installed in a bypass line downstream of the receiver. This permits replacement of the cartridge without shutdown of the system. A typical dehydrator is shown in figure 6-23. The cartridge is filled with a desiccant such as activated alumina or silica gel that adsorbs moisture and also acts as a filter. Even small amounts of moisture can cause problems such as frozen thermostatic expansion valves, so it is important to remove sufficient moisture to prevent the release of water in the low pressure portions of the system. Lower system temperatures require lower moisture contents. To obtain maximum service life from the cartridge, the dehydrator should only be in service during charging of the system or when high moisture content is suspected.

## Strainer

Strainers are commonly installed in the liquid line before the solenoid valve and expansion valve to remove foreign particles such as scale, metal chips, and dirt. Since the refrigeration system is a closed circuit and most refrigerants are excellent solvents, any solid impurities will be circulated and can cause clogging and sticking of the automatic valves. Fine mesh strainers such as are shown in figure 6-24 will remove these solid impurities. In addition to mesh strainers, filters with porous pad elements for the removal of

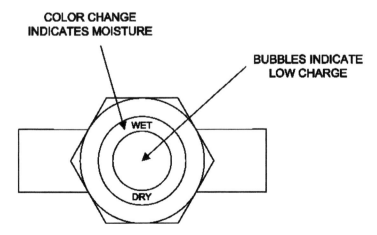

Fig. 6-22. Sight glass.

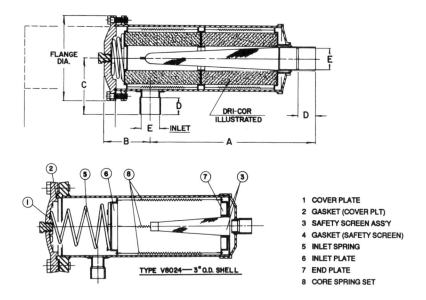

| | |
|---|---|
| 1 | COVER PLATE |
| 2 | GASKET (COVER PLT) |
| 3 | SAFETY SCREEN ASS'Y |
| 4 | GASKET (SAFETY SCREEN) |
| 5 | INLET SPRING |
| 6 | INLET PLATE |
| 7 | END PLATE |
| 8 | CORE SPRING SET |

Fig. 6-23. Dehydrator.

very fine particles are available. The strainer element can be removed for cleaning without securing the system by isolating the strainer with the hand valves and continuing to operate using the hand expansion valve.

### Ship's Stores Refrigeration System

A diagram of a ship's stores refrigeration system with typical operating controls is shown in figure 6-25. Two boxes are shown, a freeze box and a

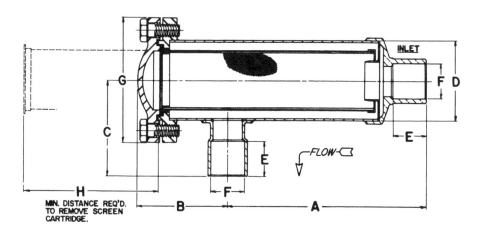

Fig. 6-24. Strainer. Courtesy Henry Valve Co.

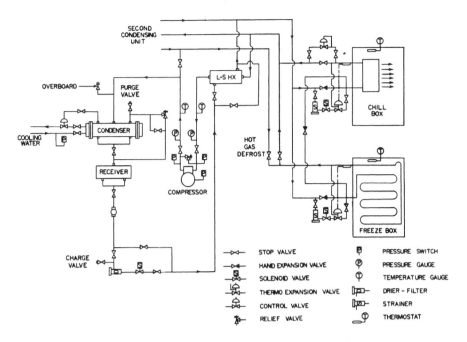

Fig. 6-25. Ship's stores refrigeration system diagram.

chill box. Each is controlled by an externally equalized expansion valve, a thermostat, and a solenoid valve. An evaporator pressure regulator is fitted to the chill box and the freeze box is piped for hot gas defrosting. High-pressure, low-pressure, water failure, and oil pressure switches are installed to automatically operate and protect the compressor. A water regulating valve is installed on the condenser cooling water outlet. Also installed are strainers at each evaporator inlet, a drier, and a refrigerant sight glass at the receiver outlet, and relief valves to protect the system from high pressures.

## PROBLEMS (ENGLISH UNITS)

6.1E  A refrigeration system using R-22 is fitted with an internally equalized thermostatic expansion valve. The evaporator inlet pressure is 55 psig and the outlet temperature is 13°F. Assuming negligible pressure drop across the evaporator, what is the superheat? What is the pressure difference across the expansion valve diaphragm being balanced by the superheat spring?

6.2E  If the pressure drop across the evaporator in the above problem is 5 psi, what is the actual superheat? If an externally actuated expansion valve with the same superheat spring pressure as in the above problem is installed, what will the superheat now be?

6.3E   A refrigeration system using R-134a is fitted with an externally equalized expansion valve. The valve is adjusted for 10°F of superheat at an evaporator temperature of 40°F. What will the superheat be if the system is operated at −10°F?

# PROBLEMS (SI UNITS)

6.1S   A refrigeration system using R-134a is fitted with an internally equalized thermostatic expansion valve. The evaporator inlet pressure is 200 kPa and the outlet temperature is −4°C. Assuming negligible pressure drop across the evaporator, what is the superheat? What is the pressure difference across the expansion valve diaphragm being balanced by the superheat spring?

6.2S   If the pressure drop across the evaporator in the above problem is 30 kPa, what is the actual superheat? If an externally actuated expansion valve with the same superheat spring pressure as in the above problem is installed, what will the superheat now be?

6.3S   A refrigeration system using R-22 is fitted with an externally equalized expansion valve. The valve is adjusted for 6°C of superheat at an evaporator temperature of 5°C. What will the superheat be if the system is operated at −25°C?

## CHAPTER 7

# Psychrometry and HVAC Processes

Psychrometry is the study of mixtures of air and water vapor. This subject is important to air-conditioning because the systems handle air-water vapor mixtures, not pure dry air. In addition to cooling and heating, some air-conditioning processes involve the removal of water from the air-water vapor mixture (dehumidification) while some involve the addition of water (humidification). Before we can proceed with an analysis of air-water vapor mixtures, we must define some important terms and properties. These include such properties as dry-bulb temperature, wet-bulb temperature, dew point, relative humidity, humidity ratio, specific volume, and enthalpy.

## DRY-BULB TEMPERATURE (DB)

The temperature of the air as sensed by a standard thermometer is called the dry-bulb temperature.

## WET-BULB TEMPERATURE (WB)

The temperature sensed by a thermometer whose bulb is wrapped in a water-soaked wick and moved rapidly in air is called the wet-bulb temperature. If the air is not saturated, some of the water will evaporate, cooling the thermometer bulb below the dry-bulb temperature. A sling psychrometer (figure 7-1) is an inexpensive device containing a standard and a wet-bulb thermometer mounted on a pivoting handle. Swinging the device rapidly produces the required air movement and allows simultaneous measurement of the wet- and dry-bulb temperatures in the space.

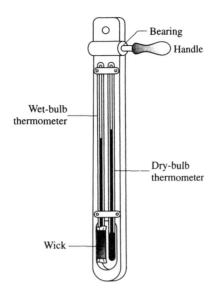

Fig. 7-1. Hand-held sling psychrometer.

## DEW POINT TEMPERATURE (DP)

Dew point temperature is the temperature at which water vapor will begin to condense if the air were cooled at constant pressure. At the dew point, the air is saturated.

## RELATIVE HUMIDITY (RH)

Relative humidity is the ratio of the mass of water vapor in the mixture divided by the mass that would exist if the air were saturated at the same dry-bulb temperature. It will be shown later it is also the ratio of the actual partial water vapor to the partial pressure at saturation. The relative humidity is commonly expressed as a percentage by multiplying the ratio by 100.

## HUMIDITY RATIO ($\omega$)

Humidity ratio (also called absolute humidity) is the ratio of the mass of water vapor in the air to the mass of dry air. It is expressed in pound/pound dry air, or grains/pound of dry air (7,000 grains = 1 pound), or kilogram/kilogram of dry air.

## SPECIFIC VOLUME ($\rho$)

Specific volume is the volume occupied by one pound or one kilogram of air. The units are cubic feet/pound or cubic meters/kilogram.

## ENTHALPY *(h)*

Enthalpy is the thermal energy content of the air-water vapor mixture expressed in Btu/pound or kilojoule/kilogram.

## CALCULATING THE PROPERTIES OF AIR-WATER VAPOR MIXTURES

Consider the piston-cylinder system shown in figure 7-2 containing a mixture of air and water vapor at atmospheric pressure. Dalton's law states

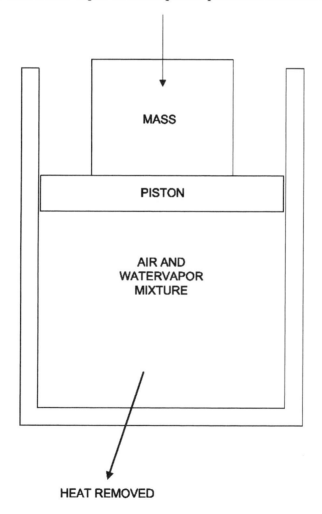

Fig. 7-2. Piston-cylinder system maintaining constant pressure.

the total pressure must equal the sum of the partial pressures. In our example, the partial pressure of the air plus the partial pressure of the water vapor must equal the cylinder pressure, that is, atmospheric pressure. Assume the water vapor in the cylinder is superheated. This means the temperature of the water vapor is above the saturation pressure corresponding to the vapor partial pressure. Now let's gradually remove heat from the cylinder. As heat is removed, the temperature of the air and water vapor will drop, and the volume of gas and vapor will decrease. The piston on the top of the cylinder will drop to maintain the total pressure constant. At some point, the water vapor will become saturated, and any further removal of heat will result in some of the vapor condensing. The temperature at this point is called the dew point. The steam tables are used to determine the saturation temperature at the water vapor pressure.

It is important to recognize that the amount of water vapor that can mix with the air is dependent only on the dry-bulb temperature of the air. The vapor partial pressure at this saturated condition will be equal to the saturation pressure corresponding to the dry-bulb temperature. If the dry-bulb temperature is increased, the air can contain more water vapor at saturation. If the temperature is decreased, the air cannot contain as much.

From the definitions above, it can be seen that relative humidity compares the mass of water vapor in the mixture to the amount that would exist at saturation. Since the vapor pressures are low, the water vapor can be considered to behave like an ideal gas. The ideal gas equation is:

$$p V = m\, R\, T \qquad\qquad (7.1)$$

where

$p$ = absolute pressure, in lbf/ft$^2$ or kPa
$V$ = volume, in ft$^3$ or m$^3$
$m$ = mass, in lbm or kg
$R$ = the individual gas constant, in ft-lbf/lbm-°R or kJ/kg-°K
$T$ = the absolute temperature, in °R or °K

The ideal gas equation can be use to calculate the specific volume and density of a gas. Remembering that the specific volume is the volume per unit mass and the density is the mass per unit volume:

$$v = \frac{V}{m} = \frac{R\,T}{p}$$

$$\rho = \frac{m}{v} = \frac{p}{R\,T}$$

Solving the ideal gas equation for the mass gives the following:

$$m = pV/RT$$

Using the ideal gas equation to determine the mass of water vapor, with the subscript "v" used for the actual water vapor properties, and "s" for the water vapor properties at saturation, the relative humidity is thus:

$$RH = \frac{m_v}{m_s} = \frac{p_v\,V/R_v\,T_v}{p_s\,V/R_s\,T_s}$$

Since the volumes, gas constants, and temperatures are the same for the actual and saturated vapor states:

$$RH = \frac{p_v}{p_s} \tag{7.2}$$

---

EXAMPLE PROBLEM 7.1. Air has a dry-bulb temperature of 80°F and the water vapor has a partial pressure of 0.25 psia. What is the dew point temperature and the relative humidity? If the dry-bulb temperature is reduced to 70°F, what will the relative humidity be?

SOLUTION.

SKETCH AND GIVEN DATA:

ASSUMPTIONS:

1. The total pressure of the air-water vapor mixture is 14.7 psia.
2. The air and water vapor can be considered to behave as ideal gases.

ANALYSIS:

From the steam tables at a pressure of 0.25 psia, Tsat = 59.3°F (interpolating). This is the dew point.

From the steam tables at 80°F, the saturation pressure is 0.50792 psia. The relative humidity is thus:

$$RH = \frac{0.25}{0.50792} = 0.492 = 49.2\%$$

From the steam tables at 70°F, the saturation pressure is 0.38369 psia. The relative humidity is thus:

$$RH = \frac{0.25}{0.36369} = 0.687 = 68.7\%$$

COMMENTS:

The relative humidity increased as the dry-bulb temperature decreased because air at the lower temperature cannot contain as much moisture when saturated.

---

The humidity ratio of an air-water vapor mixture, or absolute humidity, is defined above as the ratio of the mass of water vapor in a given volume of mixture to the mass of air in the same volume. Note that the subscript "v" is used for the actual water vapor properties, and "a" for the air (without the vapor) present in the mixture. Thus, using the ideal gas law to calculate the mass:

$$\omega = \frac{m_v}{m_a} = \frac{p_v V / R_v T_v}{p_a V / R_a T_a} = \frac{R_a \, p_v}{R_a \, p_a} \tag{7.3}$$

where the individual gas constants for air and water vapor are:

$$R_a = 53.34 \text{ ft-lbf/lbm-}^\circ\text{R} \quad \text{or} \, 0.287 \text{ kJ/kg-}^\circ\text{K}$$
$$R = 85.77 \text{ ft-lbf/lbm-}^\circ\text{R} \quad \text{or} \, 0.4615 \text{ kJ/kg-}^\circ\text{K}$$

therefore, since the volumes and temperatures are the same:

$$\omega = 0.622 \frac{p_v}{p_a} \tag{7.4}$$

Combining equations 7.2 and 7.4, the following relationship between the relative humidity and the humidity ratio can be derived:

$$RH = \frac{\omega \, p_a}{0.622 \, p_s} \tag{7.5}$$

---

EXAMPLE PROBLEM 7.2. Air has a dry-bulb temperature of 25°C and a dew point of 15°C. Calculate the relative humidity and the humidity ratio.

SOLUTION.

SKETCH AND GIVEN DATA:

DB = 25°C          RH = ?

DP = 15°C          ω = ?

ASSUMPTIONS:
1. The total pressure of the air-water vapor mixture is 1.1.325 kPa.
2. The air and water vapor can be considered to behave as ideal gases.

ANALYSIS:
From the steam tables at 25°C, the saturated pressure is 3.1728 kPa.
From the steam tables at 15°C, the saturated pressure is 1.7071 kPa.
Using the definition relative humidity, equation 7.2:

$$RH = \frac{1.7071}{3.1728} = 0.538 = 53.8\%$$

Using equation 7.4:

$$\omega = 0.622 \frac{1.7071}{101.325 - 1.7071} = 0.01065 \text{ kg vapor/kg dry air}$$

COMMENTS:
The partial pressure of the dry air is the total pressure minus the vapor partial pressure from Dalton's Law.

The use of the ideal gas equation to calculate water vapor properties above requires some comment. You can use the ideal gas law to describe the behavior of water vapor up to temperatures of about 150°F or 65°C with good accuracy. Above this temperature, the saturation pressure of the water vapor in the air becomes high enough that the nonideal behavior of the vapor-gas mixture causes unacceptable errors, and the steam tables must be used. Most HVAC processes operate at temperatures below this limit, so this does not become a problem in normal practice.
The total thermal energy of a mixture of air and water vapor $(Q_t)$ is the sum of the energy of the dry air (the sensible energy, $Q_s$) plus the energy of the water vapor (the latent energy, $Q_l$):

$$Q_t = Q_s + Q_l$$

Since the thermal energy is the mass times the enthalpy:

$$m\,h = m_a\,h_a + m_a\,h_v$$

And using the humidity ratio to determine the mass of water vapor:

$$m\,h = m_a\,h_a + m_v\,\omega\,h_v$$

Since the mass of the water vapor is small, the mass of the air and the mass of the mixture are almost identical. Dividing by the mass of the mixture, a relationship for the total mixture enthalpy is thus:

$$h = h_a + \omega \, h_v$$

The specific heat of air at constant pressure can be used to calculate the gas enthalpy. Even though the water vapor is slightly superheated in most cases, the enthalpy of the water vapor is very close to the enthalpy of saturated steam at the dew point temperature, in general, within 0.1 to 0.2 Btu/lbm. Thus the mixture enthalpy can be expressed as:

$$h = C_p \, T_a + \omega \, h_{g@dp}$$

Since the $C_p$ for air is 0.24 Btu/lbm-°R or 1.0047 kJ/kg-°K and recognizing that the air temperature is the dry-bulb temperature:

$$h = 0.24 \, DB + \omega \, h_{g@dp} \text{ (in Btu/lbm)} \qquad (7.6a)$$

$$h = 1.0047 \, DB + \omega \, h_{g@dp} \text{ (in kJ/kg)} \qquad (7.6b)$$

Note that since the $DB$ temperature is in units of °F or °C, the enthalpy of the dry air will be zero at 0°F for English units and at 0°C for SI units. The references used in the steam tables are zero enthalpy for liquid water at 32°F or 0°C. This means that unit conversions for enthalpy cannot be made between English and SI units without taking these references into account.

Consider the spray chamber shown in figure 7-3. Air enters the unit where it is exposed to a spray of liquid water. A pump continuously recirculates the water from the collection sump back to the spray nozzles. If the entering air is not saturated, water will evaporate, raising the humidity ratio and the relative humidity of the air. Since no heat is being added during this process (that is, the process is adiabatic), the energy for the vaporization of the water comes from the air, and its temperature drops. If the air is saturated when it leaves the unit, the temperature of the exiting mixture is at the wet-bulb temperature. This is because the process taking place in the spray chamber is very similar to what takes place on the wick of a sling psychrometer. This is called an adiabatic saturation process.

Note that since energy is not added or removed in this process, the total enthalpy of the air mixture remains constant as the adiabatic saturation process takes place. Since both the enthalpy and wet-bulb temperature are constant, the wet-bulb temperature is directly related to the total enthalpy of the mixture. Note also that the lower the relative humidity, the more water vapor will be evaporated, and the lower the final temperature of the saturated mixture. Thus if you have two air samples at the same dry-bulb temperature but different relative humidities, the one with the lower relative humidity will have a lower wet-bulb temperature. It is also important to note that if the relative humidity is below 100 percent, the wet-bulb temperature will be lower than the dry-bulb temperature, but higher than the

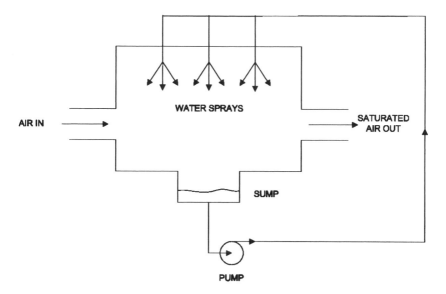

Fig. 7-3. Adiabatic saturation.

dew point. If the air is saturated (100 percent relative humidity), the dry-bulb, wet-bulb, and dew point temperatures will all be identical.

---

EXAMPLE PROBLEM 7.3. Air has a dry-bulb temperature of 85°F and a relative humidity of 40 percent. Calculate (a) the total enthalpy, (b) the humidity ratio, and (c) the dew point.

SOLUTION.
  SKETCH AND GIVEN DATA:

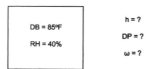

DB = 85°F

RH = 40%

h = ?

DP = ?

ω = ?

  ASSUMPTIONS:
  1. The total pressure of the air-water vapor mixture is 14.7 psia.
  2. The air and water vapor can be considered to behave as ideal gases.
  ANALYSIS:
  From the steam tables at a temperature of 85°F, the saturation pressure is 0.597 psia.

The vapor partial pressure is thus 0.597 psia × 0.4 = 0.239 psia

From the steam tables at 0.239 psia, the saturated temperature is 58°F. Therefore, the dewpoint temperature (c) is 58°F. Also from the steam tables at that presssure, the enthalpy of the saturated vapor $(h_g)$ is 1086.9 Btu/lbm. Using equation 7.4:

$$\omega = 0.622 \frac{p_v}{p_a}$$

$$\omega = 0.622 \frac{0.239}{14.7 - 0.239} = 0.0102 \ \text{lbm vapor/lbm dry air} \qquad \text{(b)}$$

Using equation 7.6a:

$$h = 0.24 \ DB + \omega \ h_{g@dp}$$
$$h = (0.24)(85) + (0.0102)(1{,}086.9) = 31.49 \ \text{Btu/lbm} \qquad \text{(a)}$$

COMMENTS:

The humidity ratio was needed to calculate the enthalpy, so it had to be calculated first.

---

## THE PSYCHROMETRIC CHART

While the above procedures can be used to calculate the properties of air-water vapor mixtures and analyze HVAC processes, it can be time consuming. A more convenient way to represent the properties of air-water vapor mixtures is on something called the psychrometric chart. The equations above can be used to determine the properties at a range of conditions and the results plotted. The final product is the psychrometric chart, figures 7-4a and 7-4b. In order to locate any condition of air on the chart, two independent properties must be known. With these two properties, the air condition point can then be plotted on the chart, and all other properties can then be read. Note that the horizontal axis of the psychrometric chart is the dry-bulb temperature, and the vertical axis is the humidity ratio.

Refer to figure 7-5 for assistance in plotting and reading air conditions on the psychrometric chart. Note that the lines of constant dry-bulb temperature are vertical and can be read using the scale on the bottom of the graph. The lines of constant humidity ratio are horizontal and can be read using the scale on the right side of the graph. Lines of constant wet-bulb temperature and dry air specific volume are labeled in the body of the

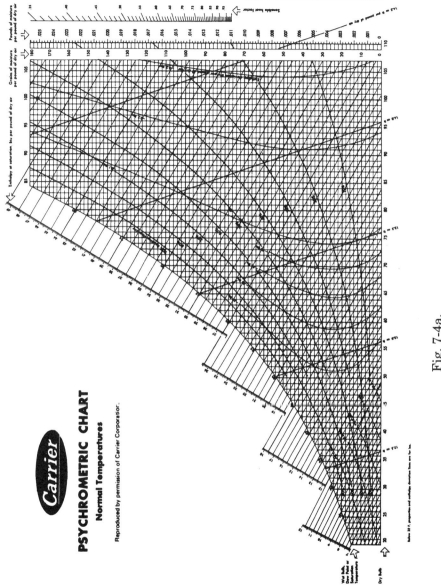

Fig. 7-4a.

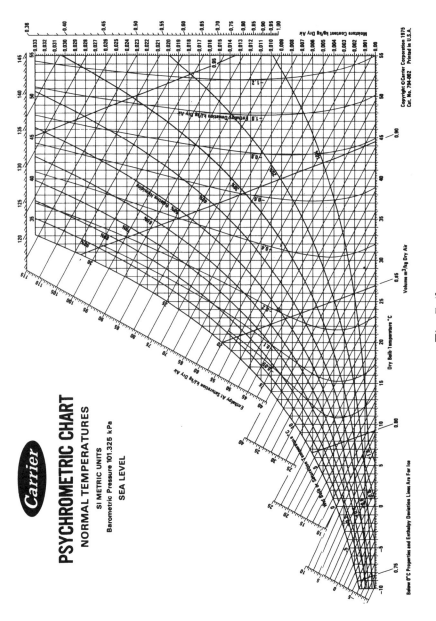

Fig. 7-4b.

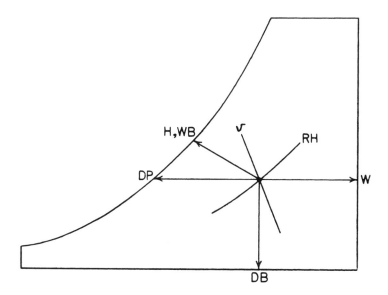

Fig. 7-5. Reading the psychrometric chart.

chart, and run diagonally up from right to left. The lines of constant specific volume are steeper than those for wet-bulb temperature. Note that the lines of constant relative humidity are curved and rise from left to right.

The curved line that defines the upper left side of the graph is the saturation line. Along this line are scales for temperature and enthalpy. To read the dew point of a mixture, proceed horizontally to the left (constant humidity ratio and decreasing dry-bulb temperature) until you reach the saturation line and read the dew point off the temperature scale. To read the wet-bulb temperature and enthalpy of a mixture, follow the constant wet-bulb line up and to the left until you reach the saturation line and read the values. As was noted in the above section on calculating enthalpy, the water vapor is typically slightly superheated, and thus using the saturated vapor enthalpy results in a slight error, typically 0.1 to 0.2 Btu/lbm. This "enthalpy deviation" is plotted on the chart and can be used to adjust the enthalpy value to improve accuracy.

EXAMPLE PROBLEM 7.4. The readings taken with a sling psychrometer are 78°F dry-bulb temperature and 65°F wet-bulb temperature. Use the psychrometric chart to determine (a) the relative humidity, (b) the dew point, (c) the humidity ratio, and (d) total enthalpy.

SOLUTION.

SKETCH AND GIVEN DATA:

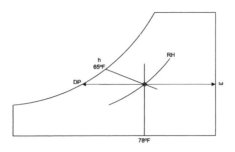

ASSUMPTIONS:
1. The air and water vapor can be considered to behave as ideal gases.
2. The sling psychrometer was able to obtain adiabatic saturation conditions on the wet-bulb wick.

ANALYSIS:
Plotting the condition point on the psychrometric chart using the dry- and wet-bulb temperatures, and then reading the other properties:

$$RH = 50\%$$
$$DP = 58°F$$
$$\omega = 0.0102 \text{ lbm vapor/lbm dry air}$$
$$h = 30.1 \text{ Btu/lbm}$$

COMMENTS:
None.

# HVAC PROCESSES

The air inside spaces occupied by humans must be conditioned for human comfort and safety. This can involve controlling temperature and humidity, maintaining air quality by ventilation and filtering, and providing air circulation. The requirements of these heating, ventilation and air-conditioning (HVAC) systems will be discussed in more detail in chapters 8 and 9. At this point the concern is about understanding how to analyze processes that involve heating, cooling, humidification, dehumidification, and mixing. In most cases, it is convenient to use the psychrometric chart to analyze these HVAC processes.

## Mixing Processes
The mixing of two air streams is a common process in HVAC systems. This process can be analyzed by applying the laws of conservation of

mass and energy to the process. Figure 7-6(a) shows two air streams
mixing together into a single combined stream. Writing the mass and
energy balances:

$$m_1 + m_2 = m_3$$
$$m_1 h_1 + m_2 h_2 = m_3 h_3$$

The energy balance equation can be written based on the total enthalpy
at each point, or based on the sensible or latent heat components separately. If the energy balance equation is written based on the sensible heat
components:

$$m_1\, Cp\, T_1 + m_2\, Cp\, T_2 = m_3\, Cp\, T_3 = (m_1 + m_2)\, Cp\, T_3$$

Dividing the equation by $Cp$ and solving for the outlet temperature $(T_3)$:

$$T_3 = \frac{m_1\, T_1 + m_2\, T_2}{m_1 + m_2} \qquad (7.7)$$

If the energy balance equation is written based on the latent heat components, the following result will be obtained:

$$m_1\, \omega_1 + m_2\, \omega_2 = m_3\, \omega_3$$
$$\omega_3 = \frac{m_1\, \omega_1 + m_2\, \omega_2}{m_1 + m_2} \qquad (7.8)$$

If a mixing process is plotted on the psychrometric chart, each of the
three points will lie along a straight line as shown on figure 7- 6(b). The location of the outlet point will depend on the relative magnitude of the two
entering flows. If both entering flows are equal, the outlet point will lie
midway between the two inlet points on the chart. If they are not equal, the
outlet point will lie closer to the larger flow. The approach outlined above
can be used to analyze processes with more inlet or outlet flows, or situations where a single flow is split into two or more outlet flows.

---

EXAMPLE PROBLEM 7.5. Ten m$^3$/sec of air at 35°C dry-bulb temperature and a
humidity ratio of 0.018 kg/kg mixes with 20 m$^3$/kg at 20°C and a humidity
ratio of 0.009 kg/kg. Determine the dry-bulb temperature and humidity ratio of the mixture.

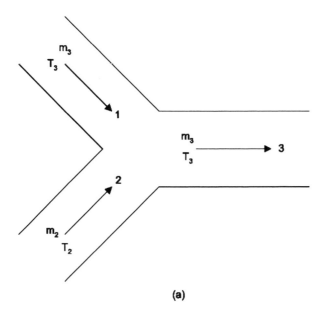

(a)

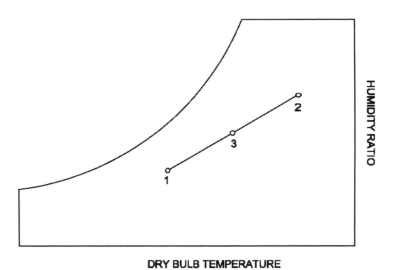

DRY BULB TEMPERATURE

Fig. 7-6. Mixing process.

Solution.

SKETCH AND GIVEN DATA:

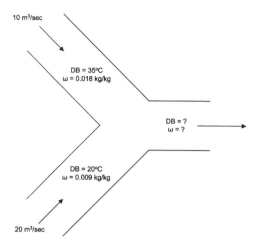

ASSUMPTIONS:

1. The air and water vapor behave as ideal gases.
2. The process is steady-state.
3. The changes in kinetic and potential energies may be neglected.

ANALYSIS:

Plotting the two conditions on the psychrometric chart and reading the specific volumes:

$$v_1 = 0.9 \text{ m}^3/\text{kg} \qquad v_2 = 0.84 \text{ m}^3/\text{kg}$$

Calculating the two mass flows:

$$m_1 = \frac{10 \, m^3/\text{sec}}{0.9 \, m^3/\text{kg}} = 11.1 \text{ kg/sec}$$

$$m_1 = \frac{20 \, m^3/\text{sec}}{0.84 \, m^3/\text{kg}} = 23.8 \text{ kg/sec}$$

Using equation 7.7:

$$T_3 = \frac{m_1 \, T_1 + m_2 \, T_2}{m_1 + m_2}$$

$$T_3 = \frac{(11.1 \text{ kg/sec})(35^\circ \text{C}) + (23.8 \text{ kg/sec})(20^\circ \text{C})}{11.1 \text{ kg/sec} + 23.8 \text{ kg/sec}} = 24.8^\circ \text{C}$$

Using equation 7.8:

$$\omega_3 = \frac{m_1\,\omega_1 + m_2\,\omega_2}{m_1 + m_2}$$

$$\omega_3 = \frac{(11.1\ \text{kg/sec})(0.018\ \text{kg/kg}) + (23.8\ \text{kg/sec})(0.009\ \text{kg/kg})}{11.1\ \text{kg/sec} + 23.8\ \text{kg/sec}} = 0.019\ \text{kg/kg}$$

COMMENTS:

Note that the outlet condition will lie on a straight line between the two inlet points on the psychrometric chart and will be closer to the point with the larger mass flow.

## Sensible Heating

Sensible heating occurs when the air passed over a coil or other surface that is at a temperature higher than the DB temperature of the air. As the air absorbs heat, the temperature of the air rises. Since no moisture is added or removed, the humidity ratio and dew point of the air remain constant. Since the DB temperature increases, the WB temperature and total enthalpy will also increase. On the psychrometric chart, the process will be a horizontal line, with the outlet to the right of the inlet.

## Coil Bypass Factor

Consider a heating coil being used to heat air from 50°F to 100°F. The coil surface temperature would need to be somewhat higher than 100°F to account for the efficiency of the coil. The more efficient the coil, the closer the coil temperature can be to 100°F to maintain the required air outlet temperature. A very efficient coil would only need to be a few degrees above 100°F. A less efficient coil would need to be at a much higher temperature. In general, coils with large amounts of area and many rows of coils will have higher efficiency.

One way to express the efficiency of a heating or cooling coil is with a coil bypass factor *(BPF)*. The *BPF* can be defined by assuming that some of the air comes in intimate contact with the coil and leaves at the coil temperature. The rest of the air bypasses the coil and leaves at the inlet temperature and the two air streams mix downstream. The closer the outlet temperature approaches the coil temperature the closer the *BPF* will be to 0.0. The *BPF* is defined as follows:

$$BPF = \frac{T_{coil} - T_{out}}{T_{coil} - T_{in}} \tag{7.9}$$

where
$T_{coil}$ = mean effective temperature of the coil
$T_{in}$ = air inlet DB temperature
$T_{out}$ = air outlet DB temperature

The value of the *BPF* will be between 0.0 and 1.0. Note that the *BPF* can be used for either heating or cooling coils. In air-conditioning applications where the coil is both cooling and reducing humidity, the mean coil temperature is sometimes called the apparatus dew point (ADP).

---

EXAMPLE PROBLEM 7.6. Five thousand $ft^3$/lbm of air at 60°F and 80 percent relative humidity is heated to 90°F by passing it across a coil with a mean temperature of 105°F. Determine (a) the outlet air relative humidity, (b) the heat transferred, and (c) the coil bypass factor.

SOLUTION.

SKETCH AND GIVEN DATA:

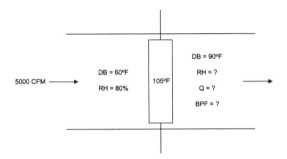

ASSUMPTIONS:
1. The air and water vapor behave as ideal gases.
2. The process is steady-state.
3. The changes in kinetic and potential energies may be neglected.

ANALYSIS:

Plot the inlet point on the psychrometric chart, then plot the outlet point at the same humidty ratio. The outlet point will lie horizontally and to the right of the inlet point.

Reading the relative humidity of the outlet from the chart,

$$RH_2 = 29\% \tag{a}$$

Reading the enthalpies of the inlet and outlet point from the chart:

$$h_1 = 24.1\,Btu/lbm \qquad h_2 = 31.5\,Btu/lbm$$

Reading the inlet specific volume from the chart and calculating the mass flow:

$$v_1 = 13.3\,\text{ft}^3/\text{lbm}$$

$$m_1 = \frac{5{,}000\,\text{ft}^3/\text{lbm}}{13.3\,\text{ft}^3/\text{lbm}} = 376\,\text{lbm/min}$$

$$Q = m\Delta h = (376\,\text{lbm/min})(31.5 - 24.1\,\text{Btu/lbm}) = 2{,}782\,\text{Btu/min} \qquad \text{(b)}$$

Using equation 7.9 to calculate the bypass factor:

$$BPF = \frac{T_{coil} - T_{out}}{T_{coil} - T_{in}} = \frac{105°\text{F} - 90°\text{F}}{105°\text{F} - 60°\text{F}} = 0.333 \qquad \text{(c)}$$

COMMENTS:
The heat transferred could have been calculated using the air specific heat and the temperature difference $(Q = m\,Cp\,\Delta T)$ since there is only a change in sensible heat across the coil.

### Sensible Cooling and Cooling with Dehumidification

Sensible cooling will occur when air is passed across a coil with a mean surface temperature below the DB temperature but above the DP temperature of the air. The air is cooled, but no moisture is removed. Since the humidity ratio remains constant, the cooling process will appear on the psychrometric chart as a horizontal line. The DP temperature will remain constant, but the RH will increase.

If the mean coil temperature is below the DP temperature of the entering air, the air will be cooled and water vapor will condense on the coil, lowering the humidity ratio. The removal of moisture is called dehumidification. Air that comes into intimate contact with the coil will initially be cooled to its saturation temperature, then as further cooling occurs, water vapor will condense on the coil, lowering the humidity ratio. This process will appear as a horizontal line from the inlet point to the saturation line, with the process path then continuing along the saturation line to the coil temperature. The actual air outlet temperature will lie on the psychrometric chart along a straight line running between the air inlet point and the coil temperature on the saturation line. The coil BPF will determine the location of the outlet point along this process line. This can be considered a mixing process between saturated air at the coil temperature and air at the inlet temperature.

In a cooling process with dehumidification, both sensible heat and latent heat are removed from the air. The slope of the coil process line on the psychrometric chart indicates the relative amounts of each. If the line is horizontal, all the heat transferred is sensible heat. A line sloping down to the left indicates latent heat has also been removed from the air. The steeper the slope, the higher the percentage of latent heat removed relative to the total heat removed. The ratio of the sensible heat $(Q_s)$ to total heat $(Q_t)$ is defined as the sensible heat factor $(SHF)$:

$$SHF = \frac{Q_s}{Q_t} = \frac{Q_s}{Q_s + Q_l} \qquad (7.10)$$

From the equations for enthalpy (7.6a and 7.6b), the sensible heat and latent heat can be calculated as follows:

$$Q_s = m\ Cp\ \Delta DB \qquad (7.11)$$

$$Q_l = m\ \Delta\!\left(\omega\ h_{g\,@dp}\right) \qquad (7.12)$$

The *SHF* can be either calculated using these equations or determined directly from the psychrometric chart. The chart contains a *SHF* scale on the right side next to the humidity ratio scale. The *SHF* scale is used in combination with the reference point in the center of the chart. To read the *SHF* using the chart, plot a reference line extending from the reference point to the *SHF* scale. This reference line must have the same slope as the coil process line. Figure 7-7 shows a cooling and dehumidification process plotted on the psychrometric chart with the *SHF* determined from the scale on the chart.

---

EXAMPLE PROBLEM 7.7. Five thousand ft³/lbm of air at 85°F dry-bulb and 70°F wet-bulb is to be cooled and dehumidified to 60°F and 80% relative humidity. Determine (a) the required mean coil temperature, (b) the required coil bypass factor, and (c) the heat transferred in the coil.

SOLUTION.
  SKETCH AND GIVEN DATA:

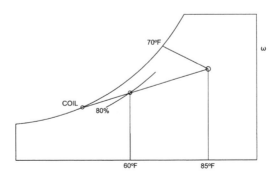

ASSUMPTIONS:
1. The air and water vapor behave as ideal gases.
2. The process is steady-state.
3. The changes in kinetic and potential energies may be neglected.

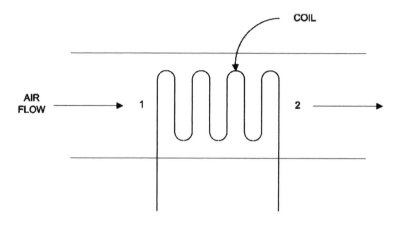

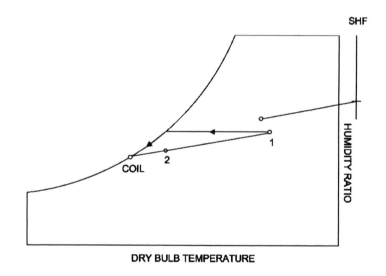

Fig. 7-7. Cooling and dehumidification process.

ANALYSIS:

Plot the inlet and outlet points on the psychometric chart. Connect the two points with a straight line and extend the line to the left until it intersects the saturation line. Reading the coil temperature:

$$T_{coil} = 47°\text{F} \tag{a}$$

Using equation 7.9 to calculate the bypass factor:

$$BPF = \frac{T_{coil} - T_{out}}{T_{coil} - T_{in}} = \frac{47°\text{F} - 60°\text{F}}{47°\text{F} - 85°\text{F}} = 0.342 \tag{b}$$

To calculate the heat transferred, you need the mass flow and the inlet and outlet enthalpies. Reading the following values from the psychrometric chart:

$$h_1 = 34.1 \,\text{Btu/lbm} \qquad h_2 = 24.1 \,\text{Btu/lbm} \qquad v_1 = 14.0 \,\text{ft}^3/\text{lbm}$$

$$Q = m \, \Delta h = \frac{5{,}000 \,\text{ft}^3/\text{min}}{14.0 \,\text{ft}^3/\text{min}} (34.1 - 24.1 \,\text{Btu/lbm}) = 3{,}571 \,\text{Btu/min} \tag{c}$$

COMMENTS:

Since the process involves both sensible and latent heat, the heat tranferred cannot be calculated using the product of the air specific heat and the temperature change.

## Humidification

In winter heating situations, it is sometimes desirable to add moisture to the air to maintain a comfortable humidity in the conditioned space. When cold winter air with a low humidity ratio is heated, a very low relative humidity can result. Moisture can be added to the air steam in two basic ways: by adding steam to the air, or spraying finely atomized liquid water in the air steam. When steam is used, the humidification process will include the addition of heat and thus the process line on the psychrometric chart will rise and move to the right. When water atomization is used, the energy to vaporize the water comes from the air, and the process is similar to the adiabatic saturation process discussed earlier with the process line following a line of constant wet-bulb temperature on the chart. The main difference is that only enough water is added to increase the humidity the desired amount. The air does not become fully saturated.

## Analyzing Actual HVAC Systems

The HVAC systems found in practice typically include combinations of the processes discussed above. For example, an air-conditioning system may include the introduction of some outside air to maintain air quality prior to the cooling and dehumidification of the air. This will result in a mixing process preceding a cooling and dehumidification process. Systems that serve multiple spaces sometimes employ reheat coils in the branch ducts serving each space, permitting independent control of the temperature in each space. This adds a sensible heating process to the system analysis. The following example problems will illustrate some of the techniques for analyzing some typical HVAC systems.

---

EXAMPLE PROBLEM 7.8. An air-conditioning system cools and dehumidifies and then reheats 2,625 ft³/min of air. The air enters the cooling coil at 80°F and 70 percent relative humidity and leaves the reheat coil at 70°F and 50 percent relative humidity. Determine (a) the temperature of the air leaving the cooling coil before being reheated, (b) the quantity of water condensed, (c) the cooling load in tons, and (d) the reheater load, in Btu/hr.

SOLUTION.
SKETCH AND GIVEN DATA:

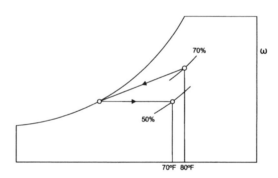

ASSUMPTIONS:
1. The air and water vapor behave as ideal gases.
2. The process is steady-state.
3. The changes in kinetic and potential energies may be neglected.
4. The air leaves the cooling coil saturated.

ANALYSIS:
Plotting the cooling coil inlet and reheat coil outlet points on the psychrometric chart, the following air properties are determined:

$$h_1 = 36.2\,\text{Btu/lbm} \qquad \omega_1 = 0.0155\,\text{lbm/lbm} \qquad v_1 = 13.95\,\text{ft}^3/\text{lbm}$$
$$h_3 = 25.4\,\text{Btu/lbm} \qquad \omega_3 = 0.0078\,\text{lbm/lbm}$$

The humidity ratio at the cooling coil outlet must be the same as the reheat coil outlet since it is a sensible heating process.

$$\omega_2 = \omega_3 = 0.0078 \text{ lbm/lbm}$$

Plotting a line horizontally to the left from the reheat coil outlet to the saturation line on the chart, the following properties can be read:

$$h_2 = 20.6 \text{ Btu/lbm} \qquad T_2 = 50.5°\text{F} \qquad\qquad \text{(a)}$$

The air mass flow rate is:

$$m_a = \frac{2,625 \text{ ft}^3/\text{min}}{13.95 \text{ ft}^3/\text{lbm}} = 188.2 \text{ lbm/min}$$

The water flow removed in the cooling coil is:

$$m_w = ma(\omega_1 - w_2) = (188.2 \text{ lbm/min})(0.0155 - 0.0078 \text{ lbm/lbm})$$
$$m_w = 1.448 \text{ lbm/min} \qquad\qquad \text{(b)}$$

Writing an energy balance around the cooling coil:

$$\text{Energy in} = \text{Energy out}$$
$$m\, h_1 = Q + m_a h_2 + m_w h_f \qquad\qquad \text{(d)}$$

where $h_f$ is from the steam tables at 70°F = 37.68 Btu/lbm

$$Q - (188.2 \text{ lbm/min})(36.2 - 20.6 \text{ Btu/lbm}) - (1.448 \text{ lbm/min})(37.65 \text{ Btu/lbm})$$
$$Q = 2,881 \text{ Btu/min} = 14.4 \text{ tons} \quad (1 \text{ ton} = 200 \text{ Btu/min}) \qquad \text{(c)}$$

Writing an energy balance around the reheat coil:

$$\text{Energy in} = \text{Energy out}$$
$$Q + m_a h_2 = m_a h_2$$
$$Q = m_a(h_3 - h_2) = (188.2 \text{ lbm/min})(25.4 - 20.6 \text{ Btu/lbm}) = 903 \text{ Btu/min} \quad \text{(d)}$$

COMMENTS:
Note it would be impossible to achieve the desired outlet conditions with only a cooling and dehumidification process. A process line drawn though the two points does not intersect the saturation line.

---

EXAMPLE PROBLEM 7.9. An air-conditioning system maintains the crew quarters of ship at 78°F and 40 percent relative humidity. The unit mixes 3,400 ft³/min of air recirculated from the quarters with 600 ft³/min of outside air at 95°F dry-bulb and 75°F wet-bulb temperature, and then cools and dehumidifies the total flow by passing it across a cooling coil with a mean temperature of 50°F. The load on the cooling coil is 120,000 Btu/hr. Determine (a) the temperature and relative humidty of the air leaving the cooling coil, (b) the quantity of water removed by the cooling coil, (c) the coil bypass factor, and (d) the sensible heat factor of the coil.

SOLUTION.

     SKETCH AND GIVEN DATA:

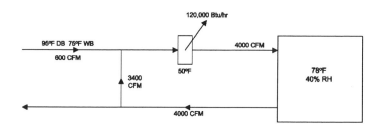

     ASSUMPTIONS:
1. The air and water vapor behave as ideal gases.
2. The process is steady-state.
3. The changes in kinetic and potential energies may be neglected.

     ANALYSIS:

Plotting the room and outside air conditions on the psychrometric chart and reading the necessary properties:

$$h_1 = 27.7\,\text{Btu/lbm} \qquad \omega_1 = 0.0082\,\text{lbm/lbm} \qquad v_1 = 13.74\,\text{ft}^3/\text{lbm}$$
$$h_2 = 38.2\,\text{Btu/lbm} \qquad \omega_2 = 0.0140\,\text{lbm/lbm} \qquad v_2 = 14.3\,\text{ft}^3/\text{lbm}$$

Calculating the mass flows:

$$m_1 = \frac{3{,}400\,\text{ft}^3/\text{min}}{13.74\,\text{ft}^3/\text{lbm}} = 247.5\,\text{lbm/min}$$

$$m_2 = \frac{600\,\text{ft}^3/\text{min}}{14.3\,\text{ft}^3/\text{lbm}} = 41.9\,\text{lbm/min}$$

From the energy balance for the mixing process, the mixture enthalpy can be calculated:

$$m_1\,h_1 + m_2\,h_2 = m_3\,h_3$$

$$h_3 = \frac{m_1\,h_1 + m_2\,h_2}{m^3} = \frac{(247.5)(27.7) + (41.9)(38.2)}{(247.5 + 41.9)} = 29.2\,\text{Btu/lbm}$$

From a mass balance for the water only in the mixing process:

$$m_1\,\omega_1 + m_2\,\omega_2 = m_3\,\omega_3$$

$$\omega_3 = \frac{m_1\,\omega_1 + m_2\,\omega_2}{m_1 + m_2} = \frac{(247.5)(0.0082) + (41.9)(0.014)}{(247.5 + 41.9)} = 0.009\,\text{lbm/lbm}$$

From the energy balance for the cooling coil, the outlet enthalpy can be calculated:

$$m_3\,h_3 = m_4\,h_4 + Q$$

$$h_4 = \frac{m_3\,h_3 - Q}{m_4} = \frac{(289.4\,\text{lbm/min})(29.2\,\text{Btu/lbm}) + 2{,}000\,\text{Btu/min}}{(289.4\,\text{lbm/min})}$$

$$h_4 = 22.3\,\text{Btu/lbm}$$

Plot the mixing process on the psychrometric chart. The cooling and dehumidification process will run between the mixture point and the coil temperature (50°F) on the saturation line. The coil outlet point is located using the enthalpy $(h_4)$ and the other properties can be read:

$$\omega = 0.0079\,\text{lbm/lbm} \qquad DB = 57°\text{F} \qquad RH = 80\% \tag{a}$$

The water removed by the cooling coil can be calculated using the total airflow and the change in humidity ratio across the cooling coil:

$$m_w = m_a(\omega_3 - \omega_4) = (289.4\,\text{lbm/min})(0.009 - 0.0079\,\text{lbm/lbm})$$

$$m_w = 0.318\,\text{lbm/min} \tag{b}$$

The coil bypass factor can be calculated from equation 7.9, with the coil inlet read from the chart or calculated using equation 7.7:

$$BPF = \frac{T_{coil} - T_{out}}{T_{coil} - T_{in}} = \frac{50°\text{F} - 57°\text{F}}{50°\text{F} - 78°\text{F}} = 0.25 \tag{c}$$

The coil sensible heat factor can be calculated using equation 7.10 or the scale and reference point on the psychrometric chart:

$$SHF = 0.83 \tag{d}$$

COMMENTS:
The psychrometric chart makes complex systems much easier to analyze than using only the equations.

## PROBLEMS (ENGLISH UNITS)

7.1E  A room contains air at 80°F with a 60°F dew point. Without using the psychrometric chart, determine (a) the partial pressure of the water vapor, (b) the relative humidity, and (c) the humidity ratio.

7.2E  The temperature of the inside surface of a room's exterior wall is 60°F, while the temperature of the air in the room is 73°F. Without using the psychrometric chart, determine the maximum relative humidity the air in the room can have before condensation occurs.

7.3E  A room contains atmospheric air at 77°F with a humidity ratio of 0.01 lbm vapor/lbm air. Without using the psychrometric chart, determine (a) the relative humidity and (b) the dew point.

7.4E  A flow of air, 2.6 lbm/sec, at 1 atm, 170°F, and 30% relative humidity enters a heat exchanger and is mixed with another stream of air with a flow rate of 2.0 lbm/sec, a pressure of 1 atm, a temperature of 80°F, and a relative humidity of 40%. Determine the temperature of the exiting mixture.

7.5E  Using the psychrometric chart determine (a) the humidity ratio and specific enthalpy of air 90°F dry-bulb and 60% relative humidity, (b) the dew point for air at 90°F dry-bulb and 80°F wet-bulb, and (c) the relative humidity and humidity ratio for air at 105°F dry-bulb and 75°F wet-bulb.

7.6E  Using the psychrometric chart, determine (a) the specific enthalpy and specific volume for air with a relative humidity of 60% and a dry-bulb temperature of 100°F; (b) the humidity ratio and the relative humidity, given a wet-bulb temperature of 75°F and a specific volume of 14.5 ft³/lbm; and (c) the wet-bulb and dry-bulb temperatures, given a relative humidity of 70% and a humidity ratio of 0.018 lbm vapor/lbm air.

7.7E  A small basement dehumidifier receives 35 ft³/min of air at 70°F and 70% relative humidity. The dehumidifier removes 2 qt of water in a 24-hour period. What is the humidity ratio of the air leaving the dehumidifier?

7.8E  An air-conditioning system dehumidifies and then reheats the air. The system operates with 2,625 ft³/min of air entering the dehumidifier at 80°F and 70% relative humidity. The air leaves the reheater at 70°F and 50% relative humidity. Determine (a) the temperature of the air leaving the dehumidifier before it is reheated, (b) the flow rate of the condensed water, (c) the tons of cooling required, and (d) the reheat in Btu/min.

7.9E  Outside air entering at 1,925 ft$^3$/min, 50°F, and 70% relative humidity is reheated and humidified so the air state entering the heating system is 85°F and 35% relative humidity. The humidification occurs with water at 65°F. Determine (a) the water flow rate required and (b) the heat transfer in Btu/min.

7.10E  An air-conditioning system consists of a heating section followed by a humidifying section that supplies saturated steam at 212°F. Twenty-one hundred ft$^3$/min of air enters the heating section at 50°F and 70% relative humidity. It leaves the humidifying section at 70°F and 50% relative humidity. Determine (a) the temperature of the air when it leaves the heating section, (b) the flow rate of steam required, and (c) the heat required.

7.13E  Air at 1.1 lbm/s, 95°F, and 25% relative humidity enters an adiabatic evaporative cooler. The cooler receives water at 70°F, and the air leaves saturated at 80°F. Determine the water flow rate.

7.14E  Two airstreams mix adiabatically. The first stream at 95°C and 60% relative humidity with a mass flow rate of 1 lbm/sec mixes with the second at 70°F and 50% relative humidity with a flow rate of 2 lbm/sec. Determine the exit air temperature and relative humidity.

7.15E  Air at 95°F and 40% relative humidity enters an adiabatic mixing chamber with a flow rate of 40 lbm/min and mixes with saturated air at 45°F with a flow rate of 65 lbm/min. Determine the relative humidity and temperature of the exit air.

7.16E  An airflow of 10,000 CFM of air with initial conditions of 100°F dry-bulb and 73°F wet-bulb temperatures is cooled and dehumidified to conditions of 60°F dry-bulb and 55°F wet-bulb temperatures. Determine (a) the total cooling load in Btu/hr, (b) the mass of water removed in lbm/min, (c) the coil *SHF*, (d) the mean coil temperature, and (e) the coil *BPF*.

7.17E  An air-conditioning system operating on 100 percent recirculation of the air is maintaining the conditions in an office at 80°F and 50% relative humidity. The total heat load is 3 tons and the *SHF* is 0.8. The cooling coil *BPF* is 0.1. Determine (a) the air volume flow rate, (b) the mean coil temperature, and (c) the coil outlet dry-bulb temperature and relative humidity.

7.18E  An air-conditioning unit for a series of staterooms handles 4,000 ft$^3$/min of air, 600 ft$^3$/min of which is outside air at 95°F dry-bulb and 75°F wet-bulb, while the remainder is air recirculated from the staterooms. The air in the staterooms is maintained at 78°F dry-bulb and 40% relative humidity. The mean coil temperature is 50°F and the *BPF* is 0.15. Determine (a) the total cooling load, (b) the water condensed by the air-conditioning unit in lbm/min, and (c) the coil outlet dry-bulb temperature and relative humidity.

# PROBLEMS (SI UNITS)

7.1S  A room contains air at 25°C with a 15°C dew point. Without using the psychrometric chart, determine (a) the partial pressure of the water vapor, (b) the relative humidity, and (c) the humidity ratio.

7.2S  An air-conditioning unit receives an air-water vapor mixture at 101 kPa, 35°C, and 80% relative humidity. Without using the psychrometric chart determine (a) the dew point, (b) the humidity ratio, (c) the partial pressure of air, and (d) the mass fraction of water vapor.

7.3S  Readings of sling psychrometer indicate the dry-bulb and wet-bulb temperatures of a room are 30°C and 25°C respectively. Without using the psychrometric chart, determine the relative humidity.

7.4S  A room contains atmospheric air at 25°C with a humidity ratio of 0.01 kg vapor/kg air. Without using the psychrometric chart, determine (a) the relative humidity and (b) the dew point.

7.5S  The temperature of the inside surface of a room's exterior wall is 15°C, while the temperature of the air in the room is 23°C. What is the maximum relative humidity the air in the room can have before condensation will occur on the wall?

7.6S  Using the psychrometric chart determine (a) the humidity ratio and specific enthalpy of air at 30°C dry-bulb and 60% relative humidity, (b) the dew point for air at 30°C dry-bulb and 25°C wet-bulb, and (c) the relative humidity and humidity ratio for air at 40°C dry-bulb and 25°C wet-bulb temperatures.

7.7S  Using the psychrometric chart, determine (a) the specific enthalpy and specific volume for air with a relative humidity of 60% and a dry-bulb temperature of 35°C; (b) the humidity ratio and the relative humidity, given a wet-bulb temperature of 25°C and a specific volume of 0.9 m³/kg; and (c) the wet- and dry-bulb temperatures, given a relative humidity of 70% and a humidity ratio of 0.018 kg vapor/kg air.

7.8S  Two airstreams mix adiabatically. The first stream at 35°C and 60% relative humidity with a mass flow rate of 1 kg/s mixes with the second at 20°C and 50% relative humidity with a flow rate of 2 kg/s. Determine the exit air temperature and relative humidity.

7.9S  Air at 35°C and 40% relative humidity enters an adiabatic mixing chamber with a flow rate of 0.3 kg/s and mixes with saturated air at 7°C with a flow rate of 0.5 kg/s. Determine the relative humidity and temperature of the exit air.

7.10S  A small basement dehumidifier processes receives 1 m³/min of air at 20°C and 70% relative humidity. The dehumidifier removes 2 liters of water in a 24-hour period. What is the humidity ratio of the air leaving the dehumidifier?

7.11S  An air-conditioning system cools and dehumidifies and then reheats the air. The system operates with 75 m³/min of air entering the cooling coil at 27°C and 70% relative humidity and leaving saturated. The air leaves the reheater at 22°C and 50% relative humidity. Determine (a) the mean cooling coil temperature, (b) the flow rate of the condensed water, (c) the tons of cooling required, and (d) the reheat in kW.

7.12S Outside air entering at 55 m$^3$/min, 10°C, and 70% relative humidity is reheated and humidified so the air-conditioning entering the heating system is 30°C and 35% relative humidity. The humidification occurs with water at 15°C. Determine (a) the water flow rate required and (b) the heat transfer in kW.

7.13S A heating system consists of a heating coil followed by a humidifying section using saturated steam at 100°C. One m$^3$/s of air enters the heating section at 10°C and 70% relative humidity. It leaves the humidifying section at 22°C and 50% relative humidity. Determine (a) the temperature of the air when it leaves the heating section, (b) the flow rate of steam required, and (c) the heat added by the heating coil.

7.14S Air at 0.5 kg/s, 35°C, and 25% relative humidity enters an adiabatic evaporative cooler. The cooler receives water at 20°C, and the air leaves saturated at 25°C. Determine the water flow rate.

7.15S Air enters a drier at 21°C and 25% relative humidity and leaves at 66°C and 50% relative humidity. Determine the air flow rate at 1 atm pressure if 5.44 kg/hr of water is evaporated from wet material in the drier.

7.16S Five m$^3$/sec of air with initial conditions of 40°C dry-bulb and 23°C wet-bulb temperatures is cooled and dehumidified to conditions of 15°C dry-bulb and 13°C wet-bulb temperatures. Determine (a) the total cooling load in kW, (b) the mass of water removed in kg/min, (c) the coil $SHF$, (d) the mean coil temperature, and (e) the coil $BPF$.

7.17S An air-conditioning system operating on 100 percent recirculation of the air is maintaining the conditions in an office at 26°C and 50% relative humidity. The total heat load is 10 kW and the $SHF$ is 0.8. The cooling coil $BPF$ is 0.1. Determine (a) the air volume flow rate, (b) the mean coil temperature, and (c) the coil outlet dry-bulb temperature and relative humidity.

7.18S An air-conditioning unit for a series of staterooms handles 2 m$^3$/s of air, 0.3 m$^3$/s of which is outside air at 35°C dry-bulb and 24°C wet-bulb, while the remainder is air recirculated from the staterooms. The air in the staterooms is maintained at 25°C dry-bulb and 40% relative humidity. The mean coil temperature is 10°C and the coil $BPF$ is 0.15. Determine (a) the total cooling load, (b) the water condensed by the air-conditioning unit in kg/s, and (c) the coil outlet dry-bulb temperature and relative humidity.

CHAPTER 8

# Cooling and Heating Load Calculations

One of the first steps in designing an HVAC or refrigeration system is the calculation of the cooling and/or heating loads. This is necessary to determine the required sizes and capacities of the various system components. An HVAC system on a modern vessel must satisfy the requirements for maintaining the temperature, humidity, purity, and movement of the air in the various occupied spaces. Some, like the crew's quarters on a ship, will require both heating in cold weather and cooling in warm weather for the comfort of the occupants. Others such as the ship's machinery engine spaces will have only ventilation installed to control the air conditions. The ship's stores refrigeration system requires only cooling load calculations to be performed in order to ensure the food can be kept at proper temperature and humidity for extended storage periods without spoilage.

## DESIGN CONDITIONS

One of the first things that must be established is the design inside conditions for the space and the design outside air conditions. These conditions will have a significant impact on the size of the heating or cooling load, so selection should consider the energy costs to operate the system over its useful life. Inside design temperatures for merchant ships are typically 70°F (21°C) in winter and 78°F (26°C) in summer, with naval vessels designed for 65 to 70°F (18 to 21°C) in winter and 80°F (27°C) in summer. Lower inside temperatures in winter and higher inside temperatures in summer will result in lower energy requirements. The relative humidity is typically maintained at about 50 to 60 percent in summer, with lower humidity permitted in winter. The inside design temperatures for a ship stores refrigeration system are typically 0°F for frozen food boxes, 35°F chill boxes storing fruit, vegetable and dairy products, and 40°F for thaw boxes.

In shoreside HVAC applications, the selection of the outside air conditions is based on the location of the building. ASHRAE (American Society of Heating, Refrigeration, and Air Conditioning Engineers) publishes suggested design summer dry- and wet-bulb temperatures and winter dry-bulb temperatures for many cities throughout the United States. These temperatures have been established based on historical data such that the actual conditions will be outside the design conditions only 2.5 percent of the time. The outside air conditions a ship will experience will vary based on the route the ship travels. A tanker carrying crude from Alaska will experience very different conditions than a cruise ship in the Caribbean. Since it is difficult to predict the routes a ship will travel over its entire service life, it is common to size the systems for both hot and cold extremes, thus providing flexibility on where the ship can operate. Typical design outside summer conditions for merchant vessels are 95°F (35°C) dry-bulb temperature and 82°F (28°C) wet-bulb temperature, with naval vessels designed for 90°F (32°C) dry-bulb and 81°F (27°C) wet-bulb temperature. Typical design outside winter dry-bulb temperatures for merchant vessels is 0°F (–18°C), with naval vessels designed for 10°F (–12°C).

## COMPONENTS OF THE COOLING AND HEATING LOAD

The cooling or heating load rarely results from a single source, but comes from a collection of separate sources. The sources that must be considered will vary from application to application. For example there are some sources that must be considered for cooling load estimates that are not needed for heating load estimates. When analyzing a house with large south facing windows, one would have to carefully consider their impact on the summer air-conditioning load. The load created by the occupants of a movie theatre will be a significant component of the cooling load, but would not be significant for the house occupied by only 4 or 5 people.

The components that need to be considered in estimating the cooling or heating load include the following:

1. Heat transfer through walls, floors, and ceilings due to conduction and convection.
2. Heat loss or gain due to ventilation or the infiltration of outside into the conditioned space.
3. Heat gain due to the transmission of solar energy through windows or by increasing the temperature of opaque surfaces.
4. Heat given off by equipment such as motors, lights, kitchen equipment, etc.
5. Heat given off by the occupants of the conditioned space.

6. Heat that must be removed from a product being stored in a refrigerated space to reduce its temperature to the desired value.

For most summer air-conditioning or refrigeration applications, all or most of the above need to be considered in the estimation of the cooling load. In heating applications, it is common to only consider the heat transfer due to conduction and convection and the heat loss due to infiltration and ventilation and not take credit for the heat gains such as solar, equipment, and occupants unless these conditions will always exist on a 24-hour basis. This allows the heating system to maintain the design inside conditions even when these factors are not providing heat. The following sections will discuss each of the factors listed above and present procedures for estimating each.

## THERMAL TRANSMISSION LOAD

The basic equation for determining the thermal transmission load through the surfaces of the conditioned space due to conduction and convection is:

$$Q = U \, A \, \Delta T \tag{8.1}$$

where

$Q$ = heat transferred, in Btu/hr or W
$U$ = overall heat transfer coefficient, in Btu/hr-ft$^2$-°F or W/m$^2$-°C
$A$ = area in ft$^2$ or m$^2$
$\Delta T$ = temperature difference between the air inside and outside the surfaces, in °F or °C

The value of the overall heat transfer coefficient is calculated in a similar manner as it was calculated in Chapter 5 for evaporators and condensers. The coefficient combines the effect of the convection on the inside and outside of the wall, and that of the conduction through the materials of the wall. Figure 8-1 shows a typical wall construction and the temperature distribution through the wall. The overall heat transfer coefficient can be estimated by the following equation:

$$U = \frac{1}{1/f_i + x_1/k_1 + x_2/k_2 \, t ... t \, x_n/k_n = 1/f_o} \tag{8.2}$$

where
$f_i$ and $f_o$ = inside and outside convection film coefficients, in Btu/hr-ft$^2$-°R or W/m$^2$-°K
$x$ = thickness of the materials, in feet, inches, or meters
$k$ = thermal conductivity of the materials, in Btu/hr-ft-°R, Btu/hr-ft$^2$-°R/in or W/m-°K

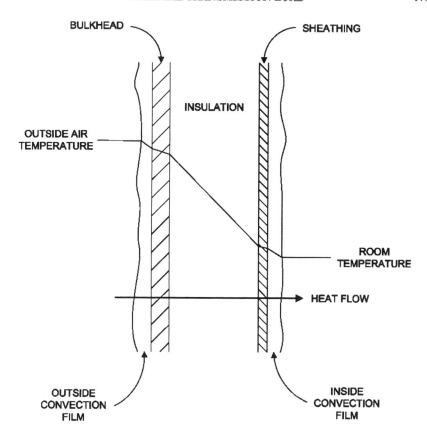

Fig. 8-1. Temperature distribution through typical wall construction.

Since it is desirable to reduce the heat gain or loss, insulating materials with good thermal resistance are typically used in the construction of the surfaces of the space to reduce the value of the overall heat transfer coefficient. This also results in the conduction through the solid materials controlling the heat transfer. The thermal resistances of the convection films are relatively small compared to the thermal resistances of the solid materials. This is unlike heat exchangers, like the condensers and evaporators discussed in chapter 5, where the convection film coefficients control the heat transfer.

In order to estimate the overall heat transfer coefficient, it is necessary to have information about the construction of the wall, floor, or ceiling. Table 8-1 contains information on the thermal conductivity and thermal resistances of some common construction materials and suggested film coefficients to use in a variety of common situations.

**TABLE 8-1**
**Thermal Conductivities and Heat Transfer Coefficients**

| Material | k (Btu/hr-ft-°F) | k (W/m-°K) |
|---|---|---|
| Steel | 28 | 48.5 |
| Aluminum alloy | 90 | 155.8 |
| Hardwood (maple. oak) | 0.092 | 0.159 |
| Softwood (pine, fir) | 0.067 | 0.116 |
| Brick, common | 0.42 | 0.73 |
| Brick, face | 0.75 | 1.3 |
| Concrete | 1.0 | 1.731 |
| Gypsum plaster | 0.0135 | 0.234 |
| Glass fiber insulation | 0.0225 | 0.039 |
| Polystyrene insulation | 0.0167 | 0.029 |
| Polyurethane insulation | 0.0133 | 0.023 |
| | | |
| Air Film Coefficients | f (Btu/hr-ft²-°F) | f (W/m²-°K) |
| Still air | 1.65 | 9.4 |
| Moving air (7.5 mph) | 4.0 | 22.7 |
| Moving air (15 mph) | 6.0 | 34 |
| | | |
| Glass Windows | U (Btu/hr-ft²-°F) | U (W/m²-°K) |
| Single pane | 1.1 | 6.2 |
| Double pane | 0.55 | 3.1 |

EXAMPLE PROBLEM 8.1. A stateroom bulkhead is constructed of a ¼ inch outside steel plate, 2 inches of glass fiber insulation and 1/16 inches of inside steel sheathing. Estimate the overall heat transfer coefficient.

SOLUTION.

SKETCH AND GIVEN DATA:

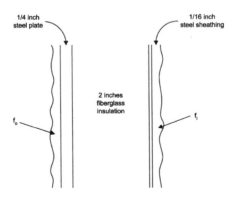

ASSUMPTIONS:
1. The material properties are uniform for each material.

2. The inside air can be considered still.

3. The outside air is moving at approximately 15 mph.

ANALYSIS:

From Table 8-1, the following values are found for the thermal conductivity of the steel and the insulation, and the film coefficients for the air on the inside and outside of the bulkhead:

For steel, $k$ = 28 Btu/hr-ft-°F

For glass fiber insulation, $k$ = 0.0225 Btu/hr-ft-°F

For still air, $f$ = 1.65 Btu/hr-ft$^2$-°F

For air with a velocity of 15 mph, $f$ = 6.0 Btu/hr-ft$^2$-°F

Substituting into equation 8.2:

$$U = \frac{1}{(1/1.65) + (0.0625/12)/28 + (2/12)/0.0225 + (0.25/12)/28 + (1/6.0)}$$

$$U = 0.122 \, \text{Btu/hr-ft}^2\text{-}°F$$

COMMENTS:

1. The steel bulkhead and sheathing have little effect on the overall heat transfer coefficient. Eliminating them would affect the answer by less than 1 percent.

2. A typical bulkhead construction would have steel stiffeners inside the insulation. Values for typical marine constructions can be found in references 2, 6, and 12.

---

# VENTILATION AND INFILTRATION LOAD

In the public spaces and stateroom on ships, outside ventilation air is introduced to maintain air quality by reducing the buildup of carbon dioxide or other contaminants. The quantity of outside air required for a space can be based on air changes per hour or CFM per person. Current practice is to calculate the requirement each way and use the higher of the two values for design purposes. Table 8-2 contains values that can be used to estimate the required quantity of outside ventilation air for common situations.

### TABLE 8-2
### Outside Air Requirements

|  | Minimum CFM / Person | Minimum Air Changes |
|---|---|---|
| Low occupancy spaces (staterooms, offices) | 15 | 2 per hour |
| High occupancy spaces (dining rooms, recreation rooms) | 12 | 3 per hour |

The quantity of conditioned supply air to the space must sufficient to maintain uniform conditions in the space. Commercial practice recommends a rate of air change of 6 minutes for high occupancy spaces and 8 minutes for all other spaces. The temperature difference between the supply air and the design room temperature should not exceed 30°F. The minimum supply airflow to any space is 35 CFM.

Even if a space is unventilated, outside air will infiltrate the conditioned space due to such causes as leaks through windows and doors, and the opening and closing of doors to enter or exit the space. In the case of food storage rooms, there are no windows and the doors are well sealed, so the infiltration is primarily due to the opening and closing of the doors. Table 8-3 can be used to estimate the infiltration in air changes per day, for rooms used for the storage of frozen food and for fruits, vegetables, and dairy products.

**TABLE 8-3**
**Air Changes per Day for Refrigerated Food Storage Boxes**

| Box Volume (ft²) | Chill Box | Freeze Box |
|---|---|---|
| 250 | 38 | 29 |
| 500 | 26 | 20 |
| 1,000 | 17.5 | 13.5 |
| 2,000 | 12 | 9.3 |
| 4,000 | 8.2 | 6.3 |
| 10,000 | 4.9 | 3.8 |
| 20,000 | 3 | 2.3 |
| 50,000 | 2 | 1.6 |
| 100,000 | 1.4 | 1.1 |

Note: Reduce the air changes by 50 percent for installations with an anteroom.

The introduction of outside air into a conditioned space, whether intentional by ventilation or unintentional by infiltration, will result in an increase in the heating or cooling load. This load can be calculated based on the total load or broken down into the sensible heat load and the latent heat load. Using the equations from chapter 7 for the sensible and latent heat:

$$Q_s = m \, Cp \, \Delta DB \tag{8.3a}$$

$$Q_l = m \, \Delta\left(\omega \, h_{g\,@dp}\right) \tag{8.3b}$$

$$Q_t = Q_s + Q_l \tag{8.3c}$$

$$Q_t = m \, \Delta h \tag{8.3d}$$

where

$Q$ = heat load in Btu/hr or kW
$m$ = mass flow of dry air in lbm/hr or kg/sec
$Cp$ = specific heat for air, 0.24 Btu/lbm-°R or 1.0047 kJ/kg-°K
$\Delta DB$ = difference in dry-bulb temperature in °F or °C
$\Delta$ = humidity ratio in lbm/lbm or kg/kg
$h_{g@dp}$ = enthalpy of the water vapor at the dew point temperature, in Btu/lbm or kW/kg
$\Delta h$ = difference in the total enthalpy in Btu/lbm or kJ/kg

For summer air-conditioning applications and refrigerated stores applications, both the sensible and latent heat components must be considered. For winter heating applications, only the sensible component needs to be considered.

---

EXAMPLE PROBLEM 8.2. A series of staterooms are air-conditioned. The outside air being supplied to maintain air quality is 1,000 CFM. Estimate the sensible and latent heat components of the ventilation load.

SOLUTION.

SKETCH AND GIVEN DATA:

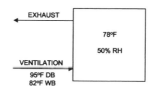

ASSUMPTIONS:
1. The room design conditions are 78°F and 50% relative humidity.
2. The outside air design conditions are 95°F DB and 82°F WB.
3. The air density is assumed to be 0.075 lbm/ft$^3$.
4. The vapor enthalpy is assumed to be 1,060 Btu/lbm.

ANALYSIS:
From the psychrometric chart, the following values for the inside and outside humidity ratios are determined:

For the inside air, $\omega$ = 72 grains/lbm = 0.0103 lbm/lbm
For the outside air, $\omega$ = 146 grains/lbm = 0.0209 lbm/lbm

Calculating the sensible heat load using equation 8.3a:

$Q_s = m\ Cp\ \Delta DB = (1{,}000 \times 0.075 \times 60\ \text{lbm/hr})(0.24\ \text{Btu/lbm-°F})(95 - 78°\text{F})$
$Q_s = 18{,}360\ \text{Btu/hr}$

Calculating the latent heat load using equation 8.3b:

$$Q_l = m \, \Delta\left(\omega \, h_{g@dp}\right)$$
$$Q_l = (1,000 \times 0.075 \times 60 \, \text{lbm/hr})(1,060 \, \text{Btu/lbm})(0.0209 - 0.0103 \, \text{lbm/lbm})$$
$$Q_l = 50,562 \, \text{Btu/hr}$$

COMMENTS:
The assumptions made about the air density and vapor enthalpy simplified the calculations, but did result in minor errors in the calculations of the heat loads. These errors are not significant in practical design calculations.

## SOLAR LOAD

When outside surfaces are exposed to the sun, radiative heat transfer will take place, which will increase the summer cooling load. The heat gain will depend on the orientation to the sun and the physical characteristics of the surface. Unlike a building on land, a ship is constantly moving and its orientation to the sun, and even its latitude, is constantly changing. This is handled by assuming a worst-case situation, and sizing the system for that load.

The solar load through transparent surfaces such as windows varies significantly based on the direction, the time of the year, the window construction, and the effect of any shades or blinds installed inside the window. The solar energy striking the glass will be either transmitted into the space, absorbed by the glass, or reflected back to the outside air as shown in figure 8-2. The solar gain into the space consists of the transmitted energy plus a fraction of absorbed energy. The solar gain in northern latitudes for unshaded single-pane windows can vary from about 250 Btu/hr-ft$^2$ for south facing windows to 20 Btu/hr-ft$^2$ for north facing windows. Since the orientation of the windows on a ship is constantly changing, it is necessary to assume the side with the greatest area is facing towards the sun for sizing purposes. Naval practice is to assume a solar load of 160 Btu/hr-ft$^2$ for all windows regardless of construction, while commercial practice is to assume 160 Btu/hr-ft$^2$ if there are windows on only one surface of the space, and 120 Btu/hr-ft$^2$ if there are windows on more than one surface.

The solar energy striking an opaque surface will be partially absorbed and partially reflected. The emissivity is a measure of the percentage of solar energy that is absorbed by the surface, with the factor varying from 0.0 to 1.0. A light shiny surface will reflect a significant amount of the energy striking it and thus will have a low emissivity. A dark dull surface will absorb most of the solar energy and will thus have a high emissivity. The effect of the absorbed energy is to raise the temperature of the surface

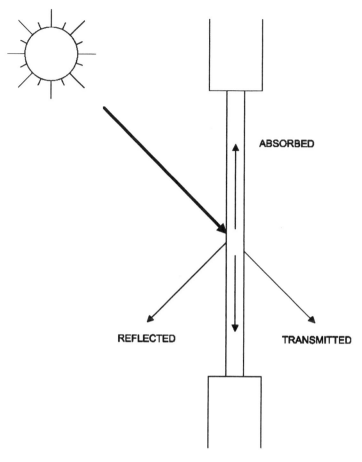

Fig. 8-2. Distribution of solar energy striking a transparent surface.

above the surrounding air temperature. It is common in marine practice to account for the solar load by assuming a temperature for surfaces exposed to the sun. Table 8-4 contains temperatures that can be assumed for weather surfaces that are exposed to the sun. The heat transmission for those weather surfaces is then calculated using the assumed surface temperature rather than using the outside air temperature and the outside film coefficient. Naval practice is to determine the surface that will have the highest solar load and ignore the effect on the other weather surfaces. Commercial practice is to consider the solar load on all weather surfaces, but lower surface temperatures are assumed when the solar loads on multiple surfaces are being considered versus a situation with only one weather surface.

**TABLE 8-4**
**Solar Load Factors (Based on 95°F DB Temperature)**

*Single Weather Boundary*
Vertical surfaces                    125°F surface temperature
Horizontal surfaces                  145°F surface temperature
Windows and glass surfaces           160 Btu/hr-ft$^2$

*Multiple Weather Boundaries*
Vertical surfaces                    115°F surface temperature
Horizontal surfaces                  130°F surface temperature
Windows and glass surfaces           120 Btu/hr-ft$^2$

If the weather surfaces are shaded by an overhang, the sun angle can be assumed to be 45°. Thus a 5 foot overhang would shade the top 5 feet of the weather surface. The load is thus calculated based on the design outside to the design inside air temperatures for the shaded portion and the solar outside surface to the inside air temperature for the portion exposed to the sun.

---

EXAMPLE PROBLEM 8.3. A stateroom has a single weather bulkhead. The bulkhead construction is the same as example 8-1 and it is 8 feet 6 inches high by 12 feet long with a 2 foot by 3 foot single pane window. Estimate the bulkhead transmission cooling load considering it is completely shaded, and if it is completely exposed to the sun.

SOLUTION.
SKETCH AND GIVEN DATA:

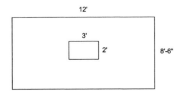

ASSUMPTIONS:
1. The bulkhead is the only surface of the stateroom exposed to the weather.
2. The inside design temperature is 78°F and the outside design temperature is 95°F.

ANALYSIS:
Calculating the areas of the solid bulkhead and the window:

$$A_{win} = (2 \text{ ft})(3 \text{ ft}) = 6 \text{ ft}^2$$
$$A_{bulk} = (8.5 \text{ ft})(12 \text{ ft}) - 6 \text{ ft}^2 = 96 \text{ ft}^2$$

Using the results from example 8.1 and the coefficient for a single pane window from table 8-1, calculate the cooling load for the shaded condition:

$$Q_{bulk} = U \ A \ \Delta T = \left(0.122\,\text{Btu/hr-ft}^2\text{-}^\circ\text{F}\right)\left(96 \ \text{ft}^2\right)(95^\circ\text{F} - 78^\circ\text{F}) = 199.1\,\text{Btu/hr}$$

$$Q_{win} = U \ A \ \ \Delta T = \left(1.1\,\text{Btu/hr-ft}^2\text{-}^\circ\text{F}\right)\left(6 \ \text{ft}^2\right)(95^\circ\text{F} - 78^\circ\text{F}) = 112.2\,\text{Btu/hr}$$

$$Q_{tot} = 199.1 + 112.2 = 311.3\,\text{Btu/hr}$$

For the unshaded condition, using the solution for example problem 8.1, calculate the overall heat transfer coefficient without the outside film coefficient. The resistances of the steel bulkhead and sheathing can be neglected since they have little effect on the value of the heat transfer coefficient.

$$U = \frac{1}{7.41 + 0.6061} = 0.125\,\text{Btu/hr-ft}^2\text{-}^\circ\text{F}$$

Calculating the heat loads for the solid bulkhead, using the factors from table 8-4 for a single weather boundary:

$$Q_{win} = F_{glass} \ A = \left(160\,\text{Btu/hr-ft}^2\right)\left(6 \ \text{ft}^2\right) = 960\,\text{Btu/hr}$$

$$Q_{bulk} = U \ A \ \ \Delta T = \left(0.125\,\text{Btu/hr-ft}^2\text{-}^\circ\text{F}\right)\left(96 \ \text{ft}^2\right)(125^\circ\text{F} - 78^\circ\text{F}) = 564\,\text{Btu/hr}$$

$$Q_{tot} = 960 + 564 = 1,524\,\text{Btu/hr}$$

COMMENTS:
If the bulkhead is partially shaded, it would be broken into two sections. One section would be calculated considering the solar effects, and the other without. A solar angle of 45° is commonly assumed.

## EQUIPMENT AND LIGHTING LOAD

The heat released by equipment and lighting installed in an air-conditioned space must be considered in the cooling load calculations. For equipment operated by motors such as fans and pumps, the heat released depends on the efficiency of the motor, where the equipment load is located, and the number of hours per day the equipment operates. If the load is located within the air-conditioned space, the electrical power consumption can simply be converted to heat and included in the overall cooling load. If the equipment's connected load is outside the conditioned space, only the equipment losses appear as heat released into the space. A factor adjusting for the location of the load and hours of use must be applied to the equipment's electric power consumption to determine the average heat load. Table 8-5 contains typical electric motor efficiencies and

other data that can be used to determine an appropriate factor to use for
estimating equipment loads.

**TABLE 8-5**
**Electric Motor Efficiencies**

| Motor Size, HP | Efficiency, % |
|:---:|:---:|
| $\frac{1}{8}$ | 50 |
| $\frac{1}{4}$ | 60 |
| $\frac{1}{2}$ | 66 |
| 1 | 71 |
| 5 | 82 |
| 10 | 85 |
| 20 | 87 |
| 50 | 89 |
| 75 | 90 |

The lighting in the space will result in a heat load that will vary based
on the type of lighting fixtures and the hours per day the lights are used.
For incandescent lights, the heat load is equal to the total electric load in
watts. For fluorescent lights, a factor of 1.25 is applied to account for the
additional load due to the ballasts. If the wattage of the lighting is not
known, table 8-6 can be used to estimate the required lighting.

**TABLE 8-6**
**Typical Space Lighting Loads (Btu/Hr per Ft$^2$ of Deck Area)**

| Space | Fluorescent | Incandescent |
|:---|:---:|:---:|
| Passenger and dept. head stateroom | 7 | 12 |
| Officer and crew stateroom | 4 | 7 |
| Mess rooms, lounges, and public spaces | 9 | 15 |
| Offices and other spaces | 7 | 12 |

## OCCUPANT LOAD

When a space is occupied, a load will result from the people inside. This
load will vary based on the activity level of the occupants and the number
of people in the space. The occupant load will have both a sensible and latent heat component as both heat and moisture are generated. The occupant load will obviously be more significant for a public space like the
dining room on a passenger ship than a stateroom occupied by one or two
people. Typical total occupant loads are 800 Btu/hr/person for higher levels of activity and 600 Btu/hr/person for normal levels of activity. As the
space temperature increases, the latent heat component increases and the

sensible heat component decreases. Table 8-7 contains the value of the sensible and latent components at a variety of space dry-bulb temperatures that can used to estimate the occupant load in common situations.

**TABLE 8-7**
**Occupant Heat Dissipation Sensible and Latent, in Btu/Hr**

| Room DB Temp (°F) | Mess and Working Sensible | Mess and Working Latent | All Others Sensible | All Others Latent |
|---|---|---|---|---|
| 75 | 360 | 440 | 300 | 300 |
| 76 | 345 | 455 | 290 | 310 |
| 77 | 330 | 470 | 275 | 325 |
| 78 | 315 | 485 | 265 | 335 |
| 79 | 300 | 500 | 250 | 350 |
| 80 | 285 | 515 | 240 | 360 |
| 81 | 270 | 530 | 230 | 370 |
| 82 | 255 | 545 | 215 | 385 |
| 83 | 240 | 560 | 205 | 395 |
| 84 | 225 | 575 | 190 | 410 |
| 85 | 210 | 590 | 180 | 420 |

EXAMPLE PROBLEM 8.4. An office serving 6 people has 300 watts of fluorescent lights, two ½ hp motors, and office equipment drawing 200 watts. Estimate the total occupant, lighting, and equipment loads.

SOLUTION.

SKETCH AND GIVEN DATA:

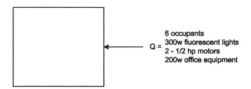

6 occupants
300w fluorescent lights
Q = 2 - 1/2 hp motors
200w office equipment

ASSUMPTIONS:
1. The load on the motors is in the cooled space.
2. All 6 occupants are in the space at the same time.
3. All equipment is on simultaneously.

ANALYSIS:
Calculating the lighting load:

$$Q_{lighting} = (0.3 \text{ kW})(1.25)(3,412 \text{ Btu/hr-kW}) = 1,279.5 \text{ Btu/hr}$$

Calculating the equipment load for the motors:

$$Q_{motors} = \frac{(2 \text{ pumps})(0.5 \text{ hp})}{(0.66)} (2{,}544.5 \text{ Btu/hp-hr}) = 3{,}855 \text{ Btu/hr}$$

Calculating the equipment load for the office equipment:

$$Q_{office} = (0.2 \text{ kW})(3{,}412 \text{ Btu/hr-kW}) = 682.4 \text{ Btu/hr}$$

Calculating the occupant load using table 8-7:

$$Q_s = (6 \text{ persons})(265 \text{ Btu/hr-person}) = 1{,}590 \text{ Btu/hr}$$
$$Q_l = (6 \text{ persons})(335 \text{ Btu/hr-person}) = 2{,}010 \text{ Btu/hr}$$

The total loads for lighting, equipment, and occupants are:

Total sensible heat load: $Q_s = 7{,}407 \text{ Btu/hr}$
Total latent heat load: $Q_l = 2{,}010 \text{ Btu/hr}$
Total heat load: $Q_t = 9{,}417 \text{ Btu/hr}$

COMMENTS:

The sensible and latent heat loads above are used in determining the cooling load for the office, but are not considered in determining the heating load.

## PRODUCT LOAD

In refrigerated food storage applications, the products being stored will contribute to the space cooling load. When product is initially loaded, it will typically need to be lowered to the desired storage temperature. The amount of heat that must be removed from the product to reduce depends on the mass of product and its specific heat. This results in what is referred as the "pulldown" condition and will typically determine the rated capacity of the condensing units. While a short pulldown period would seem desirable, it can result in very high capacity requirements for the refrigeration system. The longer the period allowed to lower the product to the storage temperature, the lower the pulldown load will be relative to the normal operating load. Products such as fruits and vegetables stored in chill boxes will release water vapor during both pulldown and storage, resulting in a latent heat load referred to as the respiration load. Table 8-8 contains typical product conditions that can be used to estimate the pulldown and respiration loads for refrigerated food storage applications.

**TABLE 8-8**
**Typical Refrigerated Storage Product Load Conditions**

|  | *Chill Box* | *Freeze Box* |
|---|---|---|
| Final space temperature | 33°F | 0°F |
| Product entering temperature | 55°F | 15°F |
| Pulldown time: | | |
|   Ship's stores | 2 days | 2 days |
|   Refrigerated cargo | 3 days | 5 days |
| Typical product density | 30 lbm/ft$^3$ | 36 lbm/ft$^3$ |
| Typical product specific heat | 0.85 Btu/lbm-°F | 0.40 Btu/lbm-°F |
| Typical product respiration rate | | |
|   @55°F | 0.14Btu/lbm-hr | — |
|   @33°F | 0.05 Btu/lbm-hr | — |
| Typical box loading factor | 65% | 65% |

# HEATING AND COOLING LOAD SIZING EXAMPLES

This section contains three examples of heating and cooling load estimates: one for a heating application, one for an air-conditioning application, and one for a refrigeration box example. The basic procedure for each is similar:

1. Determine the appropriate inside and outside design conditions for the application.
2. Based on the construction of the walls and other surfaces of the space, determine the overall heat transfer coefficient for all surfaces that have a temperature difference across them.
3. For cooling load calculations, if any surface is exposed to the sun, determine the surface temperature for opaque surfaces and the solar load factor for windows.
4. Based on the heat transfer coefficients, temperatures, and areas, calculate the transmission and solar loads.
5. Determine the ventilation or infiltration flows appropriate for the application. In general, shipboard HVAC applications will have ventilation flows and refrigeration box applications will have infiltration flows. Calculate the sensible and latent heat loads.
6. For cooling load calculations, determine what additional loads (equipment, lighting, occupant, product, etc.) are appropriate to application. Estimate each load.
7. Sum all the loads to determine the overall load for the space.
8. Repeat the procedure for each space. Sum the load for each space to determine the required system heating or cooling capacity.

EXAMPLE PROBLEM 8.5. An officer stateroom is 12 feet long by 10 feet wide by 9 feet high. There are two weather surfaces, one bulkhead 12 feet by 9 feet with an 18 inch by 24 inch widow and the overhead. The room contains 100 watts of overhead fluorescent lights and a 75-watt incandescent table lamp. The overall heat transfer coefficients for both the overhead and weather bulkhead are 0.20 Btu/hr-ft²-°F (outside air to inside air) and 0.21 Btu/hr-ft²-°F (outside surface to inside air). Estimate the heating and cooling loads for the stateroom.

SOLUTION.
    SKETCH AND GIVEN DATA:

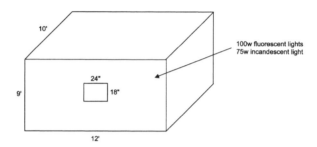

ASSUMPTIONS:
1. The weather bulkhead and overhead are completely exposed to the sun with no shading.
2. The winter inside design temperature is 70°F and the outside design temperature is 0°F.
3. The summer inside design temperature is 78°F and the outside design temperature is 95°F.

ANALYSIS:
The heating load will include only the transmission load for the weather bulkhead and the overhead. Solar effects are not included. The surfaces that must be considered are the overhead, the solid weather bulkhead, and the window.

$$Q_{ovhd} = U\ A\ \Delta T = \left(0.20\,\text{Btu/hr-ft}^2\text{-}^\circ\text{F}\right)\left(12 \times 10\ \text{ft}^2\right)\left(70 - {}^\circ\text{F}\right)$$
$$= 1{,}680\,\text{Btu/hr}$$

$$Q_{bulk} = U\ A\ \Delta T = \left(0.20\,\text{Btu/hr-ft}^2\text{-}^\circ\text{F}\right)\left(12 \times 9 - 3\ \text{ft}^2\right)\left(70 - 0\ ^\circ\text{F}\right)$$
$$= 1{,}470\,\text{Btu/hr}$$

$$Q_{win} = U\ A\ \Delta T = \left(1.1\,\text{Btu/hr-ft}^2\text{-}^\circ\text{F}\right)\left(3\ \text{ft}^2\right)\left(70 - 0\ ^\circ\text{F}\right) = 231\,\text{Btu/hr}$$

Heating load = 1,680 + 1,470 + 231 = 3,381 Btu/hr

The cooling load will consider the transmission loads, including solar effects, plus the loads for the lights and occupant loads. The transmission loads are:

$$Q_{ovhd} = U\ A\ \Delta T = \left(0.21\,\text{Btu}/\text{hr-ft}^2\text{-}°\text{F}\right)\left(12 \times 10\ \text{ft}^2\right)(130\text{-}78\ °\text{F}) = 1{,}310.4\,\text{Btu}/\text{hr}$$

$$Q_{bulk} = U\ A\ \ \Delta T = \left(0.21\,\text{Btu}/\text{hr-ft}^2\text{-}°\text{F}\right)\left(12 \times 9 - 3\ \text{ft}^2\right)(115\text{-}78\ °\text{F}) = 815.9\,\text{Btu}/\text{hr}$$

$$Q_{win} = F\ A = \left(120\,\text{Btu}/\text{hr-ft}^2\right)\left(3\ \text{ft}^2\right) = 360\,\text{Btu}/\text{hr}$$

The lighting load is:

$$Q_{light} = \left((0.10\ \text{kW})(1.25) + 0.075\ \text{kW}\right)(3{,}412\,\text{Btu}/\text{hr-kW}) = 682.4\,\text{Btu}/\text{hr}$$

The occupant sensible and latent head loads are:

$$Q_s = (1\ \text{person})(265\,\text{Btu}/\text{hr-person}) = 265\,\text{Btu}/\text{hr}$$
$$Q_l = (1\ \text{person})(335\,\text{Btu}/\text{hr-person}) = 335\,\text{Btu}/\text{hr}$$

The total sensible and latent cooling loads are:

$$Q_s = 1{,}310.4 + 815.9 + 360 + 682.4 + 265 = 3{,}433.7\,\text{Btu}/\text{hr}$$
$$Q_l = 335\,\text{Btu}/\text{hr}$$

COMMENTS:
The ventilation load is not included because it will be included in the overall system load calculation. This is because outside air is mixed with the air being recirculated from the conditioned spaces.

---

EXAMPLE PROBLEM 8.6. The air-conditioning system for the house of a tanker is being sized. The total sensible heat load is 100,000 Btu/hr and the latent heat load is 20,000 Btu/hr. The outside airflow is 1,000 CFM and total supply flow to the house spaces is 4,000 CFM. Determine: (a) the mixture DB temperature, (b) the system sensible heat factor, (c) the coil outlet temperature, and (d) the system capacity in tons.

SOLUTION.
SKETCH AND GIVEN DATA:

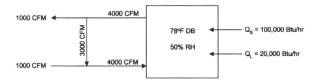

ASSUMPTIONS:

1. The inside design conditions are 78°F DB and 50 percent relative humidity.
2. The outside design conditions are 95°F DB and 82°F WB.

ANALYSIS:

From the psychrometric chart, the following values are determined:

$$\text{Outside air specific volume } (v) = 14.4 \text{ ft}^3/\text{lbm}$$
$$\text{Outside air humidity ratio } (\omega) = 0.0208/\text{lbm}$$
$$\text{Inside air humidity ratio } (\omega) = 0.0102 \text{ lbm}/\text{lbm}$$

Calculating the sensible and latent components of the outside air ventilation load:

$$Q_s = m \ Cp \ \Delta T = \frac{\left(1,000 \text{ ft}^3/\text{min}\right)\left(60 \text{ min}/\text{hr}\right)}{\left(14.4 \text{ ft}^3/\text{lbm}\right)} (0.24 \text{ Btu}/\text{lbm-}°\text{F})(95-78°\text{F})$$

$$Q_s = 17,000 \text{ Btu}/\text{hr}$$

$$Q_l = m \ h_{fg@db} \ \Delta\omega = (4,167 \text{ lbm}/\text{hr})(1,060 \text{ Btu}/\text{hr})(0.0208-0.0102 \text{ lbm}/\text{lbm})$$

$$Q_l = 46,820 \text{ Btu}/\text{hr}$$

The system sensible heat factor is thus:

$$SHF = \frac{Qs}{Qs+Q_l} = \frac{100,000+17,000}{100,000+17,000+20,000+46,820} = 0.636 \qquad \text{(b)}$$

Calculating the DB temperature of the mixture of outside and recirculation air:

$$T_M = \frac{\left(1,000 \text{ ft}^3/\text{min}\right)(95°\text{F}) + \left(3,000 \text{ ft}^3/\text{min}\right)(78°\text{F})}{\left(4,000 \text{ ft}^3/\text{min}\right)} = 82.3°\text{F} \qquad \text{(a)}$$

Calculating the cooling coil outlet temperature using the total sensible heat load.

$$Qs = m \ Cp \ \Delta T$$

$$\Delta T = \frac{(117,000 \text{ Btu}/\text{hr})}{(4,000 \times 60/14 \text{ lbm}/\text{hr})(0.24 \text{ Btu}/\text{lbm-}°\text{F})} = 28.4°\text{F}$$

$$T_C = 82.3°\text{F} - 28.4°\text{F} = 53.9°\text{F} \qquad \text{(c)}$$

The capacity of the system in tons is thus:

$$\text{Tons} = \frac{183,820\,\text{Btu/hr}}{12,000\,\text{Btu/hr-ton}} = 15.3 \text{ tons} \qquad\qquad \text{(d)}$$

COMMENTS:

The introduction of the outside ventilation air resulted in a 50 percent increase in the system load.

---

EXAMPLE PROBLEM 8.7. A freeze box for a ship's stores refrigeration system opening to an anteroom has dimensions of 20 feet by 20 feet by 7 feet has a design temperature of 0°F. One bulkhead adjoins a chill box operating at 35°F, while a second bulkhead adjoins a freeze box operating at 0°F. All the other surfaces are exposed to external temperatures. The overall heat transfer coefficients for the bulkheads and overhead are 0.06 Btu/hr-ft²-°F while the coefficient for the deck is 0.03 Btu/hr-ft²-°F. Estimate the normal and pulldown cooling loads.

SOLUTION.

SKETCH AND GIVEN DATA:

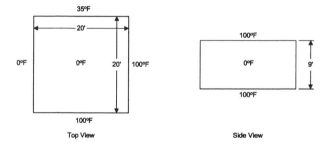

ASSUMPTIONS:

1. The air temperature on the other 4 surfaces is assumed to be 100°F.
2. The infiltration air is assumed to be 100°F and 60 percent relative humidity.
3. The product is assumed to be loaded at a temperature of 15°F.

ANALYSIS:

Calculating the freeze box volume:

$$V = (20 \text{ ft})(20 \text{ ft})(7 \text{ ft}) = 2,800 \text{ ft}^3$$

From table 8-3, the number of air changes per day is estimated based on the volume and reducing the factor by 50 percent since it opens to an anteroom:

$$\text{Air changes/day} = (8.0)(0.5) = 4.0$$

The infiltration flow rate is thus estimated as:

$$V = (2,800 \text{ ft}^3)(4.0) = 11,200 \text{ ft}^3/\text{day} = 466.7 \text{ ft}^3/\text{hr}$$

From the psychrometric chart, the enthalpy and specific volume of air at 100°F and 60 percent relative humidity is 52 Btu/lbm and 14.6 ft³/lbm. Estimating the infiltration air load:

$$Q_{inf} = m \, \Delta h = (466.7 \text{ ft}^3/\text{hr})(0.0685 \text{ lbm/ft}^3)(52 - 0 \text{ Btu/lbm}) = 1,662 \text{ Btu/hr}$$

Calculating the transmission loads for each of the six surfaces of the freeze box, using equation 8.1 ($Q = U A \, \Delta T$):

$$\text{Overhead: } (0.06 \text{ Btu/hr-ft}^2 \text{-°F})(400 \text{ ft}^2)(100°\text{F}) = 2,400 \text{ Btu/hr}$$
$$\text{Deck: } (0.03 \text{ Btu/hr-ft}^2 \text{-°F})(400 \text{ ft}^2)(100°\text{F}) = 1,200 \text{ Btu/hr}$$
$$\text{Bulkhead 1: } (0.06 \text{ Btu/hr-ft}^2 \text{-°F})(140 \text{ ft}^2)(100°\text{F}) = 840 \text{ Btu/hr}$$
$$\text{Bulkhead 2: } (0.06 \text{ Btu/hr-ft}^2 \text{-°F})(140 \text{ ft}^2)(100°\text{F}) = 840 \text{ Btu/hr}$$
$$\text{Bulkhead 3: } (0.06 \text{ Btu/hr-ft}^2 \text{-°F})(140 \text{ ft}^2)(0°\text{F}) = 0 \text{ Btu/hr}$$
$$\text{Bulkhead 4: } (0.06 \text{ Btu/hr-ft}^2 \text{-°F})(140 \text{ ft}^2)(35°\text{F}) = 294 \text{ Btu/hr}$$
$$\text{Total} = 5,574 \text{ Btu/hr}$$

The normal box load is thus:

$$1,662 + 5,574 = 7,236 \text{ Btu/hr}$$

To estimate the pulldown load, the energy required to lower the product temperature down to the storage temperature in 2 days must be added to the normal load. Estimating the load using the factors from table 8-8:

$$Q_{prod} = \frac{(2,800 \text{ ft}^3)(36 \text{ lbm/ft}^3)(0.65)(0.4 \text{ Btu/lbm-°F})(15°\text{F})}{(48 \text{ hrs})} = 8,190 \text{ Btu/hr}$$

The pulldown load is thus:

$$7,236 + 8,190 = 15,426 \text{ Btu/hr}$$

COMMENTS:
The product load is the largest component and has a significant effect on the pulldown load estimate. If product is brought in warmer than esti-

mated it can have a significant effect on the load. The use of both condensing units or permitting a longer pull-down time can handle this situation.

## PROBLEMS (ENGLISH UNITS)

8.1E   The inside bulkhead of a dining room is constructed of 3/8 inch steel. Estimate the overall heat transfer coefficient.

8.2E   The bulkhead above adjoins a storeroom with a summer design temperature of 100°F. If the dining room design temperature is 78°F, and the bulkhead is 9 feet high by 20 feet long, calculate the heat transmission gain.

8.3E   The weather bulkhead of a stateroom is 9 feet high by 10 feet long and has 3 inches of fiberglass insulation. A 24 inch by 24 inch single pane windows is located 4 feet off the deck. There is a 5 foot overhang partially shading the bulkhead. Estimate the transmission cooling and heating loads.

8.4E   The wheelhouse on a tanker is 8 feet 6 inches by 40 feet by 20 feet. Estimate the sensible and latent cooling infiltration loads assuming one air change per hour. Estimate the sensible heating infiltration load assuming 6 air changes per hour.

8.5E   A lounge has a normal occupancy of 20 crewmembers. Six fluorescent fixtures with two 40w tubes each are installed. Estimate the total occupant and lighting loads.

8.6E   The master's office is 15 feet long by 12 feet wide by 9 feet high. One bulkhead 9 feet by 15 feet and the overhead are exposed to the weather. The bulkhead has two 2 feet by 3 feet windows. The design occupancy is three persons and there are four 80W fluorescent lighting fixtures installed. The heat transfer coefficients for both the bulkhead and the overhead are 0.17 Btu/hr-ft$^2$-°F (outside air to inside air) and 0.18 Btu/hr-ft$^2$-°F (outside surface to inside air). Estimate the heating and cooling loads for the office.

8.7E   The cooling loads for the house on a containership are estimated at 180,000 Btu/hr for the sensible load and 40,000 Btu/hr for the latent heat load. The supply airflow to the house is 10,000 CFM and the outside airflow is 2,500 CFM. Determine the cooling coil outlet temperature and the system capacity in tons.

8.8E   The chill box with a design temperature of 35°F for a ship's stores refrigeration system opens into the anteroom. The box has dimensions of 25 feet by 20 feet by 7 feet. All surfaces are exposed to external temperatures except for one 25 foot by 7 foot bulkhead that adjoins a freeze box operating at 0°F and a 20 foot by 7 foot bulkhead, which opens to the anteroom. The overall heat transfer coefficients are 0.06 Btu/hr-ft$^2$-°F for the bulkheads and overhead and 0.03 Btu/hr-ft$^2$-°F for the deck. Estimate the normal and pulldown loads.

# PROBLEMS (SI UNITS)

8.1S  The inside bulkhead of a dining room is constructed of 10 mm inch steel. Estimate the overall heat transfer coefficient.

8.2S  The bulkhead above adjoins a storeroom with a summer design temperature of 38°C. If the dining room design temperature is 25°C, and the bulkhead is 2.5 m high by 10.2 long, calculate the heat transmission gain.

8.3S  The weather bulkhead of a stateroom is 2.5 m high by 3 m long and has 75 mm of fiberglass insulation. A 60 cm by 60 cm single pane windows is located 1.25 m off the deck. There is a 1.25 m overhang partially shading the bulkhead. Estimate the transmission cooling and heating loads.

8.4S  The wheelhouse on a tanker is 2.5 m by 12 m by 6 m. Estimate the sensible and latent cooling infiltration loads assuming one air change per hour. Estimate the sensible heating infiltration load assuming 6 air changes per hour.

8.5S  A lounge has a normal occupancy of 20 crewmembers. Six fluorescent fixtures with two 40W tubes each are installed. Estimate the total occupant and lighting loads.

8.6S  The master's office is 4 m long by 3 m wide by 2.75 m high. One bulkhead 2.75 m by 4 m and the overhead are exposed to the weather. The bulkhead has two 60 cm by 90 cm windows. The design occupancy is three persons and there are four 80W fluorescent lighting fixtures installed. The heat transfer coefficients for the both the bulkhead and the overhead are 1.0 $W/m^2$-°C (outside air to inside air) and 1.05 $W/m^2$-°C (outside surface to inside air). Estimate the heating and cooling loads for the office.

8.7S  The cooling loads for the house on a containership are estimated at 50 kW for the sensible load and 12 kW for the latent heat load. The supply airflow to the house is 300 $m^3$/min and the outside airflow is 70 $m^3$/min. Determine the cooling coil outlet temperature and the system capacity in tons.

8.8S  The chill box with a design temperature of 2°C for a ship's stores refrigeration system opens into the anteroom. The box has dimensions of 8 m by 6 m by 2 m. All surfaces are exposed to external temperatures except for one 8 m by 2 m bulkhead that adjoins a freeze box operating at −18°C and a 6 m by 2 m bulkhead, which opens to the anteroom. The overall heat transfer coefficients are 0.34 $W/m^2$-°C for the bulkheads and overhead and 0.17 $W/m^2$-°C for the deck. Estimate the normal and pulldown loads.

CHAPTER 9

# HVAC Systems and Components

In order to maintain the desired temperature and humidity in the conditioned spaces, the HVAC system must add or remove thermal energy to or from the space. While some heating systems may use steam space heaters and some cooling systems may use refrigerants directly, in most larger systems the heat transfer is accomplished by air or water. Air systems in common use are (1) terminal reheat, (2) dual duct, and (3) variable air volume. Water systems in common use are (1) one pipe, (2) two pipe, and (3) four pipe. These systems are designed to serve areas with more than one conditioned space or zone and where independent control of space air conditions is required. Chapter 7 describes the use of the psychrometric chart to determine the properties of air-water vapor mixtures and to analyze HVAC processes. A single zone air system will be described first to illustrate the basic principles.

## SINGLE ZONE SYSTEM

Figure 9-1 shows a single zone air system with provisions for heating, cooling, humidification, dehumidification, and the introduction of outside ventilation air. Such a system might be used to serve a single large public space such as a dining room. The supply fan delivers conditioned air to the space. An exhaust fan is commonly installed to avoid excessive positive air pressure in the space. The dampers allow the control of outside ventilation and recirculation air quantities. Control of the ventilation and recirculation quantities based on the outside air temperature can result in significant reduction in the system energy requirements. When the outside air temperature is somewhat lower than the conditioned space, increasing the ventilation air to maximum will reduce the cooling coil load. At very low or

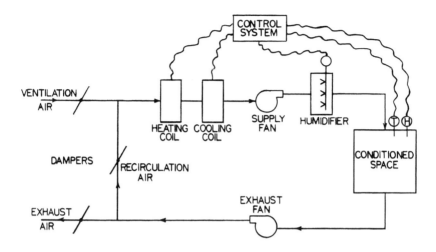

Fig. 9-1. Single zone system.

very high outside air temperatures, reducing the ventilation airflow to the minimum will result in energy reductions. Figure 9-2 is an example of a control curve, which can be programmed into the outside ventilation air control system to automatically achieve these energy savings.

During warm weather, the cooling coil dehumidifies the air in addition to the lowering air temperature. If the coil temperature is below the air dew point, water vapor will condense on the coil and air humidity will be lowered. During cold weather, the humidifier admits steam directly into the air stream, increasing humidity with little increase in dry-bulb temperature. The control system senses the space temperature and humidity and then controls the cooling and heating coils and the humidifier. In cold weather, heating and humidification will be required. In hot weather, cooling and dehumidification are needed. The space humidity during cooling can be controlled in two ways: (1) varying the cooling coil temperature, or (2) maintaining a constant low cooling coil temperature and then using the heating coil to reheat the air. The second method wastes energy and is normally only used on systems that require good humidity control or have high latent heat loads.

## MULTIPLE ZONE SYSTEMS

It is usually not economically feasible to provide a separate system for each zone. A zone is a room or group of rooms controlled by a single thermostat. The basic principles of temperature and humidity control outlined for the single zone system are expanded in the systems below to meet the requirements of multiple zone operation.

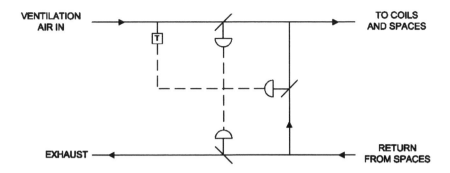

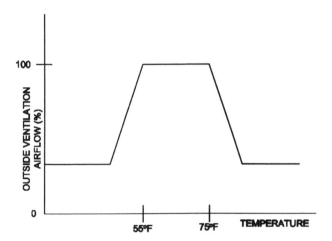

Fig. 9-2. Control of outside ventilation air.

## TERMINAL REHEAT SYSTEM

Figure 9-3 is a diagram of a simplified terminal reheat system. The supply fan delivers a fixed quantity of air, and the duct system distributes the air to the various conditioned spaces. During warm weather operation, the air leaving the cooling coil is maintained at a constant temperature, typically about 55°F (13°C). The thermostat in each zone controls the reheat coil associated with that zone to maintain the desired zone temperature. The heat source for the preheat and reheat coils may be hot water, steam, or electric power. The terminal reheat system provides good control of temperature and humidity over a wide range of loads, but is wasteful of energy since air is cooled, then heated. Increasing the cool air temperature until the lightest loaded reheat coil turns off can reduce this "thermal bucking."

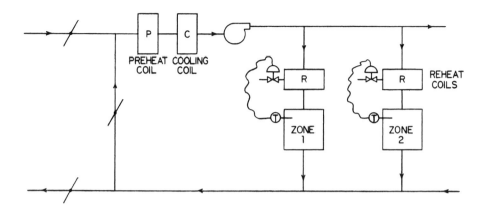

Fig. 9-3. Terminal reheat system.

The cooling system can be secured entirely when the outside air temperature drops below the design cold air duct temperature. The use of waste heat to operate the reheat coils will also reduce energy costs. During cold weather, the preheat and reheat coils supply the heating requirements. The preheat coil is designed to cut in at a temperature somewhat below the normal cooling coil temperature, thus preventing simultaneous operation of the preheater and cooling coils.

## DUAL DUCT SYSTEM

Figure 9-4 is a simplified diagram of a dual duct system. The supply fan delivers hot and cold air to the spaces through two parallel duct systems. Part of the supply airflows across the cooling coil and part across the heating coil. Each zone thermostat controls a mixing box, which proportions the warm air and cool air delivered to the zone to maintain the desired zone temperature. The total airflow to the zone remains constant. The dual duct system is responsive to load changes and can accommodate simultaneous heating in some areas and cooling in others. Since two supply ducts are required, the system is commonly designed as a high-velocity air system to reduce the duct size. However, this increases the fan head and therefore the power requirements. As with the terminal reheat system, the system permits simultaneous heating and cooling in different zones. During periods of low outside air temperature (below 55°F, 13°C), the cooling coil can be secured. During hot weather, the warm air duct temperature can be lowered or perhaps the heating coil secured. Maintaining warm duct temperatures higher than that required to maintain comfort in all zones is a

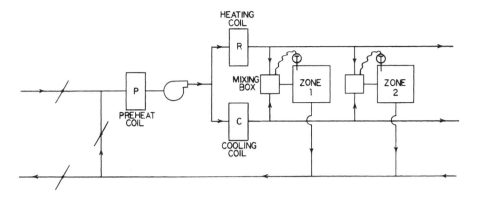

Fig. 9-4. Dual duct system.

waste of energy. Many marine systems are arranged with the cooling coil and a reheater in series. The cooling coil is installed after the supply fan, cooling the entire airflow. While less efficient due to the cooling then heating of the air for the hot air duct, this arrangement provides better dehumidification and reduces condensation problems on cold surfaces.

## VARIABLE AIR VOLUME SYSTEMS

The terminal reheat and dual duct systems described above waste energy, especially at light cooling or heating loads. Variable air volume (VAV) systems reduce this waste. While there are a number of different VAV systems, all use dampers in the supply duct to each zone to vary the airflow delivered to the zone. Figure 9-5 shows a simple VAV cooling system. The problem with this simple system is that, at low loads, the air supply is reduced to the point where poor air distribution and ventilation result. The solution to this problem is to combine the VAV technique with a terminal reheat or dual duct system.

In a VAV terminal reheat system, a damper is installed in series with the reheat coil. The zone temperature is controlled entirely by the damper when high cooling loads are high, varying the airflow to the zone as required. In low cooling load situations, once a minimum flow (perhaps 25 to 30 percent of maximum) is reached, the reheat coil is energized, and airflow remains constant at the minimum value and the reheat coil controls the zone temperature. Figure 9-6 illustrates how airflow varies with cooling load for this system. The VAV reheat system does incur some energy loss, but it is small compared to the constant volume terminal reheat system. It also overcomes the air distribution and ventilation problems of the simple VAV system.

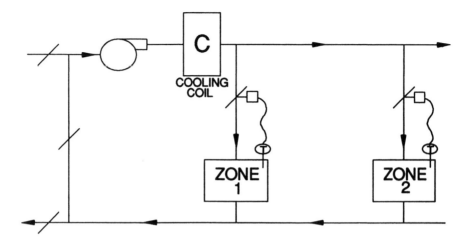

Fig. 9-5. Variable air volume system.

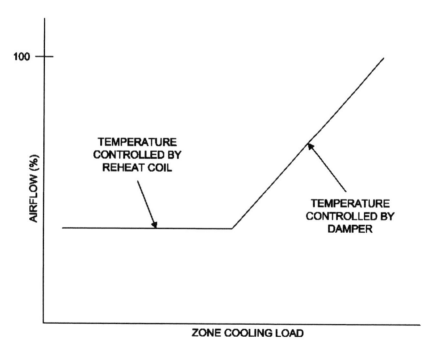

Fig. 9-6. Variation of airflow in VAV system.

In the VAV dual duct system, the mixing box characteristics are modified to reduce the cool or warm airflows before mixing the other stream. During cold weather, the warm air duct flow is modulating with no addition of cool air. During hot weather, the cool air duct flow is modulating with no addition of warm air. At moderate outside temperatures, warm and cool airflows are reduced, and air mixing of the reduced flows will occur. Figure 9-7 shows how the two airflows vary in this system and the reduced region of mixing. Like the VAV reheat system, there is still some energy waste, but it only occurs at low flows and is small compared to the constant volume dual duct system.

## WATER SYSTEMS

Water or hydronic systems accomplish heating and cooling through the distribution of hot and/or chilled water to the conditioned spaces. Water systems take up less space than air systems due to the higher density and specific heat of water. The required piping is much smaller than the ductwork required for the same capacity installation. While the initial cost of a water system may be less than an air system, the system lacks good humidity control and maintenance is higher. Hot water heating systems have many advantages over steam heating systems. Hot water provides better

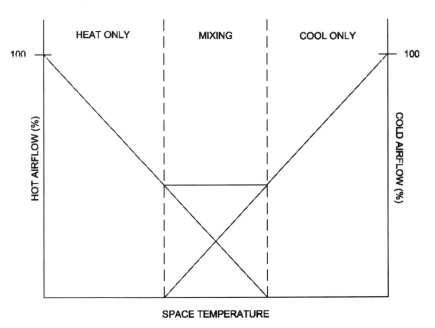

Fig. 9-7. Variation of airflow in VAV dual duct system.

control of small heating loads and eliminates the problems of condensate return, steam traps, water hammer, and corrosion in condensate return piping. Pressurized systems with closed expansion tanks commonly use water temperatures of 220°F to 240°F, while systems with open expansion tanks operate with water temperatures below 212°F.

A simple one-pipe hydronic system is shown in figure 9-8 while figure 9-9 shows a two-pipe system. In each system, hot water or chilled water is circulated to the conditioned spaces, which have fan coil units, convectors, or similar devices for exchange of heat with the air in the space. The one–pipe system reduces the amount of piping that must be installed and is suitable for large installations such as passenger ships. The two-pipe

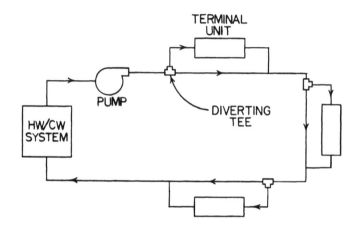

Fig. 9-8. One-pipe water system.

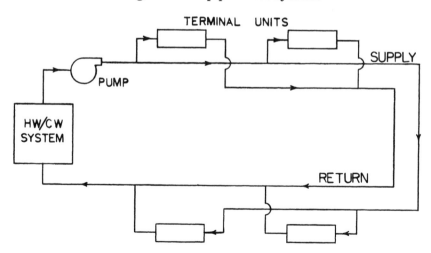

Fig. 9-9. Two-pipe water system.

system has the advantage that the water temperature at each terminal unit is the same. Two-pipe systems can be termed direct return or reversed return as shown in Figure 9-10. One advantage to a reversed return system is that the water path to and from each terminal unit is about equal. This avoids flow imbalances that can occur in a direct return system with long pipe runs. For systems with short pipe runs, a direct return system will be adequate.

The elimination of air from water systems is essential to avoid reductions in heat transfer, water circulation problems, pump cavitation, and noise. An air eliminator and float vent should be installed at the outlet of the hot water heater or chiller, and vents installed at the high points in the

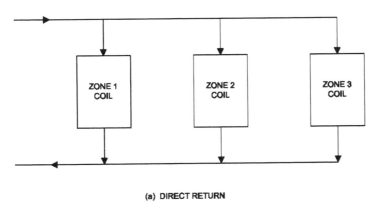

(a) DIRECT RETURN

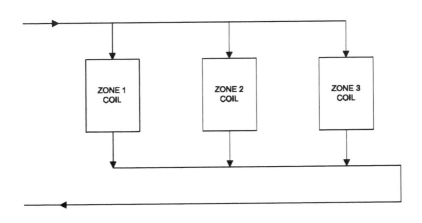

(b) REVERSED RETURN

Fig. 9-10. Direct return and reversed return water systems.

piping runs. Convectors should be down fed from above to aid in air removal back to the return line. A water velocity of at least 1 ft/sec will keep the air moving and minimize air pockets. Mains should be run as straight as possible to minimize the high points, which will require venting.

The disadvantage of the one-pipe and two-pipe systems is that heating and cooling cannot occur simultaneously in different zones. The four-pipe system shown in figure 9-11 overcomes that limitation. The terminal units are fitted with two coils, one for heating and one for cooling. The thermostat for each zone regulates the flow of hot and chilled water to the coils. Control must be sequenced so that flow is not admitted to both coils at the same time.

## UNITARY SYSTEMS

Factory assembled and packaged air-conditioning systems are available from the major air-conditioning manufacturers in sizes from about 3 to 10 tons. The units are available as a single package containing condenser, compressor, evaporator, fan, controls, and filters, or as a split unit with the condenser and compressor located separately. Both air-cooled and water-cooled systems are available. The units are low in cost due to mass production, but do not have the flexibility of a custom-designed system. On ships, they are sometimes found serving a single zone located remotely from the main conditioned spaces, such as a forward deckhouse, cargo control room, or engine room control room. Figure 9-12 shows a typical unitary system.

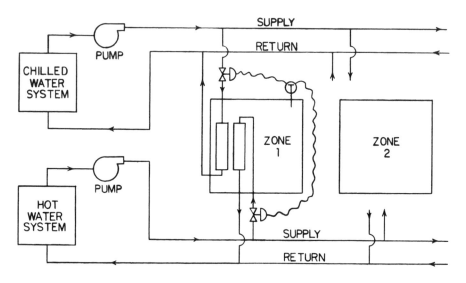

Fig. 9-11. Four-pipe water system.

Fig. 9-12. Typical unitary system.

## CARGO HOLD DEHUMIDIFICATION SYSTEMS

Cargo holds on dry cargo vessels are generally ventilated with mechanical supply and exhaust, using one air change in 20 to 30 minutes. This is done to reduce hold temperatures and condensation of moisture on hold surfaces and cargo. Introducing dry air into the holds and exhausting an equal quantity of humid air reduce condensation. One or more automatic dehumidification systems may be provided for reducing the moisture level in the holds.

Dehumidification systems use liquid or solid desiccants such as silica gel or lithium chloride. Figure 9-13 is a diagram of a liquid desiccant unit. Figure 9-14 shows a solid desiccant unit. A common feature of these systems is continuous regeneration of the water-laden desiccant by passing heated air through it. Moisture removed from the desiccant by the regeneration air is exhausted to the atmosphere. Since the moisture removal process involves the conversion of water vapor in the air to liquid in the desiccant, heat is released. A cooling coil is commonly installed to reduce the temperature of the dehumidified air.

The dew point temperature in any cargo hold is normally maintained 10°F (5.6°C) below the surface temperature of the cargo or ship structure. The cargo hold dew point temperature is usually measured in the exhaust trunk and is thus an average of the different hold levels. The ventilation and dehumidification system is designed to operate in one of four modes: ventilation without dry air, ventilation with dry air, recirculation without dry air, and recirculation with dry air. The mode of operation can be

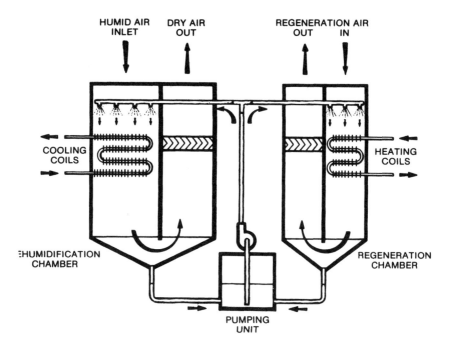

Fig. 9-13. Liquid desiccant dehumidifier.

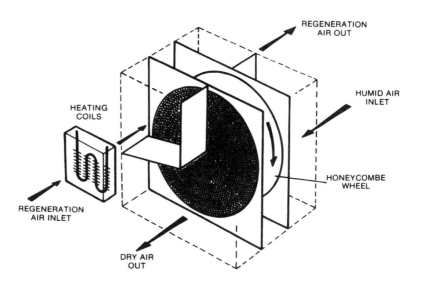

Fig. 9-14. Rotary Honeycombe dehumidifier.

selected from the wheelhouse by remote operation of pneumatically or electrically actuated control dampers.

## HVAC SYSTEM COMPONENTS

The following section describes the design and construction features of various components and equipment used in HVAC systems.

### Fans

Fans are used to distribute air through the HVAC equipment and ducts to the air-conditioned spaces. Fans used in HVAC systems may be classified as either axial flow or centrifugal. In an axial flow fan, the airflow is in the same direction as the fan shaft. In centrifugal fans, the air discharge is radial relative to the fan shaft.

Axial flow fans are termed propeller, tube-axial, or vane-axial depending on their construction. A propeller fan (figure 9-15) is merely a propeller-type wheel mounted on a supporting plate. A tube-axial fan consists of a vaned rotor mounted in a cylinder. The motor directly drives the rotor, with air drawn over the motor and discharging from the impeller end. The vane-axial fan (figure 9-16) is similar, but fixed guide vanes after the rotor convert the kinetic energy of the air into pressure and maintain axial flow, thus improving the efficiency of the fan. Propeller and tube-axial fans are limited in their ability to develop pressure, and thus cannot be used in duct systems. Vane-axial fans are commonly used in naval ducted systems due to their compact size.

Fig. 9-15. Propeller fan.

Fig. 9-16. Vane-axial fan.

Centrifugal fans are the commonly used type in merchant ship ducted air-conditioning systems. Centrifugal fans can be classified according to the shape of the impeller blades: forward-curved, radial, or backward-curved as shown in figure 9-17. In addition, high performance backward-curved blade fans are called airfoil blade fans due to the shape of the fan blades. Forward-curved blade fans are characterized by low initial cost, smaller size, lower efficiency, and an increasing power requirement with increasing airflow. Forward-curved blade fans are used primarily in small capacity applications such as fan-coil units. Backward-curved blade fans (especially airfoil types) are higher in initial cost, but have higher efficiency and thus lower operating costs, and have a nonoverloading head-capacity characteristic that eases matching of the motor to the fan. These characteristics result in backward-curved blade fans being selected for most HVAC applications. Figure 9-18 shows a typical centrifugal fan. Belt drives are commonly specified for centrifugal HVAC fans as they permit the use of less expensive high-speed motors, permit easy adjustment of fan speed by changing pulleys, and are quiet.

### CENTRIFUGAL FAN PERFORMANCE CHARACTERISTICS

The fan installed in the HVAC system must maintain the desired flow of air through the conditioned spaces while overcoming the fluid friction in the ducts and other components. The important fan performance parameters are capacity (ft$^3$/min or m$^3$/sec), static pressure head (inches or mm of water), efficiency (percent), and power (BHP or kW). Knowledge of fan performance is useful in fan selection, fan operation, and troubleshooting. Figure 9-19 shows the typical performance characteristics of a backward-curved blade centrifugal fan. Static pressure, efficiency, and brake horsepower are plotted as a function of flow rate. In general, the fan should be selected to operate near its maximum efficiency.

The fan static efficiency is defined as the power exchanged to the air divided by the power delivered to the fan by the motor.

$$\eta = \frac{Pair}{Pmotor}$$

The air horsepower can be calculated using the following equation

$$Pair = \frac{hs\,Q}{C}$$

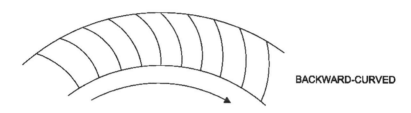

BACKWARD-CURVED

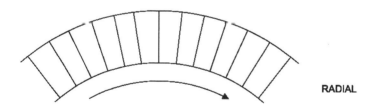

RADIAL

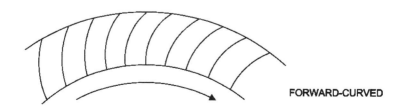

FORWARD-CURVED

Fig. 9-17. Centrifugal fan blades.

where

    $Pair$ = air power, in horsepower or kilowatts

      $hs$ = static pressure head, in inches of water or mm of water

       $Q$ – capacity, in $ft^3$/min or $m^3$/sec

       $C$ = 6,356 for English units and 102 for SI units

Fig. 9-18. Centrifugal fan. Courtesy Buffalo Forge Co.

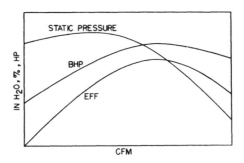

Fig. 9-19. Backward curved blade centrifugal fan
performance characteristics.

An equation for the motor power can be obtained by combining the above two relationships

$$Pmotor = \frac{hs\,Q}{C\,\eta}$$

Note that the total fan head is sometimes used instead of the static head in calculating the air horsepower. In that case the efficiency would be termed the total efficiency.

### FAN LAWS

There are several relationships that can be used to predict the behavior of fans at operating speeds other than those for which performance data are available. These relationships are:
The fan capacity varies directly with the operating speed

$$Q_2 = Q_1 \times (RPM_2/RPM_1)$$

The static head varies directly with the square of the operating speed

$$hs_2 = hs_1 \times (RPM_2/RPM_1)^2$$

The power varies with the cube of the operating speed

$$Pair_2 = Pair_1 \times (RPM_2/RPM_1)^3$$
$$Pmotor_2 = Pmotor_1 \times (RPM_2/RPM_1)^3$$

---

EXAMPLE PROBLEM 9.1. A fan is rated to deliver 8,000 CFM at a static head of 3.5 inches of water when operating at 900 RPM. The fan efficiency is 70 percent. The speed is to be changed to increase the capacity to 9,000 RPM. What is the RPM and BHP at the new operating point?

SOLUTION.
  SKETCH AND GIVEN DATA:

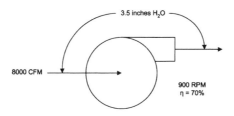

ASSUMPTIONS:

The efficiency remains constant as the operating speed is changed.

ANALYSIS:

Calculating the BHP at the rated conditions

$$Pmotor = \frac{hs\ Q}{6,356\ \eta} = \frac{(3.5\ \text{in}\ H_2O)(8,000\ \text{CFM})}{(6,356)(0.70)} = 6.29\ HP$$

$$RPM_2 = RPM_1 \times (Q_2/Q_1) = (900)(9,000/8,000) = 1,010\ RPM$$

$$BHP_2 = BHP_1 \times (RPM_2/RPM_1)^3 = (6.29)(1,010/900)^3 = 8.89\ HP$$

COMMENTS:

The large increase in horsepower may overload the fan motor. The suitablity of the motor, controller and wiring should be checked.

### CENTRIFUGAL FAN CAPACITY CONTROL

The capacity of a centrifugal fan may need to be varied to permit system balancing or for part-load operation. The capacity of a centrifugal fan can be varied in several ways: (1) varying the fan speed, (2) using outlet dampers, and (3) using inlet vanes. The simplest means of changing the speed of a belt-drive fan is to change the belt pulley diameters. This is obviously unsuitable for a system that requires frequent capacity changes but is a choice for a permanent capacity change. Many types of variable speed drives are available for variable capacity applications. A recent development is solid-state variable frequency controllers, which permit the use of standard induction motors. The fan laws can be used to predict fan operation at different operating points. Variable speed operation is the most efficient means of controlling fan capacity, but the high initial cost can offset the energy savings. With outlet damper control, the airflow is reduced by the increased pressure drop across the partially closed damper in the fan outlet duct. This represents a direct loss of energy. With inlet vane control, the partially closed vanes on the fan inlet cause the air to enter the fan impeller with "prewhirl," which reduces the fan head and thus the capacity. Inlet vane control is preferable to outlet damper control from an energy efficiency point of view, but is not as efficient as variable speed fan operation.

### Filters

Air filters are used in HVAC systems to remove dust and other particulate contaminants from the air. This is done to protect human health and comfort and maintain room cleanliness. Particles can range in size from as small as 0.1 micron to as large as 200 microns. Important performance criteria that must be considered in the selection of a filter for a particular application include the efficiency of particle removal, the pressure drop at design airflow, and the quantity of dust that can be removed before the filter needs to be cleaned or the element replaced. Filters used in marine HVAC systems are of either the dry media type or viscous media type.

Dry media filters are made of cellulose, glass fibers, specially treated paper, cotton batting, or synthetic materials. To increase surface area, the medium can be pleated in accordion form. The efficiency of dry media filter can be increased by using media with smaller densely distributed fibers. This however results in higher pressure drops and lower dust holding capacity. The dry media can be mounted in a panel or in a roll. Panel-type filters are common on smaller systems. Roll-type air filters (figure 9-20) with disposable dry media are popular for larger systems in marine service. When the media is clogged and requires changing, a new clean section is rolled into place by a motorized drive. The media roll is replaced with a new one when required. All filters on a particular ship are commonly selected with the same width to reduce the number of different replacement media that must be stocked. Filter heights of 6 feet can be accommodated.

Viscous-type air filters use a coarse media coated with a viscous substance in throwaway or cleanable element. The larger openings in the media permit higher air velocities and lower pressure drops, but the efficiency

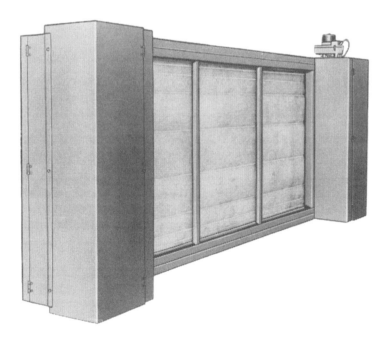

Fig. 9-20. Roll-type air filter. Courtesy The Trane Company.

is lower for removal of small particles. A common application of this type of filter is as a grease filter in galley ventilation systems and other locations where frequent replacement of disposable elements would be unacceptable. The filter element is typically fabricated of bronze or copper mesh mounted in a hot-dipped galvanized frame.

Air filters should be installed so that they are protected from the weather and are accessible for servicing by operating personnel. The length of time between filter servicing depends on many factors such as filter type, port conditions, and types of cargo handled. Filters should always be checked after dusty cargoes are handled. The pressure drop across the filter is the best means of determining the need for replacement or cleaning. A typical dry media filter will have a pressure drop of about 0.1 inches of water when clean and should be serviced when the resistance increases 2 to 3 times. Newer roll-type filters will automatically roll to a clean section when the pressure drop increases to the maximum value as sensed by a differential pressure switch.

### Heating Coils

Heating coils installed in the air ducts of marine HVAC systems may be steam, hot water, or electric resistance. Steam heating is generally cost-effective; however, it poses certain problems such as difficulty in controlling small heating capacities, condensate return, and water hammer. Hot water and electric resistance heating eliminate many of these problems. Medium temperature hot water (250° to 350°F, 121° to 177°C) is replacing auxiliary steam in many applications. Electric resistance heating is not energy efficient but may be used when adequate low-cost generating capacity is available. Electric resistance heating is particularly suited for electronics and other spaces where leakage from wet systems cannot be tolerated. Solid-state controls are available to provide excellent modulation of heat output.

Steam heating coils are usually of the header type (a header at each end of straight tubes). This avoids return bends, which may trap condensate, causing water hammer and possible freezing. If possible, the tubes should be installed vertically. Each coil should be installed with a stop valve followed by a strainer and control valve on the steam supply and a dirt pocket or strainer, trap, and a cut-out valve on the condensate outlet. At least two feet of bare pipe for cooling should be provided between the coil and the trap. Condensate lines should be level or pitched in the direction of flow and typically are connected to an atmospheric or contaminated drain tank.

Hot water heating coils are generally of the serpentine type. Header type coils have lower tube velocities, which reduce the pressure drop, but adversely affect the transfer of heat. Coils may be either bare or finned tube. Figure 9-21 shows a serpentine hot water heating coil. Air chambers

Fig. 9-21. Hot water heating coil. Courtesy The Trane Company.

and vents must be installed to eliminate air and noncondensable gases. Air trapped in the coil reduces heat transfer in the coil and causes cavitation and noise in the piping system.

The heating elements in electric resistance heating coils are usually of the tubular type with a Monel sheath. On finned elements, the fins are Monel or aluminum alloy cast integral with the sheathing.

### Cooling Coils

Either chilled water or evaporating refrigerant may be used in cooling coils installed in the ducts of HVAC systems. DX (dry expansion) is the name given to coils using evaporating refrigerant. Cooling coils are typically made of copper tubing with aluminum or copper fins arranged in a serpentine arrangement. Figure 9-22 shows a DX cooling coil while figure 9-23 shows a chilled water cooling coil. An even number of rows, usually 6 to 10, are used so that piping connections can be made to the same end of the coil. Bare tube coils are not common in cooling coils due to the small temperature difference. Fins increase the effective heat transfer area. A counterflow arrangement (figure 9-24) is commonly used for chilled water coils. In this way, the coldest water is cooling the coldest air resulting in increased heat transfer.

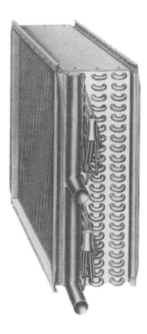

Fig. 9-22. DX cooling coil. Courtesy The Trane Company.

Fig. 9-23. Chilled water cooling coil. Courtesy The Trane Company.

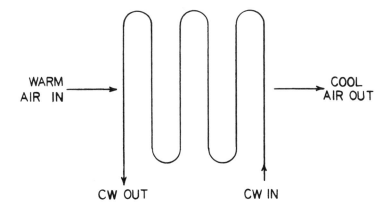

Fig. 9-24. Counterflow cooling coil arrangement.

### Radiators and Convectors

Radiators and convectors are units located directly in the heated space used to transfer the heat from circulating hot water or condensing steam to the room air. Radiators are not common on U.S. flag vessels. However, hot water radiators of embossed steel plate construction are used on many foreign flag ships. Convectors have a finned pipe heating element enclosed in a sheet metal cabinet. The elements are made of either copper or hot-dip galvanized steel. Room air enters through an opening in the bottom and leaves through an outlet grille at the top. Figure 9-25 shows some typical convectors. Convectors should be installed along weather-exposed bulkheads, under windows, and near the deck. This puts the heat where the heat loss is the greatest, and cold downdrafts are prevented. Elevating convectors off the deck decreases their capacity and stratification due to insufficient air circulation can occur.

### Unit Heaters

A unit heater consists of a finned heating coil and a fan mounted in a compact assembly. See figure 9-26. Forced circulation of air results in an increased rate of heat transfer. Unit heaters are most commonly used in steering gear rooms, shop areas, and machinery spaces of diesel ships. In large spaces where more than one unit is installed, the heaters should be directed to circulate air in the space.

### Fan-Coil Units

A fan-coil unit consists of a finned-tube coil, a small centrifugal fan, and a filter mounted in a cabinet (figure 9-27). Floor-mounted fan-coil units are

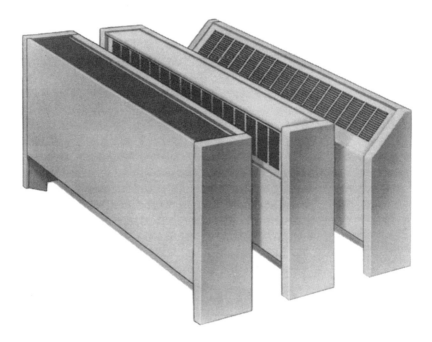

Fig. 9-25. Convectors. Courtesy The Trane Company.

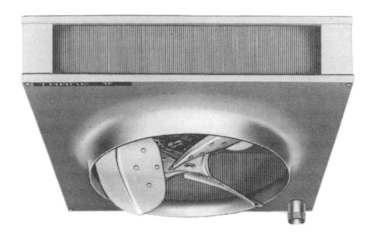

Fig. 9-26. Unit heater. Courtesy The Trane Company.

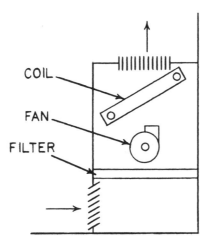

Fig. 9-27. Fan-coil unit.

externally similar in appearance to convectors. Unlike convectors, fan-coil units can be used for both cooling and heating and the fan improves the heat transfer. Heating and cooling can be accomplished by supplying either chilled or hot water to a single coil depending on the weather or by installing both a cooling and a heating coil. Fan-coil units may also be configured for mounting horizontally at ceiling levels.

### Ducts and Trunks

Conditioned air main ducts on ships are typically located in passageways with branches run to each space. The use of factory-fabricated sheet metal ducting and fittings can reduce the cost of the installation. The ducting system is hung from existing structure. Small horizontal ductwork is commonly supported by sheet metal straps, while heavier ducts require angle iron cradles suspended from rods. Occasionally built-in trunks using ship's structure to form all or part of the air passage are employed in ventilation systems. The size of trunks must be large enough to permit access to the interior for inspection and maintenance.

Ducts in cargo spaces are usually fabricated of steel plate to minimize the possibility of damage. Watertight ducts are constructed of the same material as the associated structure and must meet applicable codes. Ducts carrying heated or cooled air are covered with thermal insulation such as glass fiber or mineral wool, and covered with a vapor barrier to eliminate condensation. Insulation is available in rigid board or blanket form. Ducts can be lined with acoustic insulation to absorb sound. The acoustic insulation can also serve as the thermal insulation.

## HVAC Control Systems

The HVAC control system has the task of varying the amount of heating, cooling, dehumidification, and humidification to automatically maintain the conditioned spaces in a comfortable condition. In addition, the system must control the HVAC system in an efficient manner to minimize energy consumption.

Figure 9-28 shows a simple closed-loop control system for a hot-water heating coil. The temperature sensor senses the air temperature downstream of the coil. The controller compares the sensed temperature with the desired set point value that has been programmed into the controller. If the measured value doesn't agree with the desired value, the controller changes the signal to the control valve, opening or closing the valve and varying the amount of hot water admitted to the coil. The change in air temperature caused by the change in valve position will be sensed and additional adjustments will automatically be made as necessary.

While an HVAC control system may appear complex, it can be reduced to a series of simple system elements. The system elements are assembled from standard control devices: sensors, controllers, relays, and actuators. Pneumatic control devices have been the most common in HVAC systems because of their simplicity and low cost, though electronic control systems are now being installed on most new vessels. Pneumatic controls are typically powered by compressed air at 15 to 20 psig (103 to 138 kPa), although occasionally higher pressures are used to operate large valves and dampers. Self-actuated control valves are used in a few applications, primarily for controlling steam heating coils. Electric controls are occasionally used for simple applications where compressed air and/or suitable self-actuated devices are not available.

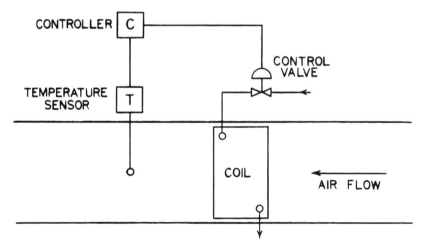

Fig. 9-28. Simple closed loop control system.

Electronic controllers have become increasingly popular for HVAC control systems as reliability and capability have increased and cost has decreased. Figure 9-29 shows a simple control system using a digital electronic controller to vary airflow to a space and maintain temperature. A thermocouple, thermistor, or resistance temperature detector (RTD) is used to sense the room temperature. The controller output is a 4–20 ma, 24-volt DC signal. Since the actuators used are still most commonly pneumatic, a current-to-pressure (I/P) transducer is necessary to convert the current output from the controller into a standard 3–15 psig pneumatic signal that the actuator is designed for. More complicated systems with multiple inputs and outputs can be controlled by a special microprocessor-based controller or a computer running process control software. Both inputs and outputs to such systems are commonly 4–20 ma current signals.

SENSORS

Sensors are used in HVAC control systems to measure a temperature, pressure, humidity, or other parameter in the system and convert it so that it can be used as an input for the controller. The sensors used in pneumatic systems convert changes in the measured parameter into a movement. This movement is used to produce a varying pneumatic pressure, usually over a range of 3 to 15 psig (20 to 100 kPa). For electronic systems, the sensor output responds to changes in an electrical property such as resistance, capacitance, voltage, or current.

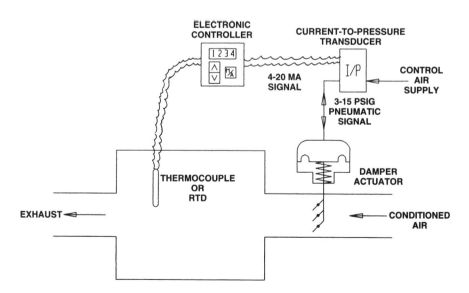

Fig. 9-29. HVAC control system with electronic controller.

The major types of temperature sensors include bimetallic, bellows, and bulb-and-capillary. The bimetallic sensor is most commonly used in room thermostats. It consists of two strips of dissimilar metals bonded together. Since the two metals expand at different rates, a temperature change causes the element to bend. The bimetallic element may be also shaped in a spiral to provide a rotary motion output. The bellows sensor is usually made of brass and filled with a vapor or gas. Temperature changes cause the bellows to expand and contract. Bulb-and-capillary elements are commonly used to sense temperatures in remote locations. The element consists of a bulb, a capillary tube, and a spring-loaded diaphragm head. The element is filled with a volatile liquid or gas. As the bulb temperature changes, the pressure exerted by the liquid or gas changes. The bulb pressure is transmitted to the diaphragm by the capillary, where the pressure change is translated into movement.

Thermocouples, resistance temperature detectors (RTDs), or thermistors are used for sensing temperature in control systems with electronic controllers. Thermocouples consist of a junction of two different metals, which produce a small voltage, generally only a few millivolts, when exposed to various temperatures. The resistance of a thermistor or RTD varies with temperature. The sensing element of an RTD is small coil of wire such as platinum, while thermistors are made of semiconductor materials. A signal conditioning circuit is necessary to linearize and convert the sensor signal into a form that can be used by the controller.

The major types of pressure sensors include diaphragms, bellows, and bourdon tubes. A diaphragm sensor is a flexible plate attached to a container. A spring balances the force caused by the pressure applied to the other side. A bellows sensor is a diaphragm connected to a container by a series of convolutions to permit an increased degree of movement. The bellows acts like a spring, or an external spring may be added to change the sensitivity. A bourdon tube sensor consists of a flattened tube bent in a circular shape. The open end is connected to the pressure source, and the closed end is free to move. An increase in pressure causes the tube to straighten out. Strain gauge pressure transducers are commonly used in systems with electronic controllers. The strain gauges change resistance as a diaphragm deflects as pressure is applied.

Humidity sensors use hygroscopic materials that change their size in response to humidity changes. One element is made of nylon bonded to a strip of metal and arranged into a coil. The nylon expands as it absorbs water, causing movement similarly to a bimetallic temperature sensor. Elements using such materials as hair, special cloth, or animal membrane that change length in response to humidity changes are also used. Electric sensors that use compounds hygroscopic materials such as lithium salt are used with electronic controllers. The material is bonded to a small circuit board in a grid arrangement and the resistance of the grid changes as water is absorbed or released.

## CONTROLLERS

The purpose of a controller is to convert the output of the temperature, pressure, or humidity sensor into a control signal (typically 3 to 15 psig for pneumatic controllers or 4-20 ma for electronic controllers) that can be used to operate valves or dampers in the HVAC system. Controllers can be termed either direct-acting or reverse-acting. A controller is direct acting when an increase in the input parameter (temperature, pressure, humidity) results in an increase in the controller output. An increase in the input to a reverse-acting controller results in a decrease in the controller output.

A pneumatic bleed-type controller is shown in figure 9-30. The right end of the flapper is moved by a sensor or air bellows and varies the amount of air exiting the nozzle. If the flapper is moved down, the nozzle exit is restricted, and the output pressure rises. If the flapper is moved up, the airflow exiting the nozzle will increase, and the output pressure drops. The arrangement of the linkage between the sensor or bellows and the flapper determines whether the controller is direct or reverse acting. For example, if an increase in the input causes the flapper to move down, the controller will be direct acting. When a bleed-type controller must deliver a large output airflow, it is commonly combined with a relay. The bleed-type controller acts as a pilot to vary the output of the relay.

Figure 9-31 is a simplified diagram of a pneumatic nonbleed controller. It demands supply air only when the outlet pressure is increasing. A downward sensor motion will cause an inward movement of the diaphragm, raising the left end of the lever and opening the supply valve. The incoming air will increase the chamber pressure, pushing up on the diaphragm to offset the input from the sensor (negative feedback). When equilibrium is attained, the supply valve closes, and the new chamber pressure becomes

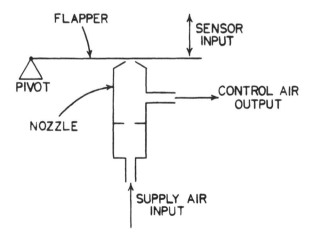

Fig. 9-30. Bleed-type controller.

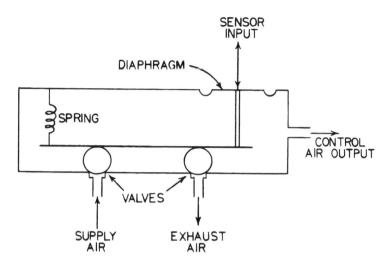

Fig. 9-31. Nonbleed controller.

the controller output pressure. A further downward sensor input will cause a rebalancing at some higher output pressure. An upward sensor movement will cause the bleed valve to open, and the controller will balance at a lower pressure. As in the bleed-type controller, the arrangement of the linkage between the sensor and the controller determines whether the controller is direct or reverse acting.

Electronic controllers used in HVAC control systems are usually microprocessor-based digital units. The built-in programming has a variety of control modes included from simple on-off control to three-mode PID (proportional-integral-derivative) control. Auto tune capability for the three-mode mode control is common. Electronic controllers are available for direct connection of various sensors or to accept standard 4-20 ma current signals as inputs. Outputs are typically 4-20 ma current signals.

### RELAYS

Relays are used in a control circuit to perform a function that is beyond the ability or capacity of the controller. Most pneumatic relays are variations of the nonbleed controller shown in figure 9-31. Some of the functions that the various relays can perform include (1) amplification (or reduction) of the input signal, (2) reversing of the input signal, (3) difference (or sum) of the input signals, (4) selection of the higher (or lower) of two input signals, (5) average of two input signals, (6) conversion to on-off operation, and (7) sequencing of two or more actuators. Figure 9-32 is a diagram of a reversing relay. It may be used to change the output from a direct-acting controller to a reverse-acting output. Figure 9-33 is a diagram of a difference relay. Its output is the difference between the two input signals. These two

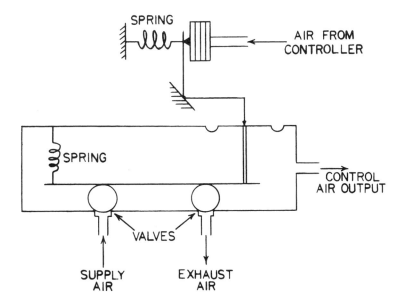

Fig. 9-32. Reversing relay.

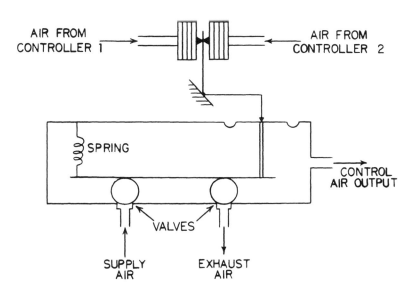

Fig. 9-33. Difference relay.

examples illustrate the modifications that can be made to a basic nonbleed controller so that it will perform various functions.

### CURRENT-TO-PRESSURE (I/P) TRANSDUCERS

These devices convert a standard 4–20 ma current signal into a standard 3–15 psig pneumatic signal. Such devices are most commonly used to interface an electronic controller to a pneumatic actuator. Figure 9-34 is a simplified schematic of an I/P transducer. It can be described as a reducing valve with the outlet pressure set point varied by a coil and magnet assembly driven by the 4–20 ma current signal. In most actual transducers, the coil and magnet assembly moves a small pilot valve, which then uses the supply air to position the main air valve. This reduces the force required from the coil and magnet assembly and improves transducer performance. Zero and span adjustments are included for calibration of the transducer.

### ACTUATORS

The function of the actuator is to convert the pneumatic signal from the control system into a movement to position a fluid valve or an air damper. A pneumatic actuator is basically a piston or diaphragm on which the control air pressure acts on one side, and spring pressure acts on the other. Figure 9-35 is a simplified schematic of a piston controller. Increasing control air pressure compresses the spring, moving the rod to the right until the spring force and the pressure times area force on the piston balance. The spring range is typically set to provide full movement over the 3 to 15

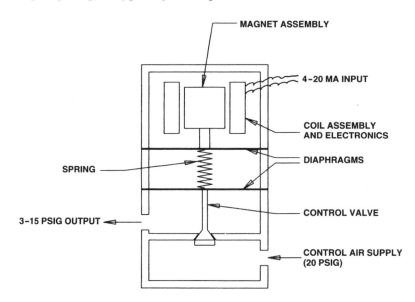

Fig. 9-34. Simplified current-to-pressure transducer.

psig (20 to 100 kPa) range of the input control air, but spring ranges for portions of the overall range are available to permit sequencing of multiple actuators. An I/P converter is necessary when pneumatic actuators are used with electronics controllers.

## POSITIONERS

Under certain conditions such as friction in the actuator or load, or large forces on the valve or damper connected, accurate positioning with a simple actuator may not be possible. The solution is to use a positioner. A positioner (or positive positioning relay) will accurately position the actuator in response to the input pressure rather than a balance of forces within the actuator. A positioner is essentially a modification of a pneumatic controller with feedback for actuator position. Use of a positioner ensures full supply air pressure is available to move the actuator even though the input control pressure may change only slightly.

## DAMPERS

Dampers are used to control the flow of air in HVAC systems. Most dampers are of the multi-leaf type. They can be described as a parallel-blade damper or an opposed-blade damper, and as normally open or normally closed. Figure 9-36 shows the operation of parallel-blade and opposed-blade dampers. Opposed-blade dampers are used in modulating applications while parallel-blade dampers are used in on-off applications. A normally open damper assumes an open position when no air pressure is applied to the actuator. A normally closed damper assumes a closed position when no air pressure is applied. The difference depends on the way the actuator is mounted, and on the way the linkage is connected to the damper.

In marine applications, outside air dampers should be made of stainless steel. Other dampers may be stainless or hot-dip galvanized steel. Damper construction should be integrally airtight without the use of nonmetallic seals.

## CONTROL VALVES

Control valves are used to control the flow of steam and water to heating and cooling coils. The size of a coil is normally based on some maximum design load, and the control valve must pass the required flow to meet that maximum load condition. However, most of the time the system is operating at part load, and the valve must satisfactorily control the fluid flow over the entire range of load conditions. Control valves are available with a number of flow-versus-lift characteristics to suit different applications. Figure 9-37 shows three common characteristics: quick opening, linear, and equal percentage. Standard globe valves typically have a quick-opening characteristic. Quick-opening valves do not modulate well at low loads because when the valve is only partially open, small valve movements

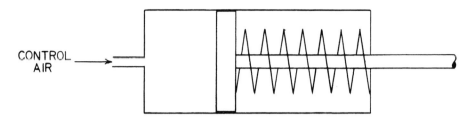

CONTROL AIR →

Fig. 9-35. Piston actuator.

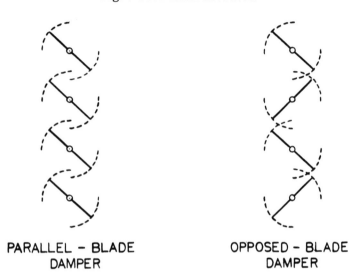

PARALLEL – BLADE DAMPER

OPPOSED – BLADE DAMPER

Fig. 9-36. Damper types.

cause large changes in flow. Valves with linear or equal-percentage characteristics are especially suitable for controlling heating and cooling coils. Valves with these characteristics are usually of the ported or cage-guided construction. See figure 9-38. By changing the shape of the ports in the plug, the flow-versus-lift characteristic of the valve may be changed.

Three-way valves are also available to control a heat exchanger by controlling the quantity of fluid bypassed around the unit. Three-way valves are available in two types: mixing and diverting. A mixing valve has two inlets and a single outlet. A diverting valve has one inlet and two outlets. Figure 9-39 shows three-way mixing and diverting valves installed to control a heat exchanger. Note that the mixing type is installed on the outlet while the diverting type is installed on the outlet.

Valves, like dampers, can be classified as normally open or normally closed. This characteristic depends on the way the actuator is connected to the valve body. A normally open valve will assume an open position with no

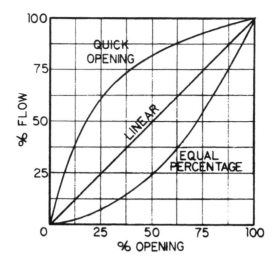

Fig. 9-37. Control valve characteristics.

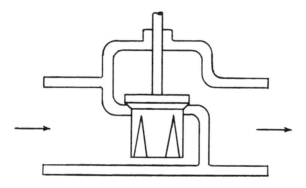

Fig. 9-38. Ported control valve.

air supply pressure to the actuator. A normally closed valve will assume a closed position with no air input.

### MATCHING CONTROLLER TO VALVES AND DAMPERS

It was noted above that controllers are either direct-acting or reverse-acting, and the dampers and control are either normally open or normally closed. It is necessary to select these characteristics to produce a system that will function properly. The valve or damper characteristic is typically selected first based on analyzing how the system will react should the control air pressure fail. Would it be preferable for the valve or damper to go fully open or fully closed? Which would cause the least system disruption?

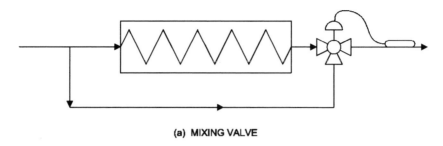

(a) MIXING VALVE

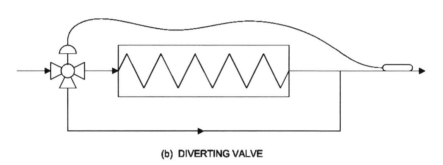

(b) DIVERTING VALVE

Fig. 9-39. Three-way valve installations.

Once the valve or damper characteristic is selected, the action of the controller is chosen to have the system respond correctly.

As an example, figure 9-40 shows a chilled water coil being used to cool air from a fan. A normally open valve has been selected so that cooling will continue if the control air pressure should be lost. In order to determine the proper controller action, assume that air temperature has risen. In order to lower the air temperature back to the desired value, the valve must open further to permit an increased cooling water flow. Since the valve has a fail open characteristic (that is will open fully on loss of air pressure), the controller air pressure must decrease to open the valve further. Note that the controller output must decrease when the temperature increases. This means the controller must be reverse-acting. Note that if a normally closed valve were selected, the controller action would need to be direct-acting.

### TERMINAL REHEAT CONTROL SYSTEM

In order to illustrate how the various control components may be connected into a complete system, a typical control system for a terminal

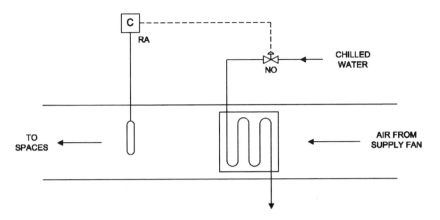

Fig. 9-40. Control of chilled water coil.

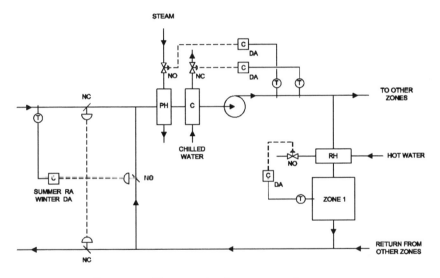

Fig. 9-41. Terminal reheat control system.

reheat air-conditioning installation will be described. Refer to figure 9-41. Thermostats in the conditioned supply duct control the steam preheater coil and chilled water cooling coil. The hot water reheater at the inlet to each conditioned space is controlled by the individual room thermostat. The preheater thermostat is set several degrees below the design chilled air (off-coil) temperature to prevent simultaneous operation of the pre-heater and cooling coil. The supply duct temperature thus remains rela-tively constant during both summer and winter operation, and the room temperature is maintained in all seasons by the reheat coil. The valve controlling the chilled water coil is normally closed, and the valves controlling the preheat and reheat coils are normally open. In the event of loss of control air pressure, the system will fail in a heating mode, thus preventing possible freezing damage. An analysis of each controller shows a direct-acting controller is needed in each application. The quantity of outside air is controlled by sensing the temperature of the outside air being mixed with the recirculation air. The three dampers must be controlled in sequence. The outside air and exhaust air dampers must open and close together, while the recirculation damper must operate opposite to the other two. This will increase recirculation when outside and exhaust airflows decrease, and vice versa. By the use of normally closed dampers in the exhaust and outside air ducts and a normally open damper in the recirculation duct, the three dampers operate in the required sequence in response to a single control air input pressure. Upon loss of control air pressure, the dampers will fail to reduce outside air to the minimum. As was discussed previously in this chapter, the quantity of outside air should be reduced during very hot or cold outside air conditions, and increased to the maximum when the outside air temperature is close to that being maintained in the conditioned spaces. This will reduce heating and cooling energy requirements. An analysis of the controller for the dampers shows that a direct-acting controller is needed in cold weather while a reverse-acting controller is need in hot weather. This can be accomplished in a number of ways such as using a reversing relay, by using separate controllers, by using a controller that can changed from direct to reverse-acting, or by using two thermostats with different actions. The changeover can be done manually or automatically by the control system.

The control systems for other types of air-conditioning systems will use many of the techniques described above, but obviously, must be adapted to suit the particular application. By breaking the system down into a series of simple elements, the operation of even the most complex control system can be understood. An understanding of the operation of the control system is essential to any attempt to adjust or troubleshoot the HVAC system.

## SYSTEM TESTING AND BALANCING

The complexity of modern HVAC systems requires careful adjustment to achieve design performance. Failure to properly adjust and balance the system can result in uncomfortable conditions in the conditioned spaces and a waste of expensive energy. The balancing process requires an understanding of the HVAC principles described in this chapter and in the references at the end of the chapter. Organized procedures must be followed to ensure a properly balanced system.

## Instrumentation

The success of system testing and balancing depends on accurate, calibrated instrumentation. These instruments are used to measure such system parameters as temperature, pressure, flow, RPM, humidity, and electrical power. Portable instruments can be used where permanently installed instruments are not available. An inexpensive pocket dial (bimetallic) thermometer or portable digital instrument is convenient for checking temperatures in air ducts. The low pressures in duct systems can be measured using a manometer or diaphragm gauge.

An important part of the system balancing process is measuring the flow rate of air in the ducts. The airflow in ducts is usually determined by measuring the air velocity using a Pitot tube or an anemometer. A Pitot tube is used in conjunction with a manometer or diaphragm gauge. It consists of two concentric tubes. The opening of the inner tube is pointed in the direction of flow, and the outer tube has holes perpendicular to the flow. The manometer or diaphragm gauge measures the difference between the total and static pressure, that is, the velocity head (pressure). This can be converted to velocity using the following equation:

$$V = 4,000 \, (Hv)^{0.5}$$

where

$V$ = air velocity, in ft/min
$Hv$ = velocity head, in inches of water

The flow rate can be calculated using the velocity and duct cross-sectional area. The average fluid velocity, determined by a number of measurements at a number of locations across the duct, should be used. The velocity measured by the Pitot tube or anemometer is converted to a flow rate using the continuity equation:

$$Q = A \, V$$

where

$Q$ = volumetric flow rate, in ft$^3$/min or m$^3$/sec
$A$ = cross-sectional area, in ft$^2$ or m$^2$
$V$ = air velocity, in ft/min or m/sec

The humidity in conditioned spaces is most commonly measured with a sling psychrometer. See figure 7-1. The instrument is spun rapidly, and the wet-bulb and dry-bulb temperatures are read. The humidity can then be read off the psychrometric chart.

It is often necessary to measure the operating RPM of rotating equipment such as fans, pumps, and compressors. If the end of the shaft is accessible, a handheld mechanical or electronic tachometer can be used. The tip of the instrument is pressed into the countersink, and the RPM is read directly. A stroboscope or photoelectric tachometer can be used where contact with the rotating shaft is difficult. A stroboscope consists of a flashing light with an adjustable frequency. The light is directed at the rotating parts and the frequency of the instrument adjusted until the equipment appears to stand still. A photoelectric tachometer measures the frequency of light reflected off the rotating shaft or coupling.

The measurement of voltage, current, and electric power supplied to motors is commonly required. A digital multimeter is very useful for checking voltages, currents, and resistances in electrical circuits. A clamp-on ammeter or wattmeter is convenient for measuring the power delivered to motors. A U-shaped jaw is opened and clipped around a single wire of the power circuit and the magnetic field created by the current flow is measured.

### Balancing an Air System
Listed below are the steps that can be followed for balancing an air system:

1. Obtain a duct system drawing and list all design velocities and flow rates. If a system drawing is not available, prepare a one-line diagram. Show the location of all balancing dampers. If design velocities or flow rates are not available, table 9-1, which lists typical design velocities in HVAC systems, can be used for estimating purposes.
2. Obtain design data for the system and all major components, that is, fans, filters, coils, dampers, mixing boxes, etc.
3. Prepare data sheets.
4. Decide on required instrumentation and on measurement locations.
5. Check the operation of all system components and controls. Check all damper positions.
6. Start the fans. Measure fan speeds and adjust RPM to design values.
7. Measure fan capacities (CFM) using a Pitot traverse of the main duct or an anemometer reading across the coils. If flow is not within 10 percent of design, check for possible problems such as closed dampers, equipment malfunction, etc. If the system is operating properly, adjust the fan speeds to obtain the proper CFM.
8. Measure the flow in the main supply and return ducts and adjust to the design value (±10 percent) with dampers.
9. Measure and adjust the flow of each outlet terminal. Work either from the farthest outlet towards the fan or from the fan outwards. Use effective outlet areas when calculating flow rates. Repeat the cycle at least once, since later adjustments will affect earlier measured flows.
10. Record all data including flows, temperatures (including WB and DB temperatures at coil inlet and outlet), and pressures. Record all performance data for all operating equipment.

## TABLE 9-1
## Typical Velocities in HVAC Systems

| Location | Velocity |
|---|---|
| Main ducts, living spaces | 800–1,500 FPM |
| Main ducts, other spaces | 1,500–2,500 FPM |
| Branch ducts | 800–1,500 FPM |
| Coils | 500–700 FPM |
| Filters | 250–350 FPM |

## Balancing a Water System

Listed below are the steps that can be followed for balancing a water system:

1. Obtain (or prepare) a piping system drawing and record design flows, temperatures, and pressures.
2. Obtain design data for the system and all major components, that is, pumps, coils, chillers, hot water heaters, and terminal units.
3. Prepare data sheets.
4. Decide on required instrumentation and on measurement locations.
5. Check operation of all pumps, valves, and controls. Check the position of all valves.
6. Start the circulating pump. Check the flow with a flowmeter or by recording the suction and discharge pressures and referring to the design head-capacity curve. Adjust flow with discharge valve to about 110 percent of design.
7. Do not balance the branches if automatic control valves are installed to vary the flow through the system coils and terminal units. If automatic control valves are not fitted, the flows in the various branches must be measured and adjusted to ±10 percent of design. Measurement of the water temperatures in and out of the coils and terminal units can be used as an additional check.
8. Measure and record all operating data including performance of all major equipment.

# PROBLEMS (ENGLISH UNITS)

9.1E  A fan is delivering 5,000 CFM at a static head of 2.5 inches of water is operating at 1,150 RPM. The electrical power into the motor is 2.5 kW. If the motor efficiency is 88 percent, what is the fan's static efficiency?

9.2E  The operating speed of the fan in the problem above is changed to 875 RPM. What is the new fan capacity and static head? How much power must be supplied to the motor?

9.3E  A stateroom served by a terminal reheat air conditioning system is to be maintained at 78°F. The airflow to the stateroom is 500 CFM and the air temperature exiting the main cooling coil is 60°F. If the room sensible heat load is 4,000 Btu/hr (a) at what temperature must air be supplied to the stateroom, and (b) what is the heat load on the reheat coil in Btu/hr.

9.4E  A dining room is being maintained at 76°F by a constant volume dual duct air-conditioning system. The sensible heat load is 18,000 Btu/hr and the design airflow is 1,750 CFM. The cold duct temperature is 60°F and the hot duct temperature is 85°F. Determine (a) the temperature of the air leaving the mixing box and (b) the flow rates of the hot and cold air being mixed together, in CFM.

# PROBLEMS (SI UNITS)

9.1S  A fan is delivering 2.5 $m^3$/sec at a static head of 60 mm of water is operating at 1,150 RPM. The electrical power into the motor is 2.5 kW. If the motor efficiency is 88 percent, what is the fan's static efficiency?

9.2S  The operating speed of the fan in the problem above is changed to 875 RPM. What is the new fan capacity and static head? How much power must be supplied to the motor?

9.3S  A stateroom served by a terminal reheat air-conditioning system is to be maintained at 25°C. The airflow to the stateroom is 15 $m^3$/min and the air temperature exiting the main cooling coil is 15°C. If the room sensible heat load is 1.25 kW (a) at what temperature must air be supplied to the stateroom and (b) what is the heat load on the reheat coil in kW.

9.4S  A dining room is being maintained at 24°C by a constant volume dual duct air-conditioning system. The sensible heat load is 5 kW and the design airflow is 50 $m^3$/min. The cold duct temperature is 15°C and the hot duct temperature is 30°C. Determine (a) the temperature of the air leaving the mixing box and (b) the flow rates of the hot and cold air being mixed together, in $m^3$/min.

## CHAPTER 10

# Absorption Systems, Multi-Pressure Systems, and Low-Temperature Systems

While the vapor compression system with a single stage reciprocating or rotary compressor is found in just about all marine refrigeration and air-conditioning applications, there are applications that require, or are better suited, to other types of systems. This chapter discusses some of those, including absorption systems, multi-pressure systems, and low-temperature systems.

## ABSORPTION SYSTEMS

The energy input to operate a vapor compression refrigeration system is the power it takes to run the compressor. Since most compressors are driven by electric motors, this energy comes from an electric generation plant that is turning the heat released by the combustion of fuel into electrical power. This process involves significant losses, with 50 percent or less of the energy supplied to the electric generation system being converted to electrical energy. The majority of the energy is lost in the exhaust to the atmosphere or rejected to the cooling or lubrication systems.

An alternative to this approach is the absorption refrigeration system in which heat rather than mechanical power is used to operate the system. This type of system uses a transport medium that will absorb the system refrigerant under certain conditions and release it under others. The two most common types of absorption systems are the ammonia-water system and the water-lithium bromide system. In the ammonia-water system, the refrigerant is ammonia and water is the transport medium. Ammonia has been used as a refrigerant for many years. It has a high latent heat but is slightly toxic and is not compatible with copper or copper alloys. Operating pressures are similar to R-12 and R-22. In the water-lithium bromide system, water is the refrigerant and lithium bromide, a hygroscopic salt, is the transport medium. Since water will freeze at 32°F, a water-lithium bromide system is limited to applications such as air-conditioning, which operate above the freezing point while ammonia-water systems can operate at temperatures well below the freezing point. A quick review of the steam tables will reveal that system operating pressures are very low with the water-lithium bromide system. For example, a 40°F evaporator temperature requires a pressure of 0.122 psia, a vacuum greater than 29.5 inches Hg.

The basic principles involved in an absorption refrigeration system can be illustrated by reference to figure 10-1 that shows a schematic diagram for a simplified ammonia-water system. The condenser, expansion valve, and evaporator function exactly as in a vapor-compression system. The absorber, generator/rectifier, regenerator, throttling valve, and circulating

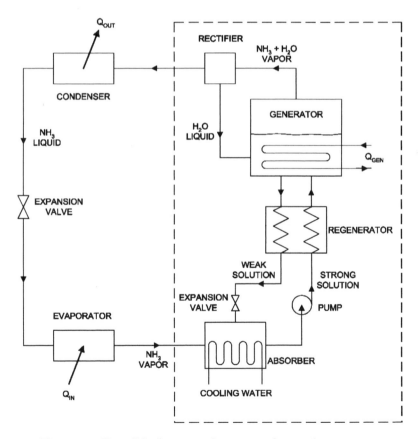

Fig. 10-1. Simplified ammonia-water absorption system.

pump basically replace the compressor in the vapor-compression system. An understanding of how these components accept low temperature and pressure vapor from the evaporator and deliver high temperature and pressure vapor to the condenser is essential to understanding how the absorption system operates.

Ammonia vapor returning from the evaporator enters the absorber where it reacts with the water, forming a liquid solution. This reaction is exothermic, so the heat released must be removed to maintain the absorber temperature as low as possible and maximize the amount of ammonia vapor absorbed. The ammonia rich solution is pumped to the generator where heat is added. This heat is the primary energy input to operate the system, as it is far larger than the power to run the pump. As the solution is heated in the generator, ammonia vapor is released, passes through a rectifier, which separates any water and returns it to the generator. The high-pressure ammonia vapor continues on to the condenser, while the hot solution, now low in ammonia, is returned to the generator through a throttling valve to begin the process again. A regenerative heat exchanger is included to improve the cycle efficiency by preheating the cool solution being pumped to the generator with the hot solution returning to the absorber. Note how the components within the dashed box function like a compressor, receiving low-pressure ammonia vapor from the evaporator and delivering high-pressure ammonia vapor to the condenser.

The performance of an absorption refrigeration system must be defined somewhat differently than it is for a vapor compression system. In chapter 3 you defined the COP of a refrigeration system as the desired effect (the cooling in the evaporator) divided by the energy input to operate the system (the compressor power). In the absorption system, the energy input to operate the system is the heat supplied to the generator. Thus

$$COP_{RH} = \frac{Q_{EVAP}}{Q_{GEN}}$$

Note that the pump power was not included in the energy input because it is small compared to the heat supplied to the generator.

The maximum possible COP for any heat-driven refrigeration system like the absorption system can be derived by considering a system consisting of a reversed Carnot cycle being driven by a Carnot engine as shown in figure 10-2. The reversed Carnot cycle, which was discussed in Chapter 2, does the cooling. The heat is supplied to the Carnot engine, which produces the power to operate the reversed Carnot cycle. Since the Carnot cycle, whether operated as an engine or a refrigeration system, is reversible, the system shown in figure 10-2 represents the ideal heat-driven refrigeration system. The COP of a reversed Carnot cycle operating as a refrigeration system is

$$COP_R = \frac{Q_L}{W} = \frac{T_L}{T_H - T_L}$$

The thermal efficiency of a Carnot cycle operating as an engine is

$$\eta_{TH} = \frac{W}{Q_H} = \frac{T_H - T_L}{T_H}$$

The COP of a heat-driven refrigeration system is the cooling effect divided by the heat supplied. Using the relationships above for the COP and thermal efficiency of the Carnot cycles and noting from figure 10-2 that for each the heat is rejected at the ambient temperature $(T_A)$.

$$COP_{RH} = \frac{Q_L}{Q_H} = COP_R \, \eta_{TH} = \frac{T_L}{(T_A - T_L)} \frac{(T_H - T_A)}{T_H} \qquad (10.2)$$

Thus for an ideal heat-driven refrigeration system, the COP will vary with the temperature at which the heat is removed from the cooled space, the temperature at which the heat is supplied to the system, and the ambient temperature. An examination of equation 10.2 shows that the COP will increase as the heat supplied temperature increases, the cooled space temperature increases, and as the ambient temperature decreases.

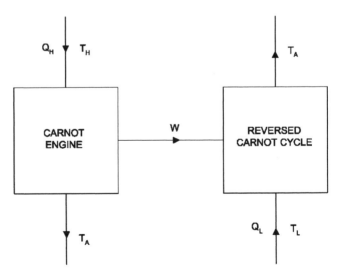

Fig. 10-2. Ideal heat-driven refrigeration system.

EXAMPLE PROBLEM 10.1. An absorption refrigeration system is to maintain a cooled space at 0°C. Heat is to be supplied to the system at 100°C and the ambient temperature is 25°C. Calculate the maximum COP for this system.

SOLUTION.
SKETCH AND GIVEN DATA:

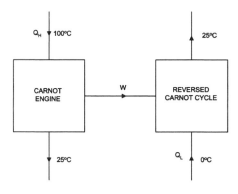

ASSUMPTIONS:
A heat-driven refrigeration system based on a Carnot engine driving a reversed Carnot cycle will have the maximum COP.

ANALYSIS:
Converting all temperature to Kelvin since absolute temperatures must be used.

$$100°C = 373°K \qquad 25°C = 298°K \qquad 0°C = 273°K$$

The maximum COP for a heat-driven refrigeration system can be calculated using equation 10.2.

$$COP_{RH} = \frac{T_L}{(T_A - T_L)} \frac{(T_H - T_A)}{T_H}$$

$$COP_{RH} = \frac{(273)(373 - 298)}{(298 - 273)(373)} = 2.19$$

COMMENTS:
The COP for an absorption system will be lower than the value calculated for the ideal system.

For typical temperatures, the COP for an ideal heat-driven refrigeration system will be about 2.0, while the COP for an actual absorption system will commonly be less than 1.0. It is important not to directly compare the COP for a heat-driven refrigeration system with that for a power-driven system because they are defined differently. However, even after adjusting for the efficiency of the process necessary to produce the power to operate the system, the power-driven system will still be more efficient. Absorption systems are also larger, more complex, and more expensive than vapor-compression systems of similar size. Absorption systems become attractive only when a source of free or inexpensive heat energy is available to operate the system. This could be waste heat from another process or solar energy. These disadvantages limit the possible marine applications of absorptions systems.

### Multi-Stage Compression

When very low evaporator temperatures are required, the compressor suction pressure decreases while the discharge pressure remains the same. As was noted in chapter 4, this increase in the compressor pressure ratio has a negative impact on reciprocating compressor performance. Due to the re-expansion of the gas trapped in the clearance volume, the volumetric efficiency decreases as the pressure ratio increases. Power requirements also increase and high discharge temperatures can cause lubrication problems. Splitting a 25:1 pressure ratio into two 5:1 steps can dramatically improve the overall volumetric efficiency. In general, maximum performance will occur when the pressure ratio of the two stages are equal. Referring to figure 10-3, the pressure ratio of the two stages are

$$PR_1 = \frac{p_i}{p_s} \qquad PR_2 = \frac{p_d}{p_i}$$

Setting the pressure ratios equal to one another and solving for the intermediate pressure.

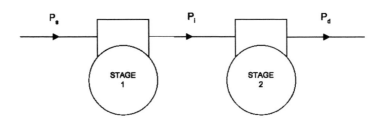

Fig. 10-3. Multi-stage compression.

$$\frac{p_i}{p_s} = \frac{p_d}{p_i}$$

$$(p_i)^2 = (p_d)(p_s)$$

$$p_i = (p_d p_s)^{0.5}$$

Multiple compression stages also permit the cooling of the gas between stages. This is referred to as intercooling. Intercooling has desirable effects including reducing the work of compression in the second stage and lowering the final discharge temperature. In air compressors, the intercooling can be done using a water-cooled or air-cooled heat exchanger, but in refrigeration compressors, the low temperatures of the gas at the intermediate pressure usually prevent that. A solution is to use liquid refrigerant to do the intercooling as shown in figure 10-4. With this technique, the gas from the first compressor stage is cooled by liquid refrigerant in an open or closed-type intercooler, or by mixing with a wet vapor from a liquid subcooler, to at or near the saturation temperature. One disadvantage of this technique is that the mass flow through the second stage is increased, resulting in greater power requirements for the second stage compressor. A second technique is to use an expansion flash chamber as shown in figure 10-5. With a flash chamber, the liquid is expanded in two steps from the condenser to the evaporator. The liquid that flashes to vapor in the first expansion is mixed with the gas entering the second compression stage. This reduces the system work because the flash gas does not need to be compressed in the first compressor stage. The mixing of the cool flash gas also reduces the second stage discharge temperature.

---

EXAMPLE PROBLEM 10.2. A reciprocating compressor is to be used in a R-134a refrigeration with an evaporator temperature of –40°F and a condensing temperature of 110°F. If a two-stage compressor is selected, determine the intermediate pressure that will result in equal pressure ratios for each stage. If the clearance volume is 4 percent of the displacement volume, estimate the clearance volumetric efficiency for the two-stage compressor and for a one-stage compressor.

SOLUTION.

SKETCH AND GIVEN DATA:

ASSUMPTIONS:

1. The compressor operates under steady-state conditions.

2. The refrigerant gas behaves like an ideal gas.

ANALYSIS:

Referring to the R-134a saturation tables, determine the evaporator and condenser pressures.

> At $-40°F$ the pressure is 7.4 psia.
>
> At $110°F$ the pressure is 161.1 psia.

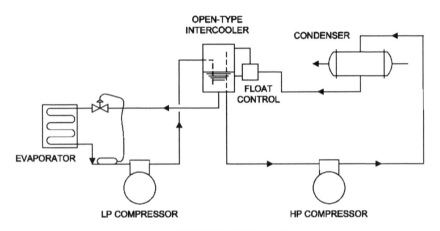

(a) OPEN-TYPE INTERCOOLER

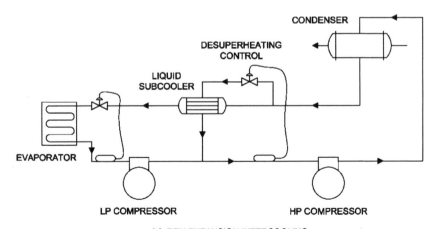

(b) DRY EXPANSION INTERCOOLING

Fig. 10-4. Liquid refrigerant intercooling.

Using equation 10.3 to determine the intermediate pressure.

$$p_i = (p_d \ p_s)^{0.5} = ((161.1)(7.4))^{0.5} = 34.5 \text{ psia}$$

The clearance volumetric efficiencies can be calculated using equation 4.3 from chapter 4.

$$\eta_{cv} = \left(1 - \left(V_{cl}/V_{dpl}\right)(P_{dis}/P_{suc} - 1)\right) \times 100$$

For the 2-stage compressor, noting that the pressure ratio is the same for each stage.

$$\eta_{cv} = \left(1 - (0.4)(161.1/34.5) - 1\right)(100) = 85.3\%$$

For the single stage compressor.

$$\eta_{cv} = \left(1 - (0.4)(161.1/7.4) - 1\right)(100) = 16.9\%$$

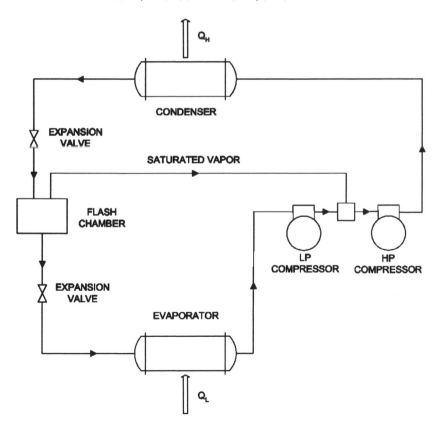

Fig. 10-5. Expansion flash chamber intercooling.

COMMENTS:
1. The high-pressure ratio results in a very low volumetric efficiency for the single-stage compressor. A two-stage compressor is a much better selection in this application.
2. With a larger clearance volume or when actual losses are considered, the volumetric efficiency of the single-stage compressor may drop to zero.

## CASCADE SYSTEMS

An alternative to multi-stage compression is the cascade system. A cascade system is essentially a series of interconnected vapor-compression systems. Figure 10-6 shows a two-stage cascade system. Note that the evaporator of the second stage is used as the condenser of the first stage. Heat removed by the first-stage system evaporator is rejected to the second-stage system.

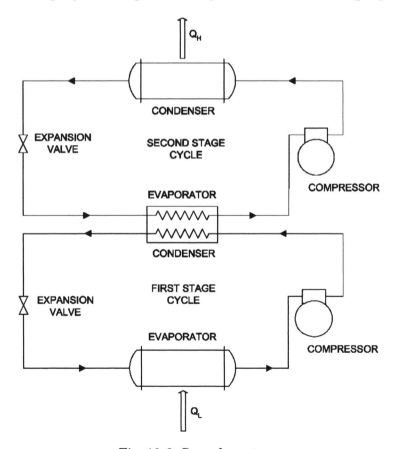

Fig. 10-6. Cascade system.

The second-stage system then rejects the heat to the cooling water in the second-stage condenser. A cascade system permits the selection of different refrigerants for each system. In order to achieve very low evaporator temperatures, a very high-pressure refrigerant is required. However, these refrigerants will have very high condenser pressures when condensed with air or water at common ambient temperatures. The use of a refrigerant such as R-22 or R-134a in a very low temperature system would result in very low evaporator pressures and large compressor displacement due to low refrigerant density. Single refrigerant systems, even when employing multi-stage compression, are generally limited to evaporator temperatures of about −100°F. At temperatures below that, the cascade system is a logical choice.

Another advantage of a cascade system is that the refrigerants in each cycle are separated. This simplifies oil return, which can be a problem in multi-stage compression systems that employ separate high-pressure and low-pressure compressors. A disadvantage of the cascade system is that the temperature difference in the evaporator/condenser connecting the systems reduces the thermal efficiency of the overall system. Cascade systems are also complex with high maintenance costs.

## LIQUEFACTION SYSTEMS

The liquefaction of gases is an important industrial process. Liquefied petroleum gas (LPG) and liquefied natural gas (LNG) are important marine cargoes, requiring special vessels equipped to handle the unique products. Current LPG and LNG carriers usually do not have liquefaction systems onboard. The cargo is liquefied ashore and loaded as liquid into insulated tanks. LNG is stored at a temperature of −259°F (−162°C), maintaining the pressure at atmospheric. The liquid vaporized due to heat transfer during the voyage (termed "boiloff") is used as fuel in the ship's boilers.

The liquefaction of gases requires the achievement of cryogenic temperatures, loosely defined as temperatures below about −150°F or −100°C. A variety of processes are available for liquefying gases. The cascade system described above is used in many large-scale LNG production facilities. Other processes available include the Hampson-Linde system, the Claude system, the closed Brayton cycle, and the auto-refrigerated cascade (ARC) cycle.

The Joule-Thomson effect is used in a number of gas liquefaction processes. At normal ambient temperatures and pressures, gases are highly superheated and behave almost like ideal gases. If an ideal gas is throttled from a high pressure to a low pressure, the temperature will theoretically remain constant, because no energy is being added or removed during the expansion. Real gases, however, will experience a change in temperature as the pressure is reduced by throttling. In some cases the temperature will drop and in others the temperature will increase. The change in temperature for a drop in pressure at constant enthalpy is termed the Joule-Thomson coefficient ($\mu$). It can be defined as a partial derivative as follows:

$$\mu = (\delta T/\delta p)_h$$

Note that if the Joule-Thomson coefficient is positive, the temperature will decrease as the gas is throttled, while if the coefficient is negative, the temperature will increase. A value of zero indicates the temperature will remain constant. The value (and sign) of the Joule-Thomson coefficient for a particular gas will vary depending on the pressure and temperature. Each gas has an inversion point at which the coefficient is zero. Above this point, the temperature will increase as the pressure drops ($\mu$ is negative), while below that point the temperature will decrease ($\mu$ is positive). The Joule-Thomson coefficient is positive for most gases at normal temperatures and pressures. Exceptions are helium, hydrogen, and neon that have very low inversion temperatures.

In order for a gas to be cooled and liquefied by throttling, it is necessary to begin the expansion at point where the Joule-Thomson coefficient is positive. A large pressure drop and, therefore, high starting pressure is necessary to achieve significant temperature reduction. For liquefaction to occur, it is necessary to cool the gas prior to throttling to have the throttling process begin at a point where the gas will expand below the saturation line. Referring to figure 10-7, note that liquefaction will not result from process A, but will for process B. Figure 10-8 shows a schematic for a simplified process based on use of the Joule-Thomson effect for gas liquefaction. Gas is compressed and then cooled, first in an aftercooler to near ambient temperature, and then in an efficient counterflow heat exchanger cooled by the cold gas returning from the separation chamber. The now high pressure and very cold gas is throttled into the saturated mixture region as shown on the T-s diagram for the process. Liquefied gas is removed in the separation chamber and the gas that did not liquefy is returned to the compressor to repeat the process.

Instead of using the boiloff from the cargo tanks as fuel in the ship's boilers, a reliquefaction system can be installed on the vessel to recondense the vapor and return the liquid to the tanks. A nitrogen expander cycle as shown in figure 10-9 is commonly recommended for systems of this size. Nitrogen is compressed and cooled several times, and the high pressure nitrogen is expanded in the turbine section of the turbo-compressor, resulting in a very low temperature gas. The cold nitrogen gas leaving the turbine is then used to cool and condense the methane vapor. Reliquefaction systems are expensive to install, operate, and maintain. The use of a reliquefaction system permits the use of efficient diesel propulsion engines burning less expensive heavy fuel oil. The increased revenue from

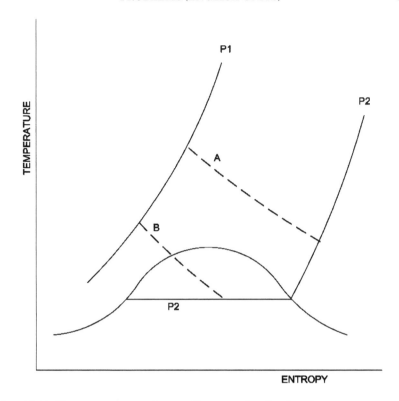

Fig. 10-7. Temperature-entropy diagram for Joule-Thomson process.

the reliquefied gas can offset the cost of installing and operating the reliquefaction system.

## PROBLEMS (ENGLISH UNITS)

10.1E  An absorption air-conditioning system uses waste heat at 220°F to maintain a refrigerated space at 0°F. If the ambient temperature is 70°F, what is the maximum COP this system can have?

10.2E  Waste heat at 240°F is being used to operate an absorption air-conditioning system. The evaporator temperature is 40°F and cooling water is available at 75°F. If the cooling load is 75 tons, what is the minimum quantity of waste heat required, in Btu/hr?

10.3E  A water-lithium bromide absorption system with a COP of 1.1 is being operated with 20 psia saturated steam (hfg = 960 Btu/lbm). The system's condenser operating at 110° is being supplied with 1,250 lbm/hr of saturated vapor

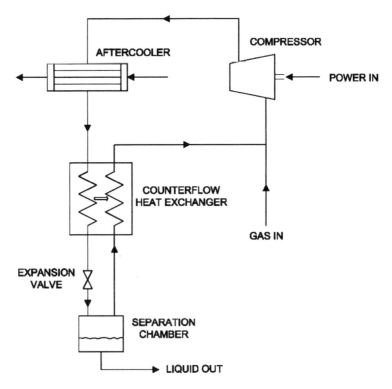

Fig. 10-8. Simplified Joule-Thomson liquefaction system.

from the generator. The evaporator is operating at 40°F and returning saturated vapor to the absorber. What quantity of steam must be supplied to the generator to operate the system?

10.4E  An R-22 refrigeration system with a refrigerant flow of 2 lbm/sec operates with an evaporator temperature of –20°F and a condensing temperature of 120°F. Determine the optimum intermediate pressure if a 2-stage reciprocating compressor is selected. For isentropic compression, calculate the compressor power without intercooling, and also with a flash intercooler, cooling the gas back to saturation.

10.5E  A 2-stage cascade vapor-compression refrigeration system uses R-22 in the low-temperature stage and R-134a in the high-temperature stage. Each stage operates on the ideal saturated cycle with an R-22 evaporator temperature of –30°F and an R-134a condenser temperature of 110°F. The R-134a compressor operates with a compression ratio of 5:1 and there is a 15°F temperature difference in the evaporator/condenser linking the stages. For a cooling capacity of 100 tons determine (a) the mass flow rates of R-22 and R-134a, (b) the power requirements for each compressor, and (c) the system COP.

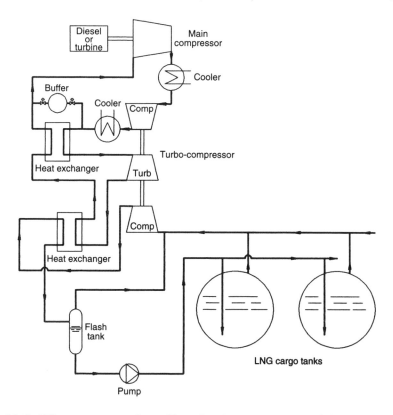

Fig 10-9. Nitrogen expander reliquefaction system simplified diagram.

## PROBLEMS (SI UNITS)

10.1S   An absorption air-conditioning system uses waste heat at 110°C to maintain a refrigerated space at –20°C. If the ambient temperature is 20°C, what is the maximum COP this system can have?

10.2S   Waste heat at 120°C is being used to operate an absorption air-conditioning system. The evaporator temperature is 10°C and cooling water is available at 25°C. If the cooling load is 100 kW, what is the minimum quantity of waste heat required, in kW?

10.3S   A water-lithium bromide absorption system with a COP of 1.1 is being operated with 120 kPa saturated steam (hfg = 2,244 kJ/kg). The system's condenser operating at 45°C is being supplied with 10 kg/min of saturated vapor from the generator. The evaporator is operating at 5°C and returning saturated vapor to the absorber. What quantity of steam must be supplied to the generator to operate the system?

**10.4S** Determine the pressure ratio for a reciprocating compressor with a clearance volume of 5 percent of the compressor displacement that will reduce the clearance volumetric efficiency to zero.

**10.5S** An R-22 refrigeration system with a refrigerant flow of 1 kg/sec operates with an evaporator temperature of −20°C and a condensing temperature of 40°C. Determine the optimum intermediate pressure if a 2-stage reciprocating compressor is selected. For isentropic compression, calculate the compressor power without intercooling, and also with a flash intercooler, cooling the gas back to saturation.

**10.6S** A 2-stage cascade vapor-compression refrigeration system uses R-22 in the low-temperature stage and R-134a in the high-temperature stage. Each stage operates on the ideal saturated cycle with an R-22 evaporator temperature of −30°C and an R-134a condenser temperature of 45°C. The R-134a compressor operates with a compression ratio of 5:1 and there is a 10°C temperature difference in the evaporator/condenser linking the stages. For a cooling capacity of 200 kW determine (a) the mass flow rates of R-22 and R-134a, (b) the power requirements for each compressor, and (c) the system COP.

CHAPTER 11

# Operation and Maintenance

The Montreal Protocol and the amendments to the Clean Air Act described in chapter 3 have mandated a number of changes to procedures for operating and maintaining refrigeration systems. Most of these changes are aimed at reducing the release of CFCs and HCFCs into the atmosphere. The regulations require that technicians involved in servicing refrigeration systems recover refrigerants rather than vent them to the atmosphere. Venting that takes place with the knowledge of the technician (other than good faith "de minimus" and other specifically permitted releases) is in violation of the regulations. The regulations also require that technicians performing maintenance, service, or repair procedures that could release CFCs or HCFCs into the atmosphere obtain certification through an EPA-approved testing organization.

## PROHIBITION ON VENTING OF REFRIGERANTS

Since July 1, 1992, it has been illegal while maintaining, servicing, repairing, or disposing of a refrigeration system to knowingly vent a CFC or HCFC into the atmosphere. On November 15, 1995, HFCs were included in this prohibition. Certain types of releases are permitted under the prohibition including the following:

1. "De minimus" quantities of refrigerant released in the course of making good faith attempts to recapture and recycle or safely dispose of refrigerant.
2. Refrigerants emitted in the course of normal operation of air-conditioning and refrigeration equipment such as from mechanical purging and leaks.

Note that the EPA requires the repair of leaks above a certain size in larger systems.

3. Releases of CFCs and HCFCs that are not used as refrigerants. For example, the release of nitrogen with a small amount of R-22 used as a leak test gas or holding charge is permitted because the R-22 is not used as a refrigerant.

4. Small releases of refrigerant that result from purging hoses or from connecting or disconnecting hoses to charge or service appliances. Recovery and recycling equipment manufactured after November 15, 1993, must be equipped with low-loss fittings.

## CERTIFICATION OF TECHNICIANS

All persons involved in the servicing of refrigeration systems that could result in the release of CFCs or HCFCs into the atmosphere must be certified through an EPA-approved certification program. Technicians must be certified for each type of equipment for which they work as follows:

Type I—small appliances. A small appliance is defined as a system containing 5 pounds or less of refrigerant.

Type II—high and very high pressure systems, including marine systems using R-12 and R-22. A high-pressure refrigerant is defined as one with a boiling point between –50°C (–58°F) and 10°C (50°F) at atmospheric pressure. A very high-pressure refrigerant is defined as one with a boiling point below –50°C (–58°F) at atmospheric pressure.

Type III—low pressure systems, including chiller units using R-11 and R-123. A low-pressure refrigerant is defined as one with a boiling point above 10°C (50°F) at atmospheric pressure.

Universal Certification—allows work on all the above system types.

Certification for each type of equipment requires passing a core multiple-choice test plus a separate multiple-choice test for each system type. Each of the four test modules consists of 25 multiple-choice questions and 70 percent correct is required for passing. Passing all four modules results in Universal Certification. More information on the certification test including sample questions is contained in the appendix.

## LEAK REPAIR

When the owner or operator of an appliance that normally contains a refrigerant charge of more than 50 pounds determines it is leaking at a rate greater than that listed in table 11-1, the owner is required to take corrective action. It is required that the leak must be repaired within 30 days from the time the leak is discovered. An alternative is to develop a dated plan to retrofit the system to an alternative refrigerant or retire the system from service, be developed, and actions completed under that plan within one year. Note that the owner or operator is required to maintain records of refrigerant additions to the system and would be expected to note leakage rates above the trigger rate. For systems with a charge under 50 pounds, there are no regulations requiring mandatory repairs of leaks.

**TABLE 11-1**
**Maximum Permitted Leakage Rates**

| Size of Charge | Type of Equipment | Maximum Leakage Rate | Repair Required? |
|---|---|---|---|
| 50 pounds or less | All | None specified | No |
| 50 pounds or more | Industrial process and commercial refrigeration equipment | 35% of charge annually | Yes |
| 50 pounds or more | Comfort cooling chillers and all other equipment | 15% of charge annually | Yes |

# RECOVER, RECYCLE, AND RECLAIM

The terms recover, recycle, and reclaim have become industry standard and their definitions and differences must be understood by those involved in the use of refrigerants. Recovery means the removal of refrigerant from a system and storage of it in an external container without necessarily testing or processing it in any way. Recycle refers to the processing of refrigerant for reuse by the removal of contaminants (moisture and particulates) through the use of devices such as filter-driers. This term usually applies to processes that can take place on site or at a local service shop. Reclaim describes the reprocessing of refrigerants back to new product specifications as defined in American Refrigeration Institute specification ARI-700. Table 11-2 summarizes the quality requirements that must be met per ARI-700. Reclamation of refrigerants typically involves a variety of processes and procedures including filtering and distillation and is normally only available at a specialized reprocessing or manufacturing facility. Most technicians involved directly in the servicing of refrigeration systems will be using only the recovery process. Refrigerant that is recovered or recycled can be returned to the system or another system of the same owner. Ownership cannot be transferred to another party. Only refrigerant that has been reclaimed and tested as meeting ARI-700 specification can be sold to another user. Details on the equipment and procedures for refrigerant recovery are discussed in the following section.

## TABLE 11-2
## ARI-700 Specifications

| Contaminant | Units | Specification |
|---|---|---|
| Air and noncondensables | % by volume at 25°C | 1.5 |
| Water | ppm by weight | 10 |
| All other impurities | % by weight | 0.50 |
| High boiling residue | % by volume | 0.01 |
| Particulates/solids | None | Visually clean |
| Acidity | ppm by weight | 1.0 |
| Chlorides | None | No visible turbidity |

## Refrigerant Recovery

The removal of refrigerant from the system can be accomplished by passive or active means. The traditional passive method is to use the pressure in the system to return refrigerant to a refrigerant storage bottle. The limitation of this method is that it is usually not possible to remove sufficient refrigerant from the system to satisfy the current regulations. Prior to opening a system containing CFCs or HCFCs, the system pressure must be reduced (evacuated) to the levels shown in table 11-3. This evacuation can only be accomplished with a refrigerant recovery unit. Note that the evacuation levels are different for recovery equipment manufactured before November 15, 1993, and equipment manufactured on or after that date. Equipment manufactured on or after November 15, 1993, must be certified by an EPA-approved organization.

## TABLE 11-3
## Required Evacuation Levels

| Type of Appliance | Using Recovery or Recycling Equipment Manufactured or Imported before Nov. 15, 1993 | Using Recovery or Recycling Equipment Manufactured or Imported on or after Nov. 15, 1993 |
|---|---|---|
| R-22 appliance containing less than 200 pounds of refrigerant | 0 inches Hg vacuum | 0 inches Hg vacuum |
| R-22 appliance containing 200 pounds or more of refrigerant | 4 inches Hg vacuum | 10 inches Hg vacuum |
| High-pressure appliance containing less than 200 pounds of refrigerant | 4 inches Hg vacuum | 10 inches Hg vacuum |
| High-pressure appliance containing 200 pounds or more of refrigerant | 4 inches Hg vacuum | 15 inches Hg vacuum |
| Very-high-pressure appliance | 0 inches Hg vacuum | 0 inches Hg vacuum |
| Low-pressure appliance | 25 inches Hg vacuum | 25 mm Hg absolute |

There are some exceptions to the evacuation levels listed in Table 11-3. If a major repair of the system is to be accomplished, the system must be evacuated to the specified levels. The EPA defines major repair as one involving removal of the compressor, condenser, evaporator, or auxiliary heat exchanger coil. For minor repairs, the component may be isolated and the pressure reduced to atmospheric. For small appliances, defined as those containing less than 5 pounds of refrigerant, 80 to 90 percent of the charge must be recovered depending on whether the system compressor is operable or not and the date of manufacture of the recovery equipment. Table 11-4 summarizes the evacuation levels for small appliances. Establishing a 4 inch Hg vacuum in the system complies with this requirement. Some small appliances do not have an access port or valve to check pressures or recover refrigerant. Piercing valves are available in clamp-on and solder-on types to gain systems. Clamp-on valves must be removed after recovery is complete. Solder-on types may be permanently left on the system. Note that the steel needle in a piercing valve is designed to be used on copper or aluminum tubing and should not be used on other tubing materials.

**TABLE 11-4**
**Evacuation Levels for Small Appliances**

| Status of Compressor | Using Recovery or Recycling Equipment Manufactured or Imported before Nov. 15, 1993 | Using Recovery or Recycling Equipment Manufactured or Imported on or after Nov. 15, 1993 |
|---|---|---|
| Operational | Recover 80% of charge | Recover 90% of charge |
| Nonoperational | Recover 80% of charge | Recover 80% of charge |

The passive recovery method involves connecting a reusable or recovery refrigerant cylinder to the receiver using a service manifold. As long as the pressure in the system receiver is higher than the pressure in the refrigerant cylinder, liquid refrigerant will flow from the receiver to the cylinder. For maximum speed of removal, the cylinder should be evacuated prior to beginning recovery and the cylinder maintained cool by an ice bath as shown in figure 11-1. Heat can be applied to system to further increase the pressure difference between the recovery cylinder and the system. If the system compressor is used to assist in the recovery, it is important to monitor the compressor temperature as overheating is possible. This is especially important with a small hermetic compressor that relies on the refrigerant to cool the motor windings. As was noted above, this method cannot reduce the system pressure to the levels of table 11-3 and a refrigerant recovery unit must be used to complete the process. A refrigerant recovery unit is basically a portable condensing unit with a compressor and air-cooled condenser and related controls. While some units are designed to recover only vapor or only liquid, most units are designed for removal of both liquids and vapors from the refrigeration system. Many units also contain oil traps and filter-driers to accomplish limited purification of the refrigerant being recovered. For maximum speed of recovery, liquid should be recovered first, and then

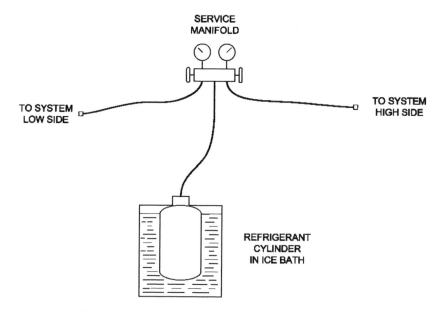

Fig. 11-1. Passive refrigerant charge recovery.

the process completed by vapor recovery. Liquid recovery is faster because of the much higher density of the liquid refrigerant compared to the vapor density.

Recovery units are designed to be used with special refrigerant recovery tanks. These tanks are similar to the cylinders used for the delivery of new refrigerant but contain separate vapor and liquid connections with shutoff valves, and a high-level cutout switch. The two separate connections permit simultaneous transfer of liquid and vapor between the unit and the system. The level switch automatically shuts the recovery unit off if the recovery tank becomes 80 percent full, preventing overfilling. Figure 11-2 shows a recovery cylinder with the gas and liquid hoses, and level switch cable connected. Figure 11-3 shows a recovery cylinder connected to a portable recovery unit.

Figure 11-4 is a diagram of a typical recovery unit and recovery tank connected to a system for refrigerant recovery. A service manifold (see figure 11-5) is used to connect the system's high side and low side connections to the recovery unit. Recovery normally consists of first recovering liquid from the unit, then proceeding with vapor recovery to lower the pressure to the required evacuation level. This unit has internal valves and controls to permit switching the unit from liquid recovery to vapor recovery without disconnecting the hoses. Some units do not have this capability and will require securing the unit after liquid recovery, reversing the hoses, and then

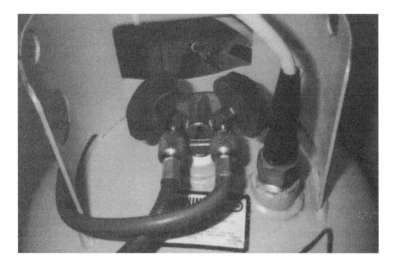

Fig. 11-2. Connections to refrigerant recovery cylinder.

Fig. 11-3. Refrigerant recovery unit and recovery cylinder.

proceeding with vapor recovery. When recovering liquid, the incoming liquid bypasses the recovery unit's compressor and is led directly to the recovery tank, and vapor exhausted from the tank is returned to the recovery unit for compression and condensation. When recovering vapor, the incoming vapor is led to the unit's compressor and condenser and the recovered refrigerant is delivered to the tank as a liquid. The change from liquid to vapor recovery is controlled by the float switch (FS2) in the inlet tank. A high level in the inlet tank will switch the unit to liquid recovery by closing solenoid valve 2 and opening solenoid valves 3 and 4. A low level in the inlet

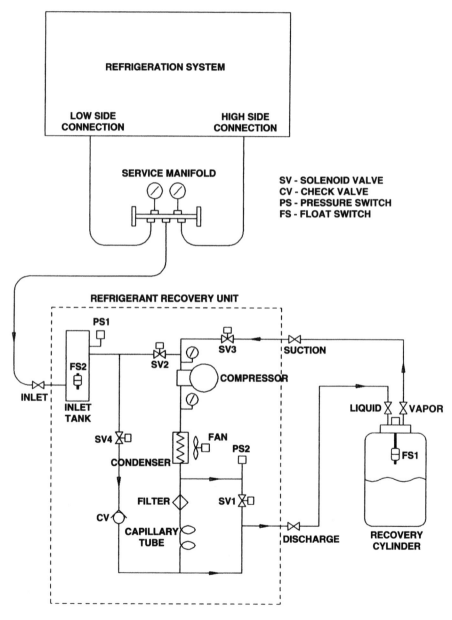

Fig. 11-4. Typical refrigerant reecovery unit.

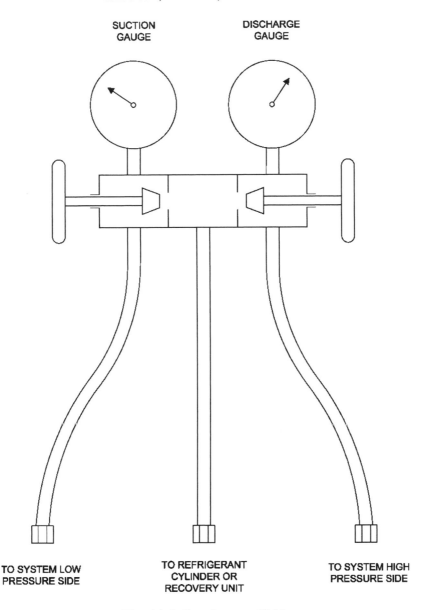

Fig. 11-5. Service manifold.

tank will switch the unit to vapor recovery by opening solenoid valve 2 and closing solenoid valves 3 and 4. Since each recovery unit is different, it is essential to read the instruction manual and carefully follow the manufacturer's operation procedures.

Regardless of the particular recovery unit being used, the following general guidelines should be followed:

1. Only use a recovery unit designed for use with the refrigerant being recovered.
2. Recover liquid first, then recover vapor. This will speed up the recovery process.
3. Do not admit liquid into the inlet of the compressor of a recovery unit as damage can result.
4. Use only approved recovery cylinders. Never use disposable refrigerant cylinders to store recovered refrigerant.
5. Never fill recovery cylinders beyond 80 percent of capacity. Overfilling can result in dangerous over pressurization of the cylinder.
6. If possible, begin recovery with a clean, dry, evacuated recovery cylinder.
7. Always use proper safety equipment such as goggles and gloves when working with refrigerants.
8. Never mix different types of refrigerants. Mixed refrigerants cannot be separated and will have to be incinerated.

### Refrigerant Cylinders

There are three types of cylinders used for the storage of refrigerants: (1) disposable cylinders, (2) returnable/reusable cylinders, and (3) recovery cylinders. It is important to be able to identify each type of cylinder. Some details of each type are discussed below.

Disposable cylinders are "one trip" and it is against the law to refill them with refrigerant. The cylinders are made of steel with a capacity up to 30 pounds and have a single plastic valve at the top. When upright, refrigerant gas is removed from the cylinder. To remove liquid refrigerant, the cylinder is inverted and rested on the handles. When the cylinder is empty, it is recycled as scrap metal. The cylinder must be released to atmospheric pressure before recycling. The cylinders are painted in a distinctive color (see table 11-5) to aid in identifying the refrigerant. The cylinder is also marked with the product number and with safety and warning information.

Returnable/reusable cylinders are larger than disposable cylinders, typically having a capacity of about 125 pounds, and with a combined liquid/vapor valve. An internal dip tube connected to the liquid valve and running to the bottom of the cylinder allows removal of liquid refrigerant without inverting the cylinder. The vapor valve is connected to the top of the cylinder. There is only one fitting for connecting the refrigerant hose and opening the appropriate valve determines if refrigerant in the liquid or vapor phase will be selected. These cylinders are also painted using the color code in table 11-5. A stamp on the shoulder of the cylinder contains information about the manufacturer, capacity, and cylinder test date.

## TABLE 11-5
### Refrigerant Cylinder Color Codes

| Refrigerant Number | Cylinder Color |
|---|---|
| R-11 | Orange |
| R-12 | White |
| R-22 | Light green |
| R-123 | Light gray |
| R-134a | Light blue |
| R-404A | Orange |
| R-407C | Brown |
| R-500 | Yellow |
| R-502 | Light purple |
| R-507 | Green/blue |
| R-717 | Silver |

Cylinders designed for use with recovery units have separate vapor and liquid valves, each with a fitting for connecting a hose. This permits simultaneous connection of the cylinder to the liquid and vapor connections of the recovery unit. Another feature is the stop-fill switch installed to automatically secure the recovery unit when the tank becomes 80 percent full. Recovery cylinders are painted gray with the top shoulder painted yellow regardless of the refrigerant in use. It is important to properly tag the cylinder to indicate the contents.

Recovery and reusable containers must be pressure tested every 5 years. The test date and tester number will be stamped on the shoulder of collar of the cylinder. For example:

$$B3$$
$$11 \quad 99$$
$$21$$

This indicates this cylinder was retested in November of 1999 by retester B321. A cylinder should not be used if the current date is more that 5 years past the dated stamped.

Certain requirements must be met when a cylinder of refrigerant is shipped. This includes used refrigerant being returned for recycling or incineration. The cylinder must be clearly labeled with the proper name of the refrigerant and the United Nations number for the refrigerant. Some examples of the required labeling are:

R-12                              R-22
Dichlorodifluoromethane          Chlorodifluoromethane
UN 1028                          UN 1018

In addition, a DOT hazard label must be attached to the cylinder. This label is a 4 inch-by-4 inch tag reading "NON-FLAMMABLE GAS." If the refrigerant is a Class I (CFC) or Class II (HCFC) substance, the cylinder must also have a warning label stating "WARNING: contains (or manufactured with) a substance that harms public health and environment by destroying ozone in the upper atmosphere."

## REFRIGERATION SYSTEM OPERATION AND MAINTENANCE

The following procedures are general in nature. They apply to typical reciprocating compressor systems with water-cooled condenser and use R-12, R-22, R-134a, and other similar fluorocarbon refrigerants. Refer to figure 6-25 for a diagram of a typical ship's stores refrigeration system.

### Safety Precautions

1. Inspect the compressor oil level and check the oil pressure periodically. The typical oil level is from one-half to three-quarters up on the sight glass. The typical oil pressure is 45 to 55 psi above the suction pressure.
2. Do not start a compressor without ensuring that shutoff valves between the compressor and the condenser are open.
3. Do not jack or turn the compressor by hand when the power is on.
4. Monitor compressor operation carefully during initial start-up. Check for proper lubrication, liquid flood back, severe vibration, or unusual noises.
5. Do not attempt to add oil to the compressor crankcase while the compressor is in operation.
6. Do not bypass or jump any protective device because it is operating improperly. Find the trouble and make the necessary corrections.
7. Do not wipe down near moving parts.
8. In case of electrical fire, secure power to the circuit and extinguish with C02 (never use water).
9. Be sure power is turned off before working on electrical equipment and circuits. Tag the circuit breaker to prevent accidental energizing of circuit.
10. Recover the charge from a system before repairs following the requirements outlined in the beginning of this chapter. If only a small section of piping is to be opened, bleed the piping sections of liquid refrigerant prior to opening for repairs. Close the inlet valve to the section being serviced, wait until the piping warms indicating liquid refrigerant removal, then close the outlet valve.
11. Do not open any part of the system to the atmosphere that is under a vacuum or air and moisture will be drawn in.
12. Drain the cooling water system to prevent a freeze-up during system shutdown in freezing weather.

13. After inspection or repair that required opening the system and prior to re-charging, evacuate the system with a vacuum pump.

14. Do not use a torch on a line that has not been bled of refrigerant since some fluorocarbons decompose into phosgene, a highly toxic gas, when exposed to high temperatures (above 1,000°F [538°C]). The area should be well-ventilated, and all isolation valves closed securely.

15. Always wear goggles and gloves when handling refrigerants. If liquid refrigerant accidentally comes in contact with the eyes, obtain medical help immediately. Do not rub or irritate the eyes, and give the following first aid treatment immediately: (a) introduce drops of sterile mineral oil into the eyes to irrigate and (b) wash the eyes with a weak boric acid solution or a sterile salt solution not to exceed 2 percent sodium chloride if irritation continues at all.

16. Treat as if the skin had been frostbitten if liquid refrigerant comes in contact with the skin.

17. Do not work in a closed area where refrigerant may be leaking unless adequate ventilation is provided. While refrigerants in common use are not toxic or flammable, it is possible to be overcome due to lack of oxygen and high concentrations of refrigerant.

18. Use care in handling and storing refrigerant cylinders. Don't subject cylinders to high temperatures. Take precautions to prevent mechanical damage. Secure cylinders carefully to avoid damage.

## Starting the System

To start up a system that has been secured, proceed as follows.

1. Check oil level in compressor crankcase.

2. Line up condenser seawater circulating system. Open valves in suction and discharge lines and close condenser water vents and drains.

3. Line up refrigerant system valves for normal system operation. Leave compressor suction stop valve closed.

4. Start seawater circulating through condenser. Vent air from condenser waterheads.

5. Start fans in refrigerated compartments (or pumps in brine or chilled water systems).

6. Check electrical power supply to compressor and solenoid valves.

7. Open compressor suction stop valve one full turn.

8. Start compressor in Auto mode.

9. Open suction valve slowly to prevent rapid pumping down of low pressure side to avoid oil foaming. If there is evidence of liquid flood back, throttle suction valve. If the compressor develops a knock, secure for five minutes and restart with suction valve throttled.

10. Observe system operation carefully for five to ten minutes.

## Normal Operation

1. Follow carefully the "Preventive Maintenance Schedule" below, including a regular check of all system pressures, temperatures, and compressor crankcase oil level.
2. Maintain proper discharge pressure by controlling seawater flow with water regulating valve.
3. Check for an open hand expansion valve or malfunctioning thermostatic valve if frosting occurs. Frost on compressor cylinders and crankcase is caused by liquid refrigerant flood back.
4. Bypass the heat interchangers if the compressor discharge gas temperature exceeds 240°F. Otherwise, the unit should be kept in operation.
5. Crack hand expansion valves and open gradually to avoid liquid flood back if valves must be used to permit inspection or repair.
6. Change over to standby compressor at least weekly during normal plant operation to equalize running times for each unit.

## Pumping Down and Securing the System

To pump down and secure a condensing unit, proceed as outlined below:

1. Close the main liquid line stop valve.
2. Let the compressor run until it cuts out on low-pressure switch.
3. Depress compressor motor controller stop button.
4. Observe the suction pressure. If it rises, restart the compressor and pump down again. Repeat until suction pressure holds steady below low-pressure cutout setting.
5. Close compressor suction and discharge stop valves.
6. Secure condenser seawater circulating system.
7. Close appropriate system refrigerant valves.

## Defrosting

When an evaporator operates below 32°F (0°C), frost forms on the coils, reducing the heat transfer. Defrosting of the coils is necessary to maintain system capacity. The two most common systems are electric defrosting and hot gas defrosting.

Systems with electric defrosting are fitted with resistance heaters on the coils, drain pan, and drain line. The defrost cycle is commonly initiated by a timer. The refrigerant solenoid closes, the evaporator fans are stopped, and the heaters are turned on. The defrost cycle can be terminated either based on time or based on sensing the rise in the evaporator temperature above freezing.

Hot gas defrosting is performed by pumping hot discharge gas from the compressor directly into the cooling coil circuit to be defrosted. The hot gas is cooled and condensed, and the frost melts off the coils. The resulting liquid refrigerant is expanded and evaporated in a second evaporator coil through a hand expansion valve. Figure 11-6 is a simplified diagram show-ing a typical hot gas defrosting system for a system with a freeze box and a chill box. During defrosting, the plant should be under normal operation. To defrost the freeze box coil by hot gas, proceed as follows:

1. Close the cut-out valve on the inlet side of the freeze box coil.
2. Allow sufficient time for all liquid refrigerant in the coil to be pumped out by the compressor. Close the coil outlet valve.
3. Close the cut-out valve on the inlet of the chill box coil. Open the hot gas supply valve for the freeze box coil.
4. Slowly open the hand expansion valve between the freeze box coil outlet and the chill box coil inlet. Throttle the hand expansion valve as necessary to prevent liquid refrigerant return to the compressor.
5. When the freeze box coil is defrosted, close the hot gas supply valve to the freeze box coil.
6. Close the hand expansion valve when all the liquid refrigerant from de-frosted coil has been removed and expanded.
7. Open the freeze box coil outlet valve and both thermal expansion valve cut-out valves.

### Preventive Maintenance Schedule
Mechanical equipment can best be kept in good repair and operating at top efficiency by strict adherence to a planned maintenance schedule. A system-atic check of operation and condition of refrigeration systems should be

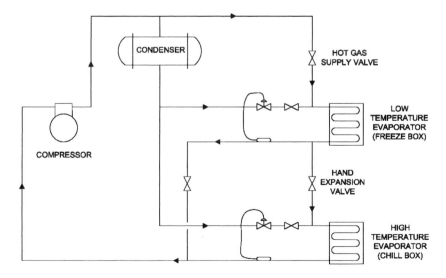

Fig. 11-6. Hot gas defrosting.

maintained. A recommended preventive maintenance schedule is outlined below. This schedule is intended only as a guide. It is not intended to replace the recommendation of the equipment manufacturer and may be altered to suit operating and maintenance conditions peculiar to the individual installation.

### ONCE PER FOUR HOUR WATCH

1. Enter all operating temperatures and pressures in a log. The log should contain columns for recording: (a) the time the check is made, (b) machinery room ambient temperature, (c) refrigerant suction pressure and temperature, (d) refrigerant discharge pressure and temperature, (e) oil pressure, (f) bull's-eye oil level (that is, low, normal, high), (g) crankcase temperature (that is, warm, cold, normal), (h) compressor noise (that is, normal, knock, or other), (i) condenser seawater supply pressure, (j) condenser seawater entering and leaving temperatures, (k) liquid refrigerant temperature, (1) liquid refrigerant condition at sight glass (that is, normal or vapor bubbles), and (m) temperature of refrigerated compartments.
2. Check motors for overheating. Get accustomed to the motor temperature by the way it feels to the hands.

### DAILY

Review hourly operating log. Note any significant changes in plant performance and take corrective action, if necessary.

### WEEKLY

1. Test refrigerant system for leaks.
2. Check for noncondensable gases in condenser. Purge, if necessary.
3. Check operation of all solenoid valves.
4. Check glands on circulating pumps.

### MONTHLY

1. Lubricate motor bearings, if necessary.
2. Blow dust out of motors and check lint screen.
3. Check contact points in motor controllers and control switches. Clean as required.
4. Check operation and settings of operating and safety control switches. Adjust as required.
5. Clean seawater strainers.
6. Check condenser zincs. Clean or replace as required.
7. If a brine is used, check brine density.

### QUARTERLY

1. Clean condenser water side.
2. Check all motors and starters.
3. Clean refrigerant liquid line strainers.

4. Check alignment of compressor and motor.

5. Check tightness of all bolts on equipment.

### ANNUALLY

1. Check calibration of all instrumentation.

2. Check onboard repair parts inventory and order parts as needed.

## Use of the Service Manifold

The service manifold shown in figure 11-5 is a useful tool for a variety of tasks in the operation and maintenance of refrigeration systems. The manifold includes high and low pressure gauges, high and low pressure valves, and three hoses. When the service manifold is connected as shown in figure 11-7, the gauges read the high and low system pressures regardless of position of the manifold valves. The manifold valves are arranged so that when the valves are closed, the refrigerant cylinder or recovery unit is isolated from the system. When one of the valves is opened, that side of the system is connected to the refrigerant cylinder or recovery unit. The procedure for connecting the service manifold and a refrigerant cylinder to the system is as follows:

1. Remove the valve stem caps from the suction line and liquid line service valves. Check that the valves are back seated.

2. Remove the caps from the service valve gauge port connections.

3. Connect the center hose to the refrigerant cylinder and open both service manifold valves.

4. Loosely connect the high and low pressure hoses to the corresponding gauge port connections.

5. Open the cylinder vapor valve for several seconds then close it, allowing the gas to escape from the loose connections. This purges the hoses of air or other contaminants. Tighten the hoses on the service valve gauge ports.

6. Back the service valves off the back seat. The manifold gauges are now reading the system pressures and the service operation can proceed.

## Refrigerant Charge

The initial refrigerant charge for the system will be given in the system instruction manual. This quantity, however, is an estimate, and the actual quantity must be determined by trial and error. A refrigerant overcharge is indicated by high discharge pressure and an increase in liquid subcooling. This is caused by liquid backing up into the condenser. A refrigerant undercharge is indicated by one or more of the following: low head pressure, low receiver level, vapor bubbles in the liquid line sight glass, compressor running continuously, short cycling, and hissing at control valves. If a system regularly requires the addition of refrigerant, the source of the leak must be located and repaired as soon as practical. If the

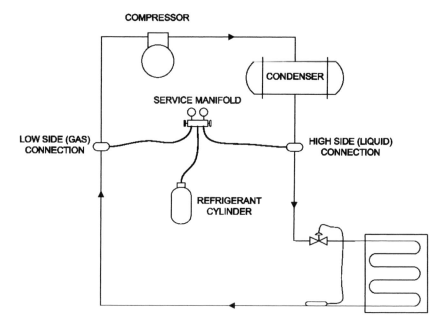

Fig. 11-7. Service manifold connection diagram.

system contains a charge of more than 50 pounds of refrigerant, the regulations require immediate action. These requirements where described earlier in this chapter.

Typical procedures for adjusting the refrigerant charge by adding or removing refrigerant are outlined in the following sections. Refrigerant can be added or removed as either a vapor or a liquid. Refrigerant addition or removal is commonly done as liquid in larger systems because it speeds up the process. Many technicians will charge smaller systems as a vapor because it is easier to control the process. When the refrigerant is a mixture (400 series or 500 series refrigerants), it is important to add or remove refrigerant only as a liquid to avoid changing the composition of the refrigerant mixture. This will occur because the most volatile component will vaporize first, followed by the less volatile components.

## Charging Refrigerant

Liquid refrigerant is charged into the system through the charging valve upstream of the filter-drier. During charging, refrigerant from the cylinder flows through the drier, passes the evaporators where it vaporizes, returns to the compressor and condenser, and is delivered to the receiver as a liquid. The outlet of the receiver must be closed during the process to prevent refrigerant from flowing from the system into the refrigerant cylinder.

This will happen because the temperature in the receiver of the operating system will be warmer than the cylinder, and thus the pressure will be higher. If a system is being charged after a major repair, the system must be leak tested, and then prepared for operation by following the procedure for starting outlined above prior to charging. To add refrigerant to an operating system, proceed as follows:

1. Close the drier bypass and open the drier inlet and outlet valves. Check to see that the solenoid valves to the evaporators are open.
2. Weigh the refrigerant drum.
3. Connect the refrigerant drum to the charging valve with a flexible charging line or using a service manifold. Crack the cylinder vapor valve briefly before tightening the line to blow out air. Observe regulations on venting CFCs and HCFCs.
4. Close the main liquid line valve between the receiver and drier and pump down the system.
5. Open the charging valve and carefully open the liquid valve on refrigerant drum. Liquid refrigerant will flow into the system.
6. Start the compressor.
7. Continue charging until required amount of refrigerant has been transferred. Check the scale reading and/or observe the liquid level in receiver to verify the proper charge.
8. When the proper charge has been achieved, close the cylinder valve and allow the compressor to stop on the low pressure switch. Close the charging valve and the drier outlet valve, and open the drier bypass valve. Open the main liquid line valve and monitor system operation. Check the level in the receiver and observe the flow through the liquid line sight glass. A low level in the receiver or bubbles in the sight glass indicate the need for further charging.
9. If the charge is complete, close the cylinder valve, and disconnect the charging line. Store the refrigerant cylinders for reuse.

## Removing Refrigerant

Refrigerant must be removed from a system that has been overcharged or prior to performing many repairs. In order to recover sufficient refrigerant to perform most repairs, a dedicated recovery unit must be used. These units were discussed earlier in this chapter including the procedures for their use in removing a refrigerant charge from a system. If only a small amount of refrigerant must be removed due to an overcharge, refrigerant may be transferred from the system to a reusable storage cylinder without use of a recovery unit as follows:

1. Secure the liquid supply to the evaporators. Close the drier bypass and drier outlet valve, and open the drier inlet valve.

2. Weigh the refrigerant cylinder and verify that it can accommodate the refrigerant to be removed from the system.
3. Connect a hose between the refrigerant cylinder and the system high-side liquid connection. Purge the hose of air with a small amount of refrigerant gas prior to final tightening.
4. Open the cylinder liquid valve and the system liquid valve with the system compressor operating automatically. Liquid refrigerant will flow from the system to the cylinder. Continue to weigh the cylinder while transferring refrigerant. Do not overfill the refrigerant cylinder.
5. Close the system valve when the required amount of refrigerant has been transferred. Allow any liquid in the hose to drain into the cylinder and then close the cylinder valve. Disconnect the hose and store the cylinder. Restore the liquid supply to the evaporators.

### Testing for Refrigerant Leaks

If a system being serviced is found to require a charge, leak detection procedures must be followed prior to the charging of additional refrigerant. A system that regularly requires a charge obviously has leaks. Adding refrigerant to such a system is a violation of the regulations. The following techniques can be used to detect leaks in refrigeration systems:

1. Visual inspection and fluorescent dyes. A simple examination of the system looking for signs of leakage such as oil at joints or seals will often reveal leaks or locations for further investigation. The charging of a fluorescent dye into the system will enhance the sensitivity of this approach, as even small leaks can be identified by brightly glowing spots.
2. Soap bubble test. This procedure is very effective in finding larger leaks. By applying a solution of soap and water to the joints, seals, and fittings of a system under pressure, gas escaping from the system will cause bubbles to form.
3. Halide torch. This device consists of a burner, needle valve, suction tube, and a chimney with a copper reaction plate. To operate, adjust the flame so that the top of the blue flame cone is level with or slightly above the reaction plate. Move the suction tube slowly along the suspected area. If refrigerant is present, it will react with the copper plate, changing color to a vivid blue with large leaks and taking on a greenish tint with small ones. The halide torch will not detect many of the new alternative refrigerants such as HFCs.
4. Electronic halide detector. A variety of leak detectors are available that use an ionization cell or other specialized sensor. Most emit a clicking sound that increases in frequency as the sample probe draws in air containing refrigerant. For visual monitoring, a series of LED lights or an LCD scale may also be included. Different models vary in sensitivity or their ability to detect different refrigerants. Many of the older units relied on detecting chlorine and will not work with HFCs. It is important to use a unit designed to detect the refrigerant used in the system.

5. Ultrasonic leak detector. This sensor detects the sound created by refrigerant leaking from a system under pressure or air leaking into a system under vacuum. Background noise can interfere with the use of this device. One advantage is that it will work in areas where air currents would upset other methods like the electronic halide detector.

6. Standing pressure test. This technique can be used on a new system or one that has been evacuated of refrigerant for repairs. Nitrogen gas is used to pressurize the system. Figure 11-8 shows a recommended arrangement for connecting the nitrogen cylinder to the system including a pressure regulator, pressure gauges to monitor the cylinder and regulator outlet pressures, and a safety valve to prevent over pressurization. If the system holds pressure, leaks are not present. If the pressure drops, an ultrasonic detector or soap bubbles can be used to find the leaks. A trace amount of R-22 gas can be added to the nitrogen charge to permit the use of electronic halide detectors.

7. Standing vacuum test. This is also a good test to use after servicing and before charging the system. The system is evacuated to a high vacuum with a vacuum pump. The ability of the system to hold vacuum is a good indication

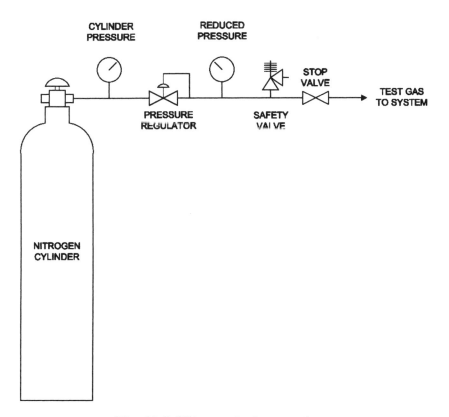

Fig. 11-8. Nitrogen test gas system.

of a tight system. The procedure for evacuation and dehydration of a refrigeration system is described in the following section.

## Evacuation and Dehydration

After initial installation or following extensive repairs, evacuation and dehydration of the system is required to prevent later troubles. Moisture in the system causes oil sludge and corrosion, and it is likely to freeze up the expansion valves of a low-temperature system. Tests and field experience have shown that most troubles with seals and internal valves are caused by moisture in the system. Proper dehydration requires a vacuum pump capable of producing a vacuum of 500 microns (0.02 inches Hg absolute or 69 Pa) and an electronic vacuum gauge. Ambient temperature must be above 60°F (15.5°C) for proper dehydration. To evacuate and dehydrate a system, proceed as follows:

1. Recover all refrigerant from the system.
2. Pressure-test the system with nitrogen to be sure it is free of leaks. Drain oil from the compressor crankcase. Replace with new oil after dehydration.
3. Release all pressure from the system. Connect a tee to the system charging valve. Connect the vacuum pump to one side of tee and the vacuum gauge to the other side, with a shutoff valve in each line.
4. Open the compressor stop valves and all line stop valves in system. Close all valves and connections to atmosphere. Be sure to open hand expansion valves, coil return valves, and any other line valves that will connect the high and low sides of the system and allow the pump to draw a vacuum on the entire system. If necessary, install a "jumper" line between the high and low sides of the system.
5. Open shutoff valve in the vacuum pump suction line, start the vacuum pump, and slowly open the system charging valve.
6. Open the shutoff valve in the gauge line occasionally and take a reading. Continue dehydrating until the vacuum gauge indicates 1,500 microns (207 Pa). The operation will probably take 18 to 72 hours depending on system size and amount of moisture in the system. Failure to achieve a reading of 1,500 microns (207 Pa) may be due to one or more of the following problems: (a) leak in system or connecting tubing, (b) closed line valve, (c) defective vacuum pump, (d) defective vacuum gauge, and (e) ambient temperature below 60°F (15.5°C).
7. Close refrigerant charging valve and vacuum gauge and pump valves and stop the vacuum pump. Disconnect vacuum line from charging valve and raise system pressure to 10 psig (69 Pa) with dry nitrogen.
8. Disconnect the refrigerant drum and release the system pressure to atmosphere. Reconnect the vacuum line, electronic vacuum gauge, and vacuum pump to charging valve. Repeat steps 5 and 6. Dehydrate system to a vacuum of 500 microns (69 Pa) instead of the 1,500 microns (207 Pa) achieved previously. Close the vacuum pump shutoff valve and stop the vacuum pump.

9. Monitor the vacuum gauge for 15 minutes to ensure system maintains vacuum. If the system holds a vacuum, the system is now ready for charging.

## Testing for Noncondensable Gases

Any air and noncondensable gases present in the system are pumped through the system and discharged by the compressor into the condenser. These gases are trapped in the condenser and cause excessive condensing pressures. When air is present, the total condenser pressure is the sum of the partial pressure of the air plus the partial pressure of the refrigerant. In order to check the condenser for the presence of air or noncondensable gases, it is essential that the gauges and thermometers used be accurate and that the system has a sufficient charge so that the liquid refrigerant present in the receiver will seal the liquid line connection. To check for noncondensable gases, proceed as follows:

1. Close the liquid line valve and allow the system to pump down.
2. Shut off compressor and close the compressor suction valve.
3. Open the condenser cooling water valves to establish maximum water flow. Monitor the condenser pressure as it gradually drops. If no discharge gauge is installed on the system, install a service manifold. When the pressure stabilizes, record the temperature from the thermometer in the liquid line at the receiver. This is the refrigerant condensing temperature. If no liquid thermometer is installed, use a contact thermometer to read the condenser shell temperature.
4. Record the condensing pressure from the discharge gauge. Refer to the appropriate table of saturated refrigerant properties in the appendix and look up the saturation temperature that corresponds to the condensing pressure.
5. Subtract the temperature recorded in step 3 from the temperature recorded in step 4. If the difference between these two temperatures is more than 5°F (2.8°C), it is necessary to purge.

## Purging Noncondensable Gases

If the above test indicates the presence of noncondensable gases, proceed as follows:

1. Close the liquid line valve and allow the system to pump down.
2. With the compressor stopped, allow water to flow through the condenser for 10 to 15 minutes until the discharge pressure stabilizes. Leave all other system valves in their normal position.
3. Open purge valve on top of condenser, and release gases for a few seconds. A small drop should be noted in the condenser pressure.
4. Since it is difficult to tell if excessive refrigerant is being purged with the noncondensables, purge slowly and continue to check the condenser for a drop in pressure after each release. Check for noncondensable gases as

explained above and continue purging until the temperature difference in step 5 drops below 5°F.

## Compressor Oil Level

A certain amount of compressor oil will always circulate through the system because oil is miscible in refrigerant. To allow for oil circulation, systems requiring a large refrigerant charge will need the addition of oil in excess of the normal compressor crankcase oil charge. When the system is first placed in operation, closely observe the oil level in the crankcase. Add oil whenever the oil level drops below normal (halfway up on the crankcase bull's-eye sight glass). Allow sufficient time for the system to balance after adding oil, since it may take some for the circulating oil to return to the compressor. Generally, the addition of one quart of oil for every fifty pounds of refrigerant charge will be an adequate allowance for oil circulation. After adding oil, if the oil level in the crankcase still falls below normal, oil is not returning to the compressor. The oil is probably being trapped in the cooling coils by an improperly adjusted thermal expansion valve. After the compressor has been stopped for several minutes, the oil level in the compressor crankcase should be about halfway up on the bull's-eye sight glass. During operation, the oil level will be slightly lower but will appear higher when oil is foaming. Check the oil level at least once per every four hours. Add or remove oil to bring the level in the crankcase to the middle of the sight glass during steady operating conditions.

## Adding Oil

The method of adding oil given below, if properly followed, will prevent air and moisture from entering the system. Since refrigerant gas is heavier than air, and the crankcase is loaded with this gas, the position of the oil-charging hole is located to prevent the admission of air. Use only clean oil from sealed containers as most refrigerant oils are highly hygroscopic and will absorb significant moisture in only a short period of time. Most of the new refrigerants are incompatible with the traditional mineral oils and require synthetic oils such as polyolester. Check the manufacturer's manual for the proper type of oil for the system. Oil can be added in several ways: using a funnel and pouring it in, using a pump, or using a vacuum to draw it in. To add oil to the system using a funnel:

1. Close the liquid line valve and pump down the system. Press the compressor stop button.
2. Remove the oil filler plug slowly.
3. Add oil to the center of bull's-eye sight glass using a clean, well-dried funnel, pouring oil from a suitable container.
4. Replace the oil filler plug tightly.
5. Restart the system.

A valved connection on the compressor crankcase will permit conveniently adding oil with a pump. After pumping down the system and stopping the compressor, the oil pump is connected to the crankcase connection and the oil is pumped in. If the compressor is run until a slight vacuum is maintained in the crankcase, a hose connected to the same crankcase connection can be used to draw oil in to the crankcase. The end of the hose must be maintained below the oil level in the container to avoid air and moisture from being drawn into the compressor crankcase. These two methods have the advantage of not opening the crankcase to the atmosphere.

### Removing Oil

Proceed as follows to remove oil from a compressor crankcase:

1. Close the liquid line valve and pump down the system.
2. Loosen the crankcase drain plug. Since the crankcase is under light pressure, do not fully remove the drain plug. Allow the required amount of oil to be drained to seep slowly around the threads of loosened plug. If a valved crankcase connection is installed on the crankcase, it can used to remove the oil.
3. Retighten the drain plug or close the valved crankcase connection.
4. Restart the system.

### Oil Pressure

Correct oil pressure will ensure adequate compressor lubrication and satisfactory operation of the compressor capacity control system. Reciprocating compressors with a forced lubrication system are typically designed to operate with a normal oil pressure of 45 to 55 psi (310 to 379 kPa) above the suction pressure. For example, if the compressor suction gauge reading is 40 psig (276 kPa), the oil pressure gauge reading should be 85 to 95 psig (586 to 655 kPa). During start-up, observe the oil pressure gauge to be sure that oil pressure develops during the first few minutes. The oil pressure may initially be low due to oil foaming, but should stabilize at normal levels when steady operating conditions have been reached. Oil foaming may last fifteen minutes or longer. Do not allow compressor to run longer than one minute if oil pressure of at least 15 psig (103 kPa) over suction pressure does not develop. Reasons for low oil pressure include the following:

1. Insufficient oil in crankcase.
2. Oil pressure regulator not seating properly.
3. Oil screen on pump suction line in bottom of crankcase clogged with dirt.
4. Oil filter clogged.
5. Oil pump worn or defective. Electric pump rotating in wrong direction.
6. Faulty oil piping.
7. Rapid pulldown of suction pressure on start-up causing excessive oil foaming.

## Compressor Overhaul and Repair

Consult the manufacturer's manual for detailed disassembly and reassembly procedures. The following are general procedures to be followed in any compressor overhaul:

1. Be sure that faulty operation of the plant is not caused by trouble in some other part of the system before dismantling a compressor.
2. Dismantle only the part of the compressor necessary to correct the fault.
3. Sweep clean the deck in the vicinity of the compressor prior to any dismantling. Remove from the area any spare parts, fittings, or tools not to be used. Obtain clean buckets or boxes in which to place disassembled components. Have on hand a supply of clean rags, as lint free as possible.
4. Spread clean canvas or heavy paper on the deck to lay out the larger parts (cylinder heads, crankshaft, etc.).
5. Maintain cleanliness during the overhaul. Clean all parts with an approved solvent after disassembly. Use a stiff brush to remove dirt from grooves and crevices. Coat all moving parts with compressor oil before reassembly.
6. Dip dismantled parts to be left overnight in clean compressor oil and wrap them in oil-soaked rags to prevent rusting.
7. Use special tools furnished by the compressor manufacturer for the particular operation involved to dismantle or reassemble a compressor.
8. Avoid damage to gaskets or gasket-seating surfaces when disassembling the compressor. These gaskets or new gaskets of identical thickness and material must be employed when reassembling. The use of discharge valve plate and compressor cylinder gaskets of proper thickness is particularly important since the thickness of these gaskets determines the clearance between the top of the pistons and discharge valve plate.
9. Mark parts carefully when disassembling the compressor so that each part removed will be replaced in its original position when reassembling.
10. Avoid filing, scraping, and grinding wherever possible when making compressor repairs or adjustments because of the danger of introducing emery or metal particles into the compressor.
11. Replace the pistons on the same rods and facing the same direction as originally during reassembly.
12. Make certain that the oil dipper on lower connecting rod bearing of splash lubricated compressors is in correct position for dipping up oil when machine is in operation.
13. Stagger the position of the ends of the piston rings so that all joints do not come on one side of the piston.
14. Clean the compressor crankcase and provide a fresh charge of proper oil.

## Analysis of Faulty Compressor Valves

Before opening a compressor for valve inspection or replacement, it should be definitely determined that the faulty operation of the system is due to the improper functioning of the valves and not to some other problem. Before assuming that compressor valves must be serviced, carefully check the system for all other possible causes of faulty operation.

Faulty compressor valves may be indicated by either a gradual or a sudden decrease in the normal compressor capacity. Either the compressor will fail to pump or the suction pressure cannot be pumped down to the designed value. This will cause the compressor to run for abnormally long intervals or even continuously. Short shutdown periods may indicate leaky compressor valves provided the faulty operation is not due to some other fault in the system.

### Testing Compressor Discharge Valves

The compressor discharge valve may be checked for leakage as follows:

1. Close liquid line valve and pump down system.
2. Stop compressor and quickly close the suction and discharge line valves.
3. If discharge pressure drops at a rate in excess of 3 psi per minute and crankcase (suction) pressure rises, there is evidence of discharge valve leakage. It may be necessary to pump down several times to remove refrigerant mixed with crankcase oil in order to obtain a true test.

If the discharge valves are found to be defective in any way, it is advisable to replace the entire valve assembly with a spare. If valve operation is faulty, chances are the discharge plate requires relapping. This process generally requires highly specialized machinery to produce a satisfactory surface and should not be attempted aboard ship except in an emergency.

### Testing Compressor Suction Valves

The compressor suction valves may be checked for leakage as follows:

1. Start the compressor under manual control.
2. Close the suction line stop valve gradually, exercising care to prevent violent oil foaming.
3. With the suction line stop valve finally closed, if a vacuum of approximately 20 inches Hg (34 kPa absolute) can be readily pumped, the suction valves may be considered satisfactory. Do not expect the vacuum to be maintained after the compressor stops due to the release of refrigerant from the oil. New valve assemblies may require a break-in period of several days before being checked.

If the test indicates a possible problem, the compressor should be pumped down, opened, and the valves inspected. Defective valves should be replaced with spare assemblies. Be sure all small pieces of a broken valve are accounted for. If any pieces are not removed, the compressor may be damaged when put back in operation. Before installing a new suction valve assembly, the piston should be checked for damage. If marred, the piston must be replaced along with the suction valve assembly.

### Alignment of Compressor Coupling

Couplings on direct drive units should be checked for proper alignment after repair or replacement. Both parallel and angular misalignment should be checked. Parallel misalignment in direct drive units is shown in figure 11-9 and angular misalignment is shown in figure 11-10. Angular misalignment can be checked with a feeler gauge or by clamping a dial indicator to the motor flange and adjusting it so the stem will contact the inside face of the compressor flange. Rotate the motor flange through 360° and record readings at 90° intervals. To check parallel misalignment, use a steel rule held against the coupling periphery, or a dial indicator clamped to the motor coupling with the stem adjusted to run on the compressor coupling

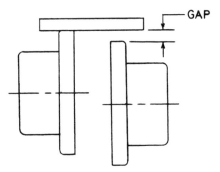

Fig. 11-9. Parallel misalignment in a direct drive unit.

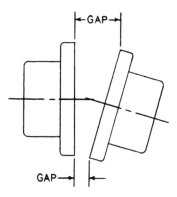

Fig. 11-10. Angular misalignment in a direct drive unit.

periphery. Shim motor feet and shift motor position as necessary to correct the misalignments. Tighten all hold-down bolts and recheck.

## Belt Drive Adjustment

The belt drive must be aligned so that there is no angular or parallel misalignment. Both alignments can be checked with a straightedge or string. Parallel misalignment in belt drive units is shown in figure 11-11, and angular misalignment is shown in figure 11-12. Correct parallel misalignment by sliding the motor pulley on its shaft. Correct angular misalignment by loosening motor hold-down bolts and turning the motor frame. Check belt tension by depressing a single belt at the center of the span with one finger. A heavier belt with a 24-inch (61 cm) span should deflect ½ to ¾ inch (13 to 19 mm). Lighter belts or longer spans should deflect proportionally more. Belts should always be replaced in sets, not singly.

## Retrofitting Refrigeration Systems

The conversion of an existing refrigeration system to another refrigerant can be a complicated and expensive process. It depends on many factors

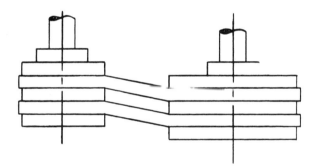

Fig. 11-11. Parallel misalignment in a belt drive unit.

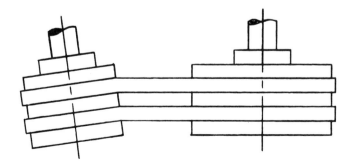

Fig. 11-12. Angular misalignment in a belt drive unit.

such as the age and condition of the system, the type of refrigerant to be used, and the compatibility of the system components with the new refrigerant and lubricating oil. In some cases it may make economic sense to replace the entire system rather than undertake a retrofit. The system manufacturer must be consulted to obtain guidance on components that will need changing and procedures to be followed.

For existing systems using R-12, there are two main refrigerant choices for retrofits: R-134a and R-22. R-134a has the advantage that its pressure-temperature relationships are very close to that of R-12. The disadvantages of an R-134a retrofit are that many systems components may be incompatible with the new refrigerant and lubricating oil and will need replacing. Careful flushing of the old oil charge before replacement is essential to avoid problems. An R-22 retrofit can be a good choice if the condensing unit was originally designed for both R-12 and R-22. Because R-22 will operate at higher pressures than R-12, the pressure rating of the condenser and receiver must be checked, and relief valves, burst disks, and expansion valves will need replacement. The compressor power requirements will increase due to the greater refrigerant density, and it may be necessary to slow the compressor speed by changing the belt pulleys or the motor to avoid motor overloading. The ability of the oil pump to properly operate at this lower speed must be verified. Permanently unloading cylinders is another possibility for reducing the compressor capacity and avoiding motor overloading.

The following procedures are typical of those required for retrofit of an R-12 reciprocating compressor system to R-134a:

1. Leak test the system and repair any leaks noted. Beginning the retrofit with a tight, properly functioning system will avoid problems during the conversion.
2. If schedule permits, begin changing the oil several weeks in advance of the conversion. At least three changes of the new POE oil will be necessary to reduce the mineral oil residual to 5 percent or less. POE oil has a substantial cleaning effect, and large volumes of debris and sludge will be dislodged from the system. The initial oil charge should remain in operation for no more than 48 hours before being changed. This initial oil charge will typically be gray-black in color with a significant amount of fine particles dispersed in it. Repeated changes are necessary until the oil remains clear and clean.
3. Recover the old refrigerant charge with a recovery unit into recovery cylinders. The weight of the refrigerant recovered should be noted to aid in recharging with the new refrigerant. Evacuate the system with a vacuum pump, and charge with clean dry nitrogen.
4. Make the hardware changes recommended by the system manufacturer. This may include the expansion valve, filter-drier, evaporator pressure regulator, suction pressure regulator, and certain seals and gaskets.

5. Evacuate the system to a hard vacuum of at least 500 microns to ensure dehydration.
6. Charge the system with the new refrigerant. Start with 90 percent of the charge removed and add additional as necessary.
7. Start system and make any necessary control and system adjustments. Carefully observe the system operation for the next couple of days. It is recommended that the oil and filter-drier be changed after 60 to 90 days of operation.

# TROUBLESHOOTING REFRIGERATION SYSTEMS

The troubleshooting charts that follow are intended as a guide for locating problems in a typical marine refrigeration or air-conditioning system with a reciprocating condenser. It is not intended to replace the detailed information provided by the manufacturer of a particular installation.

Problems with a refrigeration system can be either electrical or mechanical, although there is significant overlap between them. Electrical problems are the most common in refrigeration systems. A system wiring diagram and a digital multimeter will be adequate for troubleshooting most electrical problems. The meter can be used to test the circuits identified and locate the components suspected of causing the problem. Once the defective component is identified, repair or replace it. When troubleshooting mechanical problems, a systematic approach will help in efficiently resolving the problem. Start by collecting information about the problem. What is occurring that is not normal? Note the current operating system temperatures and pressures and compare them with the design values. Use the information collected and then consult the troubleshooting charts that follow for assistance identifying the system problem. There are a number of possible causes for most problems. It is usually necessary to use a process of elimination to narrow down the possibilities. Try the easier possibilities first, then move on to the more difficult ones. The order in which the symptoms and possible causes are presented in the troubleshooting charts does not necessarily indicate a suggested troubleshooting sequence. Note also that some problems will create multiple symptoms in the system. For example, a refrigerant undercharge can create symptoms such as low discharge pressure, high suction superheat, the compressor running continuously or short cycling, and hissing at control valves. Consider if a possible cause being considered might result in other symptoms and check to see if they are present. Once the problem is identified, correct it using the procedures outlined by the equipment manufacturer or by using the general procedures presented in this chapter.

## High Compartment Temperature

| *Possible Cause* | *Action* |
|---|---|
| Controls not functioning. | Check thermostat, solenoid valve, electrical circuits, and fuses. Check expansion valve and evaporator pressure valve operation and adjustment. |
| Coils frosted. | Check coils. Defrost, if necessary. |
| Insufficient airflow across evaporator. | Check evaporator fan operation. Check for clogged air filters. Check for blockages in air flow passages. |
| Infiltration of warm air. | Check for door ajar, poor door gaskets, or excessive traffic. |
| Recent loading of warm product. | Normal pull down. Start second condensing, if required. |

## Low Compartment Temperature

| *Possible Cause* | *Action* |
|---|---|
| Solenoid valve open. | Check for power to solenoid valve. Check thermostat for correct setting and proper operation. |
| Hand expansion valve not closed tight or leaking. | Check for open or leaking valve and correct. |

## High Compressor Discharge Pressure

| *Possible Cause* | *Action* |
|---|---|
| Air in system. | Check condenser for noncondensables. Purge, if indicated. |
| Insufficient cooling water flow. | Check for proper water supply pressure. Check that all required cooling water system valves are fully open. Check for clogged strainer. Check water regulating valve for proper operation and correct setting. Resolve all problems discovered. |
| Condenser water side dirty. | Check and clean condenser if required. |
| Refrigerant overcharge (condenser tubes partially covered. | Check for proper refrigerant charge. Remove refrigerant if overcharge is indicated. |
| Compressor discharge stop valve partially closed. | Check valve position. Open fully if necessary. |

## Low Compressor Discharge Pressure

| *Possible Cause* | *Action* |
|---|---|
| Excessive cooling water flow. | Check water regulating valve for proper operation and correct setting. Check for open bypass valve. |
| Liquid refrigerant flooding back. | Check expansion valve for proper operation and correct superheat setting. check for open or leaking hand expansion valve. |
| Compressor suction stop valve partially closed. | Check valve position. Open fully if necessary. |
| Leaking compressor valves. | Check valves for leakage. If leakage is indicated, pump system down, isolate compressor and recover refrigerant, open compressor, and inspect valves. |
| Worn piston rings or cylinder liners. | If no other reason for loss of compressor capacity can be determined, pump system down, isolate compressor and recover refrigerant, open compressor, and inspect piston rings and liners. |

## High Compressor Suction Pressure

| Possible Cause | Action |
|---|---|
| Liquid refrigerant flooding back from coils. | Check expansion valve for proper operation and correct superhead setting. |
| Leaking compressor suction valves. | Check valves for leakage. If leakage is indicated, pump system down, isolate compressor and recover refrigerant, open compressor, and inspect valves. |
| Compressor unloading at too high pressure. | Check setting and operation of low pressure cut-out. |
| Oil separator leaking discharge gas back to crankcase. | Check separator float valve for proper operation. |

## Low Compressor Suction Pressure

| Possible Cause | Action |
|---|---|
| Low pressure cut-out not stopping compressor. | Check switch for correct setting and proper operation. |
| Compressor not unloading. | Check capacity control system for correct setting and proper operation. |
| Restricted refrigerant flow to coils. | Check expansion valve for proper operation and correct superheat setting. Check solenoid valve for proper operation. Check for clogged strainer. Check for moisture in system. |
| Low refrigerant charge. | Check for correct refrigerant charge. If low, check for leaks. Repair and recharge. |

## Compressor Crankcase Sweating or Frosted

| Possible Cause | Action |
|---|---|
| Liquid refrigerant flooding back from coils. | Check expansion valve for proper operation and correct superhead setting. |
| Excessive oil in circulation. | Check for proper oil level in crankcase. Remove oil if necessary. |

## High Compressor Crankcase Temperature

| Possible Cause | Action |
|---|---|
| Clogged liquid line strainer. | Pump down system and clean strainer if required. |
| Excessive suction temperature. | Check expansion valve for proper operation and correct superhead setting. |
| Excessive discharge temperature. | Bypass heat interchanger. |
| Leaking compressor suction or discharge valves. | Check valves for leakage. If leakage is indicated, pump system down, isolate compressor and recover refrigerant, open compressor, and inspect valves. |

## Compressor Will Not Start

| Possible Cause | Action |
|---|---|
| No power to compressor. | Check circuit breaker, main setich, fuses, and wiring. Correct as necessary. |
| Motor controller overload tripped. | Reset. Check and eliminate cause of trip. |
| Compressor safety switch open. | Check if high pressure switch, water failure switch, or oil failure switch is open. Check switch setting and operation. Check for dirty contacts. Find and elinate cause of switch operation. |
| Box thermostate set too high. | Adjust set point. Check for proper operation. |
| Solenoid valve closed. | Check power to solenoid valve. If power is on but valve will not open, see "Solenoid Valve Will Not Open" below. |
| Very low refrigerant charge. | Check for proper refrigerant charge. If charge is low, check for leaks, then recharge. |

## Compressor Runs Continuously

| Possible Cause | Action |
|---|---|
| Low refrigerant charge. | Check for proper refrigerant charge. If charge is low, check for leaks, then recharge. |
| Solenoid valve leaking. | If valve will not close tightly, pump down and inspect valve. Repair or replace if necessary. |
| Compressor valves leaking. | Check valves for leakage. If leakage is indicated, pump system down, isolate compressor and recover refrigerant, open compressor, and inspect valves. |
| Worn piston rings and/or cylinder liners. | Pump down system, disassemble compressor, and inspect. Repair as required. |

## Compressor Short-cycles on High Pressure Switch

| Possible Cause | Action |
|---|---|
| High pressure switch set point is too low. | Check switch set point and adjust as necessary. |
| Compressor discharge pressure is high. | See "High Compressor Discharge Pressure" above for possible causes and actions. |

## Compressor Short-cycles on Low Pressure Switch

| Possible Cause | Action |
|---|---|
| Compressor suction pressure is low. | See "Low Compressor Suction Pressure" above for possible causes and actions. |
| Reduced evaporator capacity. | Check for frosted evaporator coils. Check for proper operation of evaporator coil fans. Check for proper operation of expansion valve. |
| Relief valve leaking slightly. | Test valve for leakage and replace if necessary. |
| Internal leak in heat interchanger. | Test for leaks and replace if necessary. |

## Loss of Oil from Compressor Crankcase

| Possible Cause | Action |
|---|---|
| Incorrect expansion valve superheat setting. | Liquid floodback will cause excessive oil loss from crankcase. Underfeeding of evaporator can inhibit oil return. Check superheat and adjust as necessary. |
| Oil return check valve stuck closed. | Pump system down, remove valve, and clean, repair, or replace. |
| Worn piston rings or cylinder liners. | Pump system down, isolate compressor and recover refrigerant, open compressor, and inspect piston rings and liner. |

## Low Oil Pressure

| Possible Cause | Action |
|---|---|
| Insufficient oil in crankcase. | Check oil level in crankcase. Add oil as required. |
| Defective oil pressure gauge. | Check gauge for proper reading. Replace if necessary. |
| Oil filter or inlet screen clogged. | Pump system down and clean as required. |
| Defective oil pump. | Check for proper rotation. Disassemble and check for wear or broken parts. |
| Defective oil pressure regulator valve. | Check and replace if defective. |
| Worn compressor bearings. | Pump system down, isolate compressor and recover refrigerant, open compressor, and inspect bearings. |

## Noisy Compressor

| Possible Cause | Action |
|---|---|
| Loose compressor mounting bolts. | Check bolts for proper tightness. Tighten if necessary. |
| Compressor drive loose, worn, or improperly aligned. | Check flexible coupling on direct-drive units. Check belts, pulleys, and flywheel on belt-drive units. |
| Liquid refrigerant flooding back. | Check for open hand expansion valve. Check expansion valve for proper operation and correction superheat setting. |
| Excessive oil in circulation. | Check for high crankcase oil level. Check for liquid floodback causing excessive oil circulation. |
| Discharge stop valve rattling. | Backseat valve fully. |
| Worn compressor main bearings, piston pins, connecting rod bearings, etc. | Pump system down, isolate compressor and receover refrigerant, open compressor, and inspect for wear. |

## Loud Hissing Noise in Refrigerant Piping

| Possible Cause | Action |
|---|---|
| Insufficient refrigerant charge. | Check for correct refrigerant charge. If low, check for leaks. Repair and recharge. |
| Obstruction in liquid line. | Check for clogged strainer, partially closed valves, or other obstructions. |

## Thermostatic Expansion Valve Underfeeding Evaporator

| Possible Cause | Action |
|---|---|
| Superheat setting too high. | Check superheat. Adjust as necessary. |
| Power assembly failure. | Check valve for proper operation of power assembly. |
| Valve orifice plugged. | Check for cause of plugging. Wax or oil indicates lubricating oil problem. Ice or debris indicates need to cut in filter-drier. |
| Low inlet pressure. | Check high side pressure. If low, check operation and set point of water regulating valve. |
| External equalizing line plugged. | Check that equalizing line is clear. |

## Thermostatice Expansion Valve Overfeeding Evaporator

| Possible Cause | Action |
|---|---|
| Superheat setting too high. | Check superheat. Adjust as necessary. |
| Remote bulb not sensing evaporator outlet temperature correctly. | Check that bulb is securely clamped to refrigerant line. Insulate bulb if exposed to high ambient temperatures. |
| Low of charge from remote bulb/power assembly. | Check valve response to different bulb temperatures. |
| External equalizing line plugged. | Check that equalizing line is clear. |
| Valve frozen open. | Apply hot rags to melt ice. If valve operation is restored, cut in filter-drier to remove moisture. |
| Valve pin and/or seat worn. | Check for tight valve shutoff. If valve doesn't close tight, inspect for warm parts. |

## Solenoid Valve Will Not Open

| Possible Cause | Action |
|---|---|
| No electric power. | Check that thermostat is funtioning and that contacts are closed. Check voltage across valve coil. If none or improper, check circuit breaker, fuses, and wiring. |
| Coil burnout or open circuit. | Check coil resistance and circuit continuity. See "Solenoid Valve Coil Burnout" below for possible causes. |
| High differentials across valve. | Check that pressure differrence across valve is not high than rated. |
| Plunger movement restricted. | Check for dirt, scale, sludge, or deformed body preventing valve movement. |

## Solenoid Valve Will Not Close

| Possible Cause | Action |
|---|---|
| Plunger movement restricted. | Check for dirt, scale, sludge, or deformed body preventing valve movement. |
| Electric power remains on. | Check voltage across coil. If not zero, check that thermostat has opened or power coming from another source. |
| Manual valve operator in open position. | Check that manual valve operator is backed out to allow valve to close. |

## Solenoid Valve Coil Burnout

| *Possible Cause* | *Action* |
|---|---|
| Incorrect voltage. | Check for high or low voltage across coil. Check for improper wiring resulting in excessive voltage drop. |
| High ambient temperature. | Check that temperature is below maximum permitted (usually 120°F). |
| Plunger movement restricted. | Check for dirt, scale, sludge, or deformed body preventing valve movement. |

# Appendix

## CONVERSION FACTORS

Area (A)
$$1 \text{ ft}^2 = 0.0929 \text{ m}^2$$
$$1 \text{ in}^2 = 645.16 \text{ mm}^2$$

Density ($\rho$)
$$1 \text{ lbm/ft}^3 = 16.018 \text{ kg/m}^3$$
$$1 \text{ slug/ft}^3 = 515.379 \text{ kg/m}^3$$

Energy (E, H, U, P.E., K.E., Q, W)
1 Btu = 1.0551 kJ
1 Btu = 778.169 ft-lbf
1 IT cal = 4.1868 J

Entropy (S)
1 Btu/°R = 1.8992 kJ/°K

Force (F)
1 lbf = 4.4482 N
$$1 \text{ dyne} = 1 \times 10^{-5} \text{ N}$$

Heat (Q) see Energy

Heat flow rate (Q)
1 Btu/hr = 0.2931 W
1 Btu/sec = 1.0551 kW

Heat transfer coefficient (f)
$$1 \text{ Btu/hr-ft}^2\text{-}°F = 5.678 \text{ W/m}^2\text{-}°K$$

Length (L)
1 ft = 0.3048 m
1 in = 2.54 cm = 0.0254 m

1 m = 39.37 in.
1 statute mile = 1.6093
  km = 5,280 ft
1 nautical mile = 6,076.1 ft

Mass (m)
1 kg = 2.20462 lbm
1 slug = 32.1739 lbm
1 tonne = 1,000 kg
1 short ton = 2,000 lbm

Power (W)
1 Btu/hr = 0.2931 W
1 Btu/sec = 1.0551 kW
1 hp = 745.7 W
1 hp = 550 ft-lbf/s
1 hp = 2,544.5 Btu/hr
1 kW = 1.341 hp

Pressure (p)
1 psia = 6.8948 kPa
1 bar = 100 kPa
1 in Hg = 0.4912 psia
1 mm Hg = 0.1333 kPa
1 atm = 101.325 kPa = 14.696
  psia
1 atm = 760 mm Hg = 29.92 in
  Hg

Specific energy (e, h, u, q, w, p.e., k.e.)
   1 Btu /lbm = 2.3261 kJ/kg

Specific entropy (s) and specific heat (Cp, Cv)
   1 Btu/lbm-°R = 4.1868 kJ/kg-°K
   1 Btu/lbm-°R = 778.169 ft-lbf/lbm-°R

Specific volume (v)
   1 ft$^3$/lbm = 0.062 428 m$^3$/kg

Temperature (T)
   °R = 1.8 °K
   °C = 5/9 (°F – 32)
   °F = (9/5 °C) + 32
   °C = °K – 273.15
   °F = °R – 459.67

Thermal conductivity (k)
   1 Btu/hr-ft-°F = 1.731 W/m-°K

Thermal diffusivity ($\alpha$)
   1 ft$^2$/sec = 0.0929 m$^2$/s
   1 ft$^2$/sec = 2.581 × 10$^{-5}$ m$^2$/s

Velocity (V)
   1 ft/sec = 0.3048 m/s
   1 mph = 0.44703 m/s

Viscosity, dynamic ($\mu$)
   1 lbm/ft-s = 1.488 N-s/m$^2$
   1 centipoise = 0.001 N-s/m$^2$

Viscosity, kinematic ($v$)
   1 ft$^2$/sec = 0.0929 m$^2$/s
   1 ft$^2$/hr = 2.581 × 10$^{-5}$ m$^2$/s

Volume (V)
   1 m$^3$ = 35.3147 ft$^3$ = 1,000 liters
   1 U.S. gal = 3.7853 liters
   1 ft$^3$ = 7.481 U.S. gal
   1 U.S. barrel = 42 gal

Work (W) see Energy

# CONSTANTS

Acceleration of gravity at sea level
   32.1739 ft/sec$^2$ = 9.807 m/s$^2$

Avogadro's number
   1 kgmol = 6.023 × 10$^{26}$ molecules

Stefan-Boltzmann constant ($\sigma$)
   5.67 × 10$^{-8}$ W /m$^2$-°K$^4$ = 0.1714 × 10$^{-8}$ Btu/hr-ft$^2$-°R$^4$

Universal gas constant (R)
   8.3143 kJ/kgmol -°K = 1,545.32 ft-lbf/pmol-°R

## Saturation Temperature Property Table for R-12 (English Units)

| Temperature (°F) | Pressure (psia) | Vapor Volume (ft³/lbm) | Liquid Density (lbm/ft³) | Liquid Enthalpy (Btu/lbm) | Vapor Enthalpy (Btu/lbm) | Liquid Entropy (Btu/lbm-°F) | Vapor Entropy (Btu/lbm-°F) |
|---|---|---|---|---|---|---|---|
| −40 | 9.3 | 3.8992 | 94.6749 | 0.00 | 73.27 | 0.0000 | 0.1746 |
| −35 | 10.6 | 3.4599 | 94.1795 | 1.05 | 73.84 | 0.0025 | 0.1739 |
| −30 | 12.0 | 3.0797 | 93.6808 | 2.10 | 74.41 | 0.0049 | 0.1732 |
| −25 | 13.5 | 2.7494 | 93.1786 | 3.15 | 74.98 | 0.0074 | 0.1726 |
| −20 | 15.2 | 2.4615 | 92.6729 | 4.21 | 75.55 | 0.0098 | 0.1720 |
| −15 | 17.1 | 2.2098 | 92.1633 | 5.28 | 76.11 | 0.0122 | 0.1715 |
| −10 | 19.2 | 1.9889 | 91.6499 | 6.35 | 76.68 | 0.0146 | 0.1710 |
| −5 | 21.4 | 1.7945 | 91.1322 | 7.42 | 77.24 | 0.0169 | 0.1705 |
| 0 | 23.8 | 1.6230 | 90.6103 | 8.51 | 77.80 | 0.0193 | 0.1700 |
| 5 | 26.4 | 1.4711 | 90.0838 | 9.59 | 78.35 | 0.0216 | 0.1696 |
| 10 | 29.3 | 1.3364 | 89.5526 | 10.68 | 78.90 | 0.0239 | 0.1692 |
| 15 | 32.4 | 1.2165 | 89.0164 | 11.78 | 79.45 | 0.0263 | 0.1688 |
| 20 | 35.7 | 1.1095 | 88.4751 | 12.88 | 80.00 | 0.0286 | 0.1685 |
| 25 | 39.3 | 1.0138 | 87.9283 | 13.99 | 80.54 | 0.0308 | 0.1681 |
| 30 | 43.1 | 0.9281 | 87.3758 | 15.10 | 81.07 | 0.0331 | 0.1678 |
| 35 | 47.2 | 0.8510 | 86.8173 | 16.22 | 81.61 | 0.0354 | 0.1675 |
| 40 | 51.6 | 0.7816 | 86.2525 | 17.35 | 82.13 | 0.0376 | 0.1673 |
| 45 | 56.3 | 0.7190 | 85.6812 | 18.48 | 82.65 | 0.0398 | 0.1670 |
| 50 | 61.3 | 0.6624 | 85.1030 | 19.62 | 83.17 | 0.0421 | 0.1668 |
| 55 | 66.6 | 0.6110 | 84.5175 | 20.77 | 83.68 | 0.0443 | 0.1665 |
| 60 | 72.3 | 0.5645 | 83.9243 | 21.92 | 84.18 | 0.0465 | 0.1663 |
| 65 | 78.4 | 0.5221 | 83.3231 | 23.08 | 84.67 | 0.0487 | 0.1661 |
| 70 | 84.8 | 0.4835 | 82.7134 | 24.25 | 85.16 | 0.0509 | 0.1659 |
| 75 | 91.5 | 0.4482 | 82.0948 | 25.43 | 85.64 | 0.0531 | 0.1657 |
| 80 | 98.7 | 0.4159 | 81.4667 | 26.61 | 86.11 | 0.0552 | 0.1655 |
| 85 | 106.3 | 0.3864 | 80.8286 | 27.80 | 86.58 | 0.0574 | 0.1653 |
| 90 | 114.3 | 0.3593 | 80.1799 | 29.01 | 87.03 | 0.0596 | 0.1651 |
| 95 | 122.7 | 0.3344 | 79.5199 | 30.22 | 87.47 | 0.0617 | 0.1649 |
| 100 | 131.6 | 0.3114 | 78.8479 | 31.44 | 87.90 | 0.0639 | 0.1648 |
| 105 | 141.0 | 0.2903 | 78.1631 | 32.67 | 88.32 | 0.0660 | 0.1646 |
| 110 | 150.8 | 0.2707 | 77.4647 | 33.91 | 88.73 | 0.0682 | 0.1644 |
| 115 | 161.1 | 0.2527 | 76.7517 | 35.16 | 89.12 | 0.0703 | 0.1642 |
| 120 | 172.0 | 0.2359 | 76.0230 | 36.43 | 89.50 | 0.0725 | 0.1640 |
| 125 | 183.3 | 0.2204 | 75.2774 | 37.70 | 89.87 | 0.0746 | 0.1638 |
| 130 | 195.2 | 0.2060 | 74.5136 | 38.99 | 90.22 | 0.0768 | 0.1636 |
| 135 | 207.7 | 0.1926 | 73.7301 | 40.30 | 90.55 | 0.0789 | 0.1634 |
| 140 | 220.7 | 0.1801 | 72.9250 | 41.61 | 90.86 | 0.0811 | 0.1632 |
| 145 | 234.4 | 0.1684 | 72.0965 | 42.95 | 91.15 | 0.0832 | 0.1629 |
| 150 | 248.6 | 0.1575 | 71.2423 | 44.30 | 91.41 | 0.0854 | 0.1627 |

## Saturation Pressure Property Table for R-12 (English Units)

| Pressure (psia) | Temperature (°F) | Vapor Volume (ft³/lbm) | Liquid Density (lbm/ft³) | Liquid Enthalpy (Btu/lbm) | Vapor Enthalpy (Btu/lbm) | Liquid Entropy (Btu/lbm-°F) | Vapor Entropy (Btu/lbm-°F) |
|---|---|---|---|---|---|---|---|
| 10 | −37.18 | 3.6432 | 94.3955 | 0.59 | 73.60 | 0.0014 | 0.1742 |
| 15 | −20.69 | 2.4988 | 92.7425 | 4.07 | 75.47 | 0.0095 | 0.1721 |
| 20 | −8.06 | 1.9107 | 91.4499 | 6.77 | 76.90 | 0.0155 | 0.1708 |
| 25 | 2.31 | 1.5506 | 90.3679 | 9.01 | 78.05 | 0.0204 | 0.1698 |
| 30 | 11.19 | 1.3066 | 89.4256 | 10.94 | 79.04 | 0.0245 | 0.1691 |
| 35 | 19.00 | 1.1299 | 88.5836 | 12.66 | 79.89 | 0.0281 | 0.1685 |
| 40 | 26.01 | 0.9958 | 87.8176 | 14.21 | 80.65 | 0.0313 | 0.1681 |
| 50 | 38.23 | 0.8053 | 86.4531 | 16.95 | 81.95 | 0.0368 | 0.1674 |
| 60 | 48.73 | 0.6762 | 85.2504 | 19.33 | 83.04 | 0.0415 | 0.1668 |
| 70 | 57.99 | 0.5826 | 84.1635 | 21.46 | 83.98 | 0.0456 | 0.1664 |
| 80 | 66.31 | 0.5116 | 83.1640 | 23.39 | 84.80 | 0.0493 | 0.1660 |
| 90 | 73.89 | 0.4557 | 82.2328 | 25.17 | 85.54 | 0.0526 | 0.1657 |
| 100 | 80.87 | 0.4106 | 81.3564 | 26.82 | 86.19 | 0.0556 | 0.1655 |
| 125 | 96.30 | 0.3282 | 79.3463 | 30.53 | 87.58 | 0.0623 | 0.1649 |
| 150 | 109.60 | 0.2723 | 77.5213 | 33.81 | 88.70 | 0.0680 | 0.1644 |
| 175 | 121.36 | 0.2316 | 75.8226 | 36.77 | 89.60 | 0.0730 | 0.1640 |
| 200 | 131.94 | 0.2007 | 74.2126 | 39.50 | 90.35 | 0.0776 | 0.1635 |
| 225 | 141.59 | 0.1763 | 72.6648 | 42.03 | 90.95 | 0.0817 | 0.1631 |

APPENDIX

## R-12 Superheat Property Table (English Units)

| Temperature (°F) | Volume (ft³/lbm) | Enthalpy (Btu/lbm) | Entropy (Btu/lbm-°F) | Volume (ft³/lbm) | Enthalpy (Btu/lbm) | Entropy (Btu/lbm-°F) |
|---|---|---|---|---|---|---|
| | 10.0 psia (−37.18°F) | | | 15.0 psia (−20.69°F) | | |
| −30 | 3.7112 | 74.54 | 0.1764 | — | — | — |
| −20 | 3.8054 | 75.87 | 0.1795 | 2.5032 | 75.56 | 0.1723 |
| −10 | 3.8992 | 77.22 | 0.1825 | 2.5676 | 76.93 | 0.1754 |
| 0 | 3.9925 | 78.57 | 0.1855 | 2.6316 | 78.30 | 0.1784 |
| 10 | 4.0855 | 79.94 | 0.1884 | 2.6951 | 79.68 | 0.1814 |
| 20 | 4.1781 | 81.32 | 0.1913 | 2.7583 | 81.07 | 0.1843 |
| 30 | 4.2705 | 82.71 | 0.1942 | 2.8212 | 82.48 | 0.1872 |
| 40 | 4.3626 | 84.11 | 0.1970 | 2.8838 | 83.89 | 0.1901 |
| 50 | 4.4545 | 85.53 | 0.1998 | 2.9462 | 85.32 | 0.1929 |
| 60 | 4.5462 | 86.96 | 0.2026 | 3.0083 | 86.76 | 0.1957 |
| | 20.0 psia (−8.06°F) | | | 25.0 psia (2.31°F) | | |
| 0 | 1.9505 | 78.02 | 0.1732 | — | — | — |
| 10 | 1.9994 | 79.42 | 0.1763 | 1.5815 | 79.15 | 0.1722 |
| 20 | 2.0479 | 80.83 | 0.1792 | 1.6214 | 80.57 | 0.1752 |
| 30 | 2.0961 | 82.24 | 0.1821 | 1.6608 | 82.00 | 0.1781 |
| 40 | 2.1441 | 83.67 | 0.1850 | 1.6999 | 83.44 | 0.1810 |
| 50 | 2.1917 | 85.11 | 0.1879 | 1.7388 | 84.89 | 0.1839 |
| 60 | 2.2391 | 86.56 | 0.1907 | 1.7774 | 86.35 | 0.1868 |
| 70 | 2.2863 | 88.02 | 0.1935 | 1.8158 | 87.82 | 0.1896 |
| 80 | 2.3334 | 89.49 | 0.1962 | 1.8540 | 89.30 | 0.1923 |
| | 30.0 psia (11.19°F) | | | 35.0 psia (19.00°F) | | |
| 20 | 1.3366 | 80.31 | 0.1718 | 1.1329 | 80.04 | 0.1688 |
| 30 | 1.3703 | 81.76 | 0.1748 | 1.1625 | 81.50 | 0.1719 |
| 40 | 1.4036 | 83.21 | 0.1777 | 1.1917 | 82.97 | 0.1748 |
| 50 | 1.4367 | 84.67 | 0.1806 | 1.2207 | 84.45 | 0.1778 |
| 60 | 1.4694 | 86.14 | 0.1835 | 1.2493 | 85.93 | 0.1807 |
| 70 | 1.5020 | 87.62 | 0.1863 | 1.2777 | 87.42 | 0.1835 |
| 80 | 1.5343 | 89.11 | 0.1891 | 1.3058 | 88.92 | 0.1862 |
| | 40 psia (26.01°F) | | | 50 psia (38.23°F) | | |
| 30 | 1.0064 | 81.24 | 0.1693 | — | — | — |
| 40 | 1.0326 | 82.73 | 0.1723 | 0.8092 | 82.22 | 0.1679 |
| 50 | 1.0585 | 84.22 | 0.1753 | 0.8309 | 83.74 | 0.1709 |
| 60 | 1.0840 | 85.71 | 0.1782 | 0.8522 | 85.27 | 0.1739 |
| 70 | 1.1093 | 87.21 | 0.1810 | 0.8733 | 86.79 | 0.1768 |
| 80 | 1.1344 | 88.72 | 0.1838 | 0.8940 | 88.32 | 0.1797 |
| 90 | 1.1592 | 90.24 | 0.1866 | 0.9146 | 89.86 | 0.1825 |
| 100 | 1.1839 | 91.76 | 0.1894 | 0.9349 | 91.40 | 0.1852 |
| 110 | 1.2085 | 93.29 | 0.1921 | 0.9551 | 92.95 | 0.1880 |
| 120 | 1.2328 | 94.83 | 0.1948 | 0.9751 | 94.50 | 0.1907 |
| | 60.0 psia (48.73°F) | | | 70.0 psia (57.99°F) | | |
| 50 | 0.6786 | 83.24 | 0.1672 | — | — | — |
| 60 | 0.6972 | 84.80 | 0.1702 | 0.5860 | 84.30 | 0.1670 |
| 70 | 0.7155 | 86.35 | 0.1732 | 0.6024 | 85.89 | 0.1700 |
| 80 | 0.7334 | 87.91 | 0.1761 | 0.6184 | 87.47 | 0.1730 |
| 90 | 0.7511 | 89.46 | 0.1790 | 0.6341 | 89.06 | 0.1759 |
| 100 | 0.7686 | 91.03 | 0.1818 | 0.6496 | 90.64 | 0.1788 |
| 110 | 0.7859 | 92.59 | 0.1846 | 0.6649 | 92.23 | 0.1816 |
| 120 | 0.8031 | 94.16 | 0.1873 | 0.6800 | 93.81 | 0.1843 |
| 130 | 0.8200 | 95.74 | 0.1900 | 0.6949 | 95.41 | 0.1871 |
| 140 | 0.8369 | 97.32 | 0.1926 | 0.7097 | 97.00 | 0.1897 |

| Temperature (°F) | Volume (ft³/lbm) | Enthalpy (Btu/lbm) | Entropy (Btu/lbm-°F) | Volume (ft³/lbm) | Enthalpy (Btu/lbm) | Entropy (Btu/lbm-°F) |
|---|---|---|---|---|---|---|
| | 80.0 psia (66.31°F) | | | 90.0 psia (73.89°F) | | |
| 70 | 0.5171 | 85.40 | 0.1672 | — | — | — |
| 80 | 0.5318 | 87.02 | 0.1702 | 0.4640 | 86.55 | 0.1676 |
| 90 | 0.5461 | 88.63 | 0.1732 | 0.4773 | 88.19 | 0.1706 |
| 100 | 0.5601 | 90.24 | 0.1761 | 0.4903 | 89.83 | 0.1736 |
| 110 | 0.5739 | 91.85 | 0.1789 | 0.5030 | 91.46 | 0.1765 |
| 120 | 0.5875 | 93.46 | 0.1817 | 0.5155 | 93.09 | 0.1793 |
| 130 | 0.6010 | 95.07 | 0.1844 | 0.5277 | 94.72 | 0.1821 |
| 140 | 0.6142 | 96.68 | 0.1872 | 0.5398 | 96.35 | 0.1848 |
| 150 | 0.6274 | 98.30 | 0.1898 | 0.5518 | 97.98 | 0.1875 |
| | 100 psia (80.67°F) | | | 125.0 psia (96.30°F) | | |
| 90 | 0.4220 | 87.73 | 0.1683 | — | — | — |
| 100 | 0.4342 | 89.40 | 0.1713 | 0.3322 | 88.24 | 0.1661 |
| 110 | 0.4460 | 91.06 | 0.1742 | 0.3427 | 89.98 | 0.1692 |
| 120 | 0.4576 | 92.71 | 0.1771 | 0.3529 | 91.71 | 0.1722 |
| 130 | 0.4690 | 94.36 | 0.1799 | 0.3628 | 93.42 | 0.1751 |
| 140 | 0.4802 | 96.01 | 0.1827 | 0.3724 | 95.12 | 0.1779 |
| 150 | 0.4912 | 97.66 | 0.1854 | 0.3818 | 96.81 | 0.1807 |
| 160 | 0.5021 | 99.31 | 0.1881 | 0.3911 | 98.51 | 0.1835 |
| 170 | 0.5129 | 100.96 | 0.1907 | 0.4002 | 100.20 | 0.1862 |
| 180 | 0.5235 | 102.62 | 0.1934 | 0.4092 | 101.89 | 0.1889 |
| | 150.0 psia (109.60°F) | | | 175.0 psia (121.36°F) | | |
| 110 | 0.2726 | 88.77 | 0.1645 | — | — | — |
| 120 | 0.2821 | 90.60 | 0.1677 | — | — | — |
| 130 | 0.2912 | 92.39 | 0.1708 | 0.2391 | 91.25 | 0.1668 |
| 140 | 0.2999 | 94.16 | 0.1738 | 0.2474 | 93.11 | 0.1699 |
| 150 | 0.3084 | 95.91 | 0.1767 | 0.2553 | 94.94 | 0.1729 |
| 160 | 0.3166 | 97.66 | 0.1795 | 0.2630 | 96.75 | 0.1759 |
| 170 | 0.3247 | 99.30 | 0.1823 | 0.2704 | 98.54 | 0.1787 |
| 180 | 0.3326 | 101.12 | 0.1850 | 0.2776 | 100.31 | 0.1815 |
| 190 | 0.3404 | 102.85 | 0.1877 | 0.2847 | 102.08 | 0.1843 |
| 200 | 0.3481 | 104.57 | 0.1903 | 0.2916 | 103.85 | 0.1870 |
| | 200.0 psia (131.94°F) | | | 225.0 psia (141.59°F) | | |
| 140 | 0.2072 | 91.95 | 0.1662 | — | — | — |
| 150 | 0.2149 | 93.88 | 0.1694 | 0.1828 | 92.69 | 0.1660 |
| 160 | 0.2222 | 95.77 | 0.1725 | 0.1990 | 94.69 | 0.1692 |
| 170 | 0.2292 | 97.62 | 0.1755 | 0.1968 | 96.64 | 0.1723 |
| 180 | 0.2360 | 99.46 | 0.1784 | 0.2033 | 98.54 | 0.1753 |
| 190 | 0.2426 | 101.28 | 0.1812 | 0.2096 | 100.42 | 0.1783 |
| 200 | 0.2490 | 103.08 | 0.1839 | 0.2156 | 102.28 | 0.1811 |
| 210 | 0.2553 | 104.88 | 0.1866 | 0.2215 | 104.12 | 0.1839 |
| 220 | 0.2614 | 106.67 | 0.1893 | 0.2273 | 105.95 | 0.1866 |
| 230 | 0.2675 | 108.46 | 0.1919 | 0.2329 | 107.77 | 0.1892 |

APPENDIX

## Saturation Temperature Property Table for R-12 (SI Units)

| Temperature (°C) | Pressure (kPa) | Vapor Volume (m³/kg) | Liquid Density (kg/m³) | Liquid Enthalpy (kJ/kg) | Vapor Enthalpy (kJ/kg) | Liquid Entropy (kJ/kg-°C) | Vapor Entropy (kJ/kg-°C) |
|---|---|---|---|---|---|---|---|
| −40.00 | 64 | 0.24342 | 1,517 | 0.00 | 170.32 | 0.0000 | 0.7305 |
| −37.50 | 72 | 0.21856 | 1,509 | 2.19 | 171.51 | 0.0093 | 0.7279 |
| −35.00 | 81 | 0.19674 | 1,502 | 4.39 | 172.71 | 0.0186 | 0.7253 |
| −32.50 | 90 | 0.17753 | 1,495 | 6.59 | 173.90 | 0.0278 | 0.7230 |
| −30.00 | 100 | 0.16057 | 1,488 | 8.81 | 175.08 | 0.0369 | 0.7207 |
| −27.50 | 111 | 0.14555 | 1,480 | 11.03 | 176.27 | 0.0460 | 0.7186 |
| −25.00 | 123 | 0.13222 | 1,473 | 13.27 | 177.45 | 0.0550 | 0.7166 |
| −22.50 | 137 | 0.12036 | 1,466 | 15.51 | 178.62 | 0.0639 | 0.7147 |
| −20.00 | 151 | 0.10978 | 1,458 | 17.76 | 179.80 | 0.0728 | 0.7129 |
| −17.50 | 166 | 0.10032 | 1,451 | 20.02 | 180.96 | 0.0817 | 0.7112 |
| −15.00 | 182 | 0.09184 | 1,443 | 22.29 | 182.13 | 0.0905 | 0.7096 |
| −12.50 | 200 | 0.08422 | 1,435 | 24.57 | 183.28 | 0.0992 | 0.7081 |
| −10.00 | 219 | 0.07737 | 1,428 | 26.87 | 184.43 | 0.1079 | 0.7067 |
| −7.50 | 239 | 0.07119 | 1,420 | 29.17 | 185.57 | 0.1166 | 0.7053 |
| −5.00 | 261 | 0.06560 | 1,412 | 31.48 | 186.71 | 0.1252 | 0.7041 |
| −2.50 | 284 | 0.06054 | 1,404 | 33.81 | 187.83 | 0.1338 | 0.7028 |
| 0.00 | 308 | 0.05595 | 1,396 | 36.14 | 188.95 | 0.1423 | 0.7017 |
| 2.50 | 334 | 0.05178 | 1,388 | 38.49 | 190.06 | 0.1508 | 0.7006 |
| 5.00 | 362 | 0.04798 | 1,380 | 40.85 | 191.16 | 0.1592 | 0.6996 |
| 7.50 | 391 | 0.04452 | 1,372 | 43.22 | 192.24 | 0.1676 | 0.6986 |
| 10.00 | 423 | 0.04135 | 1,363 | 45.61 | 193.32 | 0.1760 | 0.6977 |
| 12.50 | 456 | 0.03845 | 1,355 | 48.01 | 194.39 | 0.1844 | 0.6968 |
| 15.00 | 491 | 0.03580 | 1,346 | 50.42 | 195.44 | 0.1927 | 0.6960 |
| 17.50 | 528 | 0.03336 | 1,338 | 52.84 | 196.48 | 0.2010 | 0.6952 |
| 20.00 | 566 | 0.03112 | 1,329 | 55.28 | 197.50 | 0.2092 | 0.6944 |
| 22.50 | 607 | 0.02906 | 1,320 | 57.73 | 198.52 | 0.2174 | 0.6936 |
| 25.00 | 651 | 0.02715 | 1,311 | 60.20 | 199.51 | 0.2256 | 0.6929 |
| 27.50 | 696 | 0.02540 | 1,302 | 62.69 | 200.49 | 0.2338 | 0.6922 |
| 30.00 | 744 | 0.02377 | 1,293 | 65.19 | 201.45 | 0.2420 | 0.6915 |
| 32.50 | 794 | 0.02227 | 1,283 | 67.71 | 202.40 | 0.2501 | 0.6908 |
| 35.00 | 846 | 0.02087 | 1,274 | 70.24 | 203.32 | 0.2583 | 0.6901 |
| 37.50 | 901 | 0.01958 | 1,264 | 72.79 | 204.22 | 0.2664 | 0.6895 |
| 40.00 | 959 | 0.01838 | 1,254 | 75.36 | 205.11 | 0.2745 | 0.6888 |
| 42.50 | 1,019 | 0.01726 | 1,244 | 77.96 | 205.96 | 0.2826 | 0.6881 |
| 45.00 | 1,082 | 0.01621 | 1,234 | 80.57 | 206.80 | 0.2906 | 0.6874 |
| 47.50 | 1,148 | 0.01524 | 1,224 | 83.20 | 207.61 | 0.2987 | 0.6867 |
| 50.00 | 1,217 | 0.01433 | 1,213 | 85.86 | 208.39 | 0.3068 | 0.6860 |
| 52.50 | 1,288 | 0.01348 | 1,202 | 88.53 | 209.14 | 0.3149 | 0.6852 |
| 55.00 | 1,363 | 0.01269 | 1,191 | 91.24 | 209.86 | 0.3229 | 0.6844 |
| 57.50 | 1,441 | 0.01194 | 1,180 | 93.97 | 210.54 | 0.3310 | 0.6836 |
| 60.00 | 1,522 | 0.01124 | 1,168 | 96.73 | 211.19 | 0.3391 | 0.6827 |
| 62.50 | 1,606 | 0.01058 | 1,156 | 99.52 | 211.80 | 0.3473 | 0.6818 |
| 65.00 | 1,694 | 0.00996 | 1,144 | 102.34 | 212.37 | 0.3554 | 0.6808 |
| 57.50 | 1,785 | 0.00938 | 1,131 | 105.19 | 212.89 | 0.3636 | 0.6797 |
| 70.00 | 1,880 | 0.00883 | 1,118 | 108.08 | 213.36 | 0.3718 | 0.6786 |

## Saturation Pressure Property Table for R-12 (SI Units)

| Pressure (kPa) | Temperature (°C) | Vapor Volume (m³/kg) | Liquid Density (kg/m³) | Liquid Enthalpy (kJ/kg) | Vapor Enthalpy (kJ/kg) | Liquid Entropy (kJ/kg-°C) | Vapor Entropy (kJ/kg-°C) |
|---|---|---|---|---|---|---|---|
| 50 | −45.15 | 0.30649 | 1,531 | −4.49 | 167.86 | −0.0194 | 0.7365 |
| 100 | −30.06 | 0.16096 | 1,488 | 8.75 | 175.05 | 0.0367 | 0.7208 |
| 150 | −20.12 | 0.11026 | 1,458 | 17.65 | 179.74 | 0.0724 | 0.7130 |
| 200 | −12.49 | 0.08419 | 1,435 | 24.59 | 183.29 | 0.0993 | 0.7081 |
| 250 | −6.20 | 0.06822 | 1,416 | 30.37 | 186.16 | 0.1211 | 0.7047 |
| 300 | −0.81 | 0.05739 | 1,399 | 35.38 | 188.59 | 0.1395 | 0.7021 |
| 400 | 8.20 | 0.04360 | 1,369 | 43.89 | 192.55 | 0.1700 | 0.6984 |
| 500 | 15.65 | 0.03515 | 1,344 | 51.04 | 195.71 | 0.1948 | 0.6957 |
| 600 | 22.06 | 0.02941 | 1,322 | 57.30 | 198.34 | 0.2160 | 0.6938 |
| 700 | 27.72 | 0.02525 | 1,301 | 62.90 | 200.57 | 0.2345 | 0.6921 |
| 800 | 32.81 | 0.02209 | 1,282 | 68.01 | 202.51 | 0.2511 | 0.6907 |
| 900 | 37.45 | 0.01961 | 1,264 | 72.74 | 204.20 | 0.2662 | 0.6895 |
| 1,000 | 41.72 | 0.01760 | 1,247 | 77.15 | 205.70 | 0.2800 | 0.6883 |
| 1,200 | 49.41 | 0.01454 | 1,216 | 85.22 | 208.21 | 0.3049 | 0.6861 |
| 1,400 | 56.20 | 0.01232 | 1,186 | 92.55 | 210.19 | 0.3268 | 0.6840 |
| 1,600 | 62.32 | 0.01063 | 1,157 | 99.31 | 211.76 | 0.3467 | 0.6819 |
| 1,800 | 67.89 | 0.00929 | 1,129 | 105.64 | 212.97 | 0.3649 | 0.6796 |
| 2,000 | 73.03 | 0.00820 | 1,102 | 111.64 | 213.86 | 0.3818 | 0.6771 |

## R-12 Superheat Property Table (SI Units)

| Temperature (°F) | Volume (m³/kg) | Enthalpy (kJ/kg) | Entropy (kJ/kg-°C) | Volume (m³/kg) | Enthalpy (kJ/kg) | Entropy (kJ/kg-°C) |
|---|---|---|---|---|---|---|
| | **50 kPa (−45.15°C)** | | | **100 kPa (−30.06°C)** | | |
| −40 | 0.31395 | 170.64 | 0.7486 | — | — | — |
| −30 | 0.32833 | 176.13 | 0.7716 | 0.16100 | 175.09 | 0.7209 |
| −20 | 0.34263 | 181.72 | 0.7941 | 0.16846 | 180.79 | 0.7439 |
| −10 | 0.35685 | 187.40 | 0.8161 | 0.17582 | 186.56 | 0.7663 |
| 0 | 0.37101 | 193.19 | 0.8377 | 0.18312 | 192.42 | 0.7881 |
| 10 | 0.38512 | 199.07 | 0.8589 | 0.19037 | 198.37 | 0.8095 |
| 20 | 0.39919 | 205.05 | 0.8796 | 0.19757 | 204.41 | 0.8304 |
| 30 | 0.41322 | 211.12 | 0.9000 | 0.20473 | 210.53 | 0.8510 |
| 40 | 0.42723 | 217.29 | 0.9200 | 0.21187 | 216.73 | 0.8711 |
| 50 | 0.44121 | 223.54 | 0.9396 | 0.21898 | 223.02 | 0.8909 |
| | **150 kPa (−20.12°C)** | | | **200 kPa (−12.49°C)** | | |
| −20 | 0.11032 | 179.81 | 0.7133 | — | — | — |
| −10 | 0.11542 | 185.69 | 0.7361 | 0.08517 | 184.78 | 0.7138 |
| 0 | 0.12045 | 191.64 | 0.7582 | 0.08908 | 190.83 | 0.7364 |
| 10 | 0.12542 | 197.66 | 0.7799 | 0.09292 | 196.92 | 0.7583 |
| 20 | 0.13034 | 203.75 | 0.8010 | 0.09670 | 203.08 | 0.7796 |
| 30 | 0.13522 | 209.92 | 0.8217 | 0.10044 | 209.30 | 0.8005 |
| 40 | 0.14007 | 216.17 | 0.8420 | 0.10415 | 215.60 | 0.8210 |
| 50 | 0.14489 | 222.50 | 0.8619 | 0.10783 | 221.97 | 0.8410 |
| 60 | 0.14969 | 228.90 | 0.8814 | 0.11149 | 228.41 | 0.8606 |
| 70 | 0.15447 | 235.38 | 0.9006 | 0.11512 | 234.92 | 0.8799 |
| | **250 kPa (−6.20°C)** | | | **300 kPa (−0.81°C)** | | |
| 0 | 0.07022 | 189.98 | 0.7188 | 0.05762 | 189.10 | 0.7039 |
| 10 | 0.07339 | 196.16 | 0.7410 | 0.06035 | 195.38 | 0.7265 |
| 20 | 0.07650 | 202.39 | 0.7626 | 0.06302 | 201.68 | 0.7484 |
| 30 | 0.07956 | 208.67 | 0.7837 | 0.06563 | 208.03 | 0.7697 |
| 40 | 0.08259 | 215.02 | 0.8043 | 0.06821 | 214.43 | 0.7905 |
| 50 | 0.08559 | 221.43 | 0.8245 | 0.07075 | 220.88 | 0.8107 |
| 60 | 0.08856 | 227.91 | 0.8442 | 0.07327 | 227.40 | 0.8306 |
| 70 | 0.09151 | 234.45 | 0.8636 | 0.07577 | 233.98 | 0.8501 |
| 80 | 0.09445 | 241.06 | 0.8826 | 0.07825 | 240.62 | 0.8691 |
| 90 | 0.09736 | 247.74 | 0.9012 | 0.08071 | 247.33 | 0.8879 |
| | **400 kPa (8.20°C)** | | | **500 kPa (15.65°C)** | | |
| 10 | 0.04399 | 193.72 | 0.7025 | — | — | — |
| 20 | 0.04612 | 200.20 | 0.7250 | 0.03593 | 198.62 | 0.7058 |
| 30 | 0.04819 | 206.69 | 0.7468 | 0.03768 | 205.29 | 0.7281 |
| 40 | 0.05021 | 213.21 | 0.7679 | 0.03938 | 211.94 | 0.7497 |
| 50 | 0.05219 | 219.76 | 0.7885 | 0.04103 | 218.60 | 0.7706 |
| 60 | 0.05414 | 226.36 | 0.8086 | 0.04265 | 225.29 | 0.7910 |
| 70 | 0.05607 | 233.01 | 0.8283 | 0.04424 | 232.02 | 0.8109 |
| 80 | 0.05798 | 239.72 | 0.8476 | 0.04582 | 238.79 | 0.8304 |
| 90 | 0.05988 | 246.48 | 0.8665 | 0.04737 | 245.62 | 0.8494 |
| 100 | 0.06175 | 253.30 | 0.8850 | 0.04891 | 252.49 | 0.8681 |

| Temperature (°F) | Volume ($m^3/kg$) | Enthalpy ($kJ/kg$) | Entropy ($kJ/kg$-°C) | Volume ($m^3/kg$) | Enthalpy ($kJ/kg$) | Entropy ($kJ/kg$-°C) |
|---|---|---|---|---|---|---|
| | 600 kPa (22.06°C) | | | 700 kPa (27.72°C) | | |
| 30 | 0.03064 | 203.79 | 0.7120 | 0.02557 | 202.19 | 0.6975 |
| 40 | 0.03213 | 210.60 | 0.7341 | 0.02693 | 209.20 | 0.7202 |
| 50 | 0.03357 | 217.39 | 0.7554 | 0.02822 | 216.13 | 0.7420 |
| 60 | 0.03497 | 224.19 | 0.7761 | 0.02947 | 223.04 | 0.7631 |
| 70 | 0.03635 | 231.00 | 0.7963 | 0.03069 | 229.95 | 0.7835 |
| 80 | 0.03770 | 237.85 | 0.8160 | 0.03188 | 236.88 | 0.8034 |
| 90 | 0.03902 | 244.74 | 0.8352 | 0.03306 | 243.84 | 0.8228 |
| 100 | 0.04034 | 251.66 | 0.8540 | 0.03421 | 250.82 | 0.8418 |
| 110 | 0.04163 | 258.64 | 0.8725 | 0.03534 | 257.85 | 0.8604 |
| 120 | 0.04292 | 265.66 | 0.8905 | 0.03647 | 264.92 | 0.8786 |
| | 800 kPa (32.81°C) | | | 900 kPa (37.45°C) | | |
| 40 | 0.02300 | 207.70 | 0.7075 | 0.01991 | 206.11 | 0.6956 |
| 50 | 0.02419 | 214.81 | 0.7298 | 0.02103 | 213.42 | 0.7186 |
| 60 | 0.02533 | 221.85 | 0.7513 | 0.02210 | 220.62 | 0.7405 |
| 70 | 0.02644 | 228.87 | 0.7721 | 0.02312 | 227.75 | 0.7616 |
| 80 | 0.02752 | 235.89 | 0.7922 | 0.02412 | 234.86 | 0.7820 |
| 90 | 0.02857 | 242.91 | 0.8118 | 0.02508 | 241.97 | 0.8019 |
| 100 | 0.02961 | 249.97 | 0.8310 | 0.02602 | 249.09 | 0.8212 |
| 110 | 0.03062 | 257.05 | 0.8497 | 0.02695 | 256.23 | 0.8401 |
| 120 | 0.03163 | 264.17 | 0.8681 | 0.02786 | 263.40 | 0.8586 |
| 130 | 0.03262 | 271.32 | 0.8860 | 0.02876 | 270.60 | 0.8767 |
| | 1,000 kPa (41.72°C) | | | 1,200 kPa (49.41°C) | | |
| 50 | 0.01849 | 211.95 | 0.7079 | 0.01460 | 208.68 | 0.6876 |
| 60 | 0.01950 | 219.32 | 0.7304 | 0.01555 | 216.53 | 0.7115 |
| 70 | 0.02046 | 226.59 | 0.7519 | 0.01643 | 224.13 | 0.7340 |
| 80 | 0.02138 | 233.81 | 0.7726 | 0.01727 | 231.60 | 0.7555 |
| 90 | 0.02228 | 241.01 | 0.7927 | 0.01806 | 238.99 | 0.7761 |
| 100 | 0.02315 | 248.20 | 0.8122 | 0.01883 | 246.35 | 0.7961 |
| 110 | 0.02401 | 255.40 | 0.8313 | 0.01958 | 253.69 | 0.8155 |
| 120 | 0.02484 | 262.63 | 0.8499 | 0.02031 | 261.04 | 0.8344 |
| 130 | 0.02567 | 269.88 | 0.8681 | 0.02102 | 268.39 | 0.8529 |
| 140 | 0.02648 | 277.15 | 0.8859 | 0.02173 | 275.76 | 0.8710 |
| | 1,400 kPa (56.20°C) | | | 1,600 kPa (62.32°C) | | |
| 60 | 0.01267 | 213.37 | 0.6936 | — | — | — |
| 70 | 0.01351 | 221.43 | 0.7175 | 0.01127 | 218.42 | 0.7015 |
| 80 | 0.01429 | 229.23 | 0.7399 | 0.01203 | 226.64 | 0.7251 |
| 90 | 0.01503 | 236.86 | 0.7612 | 0.01273 | 234.59 | 0.7473 |
| 100 | 0.01573 | 244.41 | 0.7817 | 0.01339 | 242.37 | 0.7684 |
| 110 | 0.01641 | 251.91 | 0.8015 | 0.01401 | 250.05 | 0.7888 |
| 120 | 0.01706 | 259.39 | 0.8208 | 0.01462 | 257.68 | 0.8084 |
| 130 | 0.01770 | 266.86 | 0.8396 | 0.01520 | 265.28 | 0.8275 |
| 140 | 0.01833 | 274.33 | 0.8579 | 0.01577 | 272.85 | 0.8461 |
| 150 | 0.01894 | 281.81 | 0.8757 | 0.01633 | 280.43 | 0.8642 |
| | 1,800 kPa (67.89°C) | | | 2,000 kPa (73.30°C) | | |
| 70 | 0.00947 | 214.94 | 0.6853 | — | — | — |
| 80 | 0.01024 | 223.79 | 0.7108 | 0.00875 | 220.57 | 0.6963 |
| 90 | 0.01092 | 232.13 | 0.7341 | 0.00944 | 229.46 | 0.7211 |
| 100 | 0.01155 | 240.20 | 0.7560 | 0.01006 | 237.88 | 0.7440 |
| 110 | 0.01214 | 248.10 | 0.7769 | 0.01063 | 246.04 | 0.7656 |
| 120 | 0.01271 | 255.90 | 0.7970 | 0.01117 | 254.04 | 0.7862 |
| 130 | 0.01325 | 263.64 | 0.8164 | 0.01168 | 261.94 | 0.8060 |
| 140 | 0.01378 | 271.34 | 0.8353 | 0.01218 | 269.78 | 0.8252 |
| 150 | 0.01429 | 279.02 | 0.8536 | 0.01266 | 277.57 | 0.8438 |
| 160 | 0.01479 | 286.69 | 0.8715 | 0.01312 | 285.34 | 0.8620 |

## Saturation Temperature Property Table for R-22 (English Units)

| Temperature (°F) | Pressure (psia) | Vapor Volume (ft³/lbm) | Liquid Density (lbm/ft³) | Liquid Enthalpy (Btu/lbm) | Vapor Enthalpy (Btu/lbm) | Liquid Entropy (Btu/lbm-°F) | Vapor Entropy (Btu/lbm-°F) |
|---|---|---|---|---|---|---|---|
| −40 | 15.3 | 3.2872 | 87.8241 | 0.00 | 100.34 | 0.0000 | 0.2391 |
| −35 | 17.3 | 2.9181 | 87.3159 | 1.31 | 100.90 | 0.0031 | 0.2376 |
| −30 | 19.6 | 2.5984 | 86.8034 | 2.62 | 101.44 | 0.0061 | 0.2361 |
| −25 | 22.1 | 2.3204 | 86.2864 | 3.94 | 101.98 | 0.0092 | 0.2347 |
| −20 | 24.9 | 2.0779 | 85.7647 | 5.26 | 102.52 | 0.0122 | 0.2334 |
| −15 | 27.9 | 1.8656 | 85.2381 | 6.59 | 103.05 | 0.0152 | 0.2321 |
| −10 | 31.2 | 1.6792 | 84.7064 | 7.92 | 103.57 | 0.0182 | 0.2309 |
| −5 | 34.8 | 1.5150 | 84.1692 | 9.26 | 104.08 | 0.0211 | 0.2296 |
| 0 | 38.7 | 1.3701 | 83.6265 | 10.61 | 104.59 | 0.0240 | 0.2285 |
| 5 | 43.0 | 1.2417 | 83.0779 | 11.96 | 105.09 | 0.0269 | 0.2273 |
| 10 | 47.5 | 1.1276 | 82.5232 | 13.33 | 105.58 | 0.0298 | 0.2263 |
| 15 | 52.5 | 1.0261 | 81.9620 | 14.69 | 106.06 | 0.0327 | 0.2252 |
| 20 | 57.8 | 0.9354 | 81.3942 | 16.07 | 106.53 | 0.0356 | 0.2242 |
| 25 | 63.5 | 0.8543 | 80.8194 | 17.46 | 106.99 | 0.0384 | 0.2231 |
| 30 | 69.7 | 0.7815 | 80.2372 | 18.85 | 107.44 | 0.0412 | 0.2222 |
| 35 | 76.2 | 0.7161 | 79.6474 | 20.25 | 107.88 | 0.0441 | 0.2212 |
| 40 | 83.3 | 0.6572 | 79.0495 | 21.66 | 108.31 | 0.0469 | 0.2203 |
| 45 | 90.8 | 0.6040 | 78.4432 | 23.08 | 108.73 | 0.0497 | 0.2194 |
| 50 | 98.8 | 0.5558 | 77.8279 | 24.51 | 109.13 | 0.0524 | 0.2185 |
| 55 | 107.3 | 0.5122 | 77.2034 | 25.96 | 109.52 | 0.0552 | 0.2176 |
| 60 | 116.3 | 0.4725 | 76.5689 | 27.41 | 109.90 | 0.0580 | 0.2167 |
| 65 | 125.9 | 0.4364 | 75.9240 | 28.87 | 110.26 | 0.0607 | 0.2159 |
| 70 | 136.1 | 0.4035 | 75.2681 | 30.35 | 110.60 | 0.0635 | 0.2150 |
| 75 | 146.9 | 0.3734 | 74.6005 | 31.84 | 110.93 | 0.0662 | 0.2142 |
| 80 | 158.3 | 0.3459 | 73.9203 | 33.34 | 111.24 | 0.0690 | 0.2133 |
| 85 | 170.4 | 0.3207 | 73.2269 | 34.86 | 111.53 | 0.0717 | 0.2125 |
| 90 | 183.1 | 0.2975 | 72.5191 | 36.39 | 111.80 | 0.0745 | 0.2117 |
| 95 | 196.5 | 0.2762 | 71.7960 | 37.94 | 112.05 | 0.0772 | 0.2108 |
| 100 | 210.6 | 0.2566 | 71.0564 | 39.50 | 112.28 | 0.0800 | 0.2100 |
| 105 | 225.5 | 0.2385 | 70.2988 | 41.08 | 112.48 | 0.0827 | 0.2091 |
| 110 | 241.1 | 0.2217 | 69.5217 | 42.69 | 112.65 | 0.0855 | 0.2083 |
| 115 | 257.5 | 0.2062 | 68.7233 | 44.31 | 112.80 | 0.0882 | 0.2074 |
| 120 | 274.7 | 0.1918 | 67.9016 | 45.95 | 112.91 | 0.0910 | 0.2065 |
| 125 | 292.7 | 0.1785 | 67.0539 | 47.62 | 113.00 | 0.0938 | 0.2056 |
| 130 | 311.6 | 0.1660 | 66.1776 | 49.32 | 113.04 | 0.0966 | 0.2046 |
| 135 | 331.4 | 0.1544 | 65.2692 | 51.04 | 113.04 | 0.0994 | 0.2036 |
| 140 | 352.1 | 0.1435 | 64.3246 | 52.80 | 113.00 | 0.1022 | 0.2026 |
| 145 | 373.7 | 0.1334 | 63.3392 | 54.59 | 112.91 | 0.1051 | 0.2015 |
| 150 | 396.4 | 0.1238 | 62.3068 | 56.42 | 112.76 | 0.1080 | 0.2004 |

## Saturation Pressure Property Table for R-22 (English Units)

| Pressure (psia) | Temperature (°F) | Vapor Volume (ft³/lbm) | Liquid Density (lbm/ft³) | Liquid Enthalpy (Btu/lbm) | Vapor Enthalpy (Btu/lbm) | Liquid Entropy (Btu/lbm-°F) | Vapor Entropy (Btu/lbm-°F) |
|---|---|---|---|---|---|---|---|
| 20 | −29.22 | 2.5526 | 86.7234 | 2.82 | 101.53 | 0.0066 | 0.2359 |
| 30 | −11.81 | 1.7440 | 84.8998 | 7.44 | 103.38 | 0.0171 | 0.2313 |
| 40 | 1.54 | 1.3287 | 83.4576 | 11.03 | 104.75 | 0.0249 | 0.2281 |
| 50 | 12.54 | 1.0745 | 82.2388 | 14.02 | 105.83 | 0.0313 | 0.2257 |
| 60 | 21.97 | 0.9024 | 81.1685 | 16.62 | 106.72 | 0.0367 | 0.2238 |
| 70 | 30.27 | 0.7778 | 80.2051 | 18.92 | 107.47 | 0.0414 | 0.2221 |
| 80 | 37.73 | 0.6832 | 79.3225 | 21.02 | 108.12 | 0.0456 | 0.2207 |
| 100 | 50.75 | 0.5490 | 77.7354 | 24.73 | 109.19 | 0.0529 | 0.2183 |
| 120 | 61.94 | 0.4581 | 76.3197 | 27.98 | 110.04 | 0.0591 | 0.2164 |
| 140 | 71.83 | 0.3922 | 75.0258 | 30.89 | 110.72 | 0.0645 | 0.2147 |
| 160 | 80.71 | 0.3422 | 73.8227 | 33.56 | 111.28 | 0.0694 | 0.2132 |
| 180 | 88.81 | 0.3029 | 72.6892 | 36.02 | 111.74 | 0.0738 | 0.2119 |
| 200 | 96.27 | 0.2711 | 71.6104 | 38.33 | 112.11 | 0.0779 | 0.2106 |
| 250 | 112.76 | 0.2130 | 69.0844 | 43.58 | 112.74 | 0.0870 | 0.2078 |
| 300 | 126.96 | 0.1735 | 66.7135 | 48.28 | 113.02 | 0.0949 | 0.2052 |
| 350 | 139.51 | 0.1446 | 64.4192 | 52.62 | 113.01 | 0.1019 | 0.2027 |
| 400 | 150.78 | 0.1224 | 62.1412 | 56.71 | 112.73 | 0.1085 | 0.2002 |

## R-22 Superheat Property Table (English Units)

| Temperature (°F) | Volume (ft³/lbm) | Enthalpy (Btu/lbm) | Entropy (Btu/lbm-°F) | Volume (ft³/lbm) | Enthalpy (Btu/lbm) | Entropy (Btu/lbm-°F) |
|---|---|---|---|---|---|---|
| | **20 psia (–29.22°F)** | | | **30 psia (–11.81°F)** | | |
| –20 | 2.6166 | 102.90 | 0.2391 | — | — | — |
| –10 | 2.6853 | 104.40 | 0.2425 | 1.7528 | 103.66 | 0.2319 |
| 0 | 2.7534 | 105.91 | 0.2458 | 1.8005 | 105.22 | 0.2354 |
| 10 | 2.8209 | 107.42 | 0.2490 | 1.8477 | 106.78 | 0.2387 |
| 20 | 2.8880 | 108.95 | 0.2522 | 1.8944 | 108.34 | 0.2420 |
| 30 | 2.9546 | 110.48 | 0.2554 | 1.9405 | 109.91 | 0.2453 |
| 40 | 3.0209 | 112.02 | 0.2585 | 1.9863 | 111.49 | 0.2484 |
| 50 | 3.0869 | 113.58 | 0.2616 | 2.0318 | 113.08 | 0.2516 |
| 60 | 3.1526 | 115.15 | 0.2647 | 2.0769 | 114.67 | 0.2547 |
| 70 | 3.2180 | 116.73 | 0.2677 | 2.1217 | 116.27 | 0.2577 |
| | **40 psia (1.54°F)** | | | **50 psia (12.54°F)** | | |
| 10 | 1.3601 | 106.11 | 0.2311 | — | — | — |
| 20 | 1.3967 | 107.72 | 0.2344 | 1.0974 | 107.06 | 0.2283 |
| 30 | 1.4328 | 109.33 | 0.2378 | 1.1275 | 108.72 | 0.2317 |
| 40 | 1.4684 | 110.94 | 0.2410 | 1.1572 | 110.37 | 0.2351 |
| 50 | 1.5037 | 112.56 | 0.2442 | 1.1864 | 112.02 | 0.2383 |
| 60 | 1.5386 | 114.18 | 0.2474 | 1.2152 | 113.68 | 0.2416 |
| 70 | 1.5732 | 115.81 | 0.2505 | 1.2438 | 115.34 | 0.2447 |
| 80 | 1.6075 | 117.45 | 0.2536 | 1.2720 | 117.00 | 0.2478 |
| | **60 psia (21.97°F)** | | | **70 psia (30.27°F)** | | |
| 30 | 0.9235 | 108.09 | 0.2266 | — | — | — |
| 40 | 0.9492 | 109.78 | 0.2300 | 0.8002 | 109.17 | 0.2256 |
| 50 | 0.9745 | 111.47 | 0.2334 | 0.8227 | 110.90 | 0.2290 |
| 60 | 0.9993 | 113.16 | 0.2366 | 0.8448 | 112.63 | 0.2323 |
| 70 | 1.0239 | 114.85 | 0.2399 | 0.8665 | 114.35 | 0.2356 |
| 80 | 1.0481 | 116.54 | 0.2430 | 0.8879 | 116.07 | 0.2388 |
| | **80 psia (37.73°F)** | | | **100 psia (50.75°F)** | | |
| 40 | 0.6880 | 108.53 | 0.2215 | — | — | — |
| 50 | 0.7086 | 110.31 | 0.2251 | — | — | — |
| 60 | 0.7286 | 112.08 | 0.2285 | 0.5652 | 110.92 | 0.2217 |
| 70 | 0.7483 | 113.84 | 0.2318 | 0.5821 | 112.76 | 0.2252 |
| 80 | 0.7675 | 115.59 | 0.2351 | 0.5985 | 114.59 | 0.2286 |
| 90 | 0.7865 | 117.34 | 0.2383 | 0.6146 | 116.40 | 0.2319 |
| 100 | 0.8052 | 119.09 | 0.2415 | 0.6304 | 118.20 | 0.2352 |
| 110 | 0.8236 | 120.84 | 0.2446 | 0.6459 | 120.00 | 0.2384 |
| 120 | 0.8419 | 122.59 | 0.2476 | 0.6612 | 121.80 | 0.2415 |
| 130 | 0.8599 | 124.35 | 0.2506 | 0.6762 | 123.60 | 0.2446 |
| | **120 psia (61.94°F)** | | | **140 psia (71.83°F)** | | |
| 70 | 0.4704 | 111.61 | 0.2194 | — | — | — |
| 80 | 0.4851 | 113.52 | 0.2229 | 0.4034 | 112.37 | 0.2178 |
| 90 | 0.4994 | 115.41 | 0.2264 | 0.4166 | 114.35 | 0.2214 |
| 100 | 0.5134 | 117.28 | 0.2298 | 0.4293 | 116.30 | 0.2249 |
| 110 | 0.5270 | 119.13 | 0.2331 | 0.4416 | 118.22 | 0.2283 |
| 120 | 0.5403 | 120.98 | 0.2363 | 0.4537 | 120.12 | 0.2316 |
| 130 | 0.5534 | 122.82 | 0.2394 | 0.4654 | 122.02 | 0.2349 |
| 140 | 0.5663 | 124.66 | 0.2425 | 0.4770 | 123.90 | 0.2381 |
| 150 | 0.5791 | 126.50 | 0.2456 | 0.4883 | 125.78 | 0.2412 |

| Temperature (°F) | Volume (ft³/lbm) | Enthalpy (Btu/lbm) | Entropy (Btu/lbm-°F) | Volume (ft³/lbm) | Enthalpy (Btu/lbm) | Entropy (Btu/lbm-°F) |
|---|---|---|---|---|---|---|
| | **160 psia (80.71°F)** | | | **180 psia (88.81°F)** | | |
| 90 | 0.3538 | 113.22 | 0.2168 | 0.3043 | 112.00 | 0.2123 |
| 100 | 0.3657 | 115.26 | 0.2204 | 0.3158 | 114.15 | 0.2162 |
| 110 | 0.3772 | 117.26 | 0.2240 | 0.3267 | 116.24 | 0.2199 |
| 120 | 0.3884 | 119.23 | 0.2274 | 0.3372 | 118.29 | 0.2235 |
| 130 | 0.3992 | 121.18 | 0.2308 | 0.3474 | 120.30 | 0.2269 |
| 140 | 0.4098 | 123.11 | 0.2340 | 0.3572 | 122.29 | 0.2303 |
| 150 | 0.4201 | 125.04 | 0.2372 | 0.3668 | 124.27 | 0.2335 |
| | **200 psia (96.27°F)** | | | **250 psia (112.76°F)** | | |
| 100 | 0.2753 | 112.95 | 0.2121 | — | — | — |
| 110 | 0.2859 | 115.16 | 0.2160 | — | — | — |
| 120 | 0.2960 | 117.30 | 0.2198 | 0.2201 | 114.51 | 0.2109 |
| 130 | 0.3056 | 119.39 | 0.2233 | 0.2293 | 116.86 | 0.2149 |
| 140 | 0.3150 | 121.44 | 0.2268 | 0.2379 | 119.12 | 0.2187 |
| 150 | 0.3240 | 123.47 | 0.2301 | 0.2462 | 121.32 | 0.2223 |
| 160 | 0.3328 | 125.48 | 0.2334 | 0.2541 | 123.48 | 0.2258 |
| 170 | 0.3414 | 127.47 | 0.2366 | 0.2617 | 125.60 | 0.2292 |
| 180 | 0.3498 | 129.45 | 0.2397 | 0.2691 | 127.69 | 0.2325 |
| 190 | 0.3581 | 131.42 | 0.2428 | 0.2763 | 129.76 | 0.2357 |
| | **300 psia (126.96°F)** | | | **350 psia (139.51°F)** | | |
| 130 | 0.1763 | 113.84 | 0.2066 | — | — | — |
| 140 | 0.1850 | 116.44 | 0.2110 | 0.1450 | 113.16 | 0.2030 |
| 150 | 0.1931 | 118.90 | 0.2150 | 0.1536 | 116.05 | 0.2077 |
| 160 | 0.2006 | 121.26 | 0.2189 | 0.1613 | 118.72 | 0.2121 |
| 170 | 0.2078 | 123.54 | 0.2225 | 0.1684 | 121.25 | 0.2161 |
| 180 | 0.2147 | 125.78 | 0.2261 | 0.1751 | 123.68 | 0.2200 |
| 190 | 0.2213 | 127.97 | 0.2295 | 0.1814 | 126.03 | 0.2236 |
| 200 | 0.2277 | 130.13 | 0.2328 | 0.1874 | 128.32 | 0.2271 |
| 210 | 0.2339 | 132.27 | 0.2360 | 0.1932 | 130.58 | 0.2305 |
| 220 | 0.2399 | 134.39 | 0.2391 | 0.1989 | 132.79 | 0.2338 |
| | **400 psia (150.78°F)** | | | | | |
| 160 | 0.1303 | 115.70 | 0.2051 | | | |
| 170 | 0.1378 | 118.61 | 0.2097 | | | |
| 180 | 0.1446 | 121.32 | 0.2140 | | | |
| 190 | 0.1509 | 123.89 | 0.2180 | | | |
| 200 | 0.1568 | 126.36 | 0.2217 | | | |
| 210 | 0.1624 | 128.76 | 0.2253 | | | |
| 220 | 0.1677 | 131.10 | 0.2288 | | | |

## Saturation Temperature Property Table for R-22 (SI Units)

| Temperature (°C) | Pressure (kPa) | Vapor Volume (m³/kg) | Liquid Density (kg/m³) | Liquid Enthalpy (kJ/kg) | Vapor Enthalpy (kJ/kg) | Liquid Entropy (kJ/kg-°C) | Vapor Entropy (kJ/kg-°C) |
|---|---|---|---|---|---|---|---|
| −40.00 | 105 | 0.20521 | 1,407 | −0.00 | 233.24 | −0.0000 | 1.0004 |
| −37.50 | 118 | 0.18433 | 1,399 | 2.74 | 234.40 | 0.0116 | 0.9947 |
| −35.00 | 132 | 0.16598 | 1,392 | 5.48 | 235.54 | 0.0232 | 0.9892 |
| −32.50 | 147 | 0.14981 | 1,385 | 8.23 | 236.68 | 0.0346 | 0.9839 |
| −30.00 | 164 | 0.13553 | 1,377 | 11.00 | 237.80 | 0.0460 | 0.9788 |
| −27.50 | 182 | 0.12287 | 1,370 | 13.77 | 238.92 | 0.0573 | 0.9738 |
| −25.00 | 201 | 0.11163 | 1,362 | 16.55 | 240.02 | 0.0685 | 0.9690 |
| −22.50 | 223 | 0.10162 | 1,354 | 19.35 | 241.10 | 0.0797 | 0.9644 |
| −20.00 | 245 | 0.09268 | 1,347 | 22.16 | 242.18 | 0.0907 | 0.9599 |
| −17.50 | 270 | 0.08468 | 1,339 | 24.98 | 243.23 | 0.1018 | 0.9555 |
| −15.00 | 296 | 0.07751 | 1,331 | 27.81 | 244.28 | 0.1127 | 0.9512 |
| −12.50 | 324 | 0.07107 | 1,323 | 30.66 | 245.30 | 0.1236 | 0.9471 |
| −10.00 | 355 | 0.06527 | 1,315 | 33.52 | 246.31 | 0.1344 | 0.9431 |
| −7.50 | 387 | 0.06003 | 1,307 | 36.39 | 247.30 | 0.1452 | 0.9391 |
| −5.00 | 422 | 0.05529 | 1,298 | 39.28 | 248.27 | 0.1559 | 0.9353 |
| −2.50 | 459 | 0.05100 | 1,290 | 42.19 | 249.23 | 0.1666 | 0.9316 |
| 0.00 | 498 | 0.04710 | 1,282 | 45.11 | 250.16 | 0.1773 | 0.9279 |
| 2.50 | 540 | 0.04356 | 1,273 | 48.05 | 251.07 | 0.1879 | 0.9244 |
| 5.00 | 584 | 0.04034 | 1,264 | 51.01 | 251.96 | 0.1984 | 0.9209 |
| 7.50 | 631 | 0.03739 | 1,256 | 53.99 | 252.83 | 0.2089 | 0.9174 |
| 10.00 | 681 | 0.03470 | 1,247 | 56.98 | 253.67 | 0.2194 | 0.9141 |
| 12.50 | 734 | 0.03223 | 1,238 | 60.00 | 254.49 | 0.2299 | 0.9107 |
| 15.00 | 789 | 0.02997 | 1,229 | 63.03 | 255.28 | 0.2403 | 0.9075 |
| 17.50 | 848 | 0.02790 | 1,219 | 66.09 | 256.04 | 0.2507 | 0.9042 |
| 20.00 | 910 | 0.02599 | 1,210 | 69.17 | 256.77 | 0.2611 | 0.9010 |
| 22.50 | 975 | 0.02423 | 1,200 | 72.27 | 257.47 | 0.2714 | 0.8978 |
| 25.00 | 1,044 | 0.02261 | 1,191 | 75.40 | 258.14 | 0.2818 | 0.8947 |
| 27.50 | 1,116 | 0.02111 | 1,181 | 78.56 | 258.78 | 0.2921 | 0.8915 |
| 30.00 | 1,192 | 0.01972 | 1,171 | 81.74 | 259.37 | 0.3024 | 0.8884 |
| 32.50 | 1,271 | 0.01844 | 1,161 | 84.95 | 259.93 | 0.3127 | 0.8853 |
| 35.00 | 1,355 | 0.01724 | 1,150 | 88.18 | 260.45 | 0.3231 | 0.8821 |
| 37.50 | 1,442 | 0.01614 | 1,139 | 91.46 | 260.93 | 0.3334 | 0.8789 |
| 40.00 | 1,534 | 0.01511 | 1,129 | 94.76 | 261.36 | 0.3437 | 0.8757 |
| 42.50 | 1,629 | 0.01415 | 1,117 | 98.10 | 261.74 | 0.3541 | 0.8725 |
| 45.00 | 1,729 | 0.01325 | 1,106 | 101.48 | 262.07 | 0.3644 | 0.8692 |
| 47.50 | 1,834 | 0.01242 | 1,094 | 104.90 | 262.34 | 0.3749 | 0.8659 |
| 50.00 | 1,943 | 0.01163 | 1,082 | 108.36 | 262.55 | 0.3853 | 0.8624 |
| 52.50 | 2,056 | 0.01090 | 1,070 | 111.87 | 262.69 | 0.3958 | 0.8589 |
| 55.00 | 2,175 | 0.01021 | 1,057 | 115.43 | 262.76 | 0.4063 | 0.8553 |
| 57.50 | 2,299 | 0.00957 | 1,044 | 119.05 | 262.76 | 0.4170 | 0.8516 |
| 60.00 | 2,427 | 0.00896 | 1,030 | 122.73 | 262.66 | 0.4277 | 0.8477 |
| 62.50 | 2,562 | 0.00839 | 1,016 | 126.47 | 262.47 | 0.4385 | 0.8437 |
| 65.00 | 2,701 | 0.00785 | 1,001 | 130.30 | 262.18 | 0.4494 | 0.8394 |
| 67.50 | 2,846 | 0.00734 | 986 | 134.20 | 261.76 | 0.4605 | 0.8350 |
| 70.00 | 2,997 | 0.00685 | 970 | 138.21 | 261.21 | 0.4718 | 0.8302 |

## Saturation Pressure Property Table for R-22 (SI Units)

| Pressure (kPa) | Temperature (°C) | Vapor Volume ($m^3/kg$) | Liquid Density ($kg/m^3$) | Liquid Enthalpy ($kJ/kg$) | Vapor Enthalpy ($kJ/kg$) | Liquid Entropy ($kJ/kg$-°C) | Vapor Entropy ($kJ/kg$-°C) |
|---|---|---|---|---|---|---|---|
| 100 | −41.09 | 0.21523 | 1,410 | −1.19 | 232.73 | −0.0051 | 1.0029 |
| 150 | −32.08 | 0.14727 | 1,383 | 8.70 | 236.87 | 0.0366 | 0.9830 |
| 200 | −25.18 | 0.11238 | 1,363 | 16.36 | 239.94 | 0.0677 | 0.9694 |
| 250 | −19.51 | 0.09104 | 1,345 | 22.71 | 242.39 | 0.0929 | 0.9590 |
| 300 | −14.65 | 0.07658 | 1,330 | 28.20 | 244.42 | 0.1142 | 0.9506 |
| 350 | −10.38 | 0.06612 | 1,316 | 33.08 | 246.16 | 0.1328 | 0.9437 |
| 400 | −6.56 | 0.05818 | 1,303 | 37.48 | 247.67 | 0.1493 | 0.9377 |
| 500 | 0.12 | 0.04692 | 1,281 | 45.26 | 250.21 | 0.1778 | 0.9278 |
| 600 | 5.86 | 0.03929 | 1,261 | 52.03 | 252.26 | 0.2020 | 0.9197 |
| 700 | 10.92 | 0.03377 | 1,243 | 58.09 | 253.97 | 0.2233 | 0.9128 |
| 800 | 15.46 | 0.02957 | 1,227 | 63.60 | 255.42 | 0.2422 | 0.9069 |
| 900 | 19.60 | 0.02628 | 1,211 | 68.68 | 256.66 | 0.2594 | 0.9015 |
| 1,000 | 23.42 | 0.02362 | 1,197 | 73.42 | 257.72 | 0.2752 | 0.8967 |
| 1,200 | 30.26 | 0.01958 | 1,170 | 82.07 | 259.43 | 0.3035 | 0.8881 |
| 1,400 | 36.31 | 0.01666 | 1,145 | 89.89 | 260.71 | 0.3285 | 0.8804 |
| 1,600 | 41.75 | 0.01443 | 1,121 | 97.09 | 261.63 | 0.3510 | 0.8735 |
| 1,800 | 46.71 | 0.01268 | 1,098 | 103.81 | 262.26 | 0.3715 | 0.8669 |
| 2,000 | 51.27 | 0.01126 | 1,076 | 110.14 | 262.63 | 0.3906 | 0.8607 |

## R-22 Superheat Property Table (SI Units)

| Temperature (°F) | Volume (m³/kg) | Enthalpy (kJ/kg) | Entropy (kJ/kg-°C) | Volume (m³/kg) | Enthalpy (kJ/kg) | Entropy (kJ/kg-°C) |
|---|---|---|---|---|---|---|
| | 100 kPa (–41.09°C) | | | 150kPa (–32.08°C) | | |
| –40 | 0.21638 | 233.40 | 1.0058 | — | — | — |
| –35 | 0.22162 | 236.43 | 1.0187 | — | — | — |
| –30 | 0.22683 | 239.49 | 1.0314 | 0.14877 | 238.18 | 0.9884 |
| –25 | 0.23201 | 242.56 | 1.0439 | 0.15236 | 241.33 | 1.0013 |
| –20 | 0.23715 | 245.65 | 1.0562 | 0.15592 | 244.49 | 1.0139 |
| –15 | 0.24227 | 248.76 | 1.0684 | 0.15945 | 247.67 | 1.0263 |
| –10 | 0.24737 | 251.89 | 1.0804 | 0.16296 | 250.86 | 1.0386 |
| –5 | 0.25244 | 255.04 | 1.0922 | 0.16644 | 254.07 | 1.0506 |
| 0 | 0.25750 | 258.22 | 1.1040 | 0.16990 | 257.30 | 1.0626 |
| 5 | 0.26254 | 261.42 | 1.1156 | 0.17334 | 260.54 | 1.0743 |
| | 200 kPa (–25.18°C) | | | 250 kPa (–19.51°C) | | |
| –25 | 0.11248 | 240.05 | 0.9698 | — | — | — |
| –20 | 0.11526 | 243.30 | 0.9828 | — | — | — |
| –15 | 0.11800 | 246.55 | 0.9955 | 0.09309 | 245.39 | 0.9707 |
| –10 | 0.12071 | 249.81 | 1.0080 | 0.09533 | 248.72 | 0.9835 |
| –5 | 0.12340 | 253.07 | 1.0203 | 0.09755 | 252.05 | 0.9960 |
| 0 | 0.12607 | 256.35 | 1.0324 | 0.09975 | 255.39 | 1.0084 |
| 5 | 0.12872 | 259.65 | 1.0444 | 0.10192 | 258.73 | 1.0205 |
| 10 | 0.13135 | 262.96 | 1.0561 | 0.10408 | 262.09 | 1.0325 |
| 15 | 0.13396 | 266.29 | 1.0678 | 0.10622 | 265.46 | 1.0443 |
| 20 | 0.13656 | 269.63 | 1.0793 | 0.10834 | 268.85 | 1.0559 |
| | 300 kPa (–14.65°C) | | | 350 kPa (–10.38°C) | | |
| –10 | 0.07838 | 247.59 | 0.9628 | 0.06625 | 246.42 | 0.9447 |
| –5 | 0.08029 | 250.99 | 0.9756 | 0.06794 | 249.90 | 0.9578 |
| 0 | 0.08218 | 254.39 | 0.9882 | 0.06961 | 253.37 | 0.9706 |
| 5 | 0.08404 | 257.80 | 1.0005 | 0.07125 | 256.84 | 0.9832 |
| 10 | 0.08588 | 261.21 | 1.0127 | 0.07287 | 260.30 | 0.9955 |
| 15 | 0.08771 | 264.62 | 1.0246 | 0.07447 | 263.77 | 1.0077 |
| 20 | 0.08952 | 268.05 | 1.0364 | 0.07606 | 267.24 | 1.0196 |
| 25 | 0.09131 | 271.49 | 1.0481 | 0.07763 | 270.72 | 1.0314 |
| 30 | 0.09309 | 274.95 | 1.0596 | 0.07918 | 274.21 | 1.0430 |
| | 400  kPa (–6.56°C) | | | 500 kPa (0.12°C) | | |
| 0 | 0.06016 | 252.32 | 0.9547 | — | — | — |
| 5 | 0.06164 | 255.85 | 0.9677 | 0.04815 | 253.80 | 0.9408 |
| 10 | 0.06310 | 259.37 | 0.9803 | 0.04938 | 257.45 | 0.9538 |
| 15 | 0.06454 | 262.89 | 0.9926 | 0.05059 | 261.08 | 0.9665 |
| 20 | 0.06595 | 266.41 | 1.0047 | 0.05178 | 264.70 | 0.9790 |
| 25 | 0.06736 | 269.93 | 1.0166 | 0.05296 | 268.32 | 0.9912 |
| 30 | 0.06875 | 273.47 | 1.0284 | 0.05411 | 271.94 | 1.0032 |
| 35 | 0.07012 | 277.01 | 1.0400 | 0.05525 | 275.55 | 1.0151 |
| 40 | 0.07149 | 280.56 | 1.0514 | 0.05638 | 279.17 | 1.0267 |
| 45 | 0.07284 | 284.12 | 1.0627 | 0.05750 | 282.80 | 1.0382 |

| Temperature (°F) | Volume (m³/kg) | Enthalpy (kJ/kg) | Entropy (kJ/kg-°C) | Volume (m³/kg) | Enthalpy (kJ/kg) | Entropy (kJ/kg-°C) |
|---|---|---|---|---|---|---|
| | **600 kPa (5.86°C)** | | | **700 kPa (10.92°C)** | | |
| 10 | 0.04019 | 255.41 | 0.9309 | — | — | — |
| 15 | 0.04126 | 259.18 | 0.9441 | 0.03456 | 257.18 | 0.9240 |
| 20 | 0.04230 | 262.92 | 0.9570 | 0.03550 | 261.05 | 0.9374 |
| 25 | 0.04333 | 266.64 | 0.9695 | 0.03642 | 264.89 | 0.9503 |
| 30 | 0.04433 | 270.35 | 0.9819 | 0.03733 | 268.70 | 0.9630 |
| 35 | 0.04532 | 274.05 | 0.9940 | 0.03821 | 272.50 | 0.9754 |
| 40 | 0.04630 | 277.75 | 1.0059 | 0.03908 | 276.28 | 0.9876 |
| 45 | 0.04726 | 281.44 | 1.0176 | 0.03994 | 280.05 | 0.9996 |
| 50 | 0.04822 | 285.14 | 1.0291 | 0.04078 | 283.82 | 1.0113 |
| 55 | 0.04916 | 288.85 | 1.0405 | 0.04162 | 287.58 | 1.0229 |
| | **800 kPa (15.46°C)** | | | **900 kPa (19.60°C)** | | |
| 20 | 0.03037 | 259.08 | 0.9194 | 0.02635 | 256.99 | 0.9027 |
| 25 | 0.03122 | 263.06 | 0.9329 | 0.02715 | 261.13 | 0.9167 |
| 30 | 0.03205 | 266.99 | 0.9460 | 0.02792 | 265.19 | 0.9302 |
| 35 | 0.03286 | 270.88 | 0.9587 | 0.02868 | 269.21 | 0.9433 |
| 40 | 0.03365 | 274.75 | 0.9712 | 0.02941 | 273.18 | 0.9561 |
| 45 | 0.03443 | 278.61 | 0.9834 | 0.03013 | 277.12 | 0.9686 |
| 50 | 0.03519 | 282.45 | 0.9954 | 0.03083 | 281.04 | 0.9808 |
| 55 | 0.03595 | 286.28 | 1.0071 | 0.03153 | 284.95 | 0.9928 |
| 60 | 0.03669 | 290.12 | 1.0187 | 0.03221 | 288.85 | 1.0046 |
| | **1,000 kPa (23.42°C)** | | | **1,200 kPa (30.26°C)** | | |
| 30 | 0.02460 | 263.31 | 0.9153 | — | — | — |
| 35 | 0.02531 | 267.45 | 0.9289 | 0.02021 | 263.68 | 0.9020 |
| 40 | 0.02601 | 271.54 | 0.9420 | 0.02085 | 268.05 | 0.9160 |
| 45 | 0.02668 | 275.59 | 0.9549 | 0.02146 | 272.33 | 0.9296 |
| 50 | 0.02734 | 279.60 | 0.9674 | 0.02206 | 276.55 | 0.9427 |
| 55 | 0.02798 | 283.58 | 0.9796 | 0.02264 | 280.72 | 0.9555 |
| 60 | 0.02861 | 287.55 | 0.9916 | 0.02320 | 284.84 | 0.9680 |
| 65 | 0.02923 | 291.50 | 1.0034 | 0.02375 | 288.94 | 0.9802 |
| 70 | 0.02985 | 295.45 | 1.0150 | 0.02429 | 293.01 | 0.9922 |
| 75 | 0.03045 | 299.39 | 1.0264 | 0.02482 | 297.07 | 1.0039 |
| | **1,400 kPa (36.31°C)** | | | **1,600 kPa (41.75°C)** | | |
| 40 | 0.01711 | 264.20 | 0.8917 | — | — | — |
| 45 | 0.01769 | 268.79 | 0.9062 | 0.01480 | 264.87 | 0.8837 |
| 50 | 0.01825 | 273.27 | 0.9202 | 0.01534 | 269.69 | 0.8987 |
| 55 | 0.01878 | 277.66 | 0.9336 | 0.01586 | 274.36 | 0.9131 |
| 60 | 0.01930 | 281.97 | 0.9467 | 0.01635 | 278.91 | 0.9268 |
| 65 | 0.01981 | 286.24 | 0.9594 | 0.01683 | 283.37 | 0.9401 |
| 70 | 0.02030 | 290.46 | 0.9718 | 0.01729 | 287.76 | 0.9530 |
| 75 | 0.02078 | 294.65 | 0.9839 | 0.01774 | 292.11 | 0.9656 |
| 80 | 0.02126 | 298.81 | 0.9958 | 0.01817 | 296.41 | 0.9779 |
| 85 | 0.02172 | 302.96 | 1.0075 | 0.01860 | 300.67 | 0.9899 |
| | **1,800 kPa (46.71°C)** | | | **2,000 kPa (51.27°C)** | | |
| 50 | 0.01303 | 265.71 | 0.8777 | — | — | — |
| 55 | 0.01354 | 270.75 | 0.8931 | 0.01164 | 266.74 | 0.8733 |
| 60 | 0.01403 | 275.60 | 0.9078 | 0.01213 | 271.98 | 0.8891 |
| 65 | 0.01448 | 280.31 | 0.9218 | 0.01258 | 277.01 | 0.9041 |
| 70 | 0.01492 | 284.91 | 0.9354 | 0.01301 | 281.86 | 0.9184 |
| 75 | 0.01535 | 289.43 | 0.9484 | 0.01342 | 286.60 | 0.9321 |
| 80 | 0.01576 | 293.89 | 0.9611 | 0.01381 | 291.24 | 0.9453 |
| 85 | 0.01616 | 298.29 | 0.9735 | 0.01420 | 295.80 | 0.9581 |
| 90 | 0.01655 | 302.66 | 0.9856 | 0.01457 | 300.31 | 0.9706 |

## Saturation Temperature Property Table for R-134a (English Units)

| Temperature (°F) | Pressure (psia) | Vapor Volume (ft³/lbm) | Liquid Density (lbm/ft³) | Liquid Enthalpy (Btu/lbm) | Vapor Enthalpy (Btu/lbm) | Liquid Entropy (Btu/lbm-°F) | Vapor Entropy (Btu/lbm-°F) |
|---|---|---|---|---|---|---|---|
| −40 | 7.4 | 5.7839 | 88.5041 | 0.00 | 97.17 | 0.0000 | 0.2315 |
| −35 | 8.6 | 5.0544 | 88.0007 | 1.50 | 97.92 | 0.0036 | 0.2306 |
| −30 | 9.9 | 4.4330 | 87.4938 | 3.01 | 98.68 | 0.0071 | 0.2297 |
| −25 | 11.3 | 3.9014 | 86.9831 | 4.53 | 99.43 | 0.0106 | 0.2289 |
| −20 | 12.9 | 3.4449 | 86.4686 | 6.05 | 100.18 | 0.0141 | 0.2282 |
| −15 | 14.7 | 3.0514 | 85.9500 | 7.58 | 100.93 | 0.0175 | 0.2274 |
| −10 | 16.6 | 2.7109 | 88.4271 | 9.12 | 101.68 | 0.0209 | 0.2268 |
| −5 | 18.8 | 2.4154 | 84.8996 | 10.66 | 102.42 | 0.0243 | 0.2262 |
| 0 | 21.2 | 2.1579 | 84.3674 | 12.21 | 103.16 | 0.0277 | 0.2256 |
| 5 | 23.8 | 1.9330 | 83.8301 | 13.76 | 103.89 | 0.0311 | 0.2250 |
| 10 | 26.6 | 1.7537 | 83.2876 | 15.33 | 104.62 | 0.0344 | 0.2245 |
| 15 | 29.7 | 1.5623 | 82.7395 | 16.90 | 105.34 | 0.0377 | 0.2240 |
| 20 | 33.1 | 1.4094 | 82.1855 | 18.48 | 106.06 | 0.0410 | 0.2236 |
| 25 | 36.8 | 1.2742 | 81.6254 | 20.07 | 106.77 | 0.0443 | 0.2232 |
| 30 | 40.8 | 1.1543 | 81.0587 | 21.67 | 107.47 | 0.0476 | 0.2228 |
| 35 | 45.1 | 1.0478 | 80.4851 | 23.27 | 108.17 | 0.0508 | 0.2224 |
| 40 | 49.7 | 0.9528 | 79.9042 | 24.89 | 108.86 | 0.0540 | 0.2221 |
| 45 | 54.7 | 0.8680 | 79.3156 | 26.51 | 109.54 | 0.0572 | 0.2217 |
| 50 | 60.1 | 0.7920 | 78.7188 | 28.15 | 110.21 | 0.0604 | 0.2214 |
| 55 | 65.9 | 0.7238 | 78.1134 | 29.80 | 110.87 | 0.0636 | 0.2212 |
| 60 | 72.1 | 0.6625 | 77.4988 | 31.45 | 111.52 | 0.0668 | 0.2209 |
| 65 | 78.7 | 0.6072 | 76.8744 | 33.12 | 112.17 | 0.0700 | 0.2206 |
| 70 | 85.8 | 0.5572 | 76.2397 | 34.80 | 112.80 | 0.0731 | 0.2204 |
| 75 | 93.4 | 0.5120 | 75.5939 | 36.49 | 113.41 | 0.0763 | 0.2201 |
| 80 | 101.4 | 0.4710 | 74.9364 | 38.20 | 114.02 | 0.0794 | 0.2199 |
| 85 | 109.9 | 0.4338 | 74.2663 | 39.91 | 114.61 | 0.0825 | 0.2197 |
| 90 | 119.0 | 0.3999 | 73.5827 | 41.65 | 115.19 | 0.0856 | 0.2194 |
| 95 | 128.6 | 0.3690 | 72.8847 | 43.39 | 115.75 | 0.0888 | 0.2192 |
| 100 | 138.9 | 0.3407 | 72.1712 | 45.15 | 116.29 | 0.0919 | 0.2190 |
| 105 | 149.7 | 0.3148 | 71.4410 | 46.93 | 116.81 | 0.0950 | 0.2187 |
| 110 | 161.1 | 0.2911 | 70.6928 | 48.73 | 117.32 | 0.0981 | 0.2185 |
| 115 | 173.1 | 0.2693 | 69.9252 | 50.55 | 117.80 | 0.1012 | 0.2183 |
| 120 | 185.9 | 0.2493 | 69.1364 | 52.38 | 118.26 | 0.1044 | 0.2180 |
| 125 | 199.3 | 0.2308 | 68.3246 | 54.24 | 118.69 | 0.1075 | 0.2177 |
| 130 | 213.4 | 0.2137 | 67.4876 | 56.12 | 119.09 | 0.1106 | 0.2174 |
| 135 | 228.3 | 0.1980 | 66.6230 | 58.02 | 119.47 | 0.1138 | 0.2171 |
| 140 | 243.9 | 0.1833 | 65.7279 | 59.95 | 119.81 | 0.1169 | 0.2167 |
| 145 | 260.4 | 0.1697 | 64.7989 | 61.92 | 120.11 | 0.1201 | 0.2163 |
| 150 | 277.6 | 0.1571 | 63.8320 | 63.91 | 120.37 | 0.1233 | 0.2159 |

## Saturation Pressure Property Table for R-134a (English Units)

| Pressure (psia) | Temperature (°F) | Vapor Volume (ft³/lbm) | Liquid Density (lbm/ft³) | Liquid Enthalpy (Btu/lbm) | Vapor Enthalpy (Btu/lbm) | Liquid Entropy (Btu/lbm-°F) | Vapor Entropy (Btu/lbm-°F) |
|---|---|---|---|---|---|---|---|
| 10 | −29.50 | 4.3757 | 87.4425 | 3.17 | 98.76 | 0.0074 | 0.2296 |
| 15 | −14.13 | 2.9882 | 85.8588 | 7.85 | 101.06 | 0.0181 | 0.2273 |
| 20 | −2.40 | 2.2774 | 84.6239 | 11.46 | 102.80 | 0.0261 | 0.2258 |
| 25 | 7.20 | 1.8431 | 83.5923 | 14.45 | 104.21 | 0.0325 | 0.2248 |
| 30 | 15.40 | 1.5494 | 82.6953 | 17.03 | 105.40 | 0.0380 | 0.2240 |
| 35 | 22.60 | 1.3370 | 81.8948 | 19.31 | 106.43 | 0.0427 | 0.2234 |
| 40 | 29.05 | 1.1761 | 81.1673 | 21.36 | 107.34 | 0.0469 | 0.2228 |
| 50 | 40.27 | 0.9480 | 79.8729 | 24.98 | 108.89 | 0.0542 | 0.2220 |
| 60 | 49.88 | 0.7937 | 78.7333 | 28.11 | 110.19 | 0.0604 | 0.2214 |
| 70 | 58.34 | 0.6821 | 77.7041 | 30.90 | 111.31 | 0.0657 | 0.2210 |
| 80 | 65.92 | 0.5976 | 76.7582 | 33.43 | 112.28 | 0.0705 | 0.2206 |
| 90 | 72.82 | 0.5312 | 75.8770 | 35.75 | 113.15 | 0.0749 | 0.2202 |
| 100 | 79.16 | 0.4777 | 75.0479 | 37.91 | 113.92 | 0.0789 | 0.2199 |
| 125 | 93.14 | 0.3801 | 73.1459 | 42.74 | 115.54 | 0.0876 | 0.2193 |
| 150 | 105.16 | 0.3141 | 71.4180 | 46.99 | 116.83 | 0.0951 | 0.2187 |
| 175 | 115.75 | 0.2662 | 69.8084 | 50.82 | 117.87 | 0.1017 | 0.2182 |
| 200 | 125.26 | 0.2299 | 68.2816 | 54.34 | 118.71 | 0.1076 | 0.2177 |
| 225 | 133.92 | 0.2013 | 66.8127 | 57.61 | 119.39 | 0.1131 | 0.2172 |

## R-134a Superheat Property Table (English Units)

| Temperature (°F) | Volume ($ft^3$/lbm) | Enthalpy (Btu/lbm) | Entropy (Btu/lbm-°F) | Volume ($ft^3$/lbm) | Enthalpy (Btu/lbm) | Entropy (Btu/lbm-°F) |
|---|---|---|---|---|---|---|
| | **10.0 psia (−29.50°F)** | | | **15.0 psia (−14.13°F)** | | |
| −20 | 4.4856 | 100.50 | 0.2337 | — | — | — |
| −10 | 4.6001 | 102.35 | 0.2378 | 3.0212 | 101.85 | 0.2291 |
| 0 | 4.7136 | 104.21 | 0.2419 | 3.1001 | 103.75 | 0.2333 |
| 10 | 4.8262 | 106.08 | 0.2459 | 3.1781 | 105.66 | 0.2374 |
| 20 | 4.9381 | 107.98 | 0.2499 | 3.2552 | 107.59 | 0.2414 |
| 30 | 5.0493 | 109.89 | 0.2539 | 3.3316 | 109.53 | 0.2454 |
| 40 | 5.1601 | 111.83 | 0.2578 | 3.4074 | 111.49 | 0.2494 |
| 50 | 5.2704 | 113.78 | 0.2617 | 3.4828 | 113.46 | 0.2533 |
| 60 | 5.3803 | 115.75 | 0.2655 | 3.5577 | 115.45 | 0.2572 |
| 70 | 5.4898 | 117.75 | 0.2693 | 3.6323 | 117.47 | 0.2610 |
| 80 | 5.5990 | 119.76 | 0.2731 | 3.7065 | 119.50 | 0.2648 |
| | **20.0 psia (−2.40°F)** | | | **25.0 psia (7.20°F)** | | |
| 0 | 2.2922 | 103.27 | 0.2269 | — | — | — |
| 10 | 2.3531 | 105.23 | 0.2311 | 1.8572 | 104.77 | 0.2260 |
| 20 | 2.4130 | 107.19 | 0.2352 | 1.9070 | 106.77 | 0.2302 |
| 30 | 2.4721 | 109.16 | 0.2393 | 0.9560 | 108.78 | 0.2343 |
| 40 | 2.5306 | 111.14 | 0.2433 | 2.0042 | 110.79 | 0.2384 |
| 50 | 2.5886 | 113.14 | 0.2472 | 2.0518 | 112.81 | 0.2424 |
| 60 | 2.6461 | 115.15 | 0.2511 | 2.0989 | 114.84 | 0.2464 |
| 70 | 2.7032 | 117.18 | 0.2550 | 2.1456 | 116.89 | 0.2503 |
| 80 | 2.7600 | 119.23 | 0.2588 | 2.1919 | 118.95 | 0.2541 |
| | **30.0 psia (15.40°F)** | | | **35.0 psia (22.60°F)** | | |
| 20 | 1.5691 | 106.34 | 0.2260 | — | — | — |
| 30 | 1.6114 | 108.38 | 0.2302 | 1.3648 | 107.97 | 0.2265 |
| 40 | 1.6528 | 110.42 | 0.2343 | 1.4015 | 110.04 | 0.2307 |
| 50 | 1.6936 | 112.47 | 0.2384 | 1.4374 | 112.12 | 0.2348 |
| 60 | 1.7338 | 114.52 | 0.2424 | 1.4728 | 114.20 | 0.2389 |
| 70 | 1.7736 | 116.59 | 0.2463 | 1.5077 | 116.29 | 0.2429 |
| 80 | 1.8130 | 118.67 | 0.2502 | 1.5422 | 118.39 | 0.2468 |
| | **40.0 psia (29.05°F)** | | | **50.0 psia (40.27°F)** | | |
| 30 | 1.1793 | 107.54 | 0.2233 | — | — | — |
| 40 | 1.2126 | 109.66 | 0.2275 | — | — | — |
| 50 | 1.2450 | 111.76 | 0.2317 | 0.9750 | 111.02 | 0.2263 |
| 60 | 1.2768 | 113.87 | 0.2358 | 1.0019 | 113.19 | 0.2305 |
| 70 | 1.3081 | 115.98 | 0.2398 | 1.0282 | 115.35 | 0.2346 |
| 80 | 1.3389 | 118.10 | 0.2438 | 1.0540 | 117.51 | 0.2386 |
| 90 | 1.3694 | 120.23 | 0.2477 | 1.0793 | 119.68 | 0.2426 |
| 100 | 1.3995 | 122.38 | 0.2516 | 1.1043 | 121.85 | 0.2465 |
| 110 | 1.4293 | 124.53 | 0.2554 | 1.1290 | 124.04 | 0.2504 |
| 120 | 1.4589 | 126.71 | 0.2592 | 1.1534 | 126.24 | 0.2542 |
| 130 | 1.4882 | 128.89 | 0.2629 | 1.1776 | 128.45 | 0.2580 |

| Temperature (°F) | Volume (ft³/lbm) | Enthalpy (Btu/lbm) | Entropy (Btu/lbm-°F) | Volume (ft³/lbm) | Enthalpy (Btu/lbm) | Entropy (Btu/lbm-°F) |
|---|---|---|---|---|---|---|
| | 60.0 psia (49.88°F) | | | 70.0 psia (58.34°F) | | |
| 50 | 0.7940 | 110.22 | 0.2215 | — | — | — |
| 60 | 0.8179 | 112.46 | 0.2259 | 0.6857 | 111.69 | 0.2217 |
| 70 | 0.8410 | 114.68 | 0.2301 | 0.7068 | 113.99 | 0.2261 |
| 80 | 0.8636 | 116.90 | 0.2342 | 0.7271 | 116.26 | 0.2303 |
| 90 | 0.8856 | 119.11 | 0.2383 | 0.7469 | 118.51 | 0.2345 |
| 100 | 0.9073 | 121.32 | 0.2423 | 0.7662 | 120.77 | 0.2385 |
| 110 | 0.9286 | 123.54 | 0.2462 | 0.7851 | 123.02 | 0.2425 |
| 120 | 0.9496 | 125.77 | 0.2501 | 0.8037 | 125.28 | 0.2465 |
| 130 | 0.9703 | 128.00 | 0.2539 | 0.8221 | 127.54 | 0.2503 |
| 140 | 0.9908 | 130.25 | 0.2577 | 0.8401 | 129.82 | 0.2542 |
| 150 | 1.0111 | 132.52 | 0.2614 | 0.8580 | 132.10 | 0.2579 |
| | 80.0 psia (65.92°F) | | | 90.0 psia (72.82°F) | | |
| 70 | 0.6055 | 113.25 | 0.2224 | — | — | — |
| 80 | 0.6243 | 115.58 | 0.2268 | 0.5439 | 114.88 | 0.2235 |
| 90 | 0.6425 | 117.90 | 0.2310 | 0.5609 | 117.25 | 0.2278 |
| 100 | 0.6601 | 120.19 | 0.2352 | 0.5773 | 119.60 | 0.2321 |
| 110 | 0.6773 | 122.49 | 0.2392 | 0.5932 | 121.94 | 0.2362 |
| 120 | 0.6942 | 124.78 | 0.2432 | 0.6087 | 124.26 | 0.2402 |
| 130 | 0.7107 | 127.07 | 0.2471 | 0.6239 | 126.59 | 0.2442 |
| 140 | 0.7270 | 129.37 | 0.2510 | 0.6389 | 128.92 | 0.2481 |
| 150 | 0.7430 | 131.68 | 0.2548 | 0.6535 | 131.26 | 0.2520 |
| | 100.0 psia (79.16°F) | | | 125.0 psia (93.14°F) | | |
| 90 | 0.4953 | 116.58 | 0.2248 | — | — | — |
| 100 | 0.5108 | 118.98 | 0.2292 | 0.3898 | 117.31 | 0.2225 |
| 110 | 0.5257 | 121.37 | 0.2334 | 0.4033 | 119.85 | 0.2270 |
| 120 | 0.5402 | 123.74 | 0.2375 | 0.4162 | 122.34 | 0.2313 |
| 130 | 0.5544 | 126.10 | 0.2415 | 0.4286 | 124.80 | 0.2355 |
| 140 | 0.5682 | 128.46 | 0.2455 | 0.4406 | 127.25 | 0.2396 |
| 150 | 0.5818 | 130.82 | 0.2494 | 0.4523 | 129.68 | 0.2437 |
| 160 | 0.5951 | 133.18 | 0.2533 | 0.4637 | 132.12 | 0.2470 |
| 170 | 0.6083 | 135.56 | 0.2571 | 0.4749 | 134.55 | 0.2515 |
| 180 | 0.6212 | 137.94 | 0.2608 | 0.4859 | 136.98 | 0.2554 |
| 190 | 0.6040 | 140.33 | 0.2645 | 0.4967 | 139.42 | 0.2591 |
| | 150.0 psia (105.16°F) | | | 175.0 psia (115.75°F) | | |
| 110 | 0.3202 | 118.15 | 0.2211 | — | — | — |
| 120 | 0.3323 | 120.80 | 0.2257 | 0.2712 | 119.08 | 0.2203 |
| 130 | 0.3438 | 123.40 | 0.2301 | 0.2823 | 121.86 | 0.2251 |
| 140 | 0.3548 | 125.95 | 0.2344 | 0.2928 | 124.55 | 0.2296 |
| 150 | 0.3653 | 128.48 | 0.2386 | 0.3027 | 127.19 | 0.2340 |
| 160 | 0.3756 | 130.99 | 0.2427 | 0.3122 | 129.80 | 0.2382 |
| 170 | 0.3855 | 133.49 | 0.2467 | 0.3214 | 132.38 | 0.2423 |
| 180 | 0.3953 | 135.99 | 0.2506 | 0.3302 | 134.95 | 0.2464 |
| 190 | 0.4048 | 138.48 | 0.2545 | 0.3389 | 137.50 | 0.2503 |
| 200 | 0.4141 | 140.98 | 0.2583 | 0.3474 | 140.05 | 0.2542 |
| 210 | 0.4233 | 143.48 | 0.2621 | 0.3556 | 142.60 | 0.2581 |
| | 200.0 psia (125.26°F) | | | 225.0 psia (133.92°F) | | |
| 130 | 0.2351 | 120.13 | 0.2201 | — | — | — |
| 140 | 0.2454 | 123.01 | 0.2250 | 0.2076 | 121.29 | 0.2203 |
| 150 | 0.2550 | 125.80 | 0.2296 | 0.2173 | 124.27 | 0.2253 |
| 160 | 0.2641 | 128.52 | 0.2340 | 0.2262 | 127.15 | 0.2300 |
| 170 | 0.2728 | 131.20 | 0.2383 | 0.2346 | 129.94 | 0.2344 |
| 180 | 0.2811 | 133.85 | 0.2425 | 0.2426 | 132.69 | 0.2388 |
| 190 | 0.2892 | 136.48 | 0.2465 | 0.2503 | 135.40 | 0.2430 |
| 200 | 0.2970 | 139.09 | 0.2505 | 0.2577 | 138.08 | 0.2471 |
| 210 | 0.3047 | 141.69 | 0.2544 | 0.2649 | 140.75 | 0.2511 |
| 220 | 0.3121 | 144.29 | 0.2583 | 0.2718 | 143.40 | 0.2550 |
| 230 | 0.3194 | 146.89 | 0.2621 | 0.2786 | 146.05 | 0.2589 |
| 240 | 0.3266 | 149.49 | 0.2658 | 0.2853 | 148.69 | 0.2627 |

## Saturation Temperature Property Table for R-134a (SI Units)

| Temperature (°C) | Pressure (kPa) | Vapor Volume (m³/kg) | Liquid Density (kg/m³) | Liquid Enthalpy (kJ/kg) | Vapor Enthalpy (kJ/kg) | Liquid Entropy (kJ/kg-°C) | Vapor Entropy (kJ/kg-°C) |
|---|---|---|---|---|---|---|---|
| −40.00 | 51 | 0.36108 | 1,418 | 0.00 | 225.86 | 0.0000 | 0.9687 |
| −37.50 | 58 | 0.31977 | 1,410 | 3.14 | 227.44 | 0.0134 | 0.9652 |
| −35.00 | 66 | 0.28402 | 1,403 | 6.30 | 229.02 | 0.0267 | 0.9619 |
| −32.50 | 75 | 0.25298 | 1,396 | 9.47 | 230.60 | 0.0399 | 0.9588 |
| −30.00 | 84 | 0.22594 | 1,388 | 12.65 | 232.17 | 0.0530 | 0.9559 |
| −27.50 | 95 | 0.20232 | 1,381 | 15.84 | 233.74 | 0.0660 | 0.9531 |
| −25.00 | 106 | 0.18162 | 1,373 | 19.04 | 235.31 | 0.0790 | 0.9505 |
| −22.50 | 119 | 0.16343 | 1,366 | 22.26 | 236.86 | 0.0919 | 0.9480 |
| −20.00 | 133 | 0.14739 | 1,358 | 25.49 | 238.41 | 0.1046 | 0.9457 |
| −17.50 | 148 | 0.13323 | 1,351 | 28.74 | 239.95 | 0.1173 | 0.9435 |
| −15.00 | 164 | 0.12067 | 1,343 | 31.99 | 241.48 | 0.1300 | 0.9415 |
| −12.50 | 182 | 0.10952 | 1,335 | 35.27 | 243.01 | 0.1425 | 0.9396 |
| −10.00 | 201 | 0.09959 | 1,327 | 38.55 | 244.52 | 0.1550 | 0.9377 |
| −7.50 | 221 | 0.09073 | 1,319 | 41.85 | 246.02 | 0.1675 | 0.9360 |
| −5.00 | 243 | 0.08280 | 1,311 | 45.17 | 247.51 | 0.1798 | 0.9344 |
| −2.50 | 267 | 0.07569 | 1,303 | 48.51 | 248.99 | 0.1921 | 0.9329 |
| 0.00 | 293 | 0.06931 | 1,295 | 51.86 | 250.46 | 0.2044 | 0.9315 |
| 2.50 | 320 | 0.06356 | 1,286 | 55.22 | 251.91 | 0.2166 | 0.9301 |
| 5.00 | 350 | 0.05837 | 1,278 | 58.61 | 253.35 | 0.2287 | 0.9289 |
| 7.50 | 381 | 0.05369 | 1,270 | 62.01 | 254.77 | 0.2408 | 0.9276 |
| 10.00 | 415 | 0.04944 | 1,261 | 65.43 | 256.17 | 0.2529 | 0.9265 |
| 12.50 | 450 | 0.04559 | 1,252 | 68.87 | 257.56 | 0.2649 | 0.9254 |
| 15.00 | 488 | 0.04209 | 1,243 | 72.34 | 258.93 | 0.2768 | 0.9244 |
| 17.50 | 529 | 0.03890 | 1,234 | 75.82 | 260.28 | 0.2887 | 0.9234 |
| 20.00 | 572 | 0.03600 | 1,225 | 79.32 | 261.60 | 0.3006 | 0.9224 |
| 22.50 | 617 | 0.03334 | 1,216 | 82.85 | 262.91 | 0.3125 | 0.9215 |
| 25.00 | 665 | 0.03091 | 1,207 | 86.40 | 264.19 | 0.3243 | 0.9206 |
| 27.50 | 716 | 0.02869 | 1,197 | 89.98 | 265.45 | 0.3361 | 0.9197 |
| 30.00 | 770 | 0.02664 | 1,187 | 93.58 | 266.67 | 0.3479 | 0.9189 |
| 32.50 | 827 | 0.02476 | 1,178 | 97.21 | 267.87 | 0.3597 | 0.9180 |
| 35.00 | 887 | 0.02303 | 1,168 | 100.86 | 269.04 | 0.3714 | 0.9172 |
| 37.50 | 950 | 0.02144 | 1,157 | 104.55 | 270.18 | 0.3831 | 0.9163 |
| 40.00 | 1,017 | 0.01997 | 1,147 | 108.27 | 271.28 | 0.3949 | 0.9154 |
| 42.50 | 1,086 | 0.01860 | 1,136 | 112.01 | 272.35 | 0.4066 | 0.9145 |
| 45.00 | 1,160 | 0.01734 | 1,125 | 115.80 | 273.38 | 0.4183 | 0.9136 |
| 47.50 | 1,237 | 0.01617 | 1,114 | 119.62 | 274.36 | 0.4301 | 0.9127 |
| 50.00 | 1,318 | 0.01509 | 1,102 | 123.48 | 275.29 | 0.4418 | 0.9116 |
| 52.50 | 1,403 | 0.01408 | 1,090 | 127.38 | 276.18 | 0.4536 | 0.9106 |
| 55.00 | 1,492 | 0.01314 | 1,078 | 131.32 | 277.01 | 0.4654 | 0.9094 |
| 57.50 | 1,584 | 0.01226 | 1,066 | 135.32 | 277.78 | 0.4773 | 0.9082 |
| 60.00 | 1,682 | 0.01144 | 1,053 | 139.36 | 278.49 | 0.4892 | 0.9068 |
| 62.50 | 1,784 | 0.01068 | 1,039 | 143.46 | 279.12 | 0.5012 | 0.9053 |
| 65.00 | 1,890 | 0.00996 | 1,026 | 147.62 | 279.67 | 0.5132 | 0.9037 |
| 67.50 | 2,001 | 0.00929 | 1,011 | 151.84 | 280.14 | 0.5253 | 0.9020 |
| 70.00 | 2,117 | 0.00865 | 996 | 156.14 | 280.51 | 0.5376 | 0.9000 |

## Saturation Pressure Property Table for R-134a (SI Units)

| Pressure (kPa) | Temperature (°C) | Vapor Volume ($m^3/kg$) | Liquid Density ($kg/m^3$) | Liquid Enthalpy ($kJ/kg$) | Vapor Enthalpy ($kJ/kg$) | Liquid Entropy ($kJ/kg$-°C) | Vapor Entropy ($kJ/kg$-°C) |
|---|---|---|---|---|---|---|---|
| 50 | −40.45 | 0.36925 | 1,419 | −0.57 | 225.57 | −0.0024 | 0.9694 |
| 100 | −26.36 | 0.19256 | 1,378 | 17.30 | 234.46 | 0.0720 | 0.9519 |
| 150 | −17.13 | 0.13128 | 1,349 | 29.21 | 240.18 | 0.1192 | 0.9432 |
| 200 | −10.08 | 0.09988 | 1,327 | 38.45 | 244.47 | 0.1547 | 0.9378 |
| 250 | −4.28 | 0.08069 | 1,309 | 46.13 | 247.94 | 0.1834 | 0.9340 |
| 300 | 0.67 | 0.06770 | 1,293 | 52.76 | 250.85 | 0.2077 | 0.9311 |
| 400 | 8.93 | 0.05121 | 1,265 | 63.97 | 255.58 | 0.2477 | 0.9270 |
| 850 | 15.73 | 0.04112 | 1,241 | 73.36 | 259.33 | 0.2803 | 0.9241 |
| 600 | 21.57 | 0.03430 | 1,220 | 81.54 | 262.43 | 0.3081 | 0.9218 |
| 700 | 26.71 | 0.02937 | 1,200 | 88.85 | 265.05 | 0.3324 | 0.9200 |
| 800 | 31.33 | 0.02562 | 1,182 | 95.50 | 267.32 | 0.3541 | 0.9184 |
| 900 | 35.53 | 0.02269 | 1,165 | 101.64 | 269.29 | 0.3739 | 0.9170 |
| 1,000 | 39.39 | 0.02032 | 1,149 | 107.35 | 271.02 | 0.3920 | 0.9157 |
| 1,200 | 46.31 | 0.01672 | 1,119 | 117.80 | 273.90 | 0.4245 | 0.9131 |
| 1,400 | 52.42 | 0.01411 | 1,091 | 127.26 | 276.15 | 0.4533 | 0.9106 |
| 1,600 | 57.91 | 0.01213 | 1,064 | 135.97 | 277.90 | 0.4792 | 0.9079 |
| 1,800 | 62.90 | 0.01056 | 1,037 | 144.11 | 279.21 | 0.5031 | 0.9051 |
| 2,000 | 67.48 | 0.00929 | 1,011 | 151.81 | 280.14 | 0.5252 | 0.9020 |

## R-134a Superheat Property Table (SI Units)

| Temperature (°C) | Volume (m³/kg) | Enthalpy (kJ/kg) | Entropy (kJ/kg-°C) | Volume (m³/kg) | Enthalpy (kJ/kg) | Entropy (kJ/kg-°C) |
|---|---|---|---|---|---|---|
| | **50 kPa (−40.45°C)** | | | **100 kPa (−26.36°C)** | | |
| −40 | 0.37006 | 225.91 | 0.9708 | — | — | — |
| −30 | 0.38759 | 233.43 | 1.0024 | — | — | — |
| −20 | 0.40488 | 241.07 | 1.0332 | 0.19841 | 239.50 | 0.9721 |
| −10 | 0.42199 | 248.85 | 1.0633 | 0.20743 | 247.49 | 1.0030 |
| 0 | 0.43897 | 256.78 | 1.0929 | 0.21630 | 255.59 | 1.0332 |
| 10 | 0.45586 | 264.87 | 1.1220 | 0.22506 | 263.81 | 1.0628 |
| 20 | 0.47266 | 273.13 | 1.1507 | 0.23373 | 272.17 | 1.0918 |
| 30 | 0.48940 | 281.55 | 1.1789 | 0.24233 | 280.68 | 1.1203 |
| 40 | 0.50609 | 290.13 | 1.2068 | 0.25088 | 289.34 | 1.1485 |
| 50 | 0.52273 | 298.88 | 1.2343 | 0.25938 | 298.16 | 1.1762 |
| | **150 kPa (−17.13°C)** | | | **200 kPa (−10.08°C)** | | |
| 10 | 0.13582 | 246.07 | 0.9659 | 0.09991 | 244.54 | 0.9380 |
| 0 | 0.14201 | 254.35 | 0.9968 | 0.10481 | 253.05 | 0.9698 |
| 10 | 0.14808 | 262.71 | 1.0269 | 0.10955 | 261.58 | 1.0005 |
| 20 | 0.15405 | 271.19 | 1.0563 | 0.11419 | 270.19 | 1.0303 |
| 30 | 0.15995 | 279.80 | 1.0852 | 0.11874 | 278.89 | 1.0595 |
| 40 | 0.16579 | 288.54 | 1.1135 | 0.12323 | 287.72 | 1.0882 |
| 50 | 0.17158 | 297.43 | 1.1415 | 0.12766 | 296.68 | 1.1163 |
| 60 | 0.17732 | 306.46 | 1.1690 | 0.13206 | 305.78 | 1.1441 |
| 70 | 0.18304 | 315.64 | 1.1962 | 0.13642 | 315.02 | 1.1714 |
| 80 | 0.18872 | 324.98 | 1.1230 | 0.14074 | 324.40 | 1.1983 |
| | **250 kPa (−4.28°C)** | | | **300 kPa (0.67°C)** | | |
| 0 | 0.08244 | 251.69 | 0.9478 | — | — | — |
| 10 | 0.08640 | 260.41 | 0.9792 | 0.07093 | 259.19 | 0.9611 |
| 20 | 0.09024 | 269.15 | 1.0095 | 0.07425 | 268.09 | 0.9220 |
| 30 | 0.09399 | 277.97 | 1.0391 | 0.07748 | 277.03 | 1.0219 |
| 40 | 0.09768 | 286.89 | 1.0680 | 0.08063 | 286.05 | 1.0512 |
| 50 | 0.10130 | 295.93 | 1.0964 | 0.08372 | 295.16 | 1.0798 |
| 60 | 0.10489 | 305.09 | 1.1244 | 0.08677 | 304.39 | 1.1080 |
| 70 | 0.10844 | 314.38 | 1.1519 | 0.08978 | 313.74 | 1.1356 |
| 80 | 0.11195 | 323.82 | 1.1789 | 0.09276 | 323.23 | 1.1629 |
| 90 | 0.11544 | 333.39 | 1.2057 | 0.09570 | 332.84 | 1.1897 |
| | **400 kPa (8.93°C)** | | | **500 kPa (15.73°C)** | | |
| 10 | 0.05151 | 256.58 | 0.9305 | — | — | — |
| 20 | 0.05421 | 265.86 | 0.9628 | 0.04212 | 263.46 | 0.9383 |
| 30 | 0.05680 | 275.08 | 0.9937 | 0.04434 | 273.01 | 0.9703 |
| 40 | 0.05929 | 284.30 | 1.0236 | 0.04646 | 282.49 | 1.0011 |
| 50 | 0.06172 | 293.59 | 1.0528 | 0.04850 | 291.97 | 1.0309 |
| 60 | 0.06410 | 302.96 | 1.0814 | 0.05049 | 301.50 | 1.0599 |
| 70 | 0.06644 | 312.44 | 1.1094 | 0.05243 | 311.10 | 1.0883 |
| 80 | 0.06875 | 322.03 | 1.1369 | 0.05433 | 320.81 | 1.1162 |
| 90 | 0.07102 | 331.74 | 1.1640 | 0.05621 | 330.61 | 1.1436 |
| 100 | 0.07327 | 341.57 | 1.1908 | 0.05805 | 340.53 | 1.1705 |

| Temperature (°C) | Volume (m³/kg) | Enthalpy (kJ/kg) | Entropy (kJ/kg·°C) | Volume (m³/kg) | Enthalpy (kJ/kg) | Entropy (kJ/kg·°C) |
|---|---|---|---|---|---|---|
| | **600 kPa (21.57°C)** | | | **700 kPa (26.71°C)** | | |
| 30 | 0.03598 | 270.82 | 0.9499 | 0.02997 | 268.45 | 0.9313 |
| 40 | 0.03787 | 280.58 | 0.9816 | 0.03170 | 278.58 | 0.9642 |
| 50 | 0.03966 | 290.28 | 1.0121 | 0.03332 | 288.53 | 0.9954 |
| 60 | 0.04139 | 299.99 | 1.0417 | 0.03488 | 298.43 | 1.0256 |
| 70 | 0.04307 | 309.74 | 1.0705 | 0.03637 | 308.33 | 1.0549 |
| 80 | 0.04471 | 319.56 | 1.0987 | 0.03783 | 318.28 | 1.0835 |
| 90 | 0.04632 | 329.46 | 1.1264 | 0.03925 | 328.30 | 1.1114 |
| 100 | 0.04790 | 339.47 | 1.1536 | 0.04064 | 338.40 | 1.1389 |
| 110 | 0.04946 | 349.59 | 1.1803 | 0.04201 | 348.60 | 1.1659 |
| 120 | 0.05100 | 359.83 | 1.2067 | 0.04336 | 358.91 | 1.1924 |
| | **800 kPa (31.33°C)** | | | **900 kPa (35.53°C)** | | |
| 40 | 0.02704 | 276.45 | 0.9480 | 0.02337 | 274.17 | 0.9327 |
| 50 | 0.02855 | 286.70 | 0.9802 | 0.02481 | 284.77 | 0.9660 |
| 60 | 0.02997 | 296.81 | 1.0110 | 0.02615 | 295.13 | 0.9976 |
| 70 | 0.03134 | 306.88 | 1.0408 | 0.02741 | 305.39 | 1.0280 |
| 80 | 0.03266 | 316.97 | 1.0698 | 0.02863 | 315.63 | 1.0574 |
| 90 | 0.03394 | 327.11 | 1.0981 | 0.02981 | 325.89 | 1.0860 |
| 100 | 0.03519 | 337.31 | 1.1258 | 0.03095 | 336.19 | 1.1140 |
| 110 | 0.03642 | 347.59 | 1.1530 | 0.03207 | 346.57 | 1.1414 |
| 120 | 0.03763 | 357.97 | 1.1798 | 0.03316 | 357.03 | 1.1684 |
| 130 | 0.03881 | 368.46 | 1.2061 | 0.03424 | 367.58 | 1.1949 |
| | **1,000 kPa (39.39°C)** | | | **1,200 kPa (46.31°C)** | | |
| 50 | 0.02180 | 282.74 | 0.9526 | 0.01720 | 278.27 | 0.9267 |
| 60 | 0.02307 | 293.39 | 0.9850 | 0.01840 | 289.64 | 0.9614 |
| 70 | 0.02426 | 303.86 | 1.0160 | 0.01950 | 300.61 | 0.9938 |
| 80 | 0.02540 | 314.26 | 1.0458 | 0.02053 | 311.39 | 1.0248 |
| 90 | 0.02649 | 324.65 | 1.0748 | 0.02151 | 322.07 | 1.0546 |
| 100 | 0.02755 | 335.06 | 1.1031 | 0.02244 | 332.73 | 1.0836 |
| 110 | 0.02858 | 345.53 | 1.1308 | 0.02335 | 043.40 | 1.1118 |
| 120 | 0.02959 | 356.07 | 1.1580 | 0.02423 | 354.11 | 1.1394 |
| 130 | 0.03060 | 366.69 | 1.1847 | 0.02509 | 364.88 | 1.1664 |
| 140 | 0.03155 | 377.41 | 1.2109 | 0.02593 | 375.73 | 1.1930 |
| | **1,400 kPa (52.42°C)** | | | **1,600 kPa (57.91°C)** | | |
| 60 | 0.01501 | 285.47 | 0.9389 | 0.01237 | 280.69 | 0.9164 |
| 70 | 0.01606 | 297.11 | 0.9733 | 0.01343 | 293.25 | 0.9535 |
| 80 | 0.01702 | 308.34 | 1.0056 | 0.01436 | 305.07 | 0.9875 |
| 90 | 0.01792 | 319.37 | 1.0364 | 0.01522 | 316.52 | 1.0194 |
| 100 | 0.01878 | 330.30 | 1.0661 | 0.01601 | 327.77 | 1.0500 |
| 110 | 0.01960 | 341.20 | 1.0949 | 0.01677 | 338.91 | 1.0795 |
| 120 | 0.02039 | 352.10 | 1.1230 | 0.01750 | 350.02 | 1.1081 |
| 130 | 0.02116 | 363.03 | 1.1504 | 0.01820 | 361.13 | 1.1360 |
| 140 | 0.02190 | 374.01 | 1.1773 | 0.01888 | 372.26 | 1.1633 |
| 150 | 0.02264 | 385.07 | 1.2038 | 0.01955 | 383.45 | 1.1900 |
| | **1,800 kPa (62.90°C)** | | | **2,000 kPa (67.48°C)** | | |
| 70 | 0.01133 | 288.93 | 0.9337 | 0.00957 | 283.92 | 0.9130 |
| 80 | 0.01226 | 301.53 | 0.9699 | 0.01054 | 297.63 | 0.9524 |
| 90 | 0.01309 | 313.49 | 1.0033 | 0.01136 | 310.24 | 0.9877 |
| 100 | 0.01385 | 325.11 | 1.0349 | 0.01210 | 322.30 | 1.0204 |
| 110 | 0.01457 | 336.54 | 1.0651 | 0.01279 | 334.07 | 1.0515 |
| 120 | 0.01525 | 347.88 | 1.0943 | 0.01344 | 345.66 | 1.0814 |
| 130 | 0.01590 | 359.17 | 1.1227 | 0.01405 | 357.16 | 1.1103 |
| 140 | 0.01653 | 370.47 | 1.1504 | 0.01464 | 368.63 | 1.1384 |
| 150 | 0.01714 | 381.79 | 1.1774 | 0.01521 | 380.10 | 1.1658 |
| 160 | 0.01773 | 393.16 | 1.2040 | 0.01576 | 391.60 | 1.1927 |

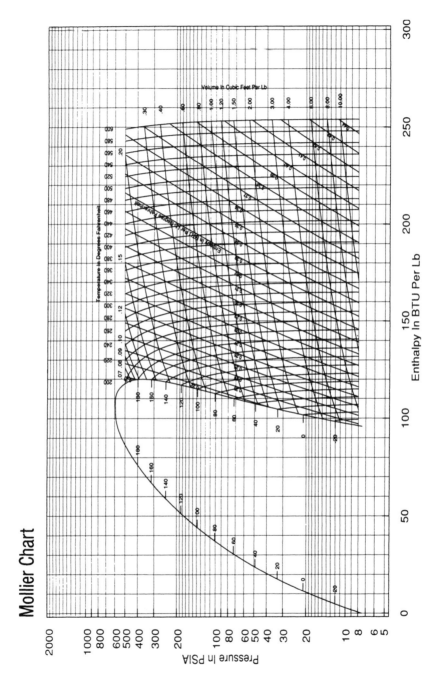

# Mollier Chart

Pressure-Enthalpy Diagram for R-134a (English Units)

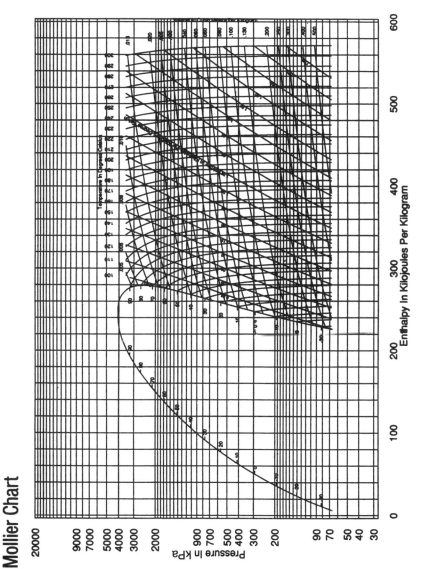

Mollier Chart

Pressure-Enthalpy Diagram for R-134a (SI Units)

APPENDIX

## Saturated Steam Properties (English Units)

| $T$ (°F) | $p$ (psia) | $v_f$ (ft³/lbm) | $v_s$ (ft³/lbm) | $h_f$ (Btu/lbm) | $h_{fg}$ (Btu/lbm) | $h_g$ (Btu/lbm) | $s_f$ (Btu/lbm-°R) | $s_{fg}$ (Btu/lbm-°R) | $s_g$ (Btu/lbm-°R) |
|---|---|---|---|---|---|---|---|---|---|
| 32 | .08856 | .016018 | 3,306.6 | −.0074 | 1075.3 | 1075.3 | −.0007 | 9.1572 | 2.1864 |
| 34 | .09599 | .016018 | 3,062.8 | 1.9365 | 1074.3 | 1076.2 | .00325 | 9.1112 | 2.1794 |
| 36 | .10397 | .016018 | 2,839.1 | 3.8863 | 1073.2 | 1077.1 | .00723 | 9.0656 | 2.1725 |
| 38 | .11253 | .016019 | 2,633.7 | 5.8415 | 1072.2 | 1078 | .0112 | 9.0202 | 2.1656 |
| 40 | .12171 | .016019 | 2,444.8 | 7.8018 | 1071.1 | 1078.9 | .01517 | 8.9752 | 2.1589 |
| 42 | .13154 | .01602 | 2,271.1 | 9.767 | 1070 | 1079.8 | .01912 | 8.9304 | 2.1521 |
| 44 | .14206 | .016021 | 2,111.1 | 11.737 | 1068.9 | 1080.7 | .02307 | 8.886 | 2.1455 |
| 46 | .15332 | .016023 | 1,963.8 | 13.711 | 1067.9 | 1081.6 | .02701 | 8.8419 | 2.1389 |
| 48 | .16535 | .016024 | 1,828. | 15.689 | 1066.8 | 1082.5 | .03093 | 8.7981 | 2.1323 |
| 50 | .17821 | .016026 | 1,702.7 | 17.671 | 1065.7 | 1083.3 | .03485 | 8.7545 | 2.1258 |
| 52 | .19194 | .016028 | 1,587.1 | 19.657 | 1064.6 | 1084.2 | .03876 | 8.7113 | 2.1194 |
| 54 | .20659 | .01603 | 1,480.2 | 21.646 | 1063.5 | 1085.1 | .04265 | 8.6684 | 2.1131 |
| 56 | .22221 | .016032 | 1,381.4 | 23.637 | 1062.4 | 1086 | .04654 | 8.6258 | 2.1068 |
| 58 | .23886 | .016035 | 1,290.1 | 25.632 | 1061.2 | 1086.9 | .05041 | 8.5834 | 2.1005 |
| 60 | .2566 | .016038 | 1,205.5 | 27.63 | 1060.1 | 1087.8 | .05428 | 8.5414 | 2.0944 |
| 62 | .27547 | .016041 | 1,127.2 | 29.63 | 1059 | 1088.6 | .05813 | 8.4996 | 2.0882 |
| 64 | .29555 | .016044 | 1,054.5 | 31.632 | 1057.9 | 1089.5 | .06196 | 8.4582 | 2.0822 |
| 66 | .3169 | .016047 | 987.19 | 33.637 | 1056.7 | 1090.4 | .06579 | 8.417 | 2.0762 |
| 68 | .33959 | .016051 | 924.68 | 35.643 | 1055.6 | 1091.3 | .06961 | 8.3761 | 2.0702 |
| 70 | .36369 | .016054 | 866.64 | 37.651 | 1054.5 | 1092.1 | .07341 | 8.3356 | 2.0643 |
| 72 | .38926 | .016058 | 812.71 | 39.661 | 1053.3 | 1093 | .0772 | 8.2952 | 2.0585 |
| 74 | .41639 | .016062 | 762.56 | 41.672 | 1052.2 | 1093.9 | .08098 | 8.255 | 2.0527 |
| 76 | .44515 | .016067 | 715.91 | 43.684 | 1051.1 | 1094.7 | .08474 | 8.2155 | 2.047 |
| 78 | .47563 | .016071 | 672.49 | 45.698 | 1049.9 | 1095.6 | .08849 | 8.176 | 2.0413 |
| 80 | .50792 | .016076 | 632.04 | 47.713 | 1048.8 | 1096.5 | .09223 | 8.1368 | 2.0357 |
| 82 | .54209 | .016081 | 594.35 | 49.728 | 1047.6 | 1097.3 | .09596 | 8.0979 | 2..0301 |
| 84 | .57825 | .016086 | 559.2 | 51.745 | 1046.5 | 1098.2 | .09967 | 8.0592 | 2.0246 |
| 86 | .61648 | .016091 | 526.4 | 53.762 | 1045.3 | 1099.1 | .10337 | 8.0208 | 2.0191 |
| 88 | .65689 | .016096 | 495.79 | 55.779 | 1044.2 | 1099.9 | .10705 | 7.9827 | 2.0137 |
| 90 | .69958 | .016102 | 467.19 | 57.798 | 1043 | 1100.8 | .11073 | 7.9448 | 2.0083 |
| 92 | .74466 | .016107 | 440.47 | 59.816 | 1041.8 | 1101.7 | .11439 | 7.9073 | 2.003 |
| 94 | .79223 | .016113 | 415.48 | 61.835 | 1040.7 | 1102.5 | .11804 | 7.8699 | 1.9977 |
| 96 | .84242 | .016119 | 392.11 | 63.854 | 1039.5 | 1103.4 | .12167 | 7.8328 | 1.9925 |
| 98 | .89533 | .016125 | 370.23 | 65.873 | 1038.4 | 1104.2 | .12529 | 7.796 | 1.9873 |
| 100 | .95109 | .016132 | 349.73 | 67.892 | 1037.2 | 1105.1 | .1289 | 7.7595 | 1.9822 |
| 102 | 1.0098 | .016138 | 330.53 | 69.911 | 1036 | 1105.9 | .13249 | 7.7231 | 1.9771 |
| 104 | 1.0717 | .016145 | 312.53 | 71.93 | 1034.9 | 1106.8 | .13607 | 7.6871 | 1.9721 |
| 106 | 1.1368 | .016152 | 295.65 | 73.949 | 1033.7 | 1107.7 | .13964 | 7.6513 | 1.9671 |
| 108 | 1.2052 | .016159 | 279.81 | 75.968 | 1032.5 | 1108.5 | .1432 | 7.6157 | 1.9622 |
| 110 | 1.2772 | .016166 | 264.93 | 77.986 | 1031.4 | 1109.4 | .14674 | 7.5804 | 1.9573 |
| 112 | 1.3529 | .016173 | 250.96 | 80.005 | 1030.2 | 1110.2 | .15027 | 7.5453 | 1.9524 |
| 114 | 1.4324 | .016181 | 237.83 | 82.022 | 1029 | 1111 | .15378 | 7.5104 | 1.9476 |
| 116 | 1.5159 | .016188 | 225.49 | 84.04 | 1027.9 | 1111.9 | .15729 | 7.4758 | 1.9428 |
| 118 | 1.6035 | .016196 | 213.88 | 86.057 | 1026.7 | 1112.7 | .16078 | 7.4414 | 1.9381 |
| 120 | 1.6955 | .016201 | 202.95 | 88.074 | 1025.5 | 1113.6 | .16425 | 7.4072 | 1.9334 |

## Saturated Steam Properties (SI Units)

| $T$ (°C) | $P$ (kPa) | $v_f$ ($m^3/kg$) | $v_g$ ($m^3/kg$) | $h_f$ ($kJ/kg$) | $h_{fg}$ ($kJ/kg$) | $h_g$ ($kJ/kg$) | $s_f$ ($kJ/kg$-°K) | $s_{fg}$ ($kJ/kg$-°K) | $s_g$ ($kJ/kg$-°K) |
|---|---|---|---|---|---|---|---|---|---|
| 0 | .6106 | .001 | 206.42 | −.0173 | 2,501.3 | 2,501.3 | −.0031 | 9.1572 | 9.1541 |
| 1 | .65657 | .001 | 192.67 | 4.0518 | 2,499.1 | 2,503.2 | .01193 | 9.1158 | 9.1277 |
| 2 | .70556 | .001 | 179.94 | 8.1318 | 2,496.9 | 2,505 | .02694 | 9.0747 | 9.1016 |
| 3 | .75776 | .001 | 168.15 | 12.222 | 2,494.7 | 2,506.9 | .04191 | 9.0338 | 9.0757 |
| 4 | .81333 | .001 | 157.22 | 16.322 | 2,492.5 | 2,508.8 | .05687 | 8.9932 | 9.05 |
| 5 | .87247 | .0010001 | 147.09 | 20.432 | 2,490.2 | 2,510.6 | .07179 | 8.9528 | 9.0246 |
| 6 | .93537 | .0010001 | 137.69 | 24.551 | 2,488 | 2,512.5 | .08668 | 8.9126 | 8.9993 |
| 7 | 1.0022 | .0010002 | 128.96 | 28.678 | 2,485.7 | 2,514.4 | .10154 | 8.8727 | 8.9743 |
| 8 | 1.0733 | .0010003 | 120.85 | 32.813 | 2,483.4 | 2,516.2 | .11636 | 8.8331 | 8.9495 |
| 9 | 1.1487 | .0010004 | 113.31 | 36.955 | 2,481.1 | 2,518.1 | .13116 | 8.7937 | 8.9248 |
| 10 | 1.2287 | .0010005 | 106.3 | 41.105 | 2,478.8 | 2,520 | .14592 | 8.7545 | 8.9005 |
| 11 | 1.3136 | .0010006 | 99.774 | 45.261 | 2,476.5 | 2,521.8 | .16064 | 8.7156 | 8.8763 |
| 12 | 1.4037 | .0010007 | 93.7 | 49.424 | 2,474.2 | 2,523.7 | .17533 | 8.6769 | 8.8523 |
| 13 | 1.4991 | .0010008 | 88.041 | 53.592 | 2,471.9 | 2,525.5 | .18998 | 8.6385 | 8.8285 |
| 14 | 1.6001 | .001001 | 82.766 | 57.767 | 2,469.6 | 2,527.4 | .20459 | 8.6003 | 8.8049 |
| 15 | 1.7071 | .0010011 | 77.846 | 61.946 | 2,467.2 | 2,529.2 | .21916 | 8.5624 | 8.7815 |
| 16 | 1.8203 | .0010013 | 73.255 | 66.13 | 2,464.9 | 2,531 | .2337 | 8.5247 | 8.7584 |
| 17 | 1.94 | .0010014 | 68.97 | 70.319 | 2,462.6 | 2,532.9 | .24819 | 8.4872 | 8.7354 |
| 18 | 2.0665 | .0010016 | 64.966 | 74.512 | 2,460.2 | 2,534.7 | .26264 | 8.4499 | 8.7126 |
| 19 | 2.2002 | .0010018 | 61.225 | 78.709 | 2,457.8 | 2,536.5 | .27706 | 8.4129 | 8.69 |
| 20 | 2.3414 | .001002 | 57.726 | 82.909 | 2,455.5 | 2,538.4 | .29143 | 8.3761 | 8.6676 |
| 21 | 2.4905 | .0010022 | 54.453 | 87.113 | 2,453.1 | 2,540.2 | .30576 | 8.3396 | 8.6454 |
| 22 | 2.6478 | .0010024 | 51.39 | 91.32 | 2,450.7 | 2,542 | .32004 | 8.3033 | 8.6233 |
| 23 | 2.8136 | .0010027 | 48.521 | 95.529 | 2,448.3 | 2,543.9 | .33429 | 8.2672 | 8.6015 |
| 24 | 2.9885 | .0010029 | 45.833 | 99.742 | 2,445.9 | 2,545.7 | .34849 | 8.2313 | 8.5798 |
| 25 | 3.1728 | .0010032 | 43.313 | 103.96 | 2,443.5 | 2,547.5 | .36265 | 8.1957 | 8.5583 |
| 26 | 3.3669 | .0010034 | 40.951 | 108.17 | 2,441.1 | 2,549.3 | .37676 | 8.1603 | 8.537 |
| 27 | 3.5713 | .0010037 | 38.734 | 112.39 | 2,438.7 | 2,551.1 | .39083 | 8.1251 | 8.5159 |
| 28 | 3.7864 | .0010039 | 36.653 | 116.61 | 2,436.3 | 2,552.9 | .40486 | 8.0001 | 8.495 |
| 29 | 4.0126 | .0010042 | 34.698 | 120.83 | 2,433.9 | 2,554.8 | .41884 | 8.0554 | 8.4742 |
| 30 | 4.2505 | .0010045 | 32.862 | 125.06 | 2,431.5 | 2,556.6 | .43278 | 8.0208 | 8.4536 |
| 31 | 4.5006 | .0010048 | 31.136 | 129.28 | 2,429.1 | 2,558.4 | .44667 | 7.9865 | 8.4332 |
| 32 | 4.7633 | .0010051 | 29.513 | 133.5 | 2,426.7 | 2,560.2 | .46052 | 7.9524 | 8.4129 |
| 33 | 5.0393 | .0010054 | 27.986 | 137.73 | 2,424.2 | 2,562 | .47433 | 7.9185 | 8.3928 |
| 34 | 5.329 | .0010058 | 26.549 | 141.96 | 2,421.8 | 2,563.8 | .48809 | 7.8848 | 8.3729 |
| 35 | 5.633 | .0010061 | 25.196 | 146.18 | 2,419.4 | 2,565.6 | .5018 | 7.8513 | 8.3532 |
| 36 | 5.9519 | .0010064 | 23.921 | 150.41 | 2,417 | 2,567.4 | .51547 | 7.8181 | 8.3336 |
| 37 | 6.2864 | .0010068 | 22.72 | 154.64 | 2,414.5 | 2,569.2 | .5291 | 7.785 | 8.3141 |
| 38 | 6.6369 | .0010072 | 21.587 | 158.86 | 2,412.1 | 2,571 | .54268 | 7.7522 | 8.2949 |
| 39 | 7.0043 | .0010075 | 20.519 | 163.09 | 2,409.7 | 2,572.7 | .55622 | 7.7195 | 8.2757 |
| 40 | 7.389 | .0010079 | 19.511 | 167.32 | 2,407.2 | 2,574.5 | .56971 | 7.6871 | 8.2568 |
| 41 | 7.7919 | .0010083 | 18.559 | 171.54 | 2,404.8 | 2,576.3 | .58316 | 7.6548 | 8.238 |
| 42 | 8.2136 | .0010087 | 17.661 | 175.77 | 2,402.3 | 2,578.1 | .59656 | 7.6228 | 8.2193 |
| 43 | 8.6548 | .0010091 | 16.812 | 180 | 2,399.9 | 2,579.9 | .60992 | 7.5909 | 8.2008 |
| 44 | 9.1163 | .0010095 | 16.01 | 184.22 | 2,397.4 | 2,581.6 | .62323 | 7.5593 | 8.1825 |
| 45 | 9.5988 | .0010099 | 15.251 | 188.45 | 2,395 | 2,583.4 | .6365 | 7.5278 | 8.1643 |
| 46 | 10.103 | .0010103 | 14.534 | 192.67 | 2,392.5 | 2,585.2 | .64793 | 7.4965 | 8.1463 |
| 47 | 10.63 | .0010108 | 13.855 | 196.89 | 2,390.1 | 2,587 | .66291 | 7.4654 | 8.1284 |
| 48 | 11.18 | .0010112 | 13.212 | 201.12 | 2,387.6 | 2,588.7 | .67605 | 7.4346 | 8.1106 |
| 49 | 11.755 | .0010116 | 12.604 | 205.34 | 2,385.1 | 2,590.5 | .68915 | 7.4038 | 8.093 |
| 50 | 12.355 | .0010121 | 12.028 | 209.56 | 2,382.7 | 2,592.2 | .7022 | 7.3733 | 8.0755 |

# EPA CERTIFICATION FOR HVACR TECHNICIANS AND PRACTICE QUESTIONS

Section 608 of the Clean Air Act requires technicians servicing air-conditioning or refrigeration equipment to obtain certification through an EPA-approved testing organization. The EPA defines a technician as any person who performs repair or maintenance that could release CFCs or HFCs into the atmosphere. The certification test consists of four modules of 25 questions each. A score of 70 percent or higher is required to pass a module, or a minimum of 18 questions answered correctly.

The four test modules are Core, Type I (Small Appliance), Type II (High Pressure), and Type III (Low Pressure). In order to achieve certification in a particular type, the technician must pass the core module plus the type module. Passing all four modules will result in Universal certification, allowing work on all three types of equipment.

The EPA web site (www.epa.gov) maintains a listing of currently approved testing organizations. Some testing organizations are open to the general public while others are limited to their members. All testing organizations use the same questions prepared by the EPA to maintain consistency.

The following section contains a listing of topics for the four test modules and sets of typical test questions. The listing of topics is that published by the EPA on its web site. Most of the relevant study material will be found in chapter 3 (refrigerants) and chapter 11 (operation and maintenance) of this text. The test questions are not directly from the EPA question bank, but are typical of what can be expected on the test.

## Core

Ozone Depletion

- Destruction of ozone by chlorine
- Presence of chlorine in CFC and HCFC refrigerants
- Identification of CFC, HCFC, and HFC refrigerants (not chemical formulas, but idea that R-12 is a CFC, R-22 is an HCFC, R-134 is an HFC, etc.)
- Idea that CFCs have higher ozone-depletion potential (ODP) than HCFCs, which in turn have higher ODP than HFCs
- Health and environmental effects of ozone depletion
- Evidence of ozone depletion and role of CFCs and HCFCs

Clean Air Act and Montreal Protocol

- CFC phaseout date
- Venting prohibition at servicing
- Venting prohibition at disposal
- Venting prohibition on substitute refrigerants in November 1995
- Maximum penalty under CAA
- Montreal Protocol (international agreement to phase out production of ozone-depleting substances)


Section 608 Regulations

- Definition/identification of high and low-pressure refrigerants
- Definition of system-dependent vs. self-contained recovery/recycling equipment
- Identification of equipment covered by the rule (all air-conditioning and refrigeration equipment containing CFCs or HCFCs except motor vehicle air-conditioners)
- Need for third-party certification of recycling and recovery equipment manufactured after November 15, 1993
- Standard for reclaimed refrigerant (ARI 700)


Substitute Refrigerants and Oils

- Absence of "drop-in" replacements
- Incompatibility of substitute refrigerants with many lubricants used with CFC and HCFC refrigerants and incompatibility of CFC and HCFC refrigerants with many new lubricants (includes identification of lubricants for given refrigerants, such as esters with 134; alkylbenzenes for HCFCs)
- Fractionation problem—tendency of different components of blends to leak at different rates


Refrigeration

- Refrigerant states (vapor vs. liquid) and pressures at different points of refrigeration cycle; how/when cooling occurs
- Refrigeration gauges (color codes, ranges of different types, proper use)

Three Rs

- Definitions
  - Recover
  - Recycle
  - Reclaim

Recovery Techniques

- Need to avoid mixing refrigerants
- Factors affecting speed of recovery (ambient temperature, size of recycling or recovery equipment, hose length and diameter, etc.)

Dehydration Evacuation

- Need to evacuate system to eliminate air and moisture at the end of service

Safety

- Risks of exposure to refrigerant (for example, oxygen deprivation, cardiac effects, frost bite, long-term hazards)
- Personal protective equipment (gloves, goggles, self-contained breathing apparatus [SCBA] in extreme cases, etc.)
- Reusable (or "recovery") cylinders vs. disposable cylinders (ensure former DOT approved, know former's yellow and gray color code, never refill latter)
- Risks of filling cylinders more than 80 percent full
- Use of nitrogen rather than oxygen or compressed air for leak detection
- Use of pressure regulator and relief valve with nitrogen

Shipping

- Labels required for refrigerant cylinders (refrigerant identification, DOT classification tag)

## Type I (Small Appliances)

Recovery Requirements

- Definition of "small appliance"

- Evacuation requirements for small appliances with and without working compressors using recovery equipment manufactured before November 15, 1993
- Evacuation requirements for small appliances with and without working compressors using recovery equipment manufactured after November 15, 1993

Recovery Techniques

- Use of pressure and temperature to identify refrigerants and detect noncondensables
- Methods to recover refrigerant from small appliances with inoperative compressors using a system-dependent or "passive") recovery device (for example, heat and sharply strike the compressor, use a vacuum pump with nonpressurized recovery container)
- Need to install both high and low side access valves when recovering refrigerant from small appliances with inoperative compressors
- Need to operate operative compressors when recovering refrigerant with a system-dependent ("passive") recovery device
- Should remove solderless access fittings at conclusion of service
- 134a as likely substitute for 12

Safety

- Decomposition products of refrigerants at high temperatures (HCI, HFl, etc.)

## Type II (High-Pressure)

Leak Detection

- Signs of leakage in high-pressure systems (excessive superheat, traces of oil for hermetics)
- Need to leak test before charging or recharging equipment
- Order of preference for leak test gases (nitrogen alone best, but nitrogen with trace quantity of 22 better than pure refrigerant)

Leak Repair Requirements

- Allowable annual leak rate for commercial and industrial process refrigeration

- Allowable annual leak rate for other appliances containing more than 50 lbs of refrigerant

Recovery Techniques

- Recovering liquid at beginning of recovery process speeds up process
- Other methods for speeding recovery (chilling recovery vessel, heating appliance or vessel from which refrigerant is being recovered)
- Methods for reducing cross-contamination and emissions when recovery or recycling machine is used with a new refrigerant
- Need to wait a few minutes after reaching required recovery vacuum to see if system pressure rises (indicating that there is still liquid refrigerant in the system or in the oil)

Recovery Requirements

- Evacuation requirements for high-pressure appliances in each of the following situations:
  - Disposal
  - Major vs. nonmajor repairs
  - Leaky vs. nonleaky appliances
  - Appliance (or component) containing less vs. more than 200 lbs
  - Recovery/recycling equipment built before vs. after November 15, 1993
- Definition of "major" repairs
- Prohibition on using system-dependent recovery equipment on systems containing more than 15 pounds of refrigerant

Refrigeration

- How to identify refrigerant in appliances
- Pressure-temperature relationships of common high-pressure refrigerants (may use standard temperature-pressure chart—be aware of need to add 14.7 to translate psig to psia)
- Components of high-pressure appliances (receiver, evaporator, accumulator, etc.) and state of refrigerant (vapor vs. liquid) in them

Safety

- Shouldn't energize hermetic compressors under vacuum
- Equipment room requirements under ASHRAE Standard 15 (oxygen deprivation sensor with all refrigerants)

## Type III (Low-Pressure)

Leak Detection

- Order of preference of leak test pressurization methods for low-pressure systems (first: hot water method or built-in system heating/pressurization device such as Prevac; second: nitrogen)
- Signs of leakage into a low-pressure system (for example, excessive purging)
- Maximum leak test pressure for low-pressure centrifugal chillers

Leak Repair Requirements

- Allowable annual leak rate for commercial and industrial process refrigeration
- Allowable annual leak rate for other appliances containing more than 50 lbs of refrigerant

Recovery Techniques

- Recovering liquid at beginning of recovery process speeds up process
- Need to recover vapor in addition to liquid
- Need to heat oil to 130°F before removing it to minimize refrigerant release
- Need to circulate or remove water from chiller during refrigerant evacuation to prevent freezing
- High-pressure cut-out level of recovery devices used with low-pressure appliances

Recharging Techniques

- Need to introduce vapor before liquid to prevent freezing of water in the tubes
- Need to charge centrifugals through evaporator charging valve

Recovery Requirements

- Evacuation requirements for low-pressure appliances, in each of the following situations:
  - Disposal
  - Major vs. nonmajor repairs
  - Leaky vs. nonleaky appliances
  - Appliance (or component) containing less vs. more than 200 lbs

- Recovery/recycling equipment built before vs. after November 15, 1993
- Definitions of "major" and "non-major" repairs
- Allowable methods for pressurizing a low-pressure system for a nonmajor repair (controlled hot water and system heating/pressurization device such as Prevac)
- Need to wait a few minutes after reaching required recovery vacuum to see if system pressure rises (indicating that there is still liquid refrigerant in the system or in the oil)

Refrigeration

- Purpose of purge unit in low-pressure systems
- Pressure-temperature relationships of low-pressure refrigerants

Safety

- Equipment room requirements under ASHRAE Standard 15 (oxygen deprivation sensor with all refrigerants)
- Under ASHRAE Standard 15 need to have equipment room refrigerant sensor for 123

## Core Practice Questions

1. How many oxygen atoms do ozone molecules contain?
   A. One.
   B. Two.
   C. Three.
   D. Four.

2. Modern recovery systems are designed to work with:
   A. All refrigerants, including methyl chloride, sulfur dioxide, and ammonia.
   B. Fluorocarbon refrigerants only.
   C. Propane and isobutane.
   D. Disposable cylinders.

3. One of the most common types of refrigerant leaks in a system are caused by improperly made flare fittings. What steps are necessary in order to make a good fitting?
   A. Make a square cut on the tubing and remove burrs using a reamer and file.
   B. When using a flaring tool, allow tubing to extend above the block by approximately a third of the height of the flare.

C. After placing a drop of refrigerant oil on the spindle end, tighten the flaring tool against the tubing one-half turn and back off one-quarter turn. Repeat the forward movement and backing off until the flare is formed.

D. All of the above.

4. The ozone destroying chemical contained in CFCs and HCFCs is . . . ?
   A. Hydrogen.
   B. Fluorine.
   C. Chlorine.
   D. Nitrogen.

5. What health hazards are associated with working with refrigerants?
   A. Irritation and frostbite to skin and eyes from direct contact.
   B. Suffocation in an enclosed space with a large leak.
   C. Toxicity of some refrigerants.
   D. All of the above.

6. When the pressure and temperature of a substance are at the point where the addition or removal of heat to/from a substance results in the substance changing state, that substance is said to be in what condition?
   A. Saturated.
   B. Articulated.
   C. Sensible.
   D. Enthalpy.

7. What harmful type of radiation does the ozone layer filter out?
   A. Infrared.
   B. Ultraviolet.
   C. Nuclear.
   D. Atomic.

8. In order to completely recover the refrigerant charge from a low pressure system with a recovery system manufactured after November 15, 1993 it is necessary to do what?
   A. Reduce the system pressure to 25"mm hg absolute.
   B. Remove the liquid only, as this will satisfy the demands of the law.
   C. Pressurize the system with nitrogen to force out the remaining refrigerant.
   D. Distill the oil in a separate heated unit.

9. System leaks in either the condenser or evaporator may result in the component chemicals in zeotropic refrigerants leaking at uneven rates, thus changing the chemical composition of the refrigerant remaining in the system. This is due to the:
   A. Difference in the vapor pressures of the various components.
   B. Presence of contaminants.
   C. Difference in temperatures.
   D. Pressure drop through the heat exchangers.

10. Equipment warranties will remain in force when what type of refrigerant is used?
    A. Recovered.
    B. Recycled.
    C. Reclaimed.
    D. All of the above.

11. Chlorofluorocarbons (CFCs) are more stable than hydrochlorofluorocarbons (HCFCs) because . . . ?
    A. They lack a fluorine atom.
    B. They are lighter than HCFCs.
    C. They are heavier than HCFCs.
    D. They lack a hydrogen atom.

12. What is an acceptable use of recycled refrigerant?
    A. It may be put into any system.
    B. It may be used as a solvent.
    C. It may be used to shrink shafts for bearing installation.
    D. It may only be returned to the same system or another that is owned by the same person.

13. CFCs contained in a mechanical refrigeration system?
    A. Chemically break-down in the refrigeration process.
    B. Threaten the environment if handled improperly.
    C. Are consumed in the refrigeration process.
    D. Become harmless to the environment after being used in the system.

14. An important safety factor in brazing is avoiding the fumes associated with brazing. Which statement below is false?
    A. It is necessary to ensure the area is well ventilated.
    B. CFCs exposed to flames may decompose and form poisonous gases.
    C. It is permissible to solder or braze a line that contains refrigerant.
    D. In many instances it is necessary to evacuate only that part of the system upon which you will be working.

15. Information regarding the health hazards associated with different chemicals and how to safely handle them may be found where?
    A. The Allied Chemical Company.

B. Material Safety Data Sheets.

C. Chemistry textbooks.

D. Walden Book sellers.

16. Threshold exposure limits (T.E.L.), the maximum allowable long-term level of exposure to a chemical based on an average career of forty work hours per week is expressed in what units of measure?

A. Parts per million (ppm).

B. Liters per cubic meter (lpm).

C. Pounds per square inch (psi).

D. Ounces per gallon (opg).

17. Violation of the CFC and HCFC venting prohibition may result in what?

A. A prison term.

B. A fine.

C. Both A and B.

D. Neither A nor B.

18. The new generation of refrigerants, HFCs, will

A. Drop in as a substitute for existing refrigerants.

B. Not drop in as a substitute.

C. Act on a totally different theory of operation.

D. Pose a greater threat to the ozone layer than traditional refrigerants.

19. It is illegal and dangerous to refill what type of cylinder?

A. D.O.T. approved refillable cylinder.

B. Any type of cylinder.

C. Disposable cylinders.

D. An empty, clean, approved refillable cylinder.

20. Heat that results in changing the state of a substance is known as what?

A. Sensible heat.

B. Latent heat.

C. Heat transfer.

D. Enthalpy.

21. In order to test for the presence of leaks on an evacuated system, which method might be used without refrigerant?

A. Standing vacuum test.

B. Air pressure test.

C. Carbon monoxide test.

D. Halide torch test.

22. Systems that are completely constructed, hermetically sealed and charged at the factory that contain five pounds or less of refrigerant are listed as what type of appliance under the section 608 regulation?
    A. Type I.
    B. Type II.
    C. Type III.
    D. It depends on the refrigerant type.

23. R-134a is what type of refrigerant?
    A. CFC.
    B. HCFC.
    C. HFC.
    D. Ammonia.

24. The Ozone Depletion Potential (ODP) is a scale that measures the harm that specific chemicals pose to the ozone layer. The scale is setup by assigning which refrigerant a value of one?
    A. R-11.
    B. R-22.
    C. R-23.
    D. R-134a.

25. The ozone layer or stratospheric ozone is found how far above the earth's surface?
    A. 1 to 3 miles.
    B. 3 to 6 miles.
    C. 11 to 22 miles.
    D. 30 to 46 miles.

26. Approved refrigerant recovery cylinders can be identified by what color code:
    A. Green tops and gray bodies.
    B. Gray tops and yellow bodies.
    C. Blue tops and green bodies.
    D. Yellow tops and gray bodies.

27. Which of the following leak detection methods is considered to be the most effective for locating the general area of small leaks?
    A. Halide torch.
    B. Audible sound.
    C. Bubble test.
    D. Electronic/ultrasonic testers.

28. What chemical found in the upper stratosphere indicates that the ozone layer is being destroyed?
    A. Nitrous oxide.
    B. Trioxide.

C. Chlorine monoxide.

D. Carbon monoxide.

29. Which of the following is a "low-pressure refrigerant" under EPA's refrigerant recycling regulations?
    A. R-22.
    B. R-500.
    C. R-134a.
    D. R-123.

30. "System-dependent" recovery devices:
    A. Must be plugged into a power source.
    B. Are hermetically sealed units requiring special maintenance.
    C. Must be connected to the liquid port on large systems.
    D. Capture refrigerant with the assistance of components in the air conditioning and refrigeration equipment.

31. The state of the refrigerant entering the compressor of a refrigeration system is:
    A. High pressure liquid.
    B. High pressure vapor.
    C. Low pressure liquid.
    D. Low pressure vapor.

32. Blended refrigerants leak from a system:
    A. At a slower rate than other refrigerants.
    B. Only if the line breaks completely.
    C. At a faster rate than other refrigerants.
    D. In uneven amounts due to different vapor pressures.

33. The state of the refrigerant leaving the condenser of a refrigeration system is:
    A. Low pressure vapor.
    B. High pressure liquid.
    C. High pressure vapor.
    D. Low pressure liquid.

34. Definition of "recover":
    A. Process refrigerant to a level equal to new product specifications.
    B. Clean refrigerant for reuse by oil separation and single or multiple passes through moisture absorption devices.
    C. Remove refrigerant from job site for disposal.
    D. Remove refrigerant in any condition from a system and store it in an external container, without necessarily testing.

35. Which of the following is a "high-pressure refrigerant" under EPA's refrigerant recycling regulations?
    A. R-113.
    B. R-123.
    C. R-11.
    D. R-12.

36. Chlorofluorocarbon (CFC) refrigerants are so named because they contain the elements:
    A. Chlorine, fluorine, & hydrogen.
    B. Chlorine, fluorine, & carbon.
    C. Chlorine, hydrogen, & carbon.
    D. Fluorine, hydrogen, & carbon.

37. Disposing of disposable cylinders is accomplished by:
    A. Giving the cylinders away to your friends to be used as air tanks.
    B. Bleeding refrigerant to ambient air and throwing the cylinders into a trash dumpster.
    C. Ensuring that all refrigerant is recovered and that the cylinders are rendered useless, then recycling the metal.
    D. Refilling the cylinders a second time at an approved facility.

38. What is one of the most serious results of damage to the ozone layer?
    A. Higher natural background radioactivity.
    B. Increased growth of marine plants.
    C. Increased volcanic activity.
    D. Increases in human skin cancer.

39. The reason for dehydrating a refrigeration system is:
    A. To remove oil and oil vapor.
    B. To remove refrigerant and refrigerant vapor.
    C. To remove water and water vapor.
    D. None of the above.

40. How many different refrigerants may be recovered into the same cylinder?
    A. Depends on the reclaim company.
    B. Only one.
    C. Only two.
    D. Any number as long as all are CFCs.

41. An example of an HCFC refrigerant is:
    A. R-22.
    B. R-114.
    C. R-717.
    D. R-11.

42. An award of up to what amount may be paid to a person supplying information that leads to a penalty against a technician who is intentionally venting?
    A. $10,000.
    B. $25,000.
    C. $50,000.
    D. $5,000.

43. After July 1, 1992, it is illegal to:
    A. Knowingly release CFC or HCFC refrigerants during the service, maintenance, repair, or disposal of appliances.
    B. Manufacture or import CFC or HCFC refrigerants in the U.S.
    C. Use CFC or HCFC refrigerants.
    D. Do any of the above.

44. Which of the following refrigerants has the lowest ozone depletion potential?
    A. R-134a.
    B. R-502.
    C. R-22.
    D. R-123.

45. Which of the following gases help form the earth's protective shield?
    A. Stratospheric ozone.
    B. Carbon dioxide.
    C. Methane.
    D. Radon.

46. The component that changes a low-pressure vapor to a high-pressure vapor is:
    A. Compressor.
    B. Evaporator.
    C. Condenser.
    D. Cap tube.

47. Which of the following could result in violations of the Clean Air Act?
    A. Knowingly releasing CFC or HCFC refrigerants while repairing appliances.
    B. Failing to reach required evacuation levels before opening or disposing of appliances.
    C. Falsifying or failing to keep required records.
    D. All of the above.

48. The synthetic lubricant presently used with ternary blends is:
    A. Whale oil.
    B. Alkylbenzene.
    C. Glycols.
    D. Esters.

49. Reusable containers for refrigerants that are under high pressure (above 15 psig) at normal ambient temperature must be hydrostatically tested and date stamped every:
   A. 2 years.
   B. 5 years.
   C. 10 years.
   D. 1 year.

50. According to the ASHRAE refrigerant safety classification standard, which of the following designations would be the most safe?
   A. B-1.
   B. B-3.
   C. A-1.
   D. A-3.

51. As of what date did it become unlawful to release Class I and Class II refrigerants to the atmosphere?
   A. July 1, 1992.
   B. July 1, 1993.
   C. November 14, 1994.
   D. January 1, 1996.

52. The atom found in CFC and HCFC refrigerants that destroys ozone in the stratosphere is:
   A. Fluorine.
   B. Carbon.
   C. Hydrogen.
   D. Chlorine.

53. Which refrigerant is a CFC?
   A. R 134a.
   B. R-123.
   C. R-22.
   D. R-12.

54. Which refrigerant is an HFC?
   A. R-134a.
   B. R-123.
   C. R-22.
   D. R-12.

55. Which refrigerant contains no chlorine?
   A. R-134a.
   B. R-123.
   C. R-22.
   D. R-12.

56. The rule of thumb for refilling approved cylinders is a maximum of percent liquid?
    A. 60%.
    B. 70%.
    C. 80%.
    D. 90%.

57. To recover refrigerant is to:
    A. Remove refrigerant in any condition from a system in either an active or passive manner and store it in an external container without necessarily testing or processing.
    B. Reduce contaminants in used refrigerant by oil separation through filter driers.
    C. Reprocess refrigerant to new product specifications.
    D. Remove refrigerant and change ownership.

58. R-134a is a "drop-in" refrigerant for:
    A. R-12.
    B. R-22.
    C. R-11.
    D. R-134a is not a drop-in refrigerant.

59. The condition and state of the refrigerant leaving a receiver is:
    A. Subcooled liquid.
    B. Subcooled vapor.
    C. Superheated vapor.
    D. Superheated liquid.

60. The component of an air-conditioning system that changes a low-pressure vapor to a high-pressure vapor is the:
    A. Condenser.
    B. Metering device.
    C. Evaporator.
    D. Compressor.

61. Processing used refrigerant through devices that remove oil and particulates and reduce moisture and acidity is called:
    A. Restoring.
    B. Recovery.
    C. Recycling.
    D. Reclaiming.

62. Which of the following is NOT a Class I or Class II substance per Section 608 of the Clean Air Act?
    A. R-12.
    B. R-22.
    C. R-11.
    D. R-134a.

63. Which of the following should be used to pressurize a system for leak testing?
    A. Oxygen.
    B. Compressed air.
    C. The system refrigerant.
    D. Nitrogen.

64. Reclaimed refrigerant must be reprocessed in accordance with:
    A. ARI Standard 700.
    B. ASHRAE Standard 15.
    C. DOT specifications.
    D. EPA standards.

65. The tendency of a refrigerant blend to leak from a system at different rates is called:
    A. Segregation.
    B. Fragmentation.
    C. Fractionation.
    D. Separation.

66. Which of the following is NOT a synthetic oil:
    A. Naphthenetic mineral oil.
    B. Alkylbenzene oil.
    C. Polyalkylene glycol oil.
    D. Polyolester oil.

67. Which of the following gases contributes most to global warming?
    A. Carbon monoxide.
    B. Sulfur dioxide.
    C. Carbon dioxide.
    D. R-12.

68. To receive Universal certification, a technician must be certified to work on:
    A. Type I equipment.
    B. Type II equipment.
    C. Type III equipment.
    D. All of the above.

69. A small appliance is defined by the EPA as:
    A. Weighing less than 100 pounds.
    B. Weighing less than 250 pounds.
    C. Containing less than 5 pounds of refrigerant.
    D. Having a capacity less than 1 ton.

70. Refrigerant recovery during low-ambient temperatures will:
    A. Have a shortened recovery time.
    B. Have an increased recovery time.
    C. Reduce emissions.
    D. Require frequent drier changes.

71. An azeotropic mixture
    A. Is a mixture of two different refrigerants.
    B. Is mixture of three different refrigerants.
    C. Condenses at a constant temperature.
    D. Exhibits a temperature glide of more than 5°F.

72. If exposed to high temperatures, R-12 and R-22 can decompose to form:
    A. Ozone.
    B. Carbon dioxide.
    C. Phosgene gas.
    D. Carbon monoxide.

73. The process that returns a used refrigerant to the requirements of ARI-700 is called:
    A. Recovery.
    B. Recycle.
    C. Reclaim.
    D. Reprocess.

74. Disposable refrigerant cylinders are used for:
    A. Recycled refrigerant.
    B. Recovered refrigerant.
    C. New refrigerant.
    D. Contaminated refrigerant.

75. Which of the following substances have the lowest ozone depletion potential (ODP)?
    A. CFCs.
    B. HCFCs.
    C. Halons.
    D. HFCs.

# Type I (Small Appliance)
# Practice Questions

1. What is the most accurate method of charging a domestic refrigerator?
   A. Completely evacuate and recharge the system using an electronic scale.
   B. Use the frostline method.
   C. Use the superheat method.
   D. Use the subcooling method.

2. Who is ultimately responsible for ensuring that the refrigerant has been recovered from a small appliance that is being discarded?
   A. The owner of the appliance.
   B. The delivery company.
   C. The final person in the disposal chain.
   D. The EPA.

3. When recovering refrigerant from a small appliance with an operative compressor using a system-dependent recovery device, where on the system should the connection be made to the recovery device?
   A. The compressor suction.
   B. The compressor discharge.
   C. The capillary tube outlet.
   D. The process stub.

4. When recovering refrigerant from a small appliance with a plugged capillary tube, where on the system should the connection be made to the recovery device?
   A. The compressor suction.
   B. The compressor discharge.
   C. The capillary tube outlet.
   D. The process stub.

5. Many recycling and recovery systems have an oil separation capacity. The oil collector should be drained after each use on hermetic compressor systems. Why?
   A. It allows for the measuring of the amount of oil removed from the system being serviced so that the proper amount may be recharged.
   B. It prevents the contamination of the oil in the recovery unit's compressor.
   C. It allows for the removal of excess oil from the refrigeration system being repaired.
   D. Both A & B.

6. The use of R-11 as a cleaning agent for burned out systems is . . . ?
   A. Still widely used and acceptable.

B. Banned with the implementation of the venting prohibition.

C. Always used.

D. Legal as long as all of the refrigerant is allowed to evaporate to the atmosphere.

7. Component chemicals of zeotropes tend to separate during a change of state. This property is known as:

A. Fractionation.

B. Fragmentation.

C. Segregation.

D. Photodissociation.

8. A low reading from the motor windings to ground, approximately 10 megohms, in a hermetic compressor is a good indication of what condition of the refrigerant?

A. The refrigerant is in good condition.

B. The refrigerant is highly acidic from a burn-out.

C. The refrigerant has a high moisture content.

D. The refrigerant is free of chlorine and may be vented.

9. When handling refrigerant cylinders, which are acceptable practices?

A. Store cylinders in an area that is not subject to temperatures above 130°F.

B. Tap on the side of the cylinder with a hammer to determine how full the cylinder is.

C. Remove and inspect the valve assembly to ensure proper operation.

D. Allow cylinder to roll around in the back of your truck.

10. Which procedure is important when making a brazed joint?

A. Measure tubing lengths accurately.

B. Use a tubing cutter to make square cuts.

C. Avoid using too much pressure when cutting tubing in order to prevent deforming the tubing.

D. All of the above.

11. If a small appliance is found to be at atmospheric pressure with the compressor shut down, it may be assumed that:

A. All refrigerant has leaked from the system and attempted recovery is not necessary.

B. The gauge set being used is defective.

C. All refrigerant in the system is a subcooled liquid, therefore, no vapor pressure.

D. Either B or C.

12. When recovering refrigerant, it is important to do which of the following?
    A. Avoid mixing different types of refrigerant.
    B. Avoid putting the system under a vacuum with the recovery equipment.
    C. Use a torch to heat the system.
    D. Shut the recovery equipment down when the system pressure reaches 6 psi.

13. When recovering refrigerant from a small appliance, using a recovery device manufactured after November 15, 1993, what percentage of the remaining charge must be recovered if the system's compressor is in working order?
    A. 60%.
    B. 70%.
    C. 80%.
    D. 90%.

14. Oil from a burned out compressor is . . . ?
    A. Golden colored.
    B. Highly acidic.
    C. In the TEV.
    D. At the top of the condenser.

15. What differentiates "system-dependent" and "self-contained" recovery devices?
    A. System-dependent recovery devices may only be used on large chillers.
    B. Self-contained recovery devices use the compressor of the system being repaired for the recovery process.
    C. Self-contained recovery devices usually contain a compressor, system dependent recovery devices do not.
    D. A deeper vacuum must be achieved using system-dependent recovery devices than is required for self-contained recovery devices.

16. Modern recovery systems are designed to work with:
    A. All refrigerants, including methyl chloride, sulfur dioxide, and ammonia.
    B. Fluorocarbon refrigerants only.
    C. Propane and isobutane.
    D. Disposable cylinders.

17. Most of the acids and contaminants from a burn-out are found where?
    A. In the refrigerant.
    B. In the oil.
    C. In the evaporator.
    D. In the condenser.

18. When using a halide torch for leak detection it is important to do which of the following?
    A. Always move the hose along the bottom of lines suspected of having leaks.
    B. Place the hose in any position along the line.
    C. Move the hose as rapidly as possible.
    D. Use only methane, as it is the only fuel that will work with a halide torch.

19. Small appliances, including access fittings, should be leak tested:
    A. Using refrigerant pressure prior to recovery.
    B. After recovery, using nitrogen.
    C. Every time the system is shut down.
    D. Prior to disposal.

20. When making a brazed joint, you should avoid touching the cleaned metal surfaces. Why?
    A. Burrs on the ends could cut your hands.
    B. Oils from the skin might impair making a good joint.
    C. You don't know where the tubing has been.
    D. You might deform the tubing.

21. Chilling a recovery cylinder will have what effect?
    A. Cylinder pressure will be increased.
    B. Cylinder pressure will be decreased.
    C. Cylinder pressure will remain constant.
    D. Cylinder pressure will fluctuate without regard for temperature.

22. When using an electronic halide detector which procedures should be followed?
    A. Adjust the sensitivity setting to highest level possible, that does not cause the detector to alarm due to the presence of background refrigerant.
    B. Move the sensor along the bottom of the lines being tested at approximately one inch per second.
    C. Avoid exposing the sensing tip directly to moisture.
    D. All of the above.

23. Small appliances, including access fittings, should be leak tested:
    A. Using refrigerant pressure prior to recovery.
    B. After recovery, using nitrogen.
    C. Every time the system is shut down.
    D. Prior to disposal.

24. Chilling the recovery cylinder expedites the recovery process because . . . ?
    A. Lowering the cylinder's temperature reduces the cylinder's pressure, thereby increasing flow rate.
    B. It increases the pressure ratio of the recovery system.
    C. It produces a higher pressure in the cylinder.
    D. It will cause the recovery system to work harder.

25. In order to service a domestic refrigerator after November 14, 1994, a technician must be certified as a
    A. Type I technician.
    B. Type II technician.
    C. Type III technician.
    D. Either Type I or Universal technician.

26. After installing and opening a piercing access valve, if the system pressure is _____, do not begin the recovery procedure.
    A. 75 psig.
    B. 50 psig.
    C. 30 psig.
    D. 0 psig.

27. EPA regulations include which of the following in the definition of a "small appliance?"
    A. Products manufactured, charged, and hermetically sealed in a factory.
    B. Products having 5 pounds or less of refrigerant.
    C. Products with compressors under ½ horsepower.
    D. Both A and B.

28. When installing any type of access fitting onto a sealed system:
    A. The fitting should be leak tested before proceeding with recovery.
    B. It is not necessary to leak test an access fitting.
    C. The fitting need not be leak tested until the total repair is completed.
    D. The system must be pressurized with dry nitrogen before leak testing can be attempted.

29. Which conditions can cause excessive pressure conditions on the high side of a self-contained (active) recovery device?
    A. When the recovery tank inlet valve has not been opened.
    B. When there is excessive air in the recovery tank.
    C. When the recovery tank outlet valve has not been opened.
    D. Both A and B.

30. Which of the following are recommended safe work practices when recovering refrigerants?
    A. Wear safety glasses or goggles when working with any compressed gases.

B. Wear a respirator when working with any refrigerant.

C. Wear butyl-lined gloves when connecting/disconnecting hoses.

D. Both A and C.

31. The following may be present in refrigerants used in small appliances in campers or other recreational vehicles and should not be recovered with current recovery devices:

A. Ammonia.

B. Hydrogen.

C. Water.

D. All of the above.

32. After recovering refrigerant from a sealed system, if nitrogen is used to pressurize or blow debris out of the system, the nitrogen:

A. Must be recovered.

B. May be vented.

C. Should not be used.

D. Should only be used if mixed with ammonia.

33. If EPA regulations change after a technician becomes certified:

A. The technician certification is grandfathered for one year to allow time for recertification.

B. It will be the technician's responsibility to comply with any future changes in the law.

C. A new certification test must be takon to bc recertified.

D. Both A and C.

34. When R-500 is recovered from an appliance, it:

A. Can be mixed with either R-22 or R-12 during the recovery process, since R-500 is actually a mixture of the two refrigerants.

B. Can be mixed with R-12 but not R-22 during the recovery process.

C. Need not be recovered since R-500 is not one of the refrigerants covered by the Clean Air Act.

D. Must be recovered into its own recovery vessel that is clearly marked to ensure that mixing of refrigerants does not occur.

35. When you check system pressures to determine the performance of a refrigerant, it's always necessary to:

A. Release a small amount of refrigerant to check for contamination.

B. Use equipment such as hand valves or self-sealing hoses to minimize any release.

C. Recover refrigerant and recharge to specifications, even if no repairs are needed.

D. Use recovery equipment to gain access to the system during testing.

36. The Department of Transportation Regulations, 49 CFR, require which parameter to be recorded on the shipping paper for hazard class 2.2, Non-flammable Compressed Gases?
    A. Weight of each cylinder.
    B. Total cubic feet of each gas.
    C. Number of cylinders of each gas.
    D. Total weight of all cylinders.

37. Equipment manufactured after November 15, 1993, that is used to recover refrigerant from small appliances for the purpose of disposal must meet what standard?
    A. Recover 95% or the refrigerant whether or not the compressor is operative.
    B. Recover 80% of the refrigerant with an inoperative compressor.
    C. Recover 90% of the refrigerant with an operative compressor.
    D. Both B and C.

38. Portable refillable tanks or containers used to ship CFC or HCFC refrigerants obtained with recovery equipment must meet what standard(s)?
    A. Department of Transportation.
    B. Community Right-To-Know Act.
    C. Underwriters Laboratories.
    D. All of the above.

39. A refrigerant that can be used as a direct, "drop-in" substitute for R-12 in a small appliance is:
    A. R-134a.
    B. R-22.
    C. R-141b.
    D. None of the above.

40. All appliances must be equipped with a service aperture or other device that is used when adding or removing refrigerant from the appliance. For small appliances, this service port typically is:
    A. A straight piece of tubing that is entered using a piercing access valve.
    B. Located 15 inches below the compressor.
    C. Installed at the factory, has a ¼ inch diameter and machine threads.
    D. Not present because small appliances are exempt from this requirement.

41. Why should you allow refrigerant inside a recovery cylinder to stabilize at room temperature?
    A. To prevent safety valves from purging refrigerant.
    B. This is a quick check method of determining refrigerant level inside the tank.

C. The only way to read refrigerant pressure accurately is at a known temperature.

D. The recovery cylinder could explode if temperature changes too quickly.

42. Using the system-dependent (passive) recovery process, which condition requires the accessing both the high and low side of the system for refrigerant recovery:

A. When there is a leak in the system.

B. When the compressor operates normally.

C. When the compressor only runs at half speed.

D. When the compressor does not run.

43. In the event of a "large" release of R-12 or R-22 in a contained area, which of the following is true?

A. Safety goggles and lined butyl gloves are sufficient.

B. Self-contained breathing apparatus (SCBA) is required.

C. Respiratory protection is not required.

D. Local exhaust and mechanical ventilation in low places are sufficient.

44. At high temperatures, (that is, open flames, glowing metal surfaces, etc.) R-12 and R-22 can decompose to form:

A. Boric and chromic acids.

B. Sulfuric and phosphoric acids.

C. Hydrochloric and hydrofluoric acids.

D. None of the above.

45. Effective August 12, 1993, persons using recovery equipment to recover refrigerant from a small appliance must certify to EPA that they have:

A. Equipment capable of removing 90% of the refrigerant when the compressor is operating or achieving a 4 inch vacuum under conditions of ARI 740-1993.

B. Equipment capable of removing 80% of the refrigerant or achieving a 4 inch vacuum under conditions of ARI 740-1993.

C. Equipment capable of achieving a 27 inch vacuum under conditions of ARI 740-1993.

D. All of the above.

46. When using nitrogen in repairing a sealed refrigeration system, the nitrogen tank should always be equipped with a:

A. Regulator.

B. Float sensor.

C. Red top.

D. Hand valve.

47. A storage cylinder of recovered R-22 at normal room temperature (about 75°F), in the absence of noncondensables, will be pressurized to:
    A. 250 psig.
    B. 200 psig.
    C. 175 psig.
    D. 130 psig.

48. When servicing a small appliance for leak repair
    A. It is mandatory to repair the leak within 30 days.
    B. It is mandatory to repair the leak only when 35% of the charge escapes within a 12 month period.
    C. It is not mandatory to repair the leak but do so whenever possible.
    D. Both A and B.

49. To speed the recovery process and ensure that all refrigerant has been removed from a frost-free refrigerator.
    A. Cool the compressor to force liquid out of the high side.
    B. Heat the recovery cylinder to vaporize liquid refrigerant.
    C. Turn on the defrost heater to vaporize any trapped liquid.
    D. Pack ice around the evaporator to ensure maximum liquid is available.

50. Persons recovering refrigerant during maintenance, service, or repair of small appliances must be certified as a:
    A. Type II Technician.
    B. Type III Technician.
    C. Type I Technician or Universal Technician.
    D. All of the above.

51. Which best describes the definition of Type I "Small appliance," as defined by EPA?
    A. Systems manufactured, charged, and hermetically sealed with five (5) pounds or less of refrigerant.
    B. Refrigerators, freezers, room air-conditioners and central air-conditioners.
    C. Any appliance charged with more than five (5) pounds of refrigerant.
    D. Any appliance charged with less than two (2) pounds of refrigerant.

52. For small appliance use, the recovery equipment manufactured after November 15, 1993, must be capable of recovering:
    A. 80% of the refrigerant when the compressor is not operating or achieve a 4 inch vacuum under ARI 740-1993.
    B. 90% of the refrigerant when the compressor is operating or achieve a 4 inch vacuum under ARI 740-1993.
    C. 99% of the refrigerant regardless of compressor operation and achieve a 10 inch vacuum under ARI 740-1993.
    D. A and B above.

53. The sale of Class I and Class II refrigerants will be restricted to technicians certified by an EPA approved program after:
    A. July 1, 1992.
    B. November 15, 1993.
    C. August 12, 1993.
    D. November 14, 1994.

54. The release of vapor from the top of a graduated charging cylinder when filling may:
    A. Be vented to the atmosphere.
    B. Be vented if the quantity does not exceed three (3) pounds.
    C. Not be vented and must be recovered.
    D. Be vented, but not inhaled.

55. Should regulations of the Clean Air Act (CAA) change after a technician is certified:
    A. The technician must take a new test to be recertified.
    B. All technicians who previously passed with an 80% will be grandfathered.
    C. It will be the technician's responsibility to learn and comply with future changes in the law.
    D. The technician must be retested and pass the exam with an 84%.

56. System dependent (passive) refrigerant recovery of small appliances:
    A. Do not require an operating compressor.
    B. Requires 80% of the refrigerant to be recovered.
    C. Recovers refrigerant in a nonpressurized container.
    D. All of the above.

57. Before disposing of a small appliance containing R-12, it is necessary to:
    A. Pressurize with nitrogen.
    B. Recover the refrigerant.
    C. Turn upside down.
    D. Thoroughly leak check.

58. A system has been operating with a complete restriction at the capillary tube inlet, what access is required for recovery?
    A. One access valve on the low side of the system.
    B. Two access valves, high and low side of system.
    C. One access valve on the high side of the system.
    D. One access valve on the evaporator, and one on the low side.

59. CFCs will not be manufactured in the United States after:
    A. 2000.
    B. 1995.
    C. 2005.
    D. 1996.

60. To work on small appliances after November 14, 1993, a technician must be certified as:
    A. Type I.
    B. Type II.
    C. Universal.
    D. A or C above.

61. A small appliance is defined as one containing less than:
    A. 1 pound of refrigerant.
    B. 5 pounds of refrigerant.
    C. 10 pounds of refrigerant.
    D. 50 pounds of refrigerant.

62. In order to remove the charge from a small appliance, a technician must have:
    A. Type I certification.
    B. Type II certification.
    C. Type III certification.
    D. Any of the above certifications.

63. Piercing-type access valves should NOT be used on the following tube material(s):
    A. Copper.
    B. Aluminum.
    C. Steel.
    D. Any of the above.

64. The law requires that a refrigerant leak in a small appliance:
    A. Must be repaired within 30 days.
    B. Must be repaired if the leak exceeds 2 pounds per year.
    C. Must be repaired if the system contains a charge of more than 5 pounds.
    D. Does not have to be repaired.

65. Clamp-on piercing-type access valves must be removed from the system after the repair because:
    A. They will corrode and contaminate the system.
    B. Their gasket will fail over time and leak.
    C. They are expensive and can be reused.
    D. They will restrict the refrigerant flow.

66. Before disposing of a small appliance containing R-12, it is necessary to:
    A. Remove the compressor.
    B. Recover the refrigerant.
    C. Notify the EPA.
    D. Recycle the copper tubing.

67. A passive or system dependent refrigerant recovery:
    A. Uses the system compressor.
    B. Uses a nonpressurized refrigerant container.
    C. Both A and B.
    D. Neither A nor B.

68. A recovery unit manufactured after November 15, 1993, and used on small appliances:
    A. Must remove 80 percent of the charge if the compressor is not operating.
    B. Must remove 90 percent of the charge if the compressor is operating.
    C. May reduce the pressure to 4 inches of mercury vacuum to satisfy the regulations.
    D. All of the above.

69. System dependent recovery equipment *cannot* be used when:
    A. The compressor is operational.
    B. The temperature is below 40°F.
    C. The temperature is above 95°F.
    D. The refrigerant charge is greater than 15 pounds.

70. When servicing a small appliance, it is now illegal to vent the following:
    A. CFCs.
    B. HCFCs.
    C. HFCs.
    D. All of the above.

71. Recovery equipment used to recover refrigerant from small appliances must be certified by an EPA-approved organization if manufactured after:
    A. November 15, 1990.
    B. July 1, 1992.
    C. November 15, 1993.
    D. November 15, 1995.

72. The service aperture found on small appliances for refrigerant recovery is called a:
    A. Relief valve.
    B. Gate valve.
    C. Globe valve.
    D. Process stub.

73. Once it is empty a disposable refrigerant cylinder:
    A. Should be rendered useless.
    B. Can be used to store contaminated refrigerant.
    C. Can be used with a recovery unit.
    D. Can only be refilled with the same refrigerant that was shipped in it.

74. Schrader valves on small appliances and recovery equipment:
    A. Must be inspected periodically for damage.
    B. Must be capped to prevent leakage after use.
    C. Have a replaceable core.
    D. All of the above.

75. Recovery units manufactured after November 15, 1993, must
    A. Be fitted with low-loss fittings.
    B. Be fitted with quick-connect fittings.
    C. Be certified for use with all refrigerants.
    D. Be certified to meet the specified recovery rates.

## Type II (High-Pressure)
## Practice Questions

1. Increased ultraviolet radiation reaching the earth's surface may result in what?
    A. Increased incidence of skin cancer.
    B. Increased incidence of cataracts.
    C. Reduced crop production.
    D. All of the above.

2. Which of the following procedures require a chemical certification of refrigerant quality?
    A. Recover.
    B. Recycle.
    C. Reclaim.
    D. None of the above.

3. An important part of avoiding difficulties with an EPA inquiry is maintaining records of refrigerant usage. What should be included in these records?
    A. The quantity of refrigerant sent to be reclaimed.
    B. The quantity of refrigerant purchased.
    C. Service records that indicate the quantity of refrigerant recovered from systems and the quantity recharged.
    D. All of the above.

4. Inhalation of high concentrations of CFCs may have what effect?
    A. Drowsiness.
    B. Loss of concentration.
    C. Cardiac arrhythmias.
    D. All of the above.

5. ASHRAE 15 requires that refrigeration systems be protected by pressure limiting devices, including: relief valves, rupture discs and fusible plugs. If more than one relief valve is used on a system, they should be mounted:
   A. In parallel.
   B. In series.
   C. In series with a hand shut-off valve.
   D. With plugs in outlet.

6. Recovery equipment that is designated for use on R-134a systems . . . ?
   A. May be used for any other type of refrigerant.
   B. Should be steam cleaned after each recovery procedure.
   C. Generally should not be used to recover CFCs and HCFCs.
   D. Do not exist, as there is no reason to recover HFCs.

7. Which international agreement began the process of phasing out the production of CFCs?
   A. The Helsinki Accord.
   B. The Uruguay Round.
   C. The Rio de Janeiro Environmental Treaties.
   D. The Montreal Protocol.

8. In order to successfully recover refrigerant from a nonsmall appliance refrigeration system that requires minor service, that is, replacing a cartridge-type filter-drier, it is necessary to reduce the pressure in the system to what point?
   A. 5 to 8 psi.
   B. 2 to 4 psi.
   C. Atmospheric pressure.
   D. A vacuum of 10 to 20 inches of mercury.

9. Are technicians certified as Type II technicians allowed to "open" a low-pressure system for repairs?
   A. Only if the system is fully charged.
   B. Yes, as long as the refrigerant is to be sent for reclaiming.
   C. No, only technicians certified as Type III technicians may open low pressure systems.
   D. No, only Type I technicians may work on low pressure systems.

10. Mixing different types of refrigerant in a recovery cylinder...?
    A. Is not a problem if the refrigerant is to be reclaimed.
    B. Will not affect the quality of the refrigerant.
    C. Should never be done.
    D. Is not possible because of the difference in the pressures of the refrigerants.

11. The excise tax charged on refrigerants is based on a formula where the weight of the refrigerant purchased is multiplied by the base tax rate and this number is multiplied by what?
    A. The ozone depletion potential (ODP) of the refrigerant.
    B. The global warming potential (GWP) of the refrigerant.
    C. The molecular weight of the refrigerant.
    D. The market scarcity factor of the refrigerant.

12. In order to assist in the prosecution of the violators of the venting prohibitions, the EPA has been authorized to do which of the following?
    A. Forego constitutional protection afforded to other criminals.
    B. Offer rewards of up to $10,000 for information which leads to the conviction of violators.
    C. Require all refrigeration technicians be subject to lie detector tests.
    D. Establish roof-top surveillance teams to watch for violators.

13. Tropospheric (atmospheric) ozone, ozone which is at or near the earth's surface, is . . . ?
    A. Beneficial in filtering-out UV radiation.
    B. Necessary to sustain human life.
    C. A harmful photochemical pollutant which is a component of smog.
    D. An inert substance.

14. For a TXV controlled system, which symptom indicates an undercharged condition and, therefore, the likelihood of a leak?
    A. Low suction pressure.
    B. Normal suction pressure.
    C. High discharge pressure.
    D. High suction pressure.

15. When using a charging manifold that is not equipped with quick-disconnect hoses, what procedure should be used to reduce refrigerant discharge to the atmosphere when disconnecting the hoses?
    A. Close the system's high-side service valve and open both of the valves on the manifold to bleed pressure back to the low-side of the system.
    B. Allow the manifold to bleed back to the charging cylinder.
    C. Close the system's suction-side service valve and open both of the valves on the manifold to bleed the pressure back to the high-side of the system.
    D. There is no way to reduce these refrigerant emissions.

16. The regulation allows for exceptions to the required evacuation levels for recovery if system leaks prevent achieving the required evacuation levels

without seriously contaminating the refrigerant that is being recovered. What steps must be taken in this instance to comply with the regulation?

A. If possible, the leaking components should be isolated from the rest of the system.

B. In no instance should the evacuation level for the leaking components be in excess of atmospheric pressure.

C. Non-leaking components of the system that are isolated from those leaking must be evacuated to prescribed evacuation levels.

D. All of the above.

17. When using the system compressor to pump refrigerant into a chilled cylinder, special attention must be paid to what?

A. Cylinder pressure.

B. System supply voltage.

C. Cylinder weight, including weight of refrigerant.

D. Both A and C.

18. What is necessary when using nitrogen or carbon dioxide as the source of pressure for a leak test?

A. Low-pressure supply cylinders.

B. This test should only be used with a system capable of withstanding over 1,000 psi.

C. A controllable regulator.

D. Liquid nitrogen or liquid carbon dioxide supply.

19. What type of contamination will the reclamation process be unable to separate?

A. Moisture.

B. Acids.

C. Particulate matter.

D. Mixed refrigerants.

20. The speed of the recovery process may be increased by which of the following?

A. The use of short hoses with a large diameter.

B. Removing as much refrigerant as possible as a liquid.

C. Chilling the recovery cylinder.

D. All of the above.

21. What procedures would be followed to perform a low-side pump-down?

A. Close the king valve and run the compressor until pressure in the area to be serviced has been reduced to the mandated level.

B. Close compressor suction valve, run the compressor until the low-pressure cut-out point is reached and then close the king valve.

C. Allow the system to go through a normal cycle and secure necessary valves once the compressor has shut down.

D. System will always be pumped down when the system is shut down.

22. During a standing vacuum test, a rise in pressure to 2,500 microns (2.5 mm hg absolute) indicates what?
    A. Too much refrigerant in the system.
    B. An insufficient charge.
    C. A leak.
    D. A malfunction in the test equipment.

23. Very high-pressure refrigerants such as R-503 and R-13 may be recovered . . . ?
    A. To any recovery cylinder.
    B. Only to specially designated cylinders that are rated for these refrigerants.
    C. Using ordinary recovery equipment.
    D. Only if ambient temperature exceeds 80°F.

24. If you are working with refrigeration equipment that requires a charge on a monthly basis, what action should be taken?
    A. Continue to charge the system.
    B. Find the leak and repair it.
    C. Ignore the situation, as this is not a problem.
    D. Adjust the thermostat.

25. It is necessary to maintain a tight system in order to protect the environment. What is one of the ways to visually find small leaks?
    A. Look for foaming at the pipe fittings.
    B. Listen for a loud whistling noise.
    C. Look for signs of oil escaping at fittings.
    D. There is no way to find leaks without test equipment.

26. With an air-cooled condenser on the roof of a building and the evaporator on the first floor, recovery should first occur:
    A. From the discharge of the compressor.
    B. From the liquid line entering the evaporator.
    C. On the suction side of the compressor.
    D. From the vapor line entering the condenser.

27. Which of the following is *not* part of the low side of the system?
    A. Suction line.
    B. Accumulator.
    C. Evaporator.
    D. Receiver.

28. Every refrigerating system shall be protected by:
    A. Low-pressure control.
    B. Refrigerant receiver.
    C. Pressure relief device.
    D. Properly located stop valve.

29. You are going to service a residential split system, providing comfort air-conditioning. You would expect to find what type of refrigerant?
   A. R-22.
   B. R-11.
   C. R-12.
   D. R-502.

30. When using recovery and recycling equipment manufactured before November 15, 1993, technicians must evacuate an appliance containing 10 pounds of CFC-500 to the following level before disposing of the appliance:
   A. 15 inches of mercury vacuum.
   B. 0 psig.
   C. 4 inches of mercury vacuum.
   D. 10 inches of mercury vacuum.

31. You are sent out to service a 60-ton packaged roof top unit. The easiest way to check the type of refrigerant it uses is to:
   A. Look on top of the TXV.
   B. Look at the unit name plate.
   C. Use your service gauge set and a refrigerant card.
   D. Ask the owner.

32. After installation of a field-piped split system, the unit should first be:
   A. Pressurized with R-12J and leak checked.
   B. Pressurized with nitrogen and leak checked.
   C. Evacuated.
   D. Pressurized with R 22 and leak checked.

33. In a refrigeration system using a thermal expansion valve, the component directly following the condenser is the:
   A. Accumulator.
   B. Evaporator.
   C. Receiver.
   D. Metering device.

34. A moisture-indicating sight glass is useful for:
   A. Checking the refrigerants water content.
   B. Providing sub-cooling.
   C. Checking the system's charge.
   D. Both A and C.

35. A reciprocating compressor should not be energized when:
   A. The suction service valve is open.
   B. The discharge service valve is open.
   C. There is a demand for cooling.
   D. The discharge service valve is closed.

36. You provide the service work for units with R-12, R-502, and R-134a. What special precautions must you take?
    A. There is no need to take any special precautions since there is little difference between these refrigerants.
    B. Provide a special set of hoses, gauges, vacuum pump, recovery machine, and oil containers to be used with R-134a only.
    C. Provide a special set of hoses, gauges, vacuum pump, recovery machine, and oil containers to be used with R-502 only.
    D. Provide a special set of hoses, gauges, vacuum pump, recovery machine, and oil containers to be used with R-12 and R-134a only.

37. Refrigerant has been recovered from an air-conditioning system and held in a refillable cylinder, in order to replace the condenser coil. The refrigerant:
    A. Must be reclaimed.
    B. Must be destroyed.
    C. Can probably be charged back into the system.
    D. Should probably be replaced with R-123.

38. You can save time recovering the refrigerant from a system by removing as much as possible in the phase?
    A. Vapor.
    B. Final.
    C. Initial.
    D. Liquid.

39. After reaching the required recovery vacuum on an appliance, you should:
    A. Immediately break the vacuum with nitrogen and open the system for service.
    B. Immediately pressurize the system with nitrogen and perform a leak check.
    C. Immediately disconnect the recycling or recovery equipment and open the system for service.
    D. Wait for at least a few minutes to see if the system pressure rises, indicating that there is still refrigerant in liquid form or in the oil.

40. Before using a recovery unit to remove the charge, what steps should be taken?
    A. Evacuate recovery unit/receiver.
    B. Check service valve positions.
    C. Check recovery unit oil level.
    D. All of the above.

41. During service, quick couplers, self-sealing hoses, or hand valves can be used to:
    A. Simplify evacuation during recycling.
    B. Minimize refrigerant release when hoses are connected and disconnected.

C. Prevent vapor lock during liquid transfer.
D. Minimize the chance of explosion during the reclamation of mixed refrigerants.

42. When first inspecting a hermetic system known to be leaking, you should look for:
    A. Particles of filter-drier core.
    B. Traces of oil.
    C. Frost on the tubing.
    D. Puddles of refrigerant.

43. When evacuating a vapor compression system, the vacuum pump should be capable of pulling a vacuum of:
    A. 1 mm Hg.
    B. 1,000 microns.
    C. 500 microns.
    D. 2 mm Hg.

44. Noncondensables in a refrigeration system result in:
    A. Higher discharge pressure.
    B. Lower suction pressure.
    C. Higher suction pressure.
    D. Lower discharge pressure.

45. Removal of the refrigerant charge from a system can be conducted more quickly by:
    A. Using a standard vacuum pump.
    B. Heating the recovery vessel.
    C. Using a smaller recovery vessel.
    D. Packing the recovery vessel in ice.

46. Refrigerant should be removed from the condenser outlet when the:
    A. Condenser is on the roof.
    B. Compressor is inoperative.
    C. Evaporator has a small leak.
    D. Condenser is below the receiver.

47. The component directly following the evaporator of a refrigeration system is the:
    A. Accumulator.
    B. Condense.
    C. Receiver.
    D. Feed device.

48. Which of the following is an indicator of a leak in a high-pressure system?
    A. Frequent purging.
    B. High head pressure.
    C. Low water temperature.
    D. Excessive superheat.

49. Backseating a suction shutoff valve will close the:
    A. Gauge port.
    B. Suction line and compressor port.
    C. Compressor and gauge port.
    D. Compressor port.

50. Testing with soap bubbles is used:
    A. In explosive atmospheres.
    B. To detect water leaks.
    C. To determine if refrigerant leaks have occurred.
    D. To pinpoint system leaks.

51. Which refrigerant can be used for leak detection as a trace gas and pressurized with nitrogen?
    A. R-12.
    B. R-11.
    C. R-22.
    D. R-115.

52. Traces of oil around the sight glass inlet fitting of a refrigeration system might be the indication of:
    A. A leak.
    B. Excessive oil in the system.
    C. An overcharge.
    D. A restriction at the TXV.

53. Type II classification, as identified by EPA, applies to what equipment?
    A. Small appliances with five (5) pounds of refrigerant and less.
    B. Refrigerants, freezer, and vending machines appliances.
    C. Low pressure appliances.
    D. Split air-conditioning equipment with five (5) pounds of refrigerant and greater.

54. The required level of evacuation for recovery equipment manufactured after November 15, 1993, on a system containing less than 200 pounds of R-12 refrigerant is:
    A. 0 inches Hg.
    B. 4 inches Hg.
    C. 10 inches Hg.
    D. 15 inches Hg.

55. Industrial process and commercial refrigeration equipment with over 50 lbs. of refrigerant with an annual leak rate of _____% requires repair under EPA regulations:
    A. 0.
    B. 15.
    C. 35.
    D. 50.

56. Comfort cooling chillers and all other equipment with over 50 lbs. of refrigerant with an annual leak rate of ____% requires repair under EPA regulations:
    A. 0.
    B. 15.
    C. 35.
    D. 50.

57. The majority of the liquid to be recovered from a system will be found in the:
    A. Condenser.
    B. Receiver (when applied).
    C. Low side of system.
    D. Evaporator.

58. It becomes the owner's responsibility to maintain records of all refrigerant added to units that contain more than _____ pounds of refrigerant charge.
    A. 15 pounds.
    B. 20 pounds.
    C. 35 pounds.
    D. 50 pounds.

59. Exceptions to the required evacuation levels for recovery equipment that require an appliance be evacuated to only 0 psig apply to appliances that:
    A. Are being salvaged.
    B. Are filled with water or substances that would damage the recovery equipment.
    C. Have defective evaporator fan motors.
    D. Have air-cooled condensers.

60. The condition and state of the refrigerant entering the receiver are:
    A. Superheated high-pressure vapor.
    B. Superheated low-pressure vapor.
    C. Superheated high-pressure liquid.
    D. Superheated low-pressure liquid.

61. The best way to identify the type of refrigerant in a system is to:
    A. Check the stem of the TXV.
    B. Check the nameplate data.
    C. Check the high and low pressure cutout settings.
    D. Smell the refrigerant.

62. Front seating the suction service valve will close:
    A. The inlet from the evaporator.
    B. The gauge port.
    C. The outlet to the compressor.
    D. Both the inlet and gauge port.

63. Excessive superheat at the evaporator outlet may be caused by:
    A. A dirty condenser.
    B. Air in the system.
    C. High refrigerant charge.
    D. Low refrigerant charge.

64. Most of the liquid charge will be found in the:
    A. Compressor.
    B. Condenser.
    C. Receiver.
    D. Evaporator.

65. The required level of evacuation for recovery equipment manufactured before November 15, 1993, on a system containing less than 200 pounds of R-12 refrigerant is:
    A. 0 inches Hg.
    B. 4 inches Hg.
    C. 10 inches Hg.
    D. 15 inches Hg.

66. The required level of evacuation for recovery equipment manufactured after November 15, 1993, on a system containing less than 200 pounds of R-22 refrigerant is:
    A. 0 inches Hg.
    B. 4 inches Hg.
    C. 10 inches Hg.
    D. 15 inches Hg.

67. The EPA defines a "major repair" as all the following except:
    A. Replacement of the condenser.
    B. Replacement of the drier cartridge.
    C. Overhaul of the compressor.
    D. Replacement of the evaporator.

68. According to the EPA regulations, a refrigeration system containing a charge of 20 pounds of R-22 equipment must be repaired if the annual leakage exceeds:
    A. 10 percent of the charge.
    B. 15 percent of the charge.
    C. 35 percent of the charge.
    D. Is not required to be repaired.

69. A technician with Universal certification cannot legally work on the following type of system:
    A. Small appliance.
    B. High pressure system.
    C. Low pressure system.
    D. Automobile air-conditioning system.

70. It is necessary to evacuate a system after repair and prior to charging to:
    A. Prevent overcharging.
    B. Prevent undercharging.
    C. Remove air and moisture.
    D. All of the above.

71. A service manifold and recovery unit used to service R-12 systems should not be used to service systems containing:
    A. R-22.
    B. R-134a.
    C. R-500.
    D. All of the above.

72. ASHRAE Standard 15 requires an enclosed space containing an R-12 refrigeration system have:
    A. An oxygen depletion alarm.
    B. A refrigerant monitor that alarms below the AEL.
    C. Both of the above.
    D. None of the above.

73. The following may be vented without recovery:
    A. Nitrogen and R-22 used as a leak test gas.
    B. Nitrogen and R-22 used as a holding charge.
    C. Both A or B.
    D. Neither A and B.

74. Which of the following would NOT be effective for detecting a leak in an R-134a system:
    A. Soap bubble testing.
    B. Ultrasonic halide leak detector.
    C. Halide torch.
    D. Standing pressure test.

75. A technician holding Type II certification may NOT work on the following:
    A. An R-11 chiller unit.
    B. An R-12 refrigration system.
    C. An R-22 air conditioning system.
    D. An R-404 ice machine.

# Type III (Low-Pressure)
# Practice Questions

1. In the refrigeration cycle, which component acts as a heat exchanger where the refrigerant accepts the heat of the space to be cooled?
   A. The metering device.
   B. The compressor.
   C. The evaporator.
   D. The condenser.

2. What is meant by the term "high efficiency purge unit?"
   A. Those purge units that discharge the highest percentage of refrigerant with the air that they remove.
   B. Those purge units that discharge very little refrigerant with the air that they remove.
   C. Those purge units that draw very little electrical power.
   D. None of the above.

3. After November 14, 1994, the sale of chlorinated refrigerants shall be restricted. Who will be allowed to purchase these compounds?
   A. Only technicians who have received EPA certification.
   B. Anyone can buy the refrigerant, but only technicians can charge the system.
   C. Only technicians can buy refrigerant in quantities of less than fifty pounds.
   D. None of the above.

4. Bill of Lading forms that list the number of cylinders, their sizes, and the type of refrigerant that they contain are required during the transportation of used refrigerant by:
   A. Department of Transportation.
   B. Environmental Protection Agency.
   C. Department of the Interior.
   D. Department of Treasury.

5. Inspection of water-sides for chillers and condensers for leaking tubes should be conducted on a regular basis. These inspections should be conducted how frequently on a minimum basis?
   A. Once a month.
   B. Once every six months.
   C. Once a year.
   D. Once every other year.

6. What type of device is very effective for removing liquid refrigerant from a low pressure system?
   A. Hand-actuated recovery device.

B. System-dependent recovery unit.

C. A pump.

D. None of the above.

7. What steps may be taken to prevent air accumulation on an idle low-pressure refrigeration system?

   A. Leave the purge unit online at all times.

   B. System pressure should be maintained slightly above atmospheric by heating the refrigerant.

   C. Open the air vents on the condenser.

   D. Intermittently operate the system with no load.

8. In addition to CFCs and HCFCs, what other substances are affected by regulations under the Clean Air Act?

   A. Carbon tetrachloride.

   B. Methyl chloroform.

   C. Halons.

   D. All of the above.

9. When a severe electrical failure occurs in a hermetic compressor, this condition is known as what?

   A. A hot compressor.

   B. An hysterisis condition.

   C. A burn-out.

   D. A electrostatic condition.

10. Soap bubbles should never be used to locate system leaks on refrigeration systems that . . ?

   A. Have a discharge pressure above 175 psi.

   B. Use R-22 as the refrigerant.

   C. Are operating at a pressure below atmospheric.

   D. Use copper tubing in their construction.

11. Who or what should be consulted prior to beginning the conversion of an existing CFC-11 system over to HCFC-123?

   A. The general conversion sequence contained in the text for this course.

   B. The system's manufacturer.

   C. The EPA.

   D. It is not a complicated procedure, therefore, consultation is not necessary.

12. R-11 and R-113 may be recovered only into drums that are...?

   A. Designated for that type of refrigerant.

   B. Have been painted yellow and grey.

   C. Were used to deliver these compounds for use as a refrigerant.

   D. All of the above.

13. Using a recovery system with a larger condenser will have what effect?
   A. It will reduce the pressure ratio experienced by the compressor of the recovery system.
   B. It will slow the recovery process.
   C. Condenser size has very little impact on the recovery process.
   D. It will increase the wear and tear on the recovery system's compressor.

14. What is meant by the phrase "opening an appliance" as it is used in the Section 608 regulation?
   A. Any service that could be reasonably expected to release refrigerant from the appliance to the atmosphere unless the refrigerant had previously be recovered.
   B. Removing the heads from an open-drive compressor.
   C. Removing sections of line that lead to the four major system components.
   D. None of the above.

15. Excessive running of the purge system generally indicates what condition?
   A. Faulty air sensors.
   B. System leaks.
   C. High ambient temperature.
   D. The use of a low-efficiency purge system.

16. What must be done to use standard leak detection methods on a low-pressure system?
   A. Lower the pressure of the system below atmospheric pressure.
   B. Raise the pressure of the system above atmospheric pressure.
   C. Cool the refrigerant.
   D. Run the purge unit.

17. In the event that system leaks prevent achieving the required evacuation level for the system being serviced, the regulation permits the technician using his best judgment to determine the lowest achievable evacuation level where the recovered refrigerant will not be significantly contaminated. In no instance shall this pressure exceed atmospheric. How would you determine that system leaks were having a significant impact on the recovery procedure?
   A. If, after system pressure is reduced below atmospheric, the recovery cylinder's pressure continues to rise.
   B. If the suction pressure gauge on the recovery unit fluctuates.
   C. If the recovery cylinder's pressure begins to fall.
   D. If the recovery unit begins to vibrate excessively.

18. Which component is particularly susceptible to leaks in low-pressure refrigeration systems with open drive type compressors?
   A. Chiller tubes.

B. Shaft seal.
C. Charging connections.
D. Shaft bearings.

19. When recovering refrigerant from a low-pressure system it is important to do what?
    A. Run the compressor during the recovery process.
    B. Pull a deeper vacuum on these systems than is necessary on high-pressure systems.
    C. Maintain a positive system pressure throughout the recovery process.
    D. These systems do not require having the refrigerant recovered for any service procedures.

20. Which of the following procedures is not considered a de minimis release of refrigerant?
    A. Purging air from manifold and hoses.
    B. Purging the nitrogen used to pressurize refrigerant vapor in a low pressure system after the liquid has been recovered.
    C. The puff of vapor lost when attaching hoses to a Schrader valve.
    D. All of the above.

21. Minor repairs may be performed on low-pressure refrigeration systems without recovering the refrigerant charge if the pressure in the system is raised to atmospheric. How may this be accomplished?
    A. Heat the refrigerant.
    B. Pressurize the system with nitrogen.
    C. Charge the system until it is completely filled with liquid refrigerant.
    D. Open system vents to the atmosphere and allow the pressure to equalize.

22. For a refrigerant to be certified as meeting the new product specifications, it must meet which standard?
    A. Shown to be free of acidity and moisture on a commercially available test kit.
    B. ARI 700-88.
    C. Visible inspection for clarity.
    D. RSES 8300.

23. Which of the following may be used on the job site to give a rough indication of the condition of the refrigerant?
    A. An acid-moisture test kit.
    B. An amino test kit.
    C. A flammability test.
    D. A capacitance tester.

24. What precautions must be taken to avoid freeze-up when recovering refrigerant from a chiller system that uses water as a heat transfer medium for either the chiller or the condenser.
    A. Maximize the recovery of refrigerant in the liquid phase.
    B. Recovery procedures should be conducted intermittently.
    C. Ensure that circulation pumps are running and monitor the water temperature, in systems where the water-sides have not been drained.
    D. A or C.

25. Low-pressure chillers typically use a rupture disc mounted on the evaporator housing to protect the system from over-pressurization. The discharge from a rupture disc should be piped so that it vents where?
    A. Outdoors.
    B. Inside the machinery room.
    C. To the evaporator.
    D. To the duct system.

26. During vapor removal from the refrigeration system:
    A. The system water pumps should be on, the recovery compressor should be on, and the recovery condenser water should be off.
    B. The system water pumps, the recovery compressor, and the recovery condenser water should all be on.
    C. The system water pumps should be off, and the recovery compressor should be on.
    D. The system water pumps should be on, and the recovery compressor should be off.

27. Refrigerant-11 at 14.7 psia will boil at approximately:
    A. 80.2°F.
    B. 60.3°F.
    C. 74.5°F.
    D. 79.7°F.

28. A centrifugal chiller's purge condensing unit:
    A. Takes its suction from the top of the condenser.
    B. Removes air and noncondensables from the system.
    C. Returns recycled refrigerant to the unit.
    D. All of the above.

29. A hydrostatic tube test kit will:
    A. Remove water from a machine.
    B. Vent refrigerant to the atmosphere.
    C. Determine if a tube leaks.
    D. Blow all water out of tubes.

30. EPA regulations require that all appliances containing more than 50 pounds of refrigerant (except for commercial and industrial process refrigeration) be repaired when the leak rate exceeds ____ percent of the charge per year.
    A.  35.
    B.  0.
    C.  15.
    D.  25.

31. When using recovery or recycling equipment manufactured before November 15, 1993, technicians must evacuate low-pressure appliances to the following level before making a major repair.
    A.  25 inches of mercury vacuum.
    B.  29 inches of mercury vacuum.
    C.  0 psig.
    D.  15 inches of mercury vacuum.

32. Charging refrigerant liquid into a refrigeration system under a 29 inch Hg vacuum can cause the:
    A.  Refrigerant liquid to freeze.
    B.  Liquid to absorb excess moisture.
    C.  Purge unit to operate.
    D.  System water to freeze.

33. Leak testing a low-pressure refrigeration system with nitrogen in excess of 10 psig could cause which of the following to fail?
    A.  Purge unit shells.
    B.  Evaporator tubes.
    C.  Rupture disc.
    D.  Condenser tubes.

34. Which of the following statements is *not* true of recycling and recovery equipment manufactured after November 15, 1993?
    A.  It must be able to handle more than one refrigerant.
    B.  It must be tested by an EPA-approved third party.
    C.  It must meet vacuum standards more stringent than those met by equipment manufactured before November 15, 1993.
    D.  It must be equipped with low-loss fittings.

35. Identify the pressure corresponding to 32°F for R-123:
    A.  17 inches of mercury vacuum.
    B.  11 inches of mercury vacuum.
    C.  23 inches of mercury vacuum.
    D.  20 inches of mercury vacuum.

36. As defined by ASHRAE Standard 15, a sensor and alarm are required for
    A1 refrigerants to sense:
    A. CFC contamination.
    B. Oxygen deprivation.
    C. HCFC leaks.
    D. Ozone.

37. When evacuating the refrigerant from a low-pressure chiller, the recovery
    unit's high pressure cut-out is set for ＿＿＿＿ psig?
    A. 10.
    B. 15.
    C. 2.
    D. 5.

38. On low pressure chillers, moisture *most frequently* enters the refrigerant
    system through:
    A. Air leaks from gasketed areas or fittings.
    B. Air leaks from the charging valve.
    C. Air leaks in the rupture disc assembly.
    D. Tube leaks.

39. Which of the following repairs would *always* be considered "major" under
    EPA's regulations?
    A. Replacement of a switch.
    B. Replacement of a condenser fan motor.
    C. Replacement of an evaporator coil.
    D. Replacement of a filter-drier.

40. Refrigerant is added to a centrifugal machine through the:
    A. Compressor service valve.
    B. Condenser charging valve.
    C. Evaporator charging valve.
    D. Float valve.

41. The *primary* purpose of a purge unit on a CFC-11 chiller is to:
    A. Condense air out of the system.
    B. Condense water out of the system.
    C. Remove noncondensables from the system.
    D. Remove CFCs from the system.

42. Charged low pressure refrigeration machines may be most efficiently leak
    checked by using:
    A. The purge system.
    B. Dry nitrogen.
    C. HCFC-22.
    D. Controlled hot water.

43. Under EPA's regulations, which of the following methods can be used to pressurize a system for the purpose of opening the system for a non-major repair?
A. Controlled hot water.
B. Add compressed air.
C. Add carbon dioxide.
D. Add nitrogen.

44. EPA regulations require that leaking commercial and industrial process refrigeration be repaired when the leak rate exceeds _____ percent of the charge per year.
A. 15.
B. 25.
C. 35.
D. 0.

45. For what refrigerant is an equipment room refrigerant sensor required under ASHRAE Standard 15?
A. R-11.
B. R-134a.
C. R-12.
D. R-123.

46. When using recovery and recycling equipment manufactured *after* November 15, 1993, technicians must evacuate low-pressure appliances to the following level before disposing of the appliance:
A. 29 inches of mercury vacuum.
B. 0 psig.
C. 15 inches of mercury vacuum.
D. 5 inches of mercury vacuum.

47. What is the primary water source for a recovery unit condensing coil?
A. Local municipal water supply.
B. De-ionized water.
C. Chilled water.
D. Condenser water.

48. How do you determine when enough vapor has entered the refrigeration system before you charge refrigerant liquid?
A. Recovery unit liquid level drops.
B. Vapor charge for 15 minutes.
C. Recovery unit pressure drops.
D. Refrigerant saturation temperature increases to 36°F.

49. A centrifugal chiller's rupture disk is connected to the chiller's:
    A. Economizer.
    B. Condenser.
    C. Evaporator.
    D. Liquid line.

50. A rupture disc on a recovery vessel for low pressure refrigerants relieves at:
    A. 20 psig.
    B. 5 psig.
    C. 10 psig.
    D. 15 psig.

51. Recovery machines using water as the condensing medium would generally use:
    A. Cooling tower water.
    B. Municipal water supply.
    C. Condensate water.
    D. Ice water.

52. Frost would be best removed from a sight glass by:
    A. Reversing the cycle.
    B. Chip the ice off.
    C. Spraying with alcohol.
    D. Turn the water supply off.

53. The maximum pressure that should be applied to a low-pressure chiller when leak checking with controlled nitrogen is:
    A. 3 psig.
    B. 10 psig.
    C. 20 psig.
    D. 30 psig.

54. Water tube leaks in a low-pressure chiller are usually found with:
    A. Water puddles.
    B. Frosted coils.
    C. A hydrostatic tube test.
    D. Leak detector.

55. To prevent freezing of the water coils of a low-pressure chiller, it is recommended:
    A. When charging, begin with vapor phase.
    B. Circulate water through the chiller.
    C. Do not inject liquid during charging until saturation temperature is above 32°F.
    D. All of the above.

56. Under ASHRAE Standard 15, what refrigerant requires equipment room sensors?
    A. R-12.
    B. R-500.
    C. R-123.
    D. R-134a.

57. Under ASHRAE Standard 15, the following refrigerants require equipment room oxygen deprivation sensors:
    A. R-11.
    B. R-12.
    C. R-134a.
    D. All the above.

58. Low-pressure chillers require purge units because:
    A. They operate below atmospheric pressure.
    B. They draw noncondensables through gaskets and seals.
    C. A and B above.
    D. They don't require purge units.

59. The purge unit draws from the:
    A. Top of the condenser.
    B. Suction of the compressor.
    C. Evaporator.
    D. Rupture disk.

60. If excessive nitrogen pressure is exerted within a low-pressure chiller, what component would fail first?
    A. Evaporator coil.
    B. Rupture disk.
    C. Compressor seals.
    D. Cooling tower.

61. When using recovery or recycling equipment manufactured *after* November 15, 1993, technicians must evacuate low-pressure appliances to the following level before making a major repair.
    A. 25 inches of mercury vacuum.
    B. 25 mm of mercury absolute.
    C. 0 psig.
    D. 15 inches of mercury vacuum.

62. The rupture disk of an R-11 chiller is commonly designed to burst at:
    A. 0 psig.
    B. 5 psig.
    C. 15 psig.
    D. 50 psig.

63. A technician recovering the charge from an R-11 chiller must have:
    A. Type I certification.
    B. Type II certification.
    C. Type III certification.
    D. All of the above.

64. The refrigerant being considered as a replacement for R-11 in chillers is:
    A. R-22.
    B. R-123.
    C. R-134a.
    D. R-404.

65. An air-conditioning chiller using R-11 must be repaired when the annual leakage rate exceeds:
    A. 5 percent of the charge per year.
    B. 15 percent of the charge per year.
    C. 35 percent of the charge per year.
    D. 15 pounds per year.

66. R-123 is classified under ASHRAE Standard 34 as being in the following safety group:
    A. A1.
    B. A2.
    C. B1.
    D. B2.

67. If excessive pressure was applied during nitrogen gas leak testing, the following component would fail first:
    A. Compressor seals.
    B. Purge unit.
    C. Rupture disk.
    D. Condenser gasket.

68. To prevent freezing of the water in the coils of a low-pressure chiller during charging, do all the following *except:*
    A. Begin charging as a vapor.
    B. Only charge when the ambient temperature is above 32°F.
    C. Begin charging liquid only when the pressure is above a saturation temperature of 32°F.
    D. Run the circulating pumps.

69. A refrigerant with a safety group of B1 has:
    A. Lower toxicity and lower flammability.
    B. Higher toxicity and no flame propagation.
    C. Higher toxicity and higher flammability.
    D. Lower toxicity and higher flammability.

70. The recommended method of raising the pressure of a low-pressure chiller for a minor repair is:
    A. Pressurizing with nitrogen.
    B. Heating the evaporator shell with an electric heater.
    C. Circulating hot water through the evaporator tubes.
    D. None of the above.

71. When raising the pressure of an R-11 chiller for maintenance, do not exceed:
    A. 0 psig.
    B. 10 psig.
    C. 15 psig.
    D. 50 psig.

72. After reaching the required evacuation pressure, the recovery machine is secured. After a few minutes, the pressure rises. This may be an indication of:
    A. Liquid refrigerant remaining in the system.
    B. Liquid refrigerant in the compressor oil.
    C. A leak in the system.
    D. All of the above.

73. To speed recovery of the refrigerant charge from a low-pressure chiller:
    A. Secure the circulating pumps.
    B. Secure the purge unit.
    C. Recover vapor first, then recover liquid.
    D. Recovery liquid first, then recover vapor.

74. The refrigerant cylinder used with recovery unit:
    A. Can only be used once.
    B. Must be pressure tested every 5 years.
    C. Must be discarded after 5 years of use.
    D. Must have a relief valve installed to prevent bursting.

75. Refrigerant recovered from a chiller unit may be:
    A. Returned to the same system.
    B. Used in another system owned by the same person.
    C. Sold if tested for contamination.
    D. Both A and B.

# References

Air-Conditioning and Refrigeration Institute. 1998. *Refrigeration and Air Conditioning.* 3rd ed. New Jersey: Prentice Hall.

Burghardt, M. D. and J. A. Harbach. 1993. *Engineering Thermodynamics,* 4th ed. Maryland: Cornell Maritime Press.

*Calculations for Merchant Ship Heating, Ventilation and Air Conditioning Design.* Technical and Research Bulletin 4-16. New Jersey: Society of Naval Architects and Marine Engineers.

Dossat, R. J. and T. J. Horan. 2002. *Principles of Refrigeration,* 5th ed. New Jersey: Prentice Hall.

*Handbook and Product Directory.* 4 vols. American Society of Heating, Refrigerating, and Air Conditioning Engineers. Atlanta, Ga.

Harrington, R. L. (ed.), 1992. *Marine Engineering,* Ch. XXI, New Jersey: Society of Naval Architects and Marine Engineers.

*Heat Transfer Coefficients.* NAVSEA Design Data Sheet, DDS 511-2. Washington, D.C.: Naval Sea Systems Command.

*Naval Ships Technical Manual.* December 1997. Refrigeration Systems. Chapter 516, 4th revision. S9086-RW-STM-010. Washington, D.C.: Naval Sea Systems Command.

*Naval Ships Technical Manual.* February 1995. Heating, Ventilating, and Air Conditioning Systems for Surface Ships. Chapter 510, 2nd revision. S9086-RQ-STM-010. Washington, D.C.: Naval Sea Systems Command.

*NAVSEA Design Practices and Criteria Manual for Air Conditioning, Ventilation, and Heating of Surface Ships.* Chapter 510, T9500-AA-PRO- 130. Washington, D.C.: Naval Sea Systems Command.

*Refrigeration Equipment for Storage Compartments—Heat Load Calculation and Selection.* NAVSEA Design Data Sheet, DDS 516-1. Washington, D.C.: Naval Sea Systems Command.

Stoecker, W. F. and J. W. Jones. 1998. *Refrigeration and Air Conditioning.* 3rd. ed. New Jersey: Prentice Hall.

*Thermal Insulation Report.* Technical and Research Bulletin 4-7. New Jersey: Society of Naval Architects and Marine Engineers.

# Index

# About the Author

James A. Harbach is a Professor at the United States Merchant Marine Academy at Kings Point, New York, teaching courses in marine engineering, thermodynamics, and refrigeration and air conditioning. He received a B.S. degree in Marine Engineering from Kings Point and graduate degrees in Mechanical Engineering from Cornell University and Polytechnic University. Professor Harbach holds a Professional Engineer license and a USCG license as First Assistant Engineer. Prior to joining the faculty at Kings Point, he sailed as an engineer on a variety of U.S. flag merchant vessels, and worked as an engineer involved in designing ships for the U.S. Navy and in designing systems for a nuclear power plant. He has co-authored a textbook on thermodynamics and contributed six chapters to Modern Marine Engineers Manual, Volumes I and II.

 More Titles from Cornell Maritime Press

*American Merchant Seaman's Manual*
William B. Hayler, Editor in Chief
ISBN 10: 0-87033-549-9, ISBN 13: 978-0-87033-549-5

*Applied Naval Architecture*
Robert B. Zubaly, ISBN 10: 0-87033-475-1, ISBN 13: 978-0-87033-475-7

*Behavior and Handling of Ships*
Henry H. Hooyer, ISBN 0-87033-306-2, ISBN 13: 978-0-87033-306-4

*Business of Shipping*
Lane C. Kendall and James J. Buckley
ISBN 0-87033-526-X, ISBN 13: 978-0-87033-526-6

*Cornell Manual, The*
John M. Keever, ISBN10: 0-87033-559-6, ISBN 13: 978-0-87033-559-4

*Diesel Engines*
Leo Block, P.E., ISBN 10: 0-87033-418-2, ISBN 13: 978-0-87033-418-4

*Formulae for the Mariner*
Richard M. Plant, ISBN10: 0-87033-361-5, ISBN 10: 13: 0-87033-361-3

*Handbook of Rights and Concerns for Mariners*
Roberto Tiangco and Russ Jackson
ISBN 0-87033-530-8, ISBN 13: 978-0-87033-530-3

*Marine Cargo Operations*
Robert J. Meurn and Charles L. Sauerbier
ISBN 10: 0-87033-550-2, ISBN 13: 978-0-87033-550-1

*Marine Radionavigation and Communications*
Jeffrey W. Monroe and Thomas L. Bushy
ISBN 10: 0-87033-510-3, ISBN 13: 978-0-87033-510-5

*Master's Handbook on Ship's Business*
Tuuli Anna Messer
ISBN 10: 0-87033-531-6, ISBN 13: 978-0-87033-531-0